GENERAL SCIENCE

Dhrubadas Chakraborty has done his Ph.D. from the Department of Chemistry, Faculty of Science, Banaras Hindu University. He has done his postdoctoral research from the Department of Chemistry, Indian Institute of Technology, Kanpur. His research interest was in the field of theoretical and computational chemistry. Ever since he finished his research work, he has been teaching chemistry and science in various capacities. He has authored several research papers, and has edited several science and technology books.

GENERAL SCIENCE
SUCCESS IN COMPETITION

DHRUBADAS CHAKRABORTY

RUPA

Published by
Rupa Publications India Pvt. Ltd 2020
7/16, Ansari Road, Daryaganj
New Delhi 110002

Sales Centres:
Allahabad Bengaluru Chennai
Hyderabad Jaipur Kathmandu
Kolkata Mumbai

ISBN: 978-93-5333-864-0

First impression 2020

10 9 8 7 6 5 4 3 2 1

Printed at Yash Printographics, Noida

CONTENTS

SECTION III
BIOLOGY

SECTION IV
COMPUTER SCIENCE

SECTION I

PHYSICS

1

UNITS AND MEASUREMENT

INTRODUCTION

In physics we study energy and forces; we also study about laws of nature. In studying the laws of nature, we make measurements. Measurement is necessary to report the value of a parameter, compare it with another, and to differentiate the value of one quantity from another. Thus, correct measurement of the quantity is very important. Measurement of a physical quantity has two parts—a number and a unit. The number that signifies the amount does not make any meaningful scientific statement if it is not associated with a unit. A unit is a standard of measurement which everyone agrees to accept. A measurement using a unit means how many times that standard (represented by the unit) the actual measurement is. In this chapter we will study about different units that we use in physics.

TYPES OF PHYSICAL QUANTITIES

There are three types of physical quantities.

Fundamental or Base Quantities

Certain physical quantities that do not depend on other physical quantities and whose units are used for expressing all the physical quantities are known as fundamental quantities. They are also known by the terms absolute or base quantities. Length, mass, time, electric current, temperature, amount of substance and luminous intensity are fundamental quantities.

Derived Quantities

All other quantities which are not fundamental but can be derived from the fundamental quantities are known as derived quantities. Examples of derived quantities are area, volume, pressure, force, energy, etc.

Supplementary Quantities

There are two quantities that are neither fundamental nor derived, and are known as supplementary quantities. These are plane angle and solid angle.

On the basis of direction and magnitude, a physical quantity can be either scalar or vector.

Scalar Quantity

A quantity which has magnitude only but no direction is called a scalar quantity. Examples of scalar quantities are mass, speed, temperature, etc.

Vector Quantity

Vector quantities are the quantities which require both magnitude and direction. Examples of vector quantities are velocity, acceleration, electric field, magnetic field, etc.

SI UNITS

The system of units of measurement we use widely today is known as the SI system.

The International System of Units (Le Systeme International d'Unités in French–abbreviated as SI) was established by the 11th General Conference on Weights and Measures (CGPM from Conference Generale des Poids et Measures). The SI system has seven base units and they are listed in Table 1.1. These units pertain to the seven fundamental scientific quantities. The other physical quantities such as speed, volume, density, etc. can be derived from these quantities.

Table 1.1: SI base units

Base quantity	Name	Symbol
Length	Metre	m
Mass	Kilogram	kg
Time	Second	s
Electric current	Ampere	A
Thermodynamic temperature	Kelvin	K
Amount of substance	Mole	mol
Luminous intensity	Candela	cd

The definitions of the SI base units are given below.

METRE:

The distance travelled by light in vacuum in 1/299,792,458th of a second is 1 m.

KILOGRAM:

The mass of a cylinder made of platinum–iridium alloy kept at the International Bureau of Weights and Measures is defined as 1 kg.

SECOND:

A particular radiation of Cesium-133 or Cs-133 is selected, which corresponds to the transition between the two hyperfine levels of the ground state of Cs-133. Each radiation has a time period of repetition of certain characteristics. The time duration in 9,192,631,770 time periods of the selected transition is defined as 1 s.

AMPERE:

Suppose two long straight wires with negligible cross section are placed parallel to each other in vacuum at a separation of 1 m and electric currents are established in the two in the same direction. If equal currents are maintained in the two wires so that the force between them is 2×10^{-7} newton per metre of the wire, then the current in any of the wires is called 1 A. Here, newton is the SI unit of force.

KELVIN:

The fraction 1/273.16 of the thermodynamic temperature of triple point of water is called 1 K.

MOLE:

The amount of a substance that contains as many elementary entities (molecules, or atoms if the substance is monoatomic) as there are number of atoms in 0.012 kg of carbon-12 is called a mole. This number (number of atoms in 0.012 kg of carbon-12) is called the Avogadro constant and its best available value is 6.022045×10^{23}.

CANDELA:

The candela is the luminous intensity, in a given direction, of a source that emits monochromatic radiation of frequency 5.40×10^{14} hertz and that has a radiant intensity in that direction of 1/683 watt per steradian.

Prefixes Used in SI Units

The SI system allows the use of prefixes to indicate the multiples or submultiples (fractions) of a unit. These prefixes are listed in Table 1.2.

Table 1.2: Standard prefixes for the SI units of measure

			deca	hecto	kilo	mega	giga	tera	peta	exa	zetta	yotta
Multiples	Prefix name		deca	hecto	kilo	mega	giga	tera	peta	exa	zetta	yotta
	Prefix symbol		da	h	k	M	G	T	P	E	Z	Y
	Factor	10^0	10^1	10^2	10^3	10^6	10^9	10^{12}	10^{15}	10^{18}	10^{21}	10^{24}
Fractions	Prefix name		deci	centi	milli	micro	nano	pico	femto	atto	zepto	yocto
	Prefix symbol		d	c	m	μ	n	p	f	a	z	y
	Factor	10^0	10^{-1}	10^{-2}	10^{-3}	10^{-6}	10^{-9}	10^{-12}	10^{-15}	10^{-18}	10^{-21}	10^{-24}

General Rules for Writing SI Units

➤ The value of a quantity is written as a number followed by a space and a unit symbol; e.g., 1.52 kg, 7.3×10^2 m^2, 22 K. This rule also applies to the per cent sign (%) and the symbol for degrees of temperature (°C). Exceptions are the symbols for plane angular degrees, minutes and seconds (°, ', and "), which are placed immediately after the number with no space after the number.

➤ There is no degree sign before the unit of temperature in K.

➤ Symbols are mathematical entities and not abbreviations. Therefore, symbols do not have to be ended with a period/full stop (.) while used, unless the rules of grammar demand a full stop or period for another reason, say, to denote the end of a sentence.

- A prefix is part of the unit, hence it is written with the symbol of the unit without a separator or space in between. For example, k in km, M in MPa and G in GHz. Compound prefixes are not allowed.

- Symbols for derived units formed by multiplication are joined with a center dot (·) or a non-breaking space (meaning, there should not be a line break between the two parts of the unit; this also means one part of the unit should not appear in one line and the other part in the next line); e.g., N·m or N m.

- Symbols for derived units formed by division are joined with a solidus (/), or given as a negative exponent. For example, the 'metre per second' can be written as m/s, m s^{-1}, or m·s^{-1}. Only one solidus should be used; e.g., kg/(m·s^2) and kg·m^{-1}·s^{-2} are acceptable, but kg/m/s^2 is ambiguous, hence not acceptable.

- The first letter of symbols for units, if derived from the name of a person, is written in upper case; otherwise, it is written in lowercase. For example, the unit of pressure is named after Blaise Pascal, so its symbol is written as 'Pa', that of force is 'N', derived from Newton, but the symbol for mole is written as 'mol'. Thus, 'T' is the symbol for tesla, a measure of magnetic field strength, and 't' the symbol for tonne, a measurement of mass. Although the symbol of litre may be written using either an uppercase 'L' or a lowercase 'l', due to the similarity of the lowercase letter 'l' to the numeral '1', especially with certain typefaces or English-style handwriting, it is recommended by the American NIST that within the United States, 'L' be used rather than 'l'. Others also more or less follow the same convention.

- Symbols of units do not have a plural form; e.g., 12 kg, but not 12 kgs.

- Uppercase and lowercase prefixes are not interchangeable and have to be used carefully, as each prefix may mean a particular multiplicative factor. For example, the quantities 1 mW and 1 MW represent two different quantities; the lowercase m stands for milli; 1 milliwatt equals 0.001 watt; and the uppercase M stands for mega; 1 megawatt equals 1000000 watt.

- A space between the number and the unit symbol (i.e., no hyphen) is specified when the combination is used as an adjective. For example, 'a 12 kg sphere'. However, in English, a hyphen would be used as normal in this context if the unit name is spelt out, e.g., 'a 12-kilogram sphere'.

Table 1.3: Supplementary units and their symbols in SI system

Quantity	Quantity symbol	SI unit name	Unit symbol
plane angle	$\alpha, \beta, \gamma, \theta, \Phi$	radian	rad
solid angle	ω, Ω	steradian	sr

Table 1.4: Derived SI units with special names

Physical quantity	Quantity symbol	SI unit	Unit symbol	Expression in SI base units	Alternative expressions
frequency	v, f	Hertz	Hz	s^{-1}	–
force	F	Newton	N	$kg\ m\ s^{-2}$	$J\ m^{-1}$
pressure	p	Pascal	Pa	$kg\ m^{-1}\ s^{-2}$	$N\ m^{-2}$
energy (all forms)	E, U, V, W, etc.	Joule	J	$kg\ m^2\ s^{-2}$	$N\ m = C\ V = V\ A\ s$
power	P	Watt	W	$kg\ m^2\ s^{-3}$	$J\ s^{-1} = V\ A$
electric charge	Q	Coulomb	C	$A\ s$	–
electric potential difference	E, ϕ, ζ, Φ, η, etc.	Volt	V	$kg\ m^2\ s^{-3}\ A^{-1}$	$J\ A^{-1}\ s^{-1} = J\ C^{-1}$
electrical capacitance	C	Farad	F	$A^2\ s^4\ kg^{-1}\ m^{-2}$	$C\ V^{-1}$
electrical resistance	R	Ohm	Ω	$kg\ m^2\ s^{-3}\ A^{-2}$	$V\ A^{-1}$
electrical conductance	G	Siemens	S	$A^2\ s^3\ kg^{-1}\ m^{-2}$	$A\ V^{-1} = \Omega^{-1}$
magnetic flux	Φ	Weber	Wb	$kg\ m^2\ s^{-2}\ A^{-1}$	$V\ s = T\ m^2$
magnetic induction	B	Tesla	T	$kg\ s^{-2}\ A^{-1}$	$Wb\ m^{-2} = N\ A^{-1}\ m^{-1}$
inductance	L, M	Henry	H	$kg\ m^2\ s^{-2}\ A^{-2}$	$V\ A^{-1}\ s = Wb\ A^{-1}$
luminous flux	Φ	Lumen	lm	$cd\ sr$	–
illumination	E	Lux	lx	$cd\ sr\ m^{-2}$	$lm\ m^{-2}$
activity (of a radionuclide)	A	Becquerel	Bq	$s-1$	–
absorbed dose	D	Gray	Gy	$m^2\ s^{-2}$	$J\ kg^{-1}$
dose equivalent	H	Sievert	Sv	$m^2\ s^{-2}$	$J\ kg^{-1}$
catalytic activity	z	Katal	kat	$mol\ s^{-1}$	–
Celsius temperature	t	degree Celsius	°C	K	–
plane angle	$\alpha, \beta, \gamma, \theta, \Phi$	Radian	rad	$m\ m^{-1}$	dimensionless
solid angle	ω, Ω	Steradian	sr	$m^2\ m^{-2}$	dimensionless

Table 1.5: Derived SI units expressed in terms of SI base units

Derived quantity	Quantity symbol	Name	Expression in SI base units
area	A	square metre	m^2
volume	V	cubic metre	m^3
speed, velocity	u, v, c	metre per second	$m\ s^{-1}$
acceleration	a, g (free fall)	metre per second squared	$m\ s^{-2}$
moment of inertia	I	kilogram square metre	$kg\ m^2$
kinematic viscosity	V	square metre per second	$m^2\ s^{-1}$
wave number	σ, ϕ	reciprocal metre	m^{-1}
mass density	P	kilogram per cubic metre	$kg\ m^{-3}$
specific volume	. V	cubic metre per kilogram	$m^3\ kg^{-1}$
current density	j, i	ampere per square metre	$A\ m^{-2}$
magnetic field strength	H	ampere per metre	$A\ m^{-1}$
concentration of substance B	cB, [B]	mole per cubic metre	$mol\ m^{-3}$
molar mass	M	kilogram per mole	$kg\ mol^{-1}$
molar volume	Vm	cubic metre per mole	$m^3 mol^{-1}$
luminance	L	candela per square metre	$cd\ m^{-2}$
mass fraction	W	kilogram per kilogram	dimensionless

Metric Prefixes for Power of 10

Some units are very large or some may be very small when expressed in SI units. A multiplicative constant of that unit is used at that time. Depending on whether a bigger or a smaller unit is required, certain prefixes are used with the unit. In Table 1.6 these prefixes and the corresponding multiplicative factor due to them are given.

8

PHYSICS

Table 1.6: Prefixes and the corresponding multiplicative factor

Prefix	Symbol	Multiplicative factor
yotta	Y	$= 10^{24}$
zetta	Z	$= 10^{21}$
exa	E	$= 10^{18}$
peta	P	$= 10^{15}$
tera	T	$= 10^{12}$
giga	G	$= 10^{9}$
mega	M	$= 10^{6}$
kilo	k	$= 10^{3}$
hecto	h	$= 10^{2}$
deca	da	$= 10^{1}$
----------	----------	----------
deci	d	$= 10^{-1}$
centi	c	$= 10^{-2}$
milli	m	$= 10^{-3}$
micro	μ	$= 10^{-6}$
nano	n	$= 10^{-9}$
pico	p	$= 10^{-12}$
femto	f	$= 10^{-15}$
atto	a	$= 10^{-18}$
zepto	z	$= 10^{-21}$
yocto	y	$= 10^{-24}$

DIMENSIONS

So far we have learnt about physical quantities and their units. We have also learnt that there are base quantities and there are derived quantities. Derived quantities are so named because they are derived from the fundamental quantities. The basic quantities in physics are mass, length, time, electric current, temperature, luminous intensity and amount of a substance. Other related quantities such as energy, acceleration and so on can be derived from combinations of these basic quantities. The way in which a derived quantity is related to its base quantity or quantities can be shown by the dimensions of the quantity. In other words, the dimension of a physical quantity is the power to which the base quantity or quantities are raised to express that quantity.

- The dimension of mass is [M]
- The dimension of length is [L]
- The dimensions of time is [T]
- The dimension of current is [A]
- The dimension of temperature is [K]
- The dimension of amount of substance is [mol]
- The dimension of luminous intensity is [cd]

Now, here are a few examples of dimensions of a derived quantity. Surface area of an object involves the product of two lengths and therefore, the dimension of surface area is $[L]^2$. In the same way the dimension of speed is $[L][T]^{-1}$ as speed is expressed as distance traversed (which is nothing but length) in unit time. Here is another example. Let us find out the dimension of force. Force is defined as: $F = m*a$

The dimension of acceleration, a derived dimensional quantity that is defined as a change of velocity per unit time, is the ratio of velocity to time. Velocity is another derived quantity, being the ratio of length and time.

$F = [M][a] = [M][vT^{-1}]$

$F = [M][L^{T-1}T^{-1}] = [MLT^{-2}]$

Dimensions of some of the derived quantities are given in Table 1.7 below.

Table 1.7: Dimensions of derived quantities

Quantity	Formula	Dimensions
Area	Length × Length	$[L]^2$
Volume	Length × Length × Length	$[L]^3$
Velocity	Length/Time	$[L][T]^{-1}$
Acceleration	Velocity/Time	$[L][T]^{-2}$
Force	Mass × Acceleration	$[M][L][T]^{-2}$
Energy	Force × Length	$[M][L]^2[T]^{-2}$
Power	Energy/Time	$[M][L]^2[T]^{-3}$
Pressure	Force/Area	$[M][L]^{-1}[T]^{-2}$
Momentum	Mass × Velocity	$[M][L][T]^{-1}$

UNCERTAINTY IN MEASUREMENTS
AND SIGNIFICANT FIGURES

In physics, one has to deal with measurements and report data from experiments as well as theoretical calculations. All measurements will be associated with a degree of uncertainty, regardless of precision and accuracy. The reason behind this is the following two factors: (a) The limitation of the measuring instrument (systematic error) and (b) the skill of the experimenter making the measurements (random error). However, during use of these numbers in computation or other calculations, care has to be exercised so as to handle the numbers conveniently and meaningfully, and present the data realistically with certainty to the extent possible.

One of the ways to minimize inaccuracy in calculations is to express a large (or small) number scientifically. Scientific notation is the way a number is expressed in exponential notation, in which any number can be expressed in the form $N \times 10^n$ where n is an exponent having positive or negative values and N is a number (called digit term) which varies between 1.000... and 9.999.... We are using ellipsis here to indicate the number of decimal places that will be reported in the expression of N. 1.000 and 9.999 mean the numbers are expressed up to third decimal places. For example, 10525468000 can be expressed in scientific notation as 1.0525468×10^{10}. Note that in this example, the number is reported up to seventh decimal place. Similarly, 0.00002541 can be expressed as 2.541×10^{-5}. The advantage of have a number expressed in scientific notation is that while carrying out mathematical operations like addition, subtraction, multiplication, division, etc., rules for exponential numbers apply. To illustrate:

Multiply 10525468000 with 0.00002541 means multiplication of 1.0525468×10^{10} with 2.541×10^{-5}.

Thus, $1.0525468 \times 10^{10} \times 2.541 \times 10^{-5}$ equals $2.6745214188 \times 10^{(10-5)}$, that is, 2.6745214188×10^5.

For carrying out addition and subtraction, the exponent part is to be made same for both (or all) the numbers. This we have learned in middle school mathematics. However, what is important here is to know when we report a number up to what decimal place we should report it.

That pertains to the accuracy of the measurement, which is described in the next section.

Accuracy and Precision

Precision of measurement refers to how close various measurements are to each other for the same quantity. In other words, if the same experiment is carried out more than once, how much is the reported value from these experiments differing from each other?

Accuracy, on the other hand, although incorrectly considered as synonymous to precision, indicates the agreement of a particular value to the true value of the result. For example, if the true value of a result is 4.00 cm and a student takes two measurements and reports the results as 3.95 cm and 3.93 cm, these values are precise as they are close to each other but are not accurate. Another student repeats the experiment and obtains 3.94 cm and 4.05 cm as the results of two measurements. These observations are neither precise nor accurate. When a third student repeats these measurements and reports 4.01 cm and 3.99 cm as the result, these values are both precise and accurate.

MOTION

INTRODUCTION

Anything that is moving is in a state of motion. In other words, anything that is not in a state of rest is in motion. The object can move in various trajectories—in a straight line; in a circular path; in a to-and-fro movement; it leaves the ground, goes up and comes back. In physics we deal with them in appropriate sections. First let us understand how we define or express the state of rest or motion in physics.

REST

When an object does not change its position with time, it is said to be in a state of rest. The important thing here is that the object has to be viewed with respect to its surroundings. It is important to understand the role of surroundings in dealing with the state of rest or motion because the concept of rest or motion may be relative. Let us try to understand this with an example. Suppose we are travelling in a train and two people are sitting facing each other or next to each other. If we consider one person with respect to another, both will appear to be at rest, because the position of both of them does not change with time. However, if either person is viewed with respect to the objects outside the train when the train is moving, their position will appear to be changing with time. In other words, neither person will be considered to be at rest. Hence, it is important to consider the state of rest with respect to another frame of reference.

MOTION

When the position of an object changes with time, the object is said to be in motion. Here again the object has to be viewed against a different frame of reference. If the frame of reference is the same, motion cannot be understood. Going with the same example of a train in which passengers are sitting, unless it is viewed with reference to a static object outside (in a different frame of reference), the motion of the moving train cannot be understood.

Types of Motion
There are three types of motion.

TRANSLATIONAL MOTION

When a body moves along a line, its motion is called translational motion. The line may be a straight one or a zigzag one. If the body moves in a straight line, the motion is called linear motion. If the motion happens in a zigzag path, it is called random motion.

Examples of translational motion:

Motion of a train on a straight track—linear motion

Motion of insects—random motion

ROTATIONAL MOTION

When a body moves around an axis, passing through the body, the motion is known as rotational motion or rotatory motion. An example of rotational motion is the rotation of Earth. The axis of rotation of Earth is the axis passing through the two poles of Earth. Another example of rotatory motion is a spinning top, which spins around its own axis.

A special type of rotational motion is circular motion. In circular motion, particles move in a trajectory that is circular in nature, and where the distance between the body's centre of mass and the axis of rotation remains fixed. In the example of rotation of Earth, all the particles on Earth's surface follow a circular motion while Earth itself carries out rotatory motion.

OSCILLATORY MOTION

A continuous to and fro motion of a body that takes place about a fixed point is called oscillatory motion. Example of oscillatory motion is that of a pendulum. When the amplitude of oscillation is very small, the oscillatory motion is called vibratory motion or vibration.

Motion Based on Dimension

Based on the dimensionality, motion can be categorized into one-dimensional, two-dimensional and three-dimensional.

MOTION IN ONE DIMENSION

The motion of a body is said to be in one dimension if it moves along a straight line in any direction. This type of motion is also called rectilinear or linear motion. Only one position coordinate is required to describe the position of the object.

E.g., Motion of a vehicle along a straight line

MOTION IN TWO DIMENSIONS

The motion of a body is said to be in two dimensions if the position of the object changes coordinates in two directions. In other words, two coordinates are required to describe the motion of the object.

E.g., Motion of a shell fired from a gun

MOTION IN THREE DIMENSIONS

The motion of a body is said to be in three dimensions if the object changes coordinates in three directions. In this type of motion three coordinates are required to describe the position of the particle.

Eg., Motion of a flying insect

Introduction to Some Terms Related to Motion

DISTANCE AND DISPLACEMENT

Distance is the actual length of path covered by a moving particle in a given interval of time. Distance is a scalar quantity.

Displacement is the change in position vector, i.e., a vector joining initial to final position. Displacement is a vector quantity.

SPEED AND VELOCITY

Speed is the rate of change of distance or the distance covered with time. It is a scalar quantity expressed by the symbol v.

Types of Speed

When a particle covers equal distances in equal intervals of time then its speed is said to be **uniform speed.**

When a particle covers unequal distances in equal intervals of time, its speed is said to be non-uniform or **variable speed**.

Average speed of a particle for a given interval of time is defined as the ratio of the total distance travelled during that time to the time taken.

$$\text{Average speed} = \frac{\text{Distance travelled}}{\text{Time taken}}$$

Instantaneous speed is the speed of a particle at a particular instant. In other words, the instantaneous speed is the average speed for an infinitesimally small time interval (i.e., $\Delta t \to 0$). Thus, instantaneous speed is expressed as:

$$\text{Instantaneous speed, } v = \lim_{\Delta t \to 0} \frac{\Delta s}{\Delta t} = \frac{ds}{dt}$$

Velocity is the rate of change of position, i.e., the rate of change of displacement with time. It is a vector quantity having the symbol $\vec{v}$. The arrow overhead indicates it is a vector quantity. Although sometimes we loosely interchange the words speed and velocity and thereby do not show the arrow overhead while expressing velocity, in the strict sense of physics that is wrong and should be avoided.

Types of Velocity

A particle is said to have uniform velocity if the magnitude as well as the direction of its velocity remains the same, and this is possible only when the particles move in the same straight line without changing or reversing its direction.

A particle is said to have non-uniform velocity if either the magnitude or direction (or both) of velocity changes.

Average velocity is defined as the ratio of change of displacement to the time taken by the body for that change of displacement.

Instantaneous velocity is defined as the rate of change of position of vector particles with time at a particular instant of time. Instantaneous velocity is represented as:

ACCELERATION

The rate of change of velocity of an object with time is called acceleration of the object. It is a vector quantity. Its direction is the same as that of change in velocity. It is expressed by the symbol $\vec{a}$.

Types of acceleration

A body is said to have **uniform acceleration** if the magnitude and direction of the acceleration remain constant during the motion of the particle.

A body is said to have **non-uniform acceleration** if its magnitude, or direction, or both, change during motion.

Average acceleration is defined as the ratio of change in velocity over a period of time to the time interval.

$$\text{Average acceleration, } \vec{a} = \frac{\Delta \vec{v}}{\Delta t}$$

Instantaneous acceleration is defined as the change in velocity vector at a particular instant.

$$\text{Instantaneous acceleration, } \vec{a} = \lim_{\Delta t \to 0} \frac{\Delta \vec{v}}{\Delta t} = \frac{d\vec{v}}{dt}$$

POSITION-TIME GRAPHS

In a position-time graph the position is plotted along the y-axis and the time along the x-axis. Different cases arise in the position-time graph.

Case I

Fig. 2.1

The line parallel to the time axis represents the particle at rest.

Case II

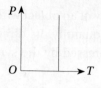

Fig. 2.2

The line parallel to the position axis represents that the particle changes its position without change in time. This is not possible.

Case III

Fig. 2.3

With change in time, the line with a constant slope represents uniform velocity of the particle.

Case IV

Fig. 2.4

The object is moving with uniform positive acceleration.

Case V

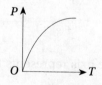

Fig. 2.5

The object is moving with negative acceleration or retardation.

VELOCITY-TIME GRAPHS

In a velocity-time graph the velocity is plotted along the y-axis and the time along the x-axis. Different cases arise in a velocity-time graph.

Case I

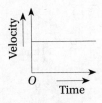

Fig. 2.6

A straight line parallel to the time axis means constant velocity with time, hence no acceleration.

Case II

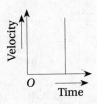

Fig. 2.7

A straight line parallel to the velocity axis means the velocity changes, but without any change in time. This is not possible.

Case III

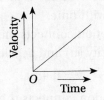

Fig. 2.8

This shows the object moving with increasing velocity with time. Therefore, it is a case of constant acceleration.

Case IV

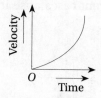

Fig. 2.9

The bending of the line with a positive slope indicates that the acceleration is increasing.

Case V

Fig. 2.10

The bending of the line with a negative slope indicates decreasing acceleration.

Equations of Motion

There are three equations of motion that deal with motion in a straight line. These equations connect initial velocity, final velocity, distance travelled and acceleration with time.

The first equation of motion connects the velocity of a body (v) after time (t) with its initial velocity (u) and acceleration (a) by the equation:

$$v = u + at$$

The second equation of motion connects the distance (s) travelled by a body in time (t), starting from initial velocity (u) and the acceleration being a.

$$s = ut + \frac{1}{2}at^2$$

The third equation of motion connects the initial velocity (u), final velocity (v), acceleration (a) and the distance travelled (s), and the form of the equation is:

$$v^2 = u^2 + 2as$$

Free-falling Objects

So far we have learnt that in motion in one dimension a body accelerates to gain speed (or velocity) with time. When a body falls freely from a vertical distance it hits the ground. A free-falling body is under the sole influence of gravity. In other words, any object that is being acted upon only by the force of gravity is said to be in a state of free fall. The equations of motion discussed in the previous section apply in case of free-falling objects also, but here the acceleration is acceleration due to gravity, g.

$$v = u + gt$$
$$s = ut + 1/2\ gt^2$$
$$v^2 = u^2 + 2gs$$

Motion in Two Dimensions

If an object moves in such a way that its position and velocity at any time can be resolved into a vertical component and a horizontal component, the body is said to be in motion in two dimensions. A projectile is an example of motion in two dimensions. Figure 2.11 shows the two components of velocity at different instants of its trajectory, when a ball is thrown upward at an angle with the ground.

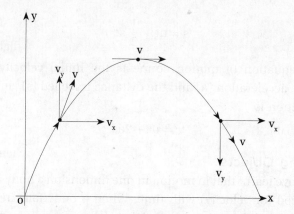

Fig. 2.11: Two components of velocity

In Figure 2.11 that shows the trajectory of a particle thrown upward at an angle with the ground, known as projectile motion, the velocity v has two components v_x and v_y. When the body is going upwards, v_y is directed upward and when it descends, the direction of v_y is downward. At the peak, there is no vertical component of the velocity. The path of the projectile is parabolic.

If the velocity v makes an angle θ with the horizontal direction, then

$v_x = v\cos\vartheta$

and

$v_y = v\sin\vartheta$

The following components of projectile motion should be remembered.

Time of ascent

It is the time during which a particle ascends. It is denoted by t_a.

$$t_a = \frac{v\sin\theta}{g}$$

TIME OF DESCENT

It is the time during which a particle descends. It is denoted by t_d.

$$t_d = \frac{v\sin\theta}{g}$$

TIME OF FLIGHT

It is the total time of ascent and descent. Therefore, time of flight, $T = t_a + t_d$

$$T = \frac{2v\sin\theta}{g}$$

MAXIMUM HEIGHT

It is the maximum height that a particle can go up to, when thrown in a projectile trajectory.

$$H = \frac{v^2\sin^2\theta}{2g}$$

RANGE

It is the horizontal component of the projectile.

$$R = \frac{v^2\sin^2\theta}{2g}$$

Uniform Circular Motion

Uniform circular motion is the motion of an object travelling at a constant speed on a circular path.

Let T be the time the object takes to travel once around the circle, that is, T is the period of the circular motion.

$$T = \frac{2\pi r}{v}$$

In uniform circular motion, the speed is constant, but the direction of the velocity vector is not constant, because being in a circular path, it is changing direction continuously.

Centripetal acceleration is expressed as:

$$a_c = \frac{v^2}{r}$$

where r is the radius of the circular path and v is the velocity of the particle.

The direction of the centripetal acceleration is towards the centre of the circle; in the same direction as the change in velocity.

3

FORCE AND GRAVITATION

INTRODUCTION

Isaac Newton, one of the greatest scientists of all time, who contributed a lot in explaining scientifically various fundamental forces and natural phenomena, was born in England in 1643. He did considerable work on motion. He propounded the three laws of motion which are, till date, considered as the foundation stone for learning about motion. These laws tell us how objects behave at rest and while in motion. These laws also tell us what happens when external force is applied on a body.

NEWTON'S FIRST LAW OF MOTION

Newton's first law of motion states that an object in a state of rest continues to be at rest, or if it is in motion, continues to remain in motion in a straight line, unless acted upon by an external unbalanced force.

In other words, the state of rest or of motion of an object does not change unless an external force causes that to change. That is why Newton's first law of motion is also known as the law of inertia.

If a book is kept on your table, it is not going to move from one place to another unless someone pushes or pulls or lifts it and places it in another position. This external action on the book which causes the change of its position is the external force acting on the book to change it from its state of rest. Similarly, a football kicked will continue to move in a straight line unless another player changes its direction or stops its motion. However, if we slide a block across a table, it eventually comes to a stop and does not continue to be in a straight line of motion forever. Why does this happen? This is because of the frictional force which opposes the movement of the block. This frictional force acts everywhere but we do not see or understand it. Remember, friction from air is also opposing this motion as well as the football in the other example. Also, in the example of football, even if another player does not stop the ball, it will not continue to move in a straight line forever. It is because of the force of friction offered by air as well as the field. Hence, even if it appears to be a case that contradicts Newton's first law of motion, it is actually not doing so. Had the frictional force between the surface of the table and the cover of the book and also friction by air not been there, the moving block on the table would have continued with its motion.

NEWTON'S SECOND LAW OF MOTION

Newton's second law of motion states that when a force acts upon an object, it will cause the object to accelerate. The larger the mass of the object, the greater will be the force needed to cause it to accelerate. This law deals with the quantitative relationship between the mass of the body, the acceleration produced and the force needed for it.

This law may be written as force = mass × acceleration,

that is,

$$F = ma$$

where F is the force, m is the mass and a is the acceleration.

Therefore, between two cars of unequal mass, the heavier car will require more force to move than the lighter car when the acceleration produced by both is the same.

NEWTON'S THIRD LAW OF MOTION

Newton's third law of motion states that for every action, there is an equal and opposite reaction.

This means that for every force there is a reactionary force that is equal in magnitude, but opposite in direction. For example, when you are standing on the ground, you are pushing down on the earth with the same magnitude of force that it is applying on you for pushing back up.

FUNDAMENTAL FORCES IN NATURE

There are four forces in nature which are called the fundamental forces or basic forces. These are the following:

Gravitational force: Weakest force; infinite in range; attractive in nature

Weak nuclear force: Weak but stronger than gravitational force; next in strength to it; very short-ranged

Electromagnetic force: Stronger than weak nuclear force; range is infinite; causes electric and magnetic effects such as the repulsion between like electrical charges or the interaction of bar magnets; can be attractive or repulsive, depending on the nature of the interacting entities

Strong nuclear force: Strongest of all; shortest in range of all the four types of fundamental forces discussed here; responsible for holding the nuclei of atoms together

MOMENTUM

Momentum is defined as the product of mass and velocity. It is a vector quantity and its SI unit is kg m s^{-1}. Therefore, if an object has mass m and is moving with velocity v, its momentum p is given by

Momentum = mass × velocity

$$p = mv$$

The equation illustrates that momentum is directly proportional to an object's mass and its velocity.

LAW OF CONSERVATION OF MOMENTUM

The law of conservation of momentum says that the total momentum of a collection of objects (a system) is conserved, that is, remains the same before and after collision. For a collision occurring between two objects, 1 and 2, in an isolated system, the total momentum of the two objects before the collision is equal to the total momentum of the two objects after the collision. That is, the momentum lost by object 1 is equal to the momentum gained by object 2.

IMPULSE

The term impulse quantifies the overall effect of a force. It is the product of force and the time during which it is exerted. It may so happen that during the time interval, force changes. Therefore, in order to find out the impulse, the average force is taken and multiplied with the time interval. It is conventionally given the symbol J and expressed in newton-second.

Mathematically, $J = F \times t$

Since, $F = ma$

and $a = \dfrac{\Delta v}{\Delta t}$

Therefore, $F\Delta t = m\Delta v = m(v_2 - v_1) = mv_2 - mv_1 = p_2 - p_1$

Thus, impulse is also measured as change in momentum.

It is an interesting and important derivation that impulse is the change of momentum. Sometimes the time of application of force is measured indirectly by measuring the change in momentum and dividing it by the average force applied.

Similarly, force can also be computed if the time of application of force is known.

FRICTION

We have learnt in Newton's first law of motion that a moving body will continue to move without changing direction unless acted upon by an unbalanced force from outside. We find, however, that this actually does not happen. If we kick a ball, it moves in a straight line for some time (depending on how hard the kick is) but comes to a stop eventually. So there must be some invisible external force that is at work. The force that opposes the motion of an object due to its contact with it is called friction. If you look at the surfaces of all objects, they are rough in nature, comprising tiny bumps and ridges. Those microscopic peaks and valleys resist the motion when two objects are moving past each other.

Here is an example. If you push your book on your desk, the book will move. The force of the push moves the book. As the book slides across the desk, it slows down and stops moving. The surface of the table opposes this motion of the book through the contact points that the book has with its surface. The force of friction acts in the opposite direction to the motion.

The equation for determining the force of friction when trying to move two objects or materials with respect to each other gives the relationship between the force of friction, the coefficient of friction and the normal force pushing the two objects together. This equation is written as:

$$F = \mu N$$

where F is the force of friction, μ is the coefficient of friction and N is the normal or the perpendicular force at the point of contact.

Types of Friction

There are three types of friction. These are discussed below.

Static Friction

If you try to slide two objects past each other, a small amount of force may not result in any motion. The force of friction under this condition is greater than the applied force. When a body is at rest, the frictional force that exists between the two surfaces in contact is called static friction.

Limiting Friction

If external force is applied to a static body, the frictional force at work stops the body from moving in the direction of the external force. The maximum amount of frictional force due to which the external force cannot move the body is called the limiting frictional force.

Kinetic Friction

The friction at play between the two contacting surfaces when they have relative motion between them is called kinetic friction. There are two types of kinetic friction—rolling friction and sliding friction. The friction opposing the motion when one body rolls over another is known as rolling friction. When the frictional force is due to sliding of one body over another, the friction is known as sliding friction.

Advantages of Friction

Friction plays an important role in our daily life. The following are some of the cases of friction where it works to our advantage.

We cannot walk steadily on a slippery road because the friction offered by a wet or slippery surface is low. It would not be possible for any vehicle to move on the road if there was no friction. If we hammer a nail in a wooden plank, it is held fixed at a position without slipping inside. This is possible due to friction.

Disadvantages of Friction

Friction offers some disadvantages also.

Friction produces undesired heat in various parts of a machine. This not only leads to wastage of energy but also faster wear and tear of machines.

It opposes motion and hence reduces speed.

Noise produced due to friction is also a disadvantage of friction.

Automobile engines (or, for that matter, any engine) require lubrication to reduce heat and increase their life.

GRAVITATION

Two objects with finite mass in this universe attract each other regardless of the distance of separation between them. The force by which they attract each other is known as the gravitational force. If the mass of the objects is small, this force is small. If the distance separating them is large, the gravitational force is again small. Objects on the earth are pulled by the earth toward its centre. This is known as gravitation force of the earth or simply the earth's gravity.

Universal Law of Gravitation

Consider two bodies with mass M and m are separated by distance r. The force of attraction between them is directly proportional to their masses and inversely proportional to the square of the distance between them. Mathematically,

$$F \alpha = \frac{Mm}{r^2}$$

or,

$$F = G\frac{Mm}{r^2}$$

where G is the universal gravitational constant. Its value is 6.67×10^{-11}

Nm^2kg^{-2}. The dimensional formula of G is $[M^{-1}L^3T^{-2}]$.

Acceleration Due to Gravity

We have already learnt that we call an object a free-falling object when it is falling under the influence of gravity only, and there is no other external force applied to it. A free-falling object has an acceleration of 9.8 m s^{-2}. This is known as the acceleration of gravity. It is denoted by the symbol g. The numerical value for the acceleration of gravity is most accurately known as 9.8 m s^{-2} or 980 cm s^{-2}. Although there will be slight variation in the numerical value of g from one place to another because of different altitudes of different places, for all practical purposes we take 9.8 m s^{-2} or 980 cm s^{-2} as the value of g.

Variations of g:

a) Acceleration due to gravity decreases as we go higher from the surface of the earth.
b) Acceleration due to gravity decreases as we go deep into the earth.
c) At the centre of the earth, the acceleration due to gravity is zero (0).
d) Acceleration due to gravity is minimum at the equator.
e) Acceleration due to gravity is maximum at the poles.
f) Acceleration due to gravity decreases due to rotation while it increases due to increase in latitude.

MASS AND WEIGHT

Mass is a measure of the amount of substance or matter an object is made up of. No matter where the object is, mass is constant, because the matter inside does not change with change in place.

Characteristics of Mass

➤ Mass is indestructible
➤ Mass can never be zero
➤ The SI unit of mass is kg

Weight of a substance is the force by which the earth attracts it to its centre. It is therefore related to gravity and hence varies from place to place as gravity varies from place to place.

Weight is measured as:

Weight = mass × acceleration due to gravity

W = mg

Characteristics of Weight

> The weight of an object changes based on its location
> Weight is a vector and its direction of pull is towards the centre of the planet
> Unlike mass, weight can be zero
> Weight is commonly measured in newton

PLANETS AND SATELLITES

A planet is a heavenly body that revolves round the sun. For example, there are nine planets that revolve round the sun. These are all members of the solar system.

A satellite is a body that revolves round another object in a fixed path, called the orbit. Typically the object around which a satellite orbits is much bigger in size than the satellite. Satellites are of two types. They may be natural ones, like the moon, which revolves around the earth, or artificial ones that are manmade and put into orbit by man. Artificial satellites have been launched for various purposes. Some of the types in which artificial satellites can be grouped into are: weather satellites, navigation satellites, communication satellites, military satellites and scientific satellites. Like we have the moon as the natural satellite to the earth, there are satellites to other planets also. With the launch of artificial communication satellites, a new revolution in communication technology has been ushered in.

GEOSTATIONARY (OR SYNCHRONOUS) SATELLITE

It is a satellite that revolves around the earth in its equatorial plane with the same angular speed and in the same direction as the earth rotates about its own axis. Since it appears stationary to an observer on the earth, it is called a synchronous or geostationary satellite. Geostationary satellites are in orbit above the equator. The height of their orbit, approximately 36,000 km, is just the right distance so that it takes them one day (24 hours) to make each orbit. This means that they stay in a fixed position over the earth's surface. Geostationary satellites always appear in the same position when seen from the ground. This is why satellite television dishes can be bolted into one position and point in one direction, and do not need to move. Geostationary satellites have uses such as communications—including satellite TV and global positioning or GPS, used for navigation systems.

POLAR SATELLITE

It is a satellite that revolves around the earth in its polar orbit (perpendicular to the equatorial plane). These satellites orbit between 100 km and 200 km above the earth's surface, taking around 90 minutes to make each orbit. The earth spins beneath the satellite as it moves, so the satellite can scan the whole surface of the earth. As the earth rotates about its axis, a polar satellite successively passes through different points on its surface, scanning the entire earth. Low orbit polar satellites have uses such as monitoring the weather, observing the earth's surface and military uses including spying, etc.

Figure 3.1 shows the two different types of path and satellites around the earth.

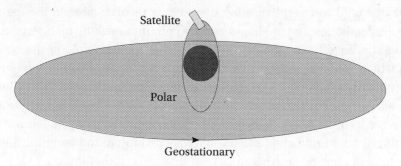

Fig. 3.1: Paths of satellites

Energy of a Satellite

A satellite revolving around the earth has potential energy as well as kinetic energy. It has potential energy because of the attractive force acting on it due to the earth, and kinetic energy because of its motion.

The total energy is given by:

$$E = - GMm/2R$$

The energy required for a satellite to leave its orbit around the earth and escape to infinity is called the binding energy. Since the total energy of a satellite revolving round the earth is—GMm/2R, in order to escape, the satellite would require GMm/2R of energy so that the total energy becomes zero. Thus, the binding energy of the satellite is + GMm/2R.

KEPLER'S LAWS OF PLANETARY MOTION

Kepler's First Law

The orbit of every planet is an ellipse with the sun at one of the two foci.

Kepler's Second Law

A line joining a planet and the sun sweeps out equal areas during equal intervals of time.

Kepler's Third Law

The square of the orbital period of a planet is directly proportional to the cube of the semi-major axis of its orbit.

ESCAPE VELOCITY

Escape velocity (or speed) is the minimum speed needed for an object to escape from the gravitational influence of a massive body. More generally, escape velocity is the speed at which the sum of an object's kinetic energy and its gravitational potential energy is equal to zero. In other words, if given escape velocity, the object will move away from the other body, continually slowing down, and will asymptotically approach zero speed as the object's distance approaches infinity, never to come back. Note that the minimum escape velocity assumes that there is no friction (e.g., atmospheric drag), which would increase the required instantaneous velocity to escape the gravitational influence, and that there will be no future sources of additional velocity (e.g., thrust), which would reduce the required instantaneous velocity. Speeds higher than escape velocity have a positive speed at infinity. The escape velocity from Earth is about 11.186 km s^{-1} at the surface.

4

ROTATIONAL MOTION

INTRODUCTION

The motion that we have studied so far is translational in nature. But there is a second kind of motion, called rotational motion, which deals with the rotation of a body about its centre of mass. The motion that we have studied so far is of a single particle. However, in reality, a particle, which is represented as a point mass and has practically no size, does not exist. Nonetheless, we applied the results of our study to the motion of bodies of finite size, assuming that motion of such bodies can be described in terms of the motion of a particle. That is, however, an idealized condition. In the real world moving bodies are in general not point masses and we have to deal with that situation. We will assume here that such an extended body is a system of particles and that this system of particles is a rigid body, meaning, the distances between all pairs of particles of such a body do not change. Again that is an idealized assumption as no real body is truly rigid, since real bodies are bound to deform under the influence of forces. But in many situations the deformations are very small, hence negligible. In this chapter, we will learn how to deal with the motion of such bodies. The concept of the centre of mass is central and very important to this chapter.

Rotational motion and translational motion have a lot in common. We will introduce some basic concepts that are distinct characteristics of rotational motion.

SOME IMPORTANT CONCEPTS

Rigid Bodies

A rigid body is an object that retains its overall shape. In other words, particles that make up the rigid body stay in the same position relative to one another even when the body is in motion. This essentially means distances between all pairs of particles of such a body do not change. Example of a rigid body is a golf ball. The shape of a golf ball does not change as it rolls and spins.

Centre of Mass

The centre of mass of a body or a system of particles is that unique single point at which the entire mass of the body or the system of particles is considered to be concentrated. It is this point that all the applied forces act on.

Since in translational motion each point on a body undergoes the same displacement with time, the motion of one particle represents the motion of the whole body. But in case of rotation or vibration of a body, only the centre of mass moves in the same way that a single particle would move under the influence of the same external forces. In other words, the centre of mass of a body is that point that moves when forces are applied on the body. The motion of a body can be described as the motion of its centre of mass. The centre of mass has translational motion under the influence of forces. If a single force acts on a body and the line of action of the force passes through the centre of the mass, the body will have linear acceleration but will possess no angular acceleration.

If we consider two masses m1 and m2 situated at a distance x1 and x2 from a fixed point, then the centre of mass can be shown to be at a point x from the same fixed point, such that,

$$x = \frac{m_1x_1 + m_2x_2}{m_1 + m_2}$$

For a set of n particles,

$$x = \frac{m_1x_1 + m_2x_2 + m_3x_3 + m_4x_4 + m_5x_5 + \ldots m_nx_n}{m_1 + m_2 + m_3 + m_4 + m_5 + \ldots m_n}$$

In other words,

$$x = \sum_{i=1}^{n} \frac{m_ix_i}{m_i}$$

The unit of x is that of distance, that is, it is expressed in metre or other units of distance.

Axis of Rotation

The rotational motion of a rigid body occurs when every point in the body moves in a circular path and the centre of the circle lies on a straight line. This line is called the axis of rotation, which cuts through the centre of mass.

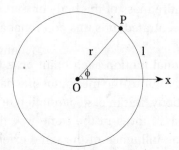

Fig. 4.1: Angular position

Conventionally, angles in a circle are measured in counterclockwise direction from the positive x-axis. The angular position of a particle is the angle subtended between the line connecting that particle (at the circumference of the circle) to the origin and the positive x-axis, measured counterclockwise. The angular position of a point does not depend on how far that point is from the origin, because it is the angle that the line joining the point with the origin makes with the x-axis. Hence all the points on that line will have the same angular position. It is connected with the radius r of the circle and the arc length l subtended by the angular position φ as:

$$\varphi = \frac{l}{r}$$

Angular Displacement

Let us imagine that the wheel is rotated counterclockwise, so that every point on line OP moves from an initial angular position of φ_i to a final angular position of φ_f. The angular displacement θ of line OP is:

$$\vartheta = \varphi_f - \varphi_i$$

It is to be noted here that both the angular positions are measured from the same x-axis line. Hence the difference will give the displacement.

Angular Velocity

Angular velocity, ω, is defined as the change in the angular displacement over time. Average angular velocity, $\bar{\omega}$, is defined by:

$$\bar{\omega} = \frac{\Delta q}{\Delta t}$$

Angular Acceleration

Angular acceleration, α, is defined as the rate of change of angular velocity over time. Average angular acceleration, $\bar{\alpha}$, is defined by:

$$\bar{\alpha} = \frac{\Delta \omega}{\Delta t}$$

Relationship Between Angular Displacement, Velocity and Acceleration to Linear Counterparts

$$l = r\theta$$
$$v = r\omega$$
$$a = r\alpha$$

where, r is the radius, l is the length of the arc, v is the linear velocity, α is the linear acceleration, α is the angular acceleration, ω is the angular velocity and θ is the angular displacement.

Torque

In order that a net force results in rotation of an object, the force has to be applied to a point other than the centre of mass of the object. Net force applied at the centre of mass does not cause rotation. Physicists call the effect of force on rotational motion as torque. Torque or the moment of a force is a measure of how much force is required to act on an object that causes rotation of that object. The object rotates about an axis, which is called the axis of rotation. Let the force be F. The distance from the axis of rotation to the point where the force acts is called the moment arm, and is denoted by r. The torque is the product of the magnitude of the force F and the perpendicular distance from the force to the axis of rotation.

$$\tau = r \times F$$

Its unit is newton metre (Nm).

Moment of Inertia

What can be the reason behind the resistance to translational motion? It is the mass of the body. Similarly, what makes a body difficult to rotate? It is the rotational equivalent of mass that causes the inertia, called the moment of inertia. It is not only mass, but the distribution of a body's mass also has a great effect on its possibility of rotation. As a general rule, a body will rotate more easily if its mass is concentrated near the axis of rotation. The moment of inertia depends on the distance from the axis. If the mass is farther away from the axis, its moment of inertia is greater.

The moment of inertia of a point mass m about an axis at a perpendicular distance of r from it is given by:

$$I = mr^2$$

Its unit is kg m^2.

The moment of inertia of rigid bodies: Suppose a body is made of 'n' number of particles of mass m_1, m_2, m_3, etc. which are at a distance of r_1, r_2, r_3, etc., respectively, from the axis of rotation, then the moment of inertia is:

$$I = \sum_{i=1}^{n} m_i r_i^2$$

The moment of inertia of some of the regular-shaped bodies is given in the figure below. The dotted line shows the axis of rotation.

Body	Figure	Moment of inertia
Solid cylinder or disc	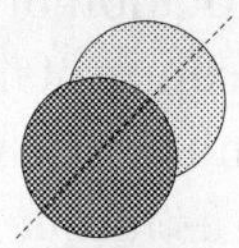	$I = \dfrac{1}{2}MR^2$
Solid sphere	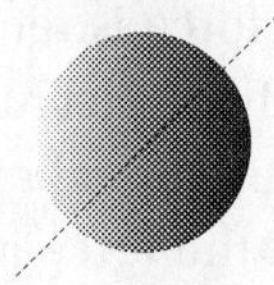	$I = \dfrac{2}{5}MR^2$
Rod with axis or rotation about centre	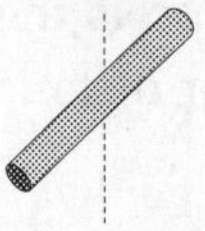	$I = \dfrac{1}{12}ML^2$ where L is the length of the rod

PHYSICS

Rod with axis of rotation at the end	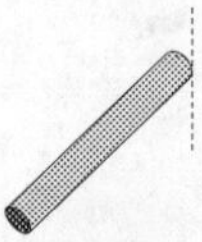	$I = \dfrac{1}{3}ML^2$
This spherical cell	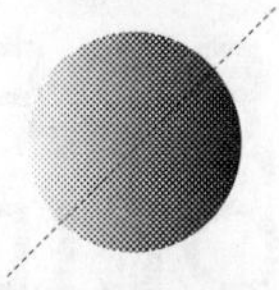	$I = \dfrac{2}{3}MR^2$

Fig. 4.2: Moment of inertia

Kinetic Energy

The kinetic energy of a rotating object is the counterpart of kinetic energy associated with linear motion. The rotational kinetic energy is expressed in terms of the moment of inertia and angular velocity. For a given fixed axis of rotation, the rotational kinetic energy can be expressed as:

$$K.E. = \frac{1}{2}I\omega^2$$

Angular Momentum

The rotational analogue of linear momentum is angular momentum, L. The angular momentum of a particle or body moving in a circular trajectory can be defined in terms of the moment of inertia and angular velocity, just as we can define linear momentum in terms of mass and velocity.

$$L = I\omega$$

Its unit is joule-second.

Conservation of Angular Momentum

The total angular momentum of a system remains constant unless acted upon by an external torque. It means the product of moment of inertia and the angular velocity always remains constant. When I increases, ω decreases to keep the product constant.

$$I_1\omega_1 = I_2\omega_2 = I_3\omega_3 = \ldots$$

5

ELASTIC PROPERTIES OF SOLIDS

INTRODUCTION

Elasticity is the property by virtue of which a body tends to retain its original shape and size after the deforming force is withdrawn. In other words, when external force is applied on a body, it causes its deformation. However, it is the property of elasticity which helps the body regain the original shape and size when the external force is withdrawn. The more the elasticity of a body, the better are the chances of regaining its original configuration.

DEFINITIONS

Perfectly Elastic Body
A body that comes back to its original shape and size completely without any part remaining deformed any more after withdrawal of a deforming force is called a perfectly elastic body.

Plastic Body
A body that does not come back to its original shape and size at all when the external deforming force is withdrawn, and hence remains in deformed shape even after withdrawal of the deforming force, is called a plastic body.

Elastic Limit
The maximum limit up to which a body can show its elastic properties after the deforming force is withdrawn, and beyond which the body remains permanently deformed, is called its elastic limit.

Stress

The effect of application of external force on a body is that to counterbalance its effect, an internal force develops and comes into play, which tries to bring the deformed configuration back to the original shape. This internal force is called stress.

It is measured as the restoring force per unit area. Its unit is Nm^{-2}.

Types of Stress

Four different types of stress can be identified. These are related to the nature of the deforming force applied on the body. These are tensile, compressive, shearing and torsional stress.

When the stress acts normal to the plane of a section, it is called a normal or direct stress. It is a term used to mean both the tensile stress and the compressive stress. Tensile and compressive stress are two types of stress a material can undergo. The type of stress is determined by the force being applied on the material. If it is a tensile (stretching) force, the material experiences a tensile stress. If it is a compressive (squeezing) force, the material experiences a compressive stress. The main difference between tensile and compressive stress is that tensile stress results in elongation, whereas compressive stress results in shortening. If the force is supplied in a horizontal direction on either side, the material tends to gain tensile stress (for stretching) and compressive stress (for squeezing).

The stress set up at the intersection of two bodies, when acting along the surface of the intersection, that is, along a direction tangential to the section, is called shear or tangential stress at the section. If the force is supplied on the surface of the material tangentially, then its angle of position changes, hence it develops shear stress.

The stress developed due to circular shaft by a twisting movement is called torsional stress.

Strain

When a deforming force is applied on a body, its configuration gets deformed. Strain is a measurement of the deformation. It is defined as:

$$\text{Strain} = \frac{\text{Change in configuration}}{\text{Dimension of the original configuration}}$$

Since strain is a ratio of the two quantities whose dimensions are the same, it has no unit. It is just a number representing the relative change in dimension of a body to its original dimension.

Depending on which part of the body is getting deformed, strain can be of different types.

Longitudinal Strain

If the deformation takes place along the length alone, then the strain is called the longitudinal strain.

$$\text{Longitudinal Strain} = \frac{\text{Change in length } (\Delta l)}{\text{Original length } (l)}$$

where change in length = final length – initial (original) length. Longitudinal strain can be either tensile (stretching) or compressive (squeezing) strain.

Shearing Strain

In case of shearing strain, the deformation takes place along a surface. It is the angle through which a face originally perpendicular to the fixed face is deformed. It is the ratio of the displacement of a layer to its distance from the fixed layer (or the width).

$$\text{Shearing Strain} = \frac{\text{Change in length of the uppermost layer of an object } (\Delta x)}{\text{Thickness of the object } (h)}$$

Volume Strain

Volume strain is defined as the change in volume due to deforming force over the original volume.

$$\text{Volume Strain} = \frac{\text{Change in volume } (\Delta v)}{\text{Original volume } (v)}$$

HOOKE'S LAW

Hooke's law deals with stress and strain. It gives a relationship between the two. According to Hooke's law, within the elastic limit, strain produced in a body is directly proportional to the stress developed. In other words,

$$\text{Stress} \propto \text{Strain}$$

Therefore,

$$\frac{\text{Stress}}{\text{Strain}} = E$$

where E is the constant of proportionality, called the modulus of elasticity. Its unit is the same as that of stress, that is, Nm^{-2}.

YOUNG'S MODULUS

Within the elastic limits, the ratio of longitudinal stress to the longitudinal strain is constant and is called Young's modulus of elasticity.

$$\text{Strain} = \frac{\text{Longitudinal stress}}{\text{Longitudinal strain}}$$

$$\frac{\frac{F}{A}}{\frac{\Delta l}{l}} = Y$$

BULK MODULUS

Within the elastic limits, the ratio of volume stress to the volume strain is constant and is called the bulk modulus of elasticity.

$$\frac{\text{Volume stress}}{\text{Volume strain}} = B$$

The bulk modulus is an extension of Young's modulus to three dimensions.

SHEAR MODULUS OR MODULUS OF RIGIDITY

The shear modulus or modulus of rigidity is defined as the shear stress over shear strain.

$$\frac{\text{Shear stress}}{\text{Shear strain}} = G$$

6

MECHANICAL PROPERTIES OF FLUIDS

INTRODUCTION

Liquids and gases are called fluids as they possess the property of flowing. In this chapter you will study about mechanical properties of fluids. Let us understand what is common in liquids and gases and how fluids are different from solids. Stress can change the volume of solids. Stress or external pressure can also change the volume of liquids and gases. However, the change in the volume of gases is much more significant than that of solids and liquids. In other words, solids and liquids are less compressible than gases.

PRESSURE

Pressure is the force applied on an object per its unit area. When an object is submerged in a fluid at rest, the fluid exerts a force on its surface. This force is always normal to the object's surface.

If F is the magnitude of this normal force on a piston of area A then the average pressure P_{av} is

$$P_{av} = \frac{F}{A}$$

Its dimensions are $[ML^{-1}T^{-2}]$.

The SI unit of pressure is Nm^{-2}. It is also called pascal (Pa) in honour of the French scientist Blaise Pascal who carried out pioneering studies on fluid pressure. A common unit of pressure is the atmosphere (atm), i.e., the pressure exerted by the atmosphere at sea level (1 atm = 1.013×10^5 Pa).

DENSITY

Density ρ is an important quantity in describing fluids. For a fluid of mass m occupying volume V, the density is defined as the mass per unit volume.

$$\rho = \frac{m}{V}$$

The dimension of density is ML^{-3}. Its SI unit is kg m^{-3}.

Liquids have their density more or less constant at all pressures because they are by and large incompressible. Gases, on the other hand, show large variation in densities with pressure. This is because gases are highly compressible.

PASCAL'S LAW

According to Pascal, the pressure in a fluid at rest is the same at all points if the points are at the same height. In other words, pressure exerted is the same in all directions in a fluid at rest. Flow of fluid from one place to another is a result of difference in pressure. Putting it differently, in the absence of flow, the pressure in the fluid must be the same everywhere. Wind is the flow of air due to differences in pressure at different places.

VARIATION OF PRESSURE WITH DEPTH

Consider a fluid at rest in a container. Let us consider two points, X and Y, of which point X is at height (h) above the point Y. The pressures at points X and Y are P_X and P_Y respectively. Consider a cylindrical element of fluid having area of base A and height (h). The difference in pressure at the two points of the cylinder, which are at a vertical separation of h, is due to their different heights. Thus, if mg is the weight of the fluid in the cylinder, we can say that the resultant force that balances the weight of the cylinder of liquid is equal. In other words,

$$(P_Y - P_X) A = mg$$

Multiplying both sides of the above expression by h,

$(P_Y - P_X) Ah = mgh$

Or, $(P_Y - P_X) V = mgh$

That is, $(P_Y - P_X) = (m/V) gh$

Or, $P = h\rho g$

This means pressure difference depends on the vertical distance h between the points (X and Y), mass density of the fluid ρ and acceleration due to gravity g.

ATMOSPHERIC PRESSURE

The pressure of the atmosphere at any point equals the weight of a column of air of unit cross-sectional area extending from that point to the top of the atmosphere. At sea level it is 1.013×10^5 Pa. This is defined as one atmospheric pressure unit or 1 atm. The mercury barometer is a device used for measuring atmospheric pressure of a place. It is found that the mercury column in the barometer has a height of about 76 cm at sea level equivalent to 1 atm. It is conventional to report pressure in terms of cm or mm of mercury (Hg). A pressure equivalent of 1 mm of Hg is called a torr (named after the Italian scientist Torricelli).

1 torr = 133 Pa

The units Hg and torr are used in medicine and physiology. In meteorology, common units are the bar and the millibar.

1 bar = 10^5 Pa

ARCHIMEDES' PRINCIPLE

Archimedes' principle states that when a body is fully or partially submerged in a fluid, the upward force, called the buoyant force, exerted on it is equal to the weight of the fluid that the body displaces and acts in the upward direction at the centre of mass of the displaced fluid. Archimedes' principle is a fundamental law of fluid mechanics. The volume of displaced fluid is equivalent to the volume of an object fully immersed in a fluid or to that fraction of the volume below the surface for an object partially submerged in a liquid. The weight of the displaced portion of the fluid is equivalent to the magnitude of the buoyant force.

FLUID IN MOTION: STREAMLINED AND TURBULENT FLOW

The study of fluids in motion is known as fluid dynamics. In the dynamics of fluid flow we study what is happening to various fluid particles at a particular point in space at a particular time. The flow of a fluid is called steady if at any given point the velocity of each passing fluid particle remains constant in time. The velocity of each particle need not be the same. However, the velocity of each particle does not change, and remains constant. Furthermore, the velocity of a particular particle may change as it moves from one point to another. That is, at some other point the particle may have a different velocity, but every other particle which passes the second point behaves exactly like the previous particle that has just passed that point. Each particle follows a smooth path, and the paths of the particles do not cross each other. These are characteristics of steady flow. When the nature of flow of a fluid is steady, its path is called a streamline. A streamline is defined as a curve whose tangent at any point is in the direction of the fluid velocity at that point. According to the equation of continuity, the product of area of cross section through which a certain volume of fluid flows, and the speed of the flow, which indicates the volume flux or flow rate of the fluid, remains constant at any point in the fluid.

A steady flow of fluids occurs when the flow speed is low. When the speed of flow of fluid particles increases and reaches beyond a limiting value, called the critical speed, steadiness ceases to exist and the flow becomes turbulent. One sees this when smoke comes out of a chimney. For the first few feet of its coming out of the chimney the flow remains laminar, but beyond a certain distance, the flow starts to be turbulent.

BERNOULLI'S THEOREM

Bernoulli's theorem, in fluid dynamics, establishes the relationship among pressure, velocity and elevation in a moving fluid (liquid or gas), when the flow of fluid is steady or laminar, and the compressibility and viscosity (internal friction) of the fluid are negligible. The theory was first derived and propounded by the Swiss mathematician Daniel Bernoulli. According to the theorem, the total mechanical energy of the flowing fluid, which comprises the energy associated with fluid pressure, the gravitational potential energy of elevation and the kinetic energy of fluid motion remain constant. Bernoulli's theorem is the principle of energy conservation for ideal fluids in a steady or streamlined flow.

Bernoulli's theorem implies, therefore, that if the fluid flows horizontally so that no change in gravitational potential energy occurs, then a decrease in fluid pressure is associated with an increase in fluid velocity. If the fluid is flowing through a horizontal pipe of varying cross-sectional area, for example, the fluid speeds up in constricted areas so that the pressure the fluid exerts is least where the cross section is smallest.

MAGNUS EFFECT

The generation of a sidewise force on a spinning cylindrical or spherical solid immersed in a fluid when there is relative motion between the spinning body and the fluid is called the Magnus effect, named after the German physicist and chemist H.G. Magnus, who first (in 1853) experimentally investigated the effect. The Magnus effect is responsible for the curve of a served tennis ball. It also affects the trajectory of a spinning artillery shell.

A spinning object moving through a fluid departs from its straight path because of pressure differences that develop in the fluid as a result of velocity changes induced by the spinning body. In the case of a ball spinning through the air, the turning ball drags some of the air around with it. Viewed from the position of the ball, the air is rushing by on all sides. The drag of the side of the ball turning into the air retards the airflow, whereas on the other side the drag speeds it up. Greater pressure on the side where the airflow is slowed down forces the ball in the direction of the low-pressure region on the opposite side, where a relative increase in airflow occurs.

TORRICELLI'S THEOREM

Torricelli's theorem establishes a relation between the speed of fluid flowing out of a small opening to the height of fluid above the opening. The law states that the speed of efflux, v, of a fluid through a sharp-edged hole at the bottom of a tank filled to a depth h is the same as the speed that a body would acquire in falling freely from a height h, i.e., v = √2gh where g is the acceleration due to gravity.

VISCOSITY

A liquid can be considered to be made up of several layers. When the liquid flows, there is friction between the layers. As a result of this, every layer below one layer opposes the forward movement of the upper layer. Viscosity is a property of the fluid which opposes the relative motion between the two layers of the fluid that are moving at different velocities. The more the viscosity of a liquid, the slower will be the movement of its layers. In other words, the more viscous a liquid is, the stickier it is, and as a result, the more difficult it is to pour it out of a container. Between water and honey, we find it is easier to pour out water from a container compared to honey. Hence honey is more viscous.

STOKES' LAW

Stokes' law deals with frictional force exerted on spherical objects in a viscous fluid. Stokes' law states that the force of viscosity on a small sphere moving through a viscous fluid is given by:

$$F = 6\pi\eta rv$$

where F is the frictional force—known as Stokes' drag—acting on the interface between the fluid and the particle, η is the dynamic viscosity, r is the radius of the spherical object and v is the flow velocity relative to the object.

TERMINAL VELOCITY

If an object is falling through a fluid (liquid or gas), as its speed increases, the drag on it will also increase. Eventually a speed will be reached where the upward force will equal the weight of the object. As there is no net force on the object, the acceleration will be zero under this condition. The object will fall at a constant velocity. This velocity is called the terminal velocity.

SURFACE TENSION

The surface of a liquid is in contact with the layer of air above it. Surface tension is the property by virtue of which the surface acts like a thin elastic sheet. The free surface of liquid at rest tends to have minimum surface area and therefore it behaves as if it is covered with a stretched membrane.

Surface tension (denoted by gamma, γ) is defined as the ratio of the surface force, F, to the length, d, along which the force acts:

$$\gamma = F/d$$

Surface tension is measured in SI units of Nm^{-1} (newton per metre).

Examples of Surface Tension

Drops of water: When using a water dropper, the water does not flow in a continuous stream, but rather in a series of drops. The shape of the drops is caused by the surface tension of the water. The only reason the drop of water isn't completely spherical is because of the force of gravity pulling down on it. In the absence of gravity, the drop would minimize the surface area in order to minimize tension, which would result in a perfectly spherical shape.

Needle (or paper clip) floating on water: Even though the density of these objects is greater than water, the surface tension along the depression is enough to counteract the force of gravity pulling down on the metal object.

ANGLE OF CONTACT

The surface of any liquid is an interface between that liquid and some other medium. The top surface of water in a test tube, for example, is an interface between the water and the air. Surface tension is thus not a property of the liquid alone, but a property of the liquid's interface with another medium. If a liquid is in a container, then besides the liquid/air interface at its top surface, there is also an interface between the liquid and the walls of the container. Where the two surfaces meet, they form a contact angle, θ. The contact angle is the angle the tangent to the surface makes with the solid surface. Note that the angle is measured through the liquid.

When water is taken in a glass vessel, the surface of the water touching the walls is concave upward, while in case of mercury in a glass vessel, the surface of mercury touching the walls is convex upward.

When the liquid surface is concave upward, the angle of contact is acute, whereas for a convex upward liquid surface, the angle of contact is obtuse. In case of an acute angle of contact, the liquid wets the glass surface, whereas for an obtuse angle of contact, the liquid does not wet the glass surface. Figure 6.1 shows the three cases of angle of contact and the nature of the meniscus of water.

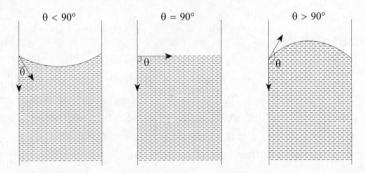

Fig. 6.1: Angle of contact and liquid meniscus

7

SIMPLE HARMONIC MOTION

INTRODUCTION

Simple harmonic motion is the type of periodic motion or oscillatory motion in which the restoring force is directly proportional to the displacement and acts in the direction opposite to that of the displacement. Since the restoring force acts in the opposite direction, the particle goes to one extreme and comes back to reach the other extreme, only to go back again to the other extreme. This goes on and on. This is therefore the to and fro motion of oscillations or vibrations.

Most common examples of simple harmonic motion are the oscillation of a spring, oscillation of a pendulum, etc. A good approximation of an oscillatory pendulum representing simple harmonic motion is when the angle of the swing is small and the mass of the bob of the pendulum is very less (ideally it should be a particle of zero mass).

PERIODIC MOTION

A motion which repeats itself at regular intervals of time is called periodic motion. Examples of periodic motion are the revolution of the earth around the sun, in which the earth repeats passing through a particular point every 365 days and the rotation of the earth around its own axis, in which it crosses a particular point every 24 hours.

Simple Harmonic Motion

The definition of simple harmonic motion states that the acceleration, a, of a particle or an object is proportional and in opposition to its displacement, x, from its equilibrium position.

A (t) ∝ -x (t)

i.e., a (t) = -kx (t)

where k is a constant of proportionality.

Since simple harmonic motion is a periodic oscillation, we can measure its period (the time it takes for one oscillation) and therefore determine its frequency (the number of oscillations per unit time, or the inverse of the period).

TIME PERIOD

The time taken for the particle to complete one oscillation, that is, the time taken for the particle to move from its starting position and return to its original position, is known as the time period, and is generally given the symbol T.

FREQUENCY

The frequency, ν (Greek letter nu), is related to the period. It is defined as the number of oscillations occurring in one second. Since the period is the time taken for one oscillation, the frequency is given by:

$$\nu = 1/T$$

The frequency is measured in s^{-1}. This unit is known as the Hertz (Hz) in honour of the physicist Heinrich Hertz. The frequency is also given the symbol f.

AMPLITUDE

The maximum displacement of the particle from its resting position is known as the amplitude. It is denoted by the symbol A.

PHASE

The phase of a particle vibrating in simple harmonic motion is the state of the particle as regards to its direction of motion and position at any instant of time. It is denoted by φ.

SIMPLE PENDULUM

A simple pendulum oscillates back and forth continuously. The time period of oscillation of a simple pendulum is

$$T = 2\pi \sqrt{\frac{l}{g}}$$

where the mass m is attached to the end of a pendulum of length l, will oscillate with a time period T and g is the gravitational acceleration.

The time period T of oscillation when a mass m attached to a spring with spring constant k will oscillate is given by

$$T = 2\pi \sqrt{\frac{m}{k}}$$

At the maximum displacement, all the energy in the system is in the form of potential energy and the velocity is zero, but this is all converted into kinetic energy once the mass reaches the equilibrium position where it has maximum velocity.

GRAPHICAL REPRESENTATION OF SIMPLE HARMONIC MOTION

Graphical representation of displacement, velocity and acceleration of a particle vibrating in simple harmonic motion with respect to time t is shown in Figure 7.1.

Displacement with time graph of a particle vibrating in simple harmonic motion shows that it is a sine curve. Maximum displacement of the particle is y = ±a (the sign signifies the alternate crest and trough nature of the curve).

TYPES OF PENDULUM

Simple Pendulum
If a point mass is hung by a weightless, inextensible and perfectly flexible string from a rigid support, then this arrangement is called a simple pendulum. If a simple pendulum has time period 2 s, then it is called a seconds pendulum.

Compound Pendulum

When a hard object is suspended from an axis and made to oscillate about that, then it is called a compound pendulum.

Physical Pendulum

When a rigid body is capable of oscillating about an axis, it is called a physical pendulum.

Conical Pendulum

When a simple pendulum fixed at one end has its bob rotating in a horizontal circle, it is called a conical pendulum.

FREE, DAMPED AND FORCED OSCILLATIONS

There are three main types of simple harmonic motion:

(i) Free oscillations: Simple harmonic motion with a constant amplitude and period and no external influences
(ii) Damped oscillations: Simple harmonic motion but with a decreasing amplitude and varying period due to external or internal damping forces
(iii) Forced oscillations: Simple harmonic motion but driven externally

Free Oscillations

The amplitude remains constant as time passes. This type of oscillation is ideal and will probably occur only in theory since in practice there will always be some damping.

In case of free oscillation, the system vibrates with its own natural frequency without the help of any external periodic force.

Forced Oscillations

When a body oscillates with the help of an external periodic force with a frequency different from the natural frequency of the body, its oscillations are called forced oscillations. A simple example of forced vibrations is a child's swing—as one pushes it, its amplitude increases.

Damped Oscillations

If the amplitude of oscillation decreases with time and finally becomes zero, the type of oscillation is called damped oscillations. These are oscillations where energy is taken from the system and so the amplitude decays. They may be of two types: natural damping and artificial damping. Figure 7.1 shows the displacement versus time curve of a damped oscillation indicating how the amplitude of vibration decreases with time.

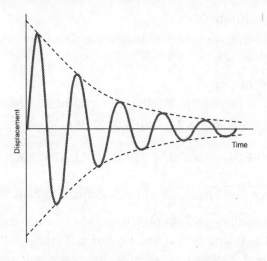

Fig. 7.1: Damped harmonic motion

RESONANCE

Resonance is a phenomenon in which a vibrating system or an external force causes another system around it to vibrate with greater amplitude at specific frequencies. The frequency at which the second body starts oscillating or vibrating at a higher amplitude is called the resonant frequency of the body. At resonant frequencies, small periodic driving forces have the ability to produce large amplitude oscillations, due to the storage of vibrational energy. Resonance occurs when a system is able to store and easily transfer energy between two or more different storage modes (such as kinetic energy and potential energy in the case of a simple pendulum). Resonance occurs with all types of vibrations or waves. Some of the instances are mechanical resonance, acoustic resonance, electromagnetic resonance, nuclear magnetic resonance (NMR), electron spin resonance (ESR), etc. Resonant systems can be used to generate vibrations of a specific frequency (for example, as in musical instruments), or pick out specific frequencies from a complex vibration containing many frequencies (for example, in filters).

PHYSICS

8

THERMAL PROPERTIES OF MATTER AND THERMODYNAMICS

INTRODUCTION

Heat is a form of energy. When heat is applied, the temperature of a body increases. When heat is withdrawn, temperature of the body decreases. In other words, temperature is the manifestation of heat. It may also be said that temperature is the effect and heat is the cause. The effect of heat is also manifested in the thermal expansion of matter. For example, when a solid or a liquid or a gas is heated, its volume expands. For example, when an iron ring is fitted into the wheel of a bullock cart, it is heated. On heating, it expands, and when it cools it contracts again, so that it fits into the wheel well. There are many other examples of practical application of heat that we have studied in middle school physics. In this chapter we will study about heat and thermal properties of matter.

HEAT AND TEMPERATURE

Temperature is a measure of hotness or coldness. An object having higher temperature than another object is said to be hotter than the latter. Although temperature can be perceived by touch, since the feeling could be relative, a thermometer is used to measure temperature. If a bowl of hot water is placed in water at room temperature taken in a bigger bowl, the water in the smaller bowl gets colder and that in the bigger bowl gets hotter until the temperature of water in both the containers becomes the same. Therefore, it can be concluded that transfer of heat takes place from a body having higher temperature to a body having lower temperature. In other words, heat flows from a hotter body to a colder body. If a cup of hot coffee is left on a table, the heat escapes to the surrounding and the coffee gets colder eventually to attain room temperature. If the cup of coffee is called the system, the medium outside it is called the surrounding. Therefore, heat transfer occurs between the system and the surrounding, until the system and the surrounding are at the same temperature. This state at which the system and the surrounding attain the same temperature is call thermal equilibrium.

So we can say that when there is temperature difference either between two (or more) systems or a system and its surroundings, heat as a form of energy is transferred between the two (or more) systems or between the system and the surrounding in the direction of higher temperature to lower temperature until both the temperatures become equal. The SI unit of heat energy is joule (J) while the SI unit of temperature is kelvin (K). Commonly used units of temperature are °C and °F. In the next section, we will discuss the relationship between different scales of measurement of temperature.

Measurement of Temperature

Temperature is measured using a thermometer. The commonly used property that is used in measuring temperature by a thermometer is the variation of the volume of a liquid with temperature. Mercury and alcohol are the liquids used in most liquid-in-glass thermometers. However, many other physical properties of materials that change sufficiently with temperature have also been used as the basis for constructing thermometers. Thermometers are calibrated so as to assign a numerical value to a given temperature. For the definition of any standard scale, two fixed reference points are needed: the upper fixed point and the lower fixed point. The most convenient upper and lower fixed points considered are the steam point and the ice point of water, also known as boiling point and freezing point, respectively. These two points are the temperatures at which pure water boils and freezes under 1 atm pressure. The two most commonly used temperature scales are the Celsius scale and the Fahrenheit scale. The freezing point and the boiling point (at 1 atm pressure) have values of 0°C and 100°C, respectively, on the Celsius scale and 32°F and 212°F, respectively, on the Fahrenheit scale. The two scales contain divisions between the two temperatures. Therefore, on the Celsius scale, there are 100 equal intervals between two reference points, and on the Fahrenheit scale this number is 180. The relationship between the two scales is:

$$\frac{C}{100} = \frac{F - 32}{180}$$

or,

$$\frac{C}{5} = \frac{F - 32}{9}$$

where C is the temperature in the Celsius scale and F is the temperature in the Fahrenheit scale.

The relationship between the Celsius scale and the Kelvin scale of temperature is:

$$T (K) = t (°C) + 273.15$$

Thermal Expansion

Change in the temperature of a body causes change in its dimensions. Expansion on heating and contraction on cooling is our common knowledge and all of us have experienced this. Most substances expand on heating and contract on cooling. The increase in the dimensions of a body due to the increase in its temperature is called thermal expansion. Thermal expansion refers to a fractional change in size of a material in response to a change in temperature. When the expansion in length takes place, it is called linear expansion. The expansion in area is called area expansion. The expansion in volume is called volume expansion.

If l is the length of a substance, Δl is the change in length, then for a small change in temperature, ΔT, the fractional change in length, $\Delta l / l$, is directly proportional to ΔT.

$$\frac{\Delta l}{l} \text{ is directly proportional to } \Delta T$$

Thus,

$$\frac{\Delta l}{l} \alpha \Delta T$$

where α is known as the coefficient of linear expansion and is characteristic of the material of the substance.

The fractional change in area due to thermal expansion, $\Delta A/A$, and the fractional change in volume due to thermal expansion, $\Delta V/V$, are connected to the coefficient of linear expansion as:

$$\frac{\Delta A}{A} = 2\alpha\Delta T$$

$$\frac{\Delta V}{V} = 3\alpha\Delta T$$

Specific Heat

The quantity of heat required to warm a given substance depends on its mass, m, the change in temperature, ΔT and the nature of the substance. Heat capacity or thermal capacity is a measurable quantity and is defined as the ratio of the heat added to (or removed from) an object for the resulting temperature change. Therefore, heat capacity, S, of a substance is defined as:

$$S = \frac{\Delta Q}{\Delta T}$$

where Q is the heat.

The specific heat per unit mass is called specific heat capacity, denoted by lowercase s.

$$S = \frac{S}{m} = \frac{1}{m}\frac{\Delta Q}{\Delta T}$$

The specific heat capacity is defined as the amount of heat per unit mass absorbed or rejected by the substance to change its temperature by one unit. It depends on the nature of the substance and its temperature. The SI unit of specific heat capacity is $J\ kg^{-1}\ K^{-1}$.

If the amount of substance is specified as the number of moles, μ, instead of mass, m, in kg, the heat capacity per mole of the substance is defined as:

$$C = \frac{S}{\mu} = \frac{1}{m}\frac{\Delta Q}{\Delta T}$$

C is called the molar specific heat capacity. The SI unit of molar specific heat capacity is $J\ mol^{-1}\ K^{-1}$. For a gas, since the change in temperature can take place at a constant volume or at a constant pressure, there are two molar heat capacities defined for a gas—molar heat capacity at constant volume, C_v, and molar heat capacity at a constant pressure, C_p.

Change of State

Normally there are three states of matter. These are solid, liquid and gas. When one state changes into another, it is called change of state of matter. Solid changes to liquid, liquid changes to gas, liquid to solid, gas to liquid, and in a few cases solid to gas and gas to solid also. These changes can occur when the exchange of heat takes place between a substance and its surroundings.

When a change of state takes place, the heat supplied does not bring about any change in temperature. Let us understand this with the help of an example. If a block of ice is heated, we will observe no change in the temperature so long as the substance is ice in the beaker. In the above process, the temperature of the system does not change, even though heat is being continuously supplied. The heat supplied is being utilized in changing the state from solid (ice) to liquid (water). It is observed that the temperature remains constant until the entire amount of the solid ice melts. The phenomenon of change of state from solid to liquid is called melting and that from liquid to solid is called freezing. The temperature at which the solid and the liquid states of a substance are in thermal equilibrium with each other is called its melting point. It depends on pressure. The melting point of a substance at 1 atm pressure is called its normal melting point.

The change of state from liquid to vapour (or gas) is called vaporization. The temperature at which the liquid and the vapour states of the substance coexist is called its boiling point. The boiling point of a substance at 1 atm pressure is called its normal boiling point. Boiling point increases with increase in pressure and decreases with decrease in pressure. It is for this reason that the pressure cooker is used for cooking at high altitudes because at high altitudes, due to low pressure, water boils at low temperature. Use of a pressure cooker makes the boiling point higher, thereby increasing the temperature, hence, cooking becomes faster.

The change from solid to vapour state directly, without passing through the liquid state, is called sublimation. The temperature at which the solid and vapour phases coexist is called the sublimation temperature.

We have already learnt that while a change of state occurs, the temperature of the system does not increase even while heating goes on. This heat is called the latent heat. Latent heat is thermal energy released or absorbed, by a body or a system, during a constant temperature process— usually during phase transition. Latent heat can therefore be understood as heat energy in hidden form which is supplied or extracted to change the state of a substance without changing its temperature.

Heat Transfer

Heat transfer is the process of transfer of heat from a body at higher temperature to that at lower temperature. Heat transfer between two bodies or between a system and its surrounding occurs when there is difference in temperature between the two bodies or between the system and the surrounding. Heat flows from the hotter body to the colder body. There are three ways by which transfer of heat takes place.

Modes of Heat Transfer

There are three modes of heat transfer between two bodies: conduction, convection and radiation.

Conduction

The transfer of heat between two solid bodies is called conduction. It depends on the difference in temperature of the two bodies or of the two parts of a body. Heat flows from the hotter part to the colder part. It occurs by the mechanism of inter-molecular energy transfer and requires a material medium. An example of conduction heat transfer is two bodies at different temperatures kept in contact with each other. Another example is heating one end of a metallic container; due to conduction the other end of the metal also gets heated.

Convection

Energy transfer across a system boundary due to a temperature difference by the combined mechanisms of intermolecular interactions and bulk transport is called convection. Convection needs fluid matter. Let us consider a vessel of water being heated. In this case heating of water due to transfer of heat from the vessel is heat transfer by convection.

Radiation

When two bodies are at different temperatures and separated by distance, the heat transfer between them is called radiation. In case of the methods of conduction and convection for heat transfer, there is a medium to transfer the heat, but in case of radiation there is no medium. The radiation heat transfer occurs due to the electromagnetic waves that exist in the atmosphere. One of the most important examples of radiation heat transfer is the heat of the sun coming to the earth.

Thermal Conductivity

Thermal conductivity is the property of a material to conduct heat. Different materials have different thermal conductivity. Heat transfer occurs at a lower rate in materials of low thermal conductivity than in materials of high thermal conductivity. Using this property, different materials find usage in different purposes. For example, materials of high thermal conductivity are widely used in heat sink applications while materials of low thermal conductivity are used as thermal insulation. The thermal conductivity of a material may depend on temperature. The reciprocal of thermal conductivity is called thermal resistivity.

Coefficient of thermal conductivity (κ) is defined as the amount of heat flowing in a second between two opposite faces of a cube of side 1 m kept at a temperature difference of 1 K.

Rate of flow of heat:

$$\frac{dQ}{dT} = \frac{\kappa A (T_1 - T_2)}{d}$$

where, κ is the coefficient of thermal conductivity, A is the area of cross section of the face and $(T_1-T_2)/d$ is the temperature gradient.

The SI unit of κ is $Js^{-1}m^{-1}K^{-1}$.

Newton's Law of Cooling

The rate of heat loss by a body or the rate of cooling of an object, that is, the rate of temperature change, is directly proportional to the difference in temperature between the body and the surroundings:

$$T = T_2 + (T_1 - T_2)e^{-kt}$$

where T_1 is the initial temperature (of the system), T_2 is the final temperature (of the surrounding), and T is the temperature after time t; k is a proportionality constant.

Thermal Radiation

Thermal radiation is the radiation that gives the sensation of warmth in our body. Any matter with temperature greater than absolute zero emits thermal radiation. This is because at absolute zero all types of motion freeze in the body. Sunrays coming to the earth are thermal radiations. Even heat emitted by a hot body is thermal radiation.

BLACK BODY

A black body is an object that absorbs all incident electromagnetic radiation, regardless of their frequency. No radiation passes through a black body and none are reflected. Because no light is reflected or transmitted, it appears black when cold. That is why the name is 'black body'. This also implies that a perfect black body has unit absorptivity. To stay in thermal equilibrium, the black body must emit radiation at the same rate as it absorbs it; so a black body also radiates well. The body is capable of emitting the full radiation spectrum. The re-radiation of energy is characteristic of the radiating system, that is the black body only, and not dependent upon the type of radiation which is incident upon it. The radiated energy can be considered to be produced by a standing wave or resonant modes of the cavity that are radiating.

Kirchoff's Law

Kirchhoff's law states that for a body of any material emitting and absorbing thermal electromagnetic radiation at every wavelength in thermodynamic equilibrium, the ratio of its emissive power to its coefficient of absorption is equal to a universal function only of radiative wavelength and temperature. That universal function describes the perfect black-body emissive power. Here, the dimensionless coefficient of absorption (or the absorptivity) is the fraction of incident light (power) that is absorbed by the body when it is radiating and absorbing in thermodynamic equilibrium.

$$\frac{e_\lambda}{a_\lambda} = E_\lambda$$

where e_λ is the emissive power of the body, a_λ is the absorptive power of the body and E_λ is a constant.

Stefan's Law

The amount of heat radiated by a unit area of surface in 1 sec is directly proportional to the fourth power of the temperature (in absolute scale) of the body.

$$E = \sigma T^4$$

where s is Stefan's constant. The unit of s is $Jm^{-2}s^{-1}K^{-4}$ or $Wm^{-2}K^{-4}$ and its value is $5.67 \times 10^{-8}\ Wm^{-2}K^{-4}$.

Wein's Displacement Law

Wien's displacement law states that the black body radiation curve for different temperatures peaks at a wavelength inversely proportional to the temperature (in absolute scale). In other words, at a particular temperature (in absolute scale), the product of maximum wavelength and temperature (in absolute scale, T) is constant.

$$\lambda_m T = b\ \text{(constant)}$$

The value of b is $2.9 \times 10^{-3}mK$, and it is called Wien's displacement constant.

THERMODYNAMICS

Thermodynamics is the study of conversion of heat energy into work and vice versa, energy transformation and its relation to matter. One of the most important things to remember is that thermodynamics is a macroscopic science. It deals with bulk systems and does not go into the molecular constituent of matter. Small-scale gas interactions are described by the kinetic theory of gases. The state of a gas in thermodynamics is specified by macroscopic variables, that is, pressure, volume, temperature and the number of moles, which are measurable and can be observed. Furthermore, there are other parameters like enthalpy, entropy, etc. which we measure in thermodynamics. There are four fundamental laws of thermodynamics. However, the numbering of these laws is somewhat confusing. They are called the zeroth law, first law, second law and third law of thermodynamics. The zeroth law of thermodynamics was propounded much later than the first and second laws of thermodynamics.

A Few Definitions

System and Surrounding

A system is defined as a region of space that contains a quantity of matter along with the energy content of that matter, or a region in space chosen for study. The mass or region immediately outside the system is called the surroundings. A system is enclosed by walls that bind it and connect it to its surroundings.

Boundary

It is the real or imaginary surface that separates the system from its surroundings. The boundaries of a system can be fixed (e.g., a constant volume reactor) or movable (e.g., a piston). Mathematically, the boundary has zero thickness, no mass and no volume. Often a wall restricts passage across it by some form of matter or energy. Ideally, a wall may be declared adiabatic, diathermal, impermeable, permeable or semi-permeable. Actual physical materials that provide walls with such idealized properties are not always readily available. The properties of the walls determine what transfers can occur.

Isolated, Closed and Open Systems

A system with walls that prevent all transfers is said to be isolated. A system whose walls allow transfer of energy as heat and as work, but not of matter, between the system and its surroundings, is called a closed system. On the other hand, the walls of an open system allow transfer, both of matter and of energy.

Thermodynamic Processes

A system is said to undergo a thermodynamic process when either there is some change in energy within the system, which is generally associated with changes in pressure, volume and temperature, or some heat transfer.

There are a few specific types of thermodynamic processes as described below.

Adiabatic process: A process with no heat transfer into or out of the system

Isochoric process: A process with no change in volume, in which case the system does no work

Isobaric process: A process with no change in pressure

Isothermal process: A process with no change in temperature

Zeroth Law of Thermodynamics

Two systems each in thermal equilibrium with a third system are in thermal equilibrium to each other. The zeroth law clearly suggests that when two systems, A and B, are in thermal equilibrium, there must be a physical quantity that has the same value for both. This thermodynamic variable whose value is equal for two systems in thermal equilibrium is called the temperature (T). Thus we mathematically express the zeroth law as:

If A and B are separately in thermal equilibrium with C, then
$T_A = T_C$ and $T_B = T_C$
This implies that $T_A = T_B$
i.e., the systems A and B are also in thermal equilibrium.

INTERNAL ENERGY

Internal energy, U, of a gas is the sum of the kinetic and potential energies of its molecules only. Kinetic energy due to various types of motion (translational, rotational and vibrational) is to be included in U. However, if the container in which the substance is kept (system) is itself moving, then its kinetic energy is neglected and not included in the internal energy of the system.

The internal energy of a system can be changed by heat and work. Heat may be supplied to the system or released by the system. Similarly, work may be done on the system or by the system.

First Law of Thermodynamics

The energy of the universe is constant. Energy can neither be created nor destroyed. However, energy can be transferred from the system to its surroundings, or vice versa. The change in the internal energy of a system is the amount of energy added to the system minus the energy spent doing work by the system.

Let
ΔQ = Heat supplied *to* the system
ΔW = Work done *on* the system
ΔU = Change in internal energy *of* the system

The general principle of conservation of energy then implies that
$\Delta U = \Delta Q + \Delta W$

i.e., the heat energy (ΔQ) supplied to the system goes in partly to increase the internal energy of the system (ΔU) and the rest in work done on the system. The above equation is known as the first law of thermodynamics.

SIGN CONVENTION FOR INTERNAL ENERGY, HEAT AND WORK

When heat and work increase the internal energy of a system ($\Delta E > 0$), they are taken to be positive. Thus when heat is supplied to the system and work is done on the system, they are taken to be positive.

When heat and work decrease the internal energy of a system ($\Delta E < 0$), they are taken to be negative. Thus when heat is released by the system and work is done by the system, they are taken to be negative.

In other words, the internal energy and temperature of a system decrease ($\Delta E < 0$) when the system either loses heat or does work on its surroundings. Conversely, the internal energy and temperature increase ($\Delta E > 0$) when the system gains heat from its surroundings or when the surroundings do work on the system.

THERMODYNAMIC PROPERTIES AND PROCESSES

An intensive property is a property of a system that does not depend on the system size or the amount of material in the system. Therefore, it is a physical property. For example, temperature, T, of a substance, density, ρ, does not depend on the quantity of substance, and hence is intensive. On the other hand, an extensive property is additive for subsystems. This means the value of the property for the system would be the sum of the property for each subsystem. Example, mass, m and volume, V.

A process in which the temperature of the system is constant throughout is called an isothermal process. A process in which the pressure is constant throughout is called an isobaric process. In an isochoric process the volume is constant. If the system is insulated from the surroundings in such a way that no heat flows between the system and the surroundings, the process is adiabatic.

Second Law of Thermodynamics
It is impossible for a process to have, as its sole result, the transfer of heat from a cooler body to a hotter one.

KELVIN-PLANCK STATEMENT

No process is possible whose sole result is the absorption of heat from a reservoir and the complete conversion of the heat into work.

CLAUSIUS STATEMENT

No process is possible whose sole result is the transfer of heat from a colder object to a hotter object.

The second law implies that no heat engine can have efficiency η equal to 1 or no refrigerator can have co-efficient of performance α equal to infinity.

Reversible and Irreversible Process

A process is reversible if both the system and the surroundings return to their original state after the process is over, with no other change anywhere else in the universe. However, a process that goes on in one direction and even if it is reversed, neither the system nor the surroundings return to the original state, is called irreversible. Spontaneous processes of nature are irreversible.

Carnot Cycle

The Carnot cycle consists of the following four processes so that the system comes back to the initial condition after four steps that take place one after another, as given below:

A reversible isothermal gas expansion process, followed by a reversible adiabatic gas expansion process, followed by a reversible isothermal gas compression process, and finally a reversible adiabatic gas compression process.

The efficiency of a Carnot engine is given by:

$$\eta = 1 - \frac{T_2}{T_1}$$

where T_1 and T_2 are the temperatures of source and sink, respectively.

Third Law of Thermodynamics

It is impossible to reduce any system to absolute zero in a finite series of operations. This means that a perfectly efficient heat engine cannot be created.

9

WAVE MOTION AND SOUND

INTRODUCTION

Wave motions are an integral part of our daily life and hence study of wave motion is very important. Examples of wave motion include waves on strings, water waves, seismic waves, sound and all electromagnetic radiation including light, heat, x-rays, etc. Although all of them are waves, there are certain common elements to all the various types of wave motion and there are also some differences. In this chapter we will learn about mechanical waves, and electromagnetic waves will be the subject matter of another chapter.

TYPES OF WAVES

There are three types of waves:

Mechanical Waves
These waves can only be created in and propagated through material medium. Mechanical waves can be either longitudinal or transverse.

Longitudinal Waves

When a wave propagates through some medium, if the particles of the medium vibrate in the same direction of travel of the disturbance, then the wave is called a longitudinal wave. Mechanical longitudinal waves are also called compressional or compression waves, because they propagate through compression and rarefaction when travelling through a medium. The region of high pressure is called compression and the region of low pressure is called rarefaction. Sometimes they are also called pressure waves, because they produce increase and decrease in pressure. A spring fixed at two ends, if pulled toward one end and released, the waves that are produced are known as longitudinal waves. Figure 9.1 shows a longitudinal wave.

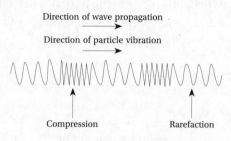

Fig. 9.1: Longitudinal wave

Longitudinal waves can travel through solids, liquids and gases.

Transverse Waves

If displacements of the medium are at right angles to the direction of propagation, the wave is called a transverse wave. Examples are waves on strings, surface waves on water, etc. That is, the wave itself travels along the string or water surface, but displacements of the medium through which the wave travels are perpendicular to the direction of the wave propagation. Figure 9.2 shows a transverse wave. Here C indicates crest and T trough. The uppermost point is called the crest and the lowest point the trough. Here, as the wave propagates from left to right, the particles of the string vibrate up and down, thus forming a transverse wave in the string.

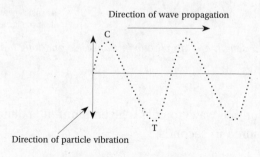

Fig. 9.2: Transverse wave

Electromagnetic Waves

These waves do not require any material medium for production and propagation.

Matter Waves

These waves are associated with moving particles like electrons, protons, etc. These waves are central to quantum mechanics that propounds all matter can exhibit wave-like behaviour.

TERMS RELATED TO WAVES

WAVELENGTH

It is the length of the repeating wave shape. It is represented by the Greek letter lambda (λ).

AMPLITUDE

It is the maximum displacement of the particles of the medium, which is determined by the energy of the wave. It is represented by A.

Figure 9.3 shows the wavelength and amplitude of transverse and longitudinal waves.

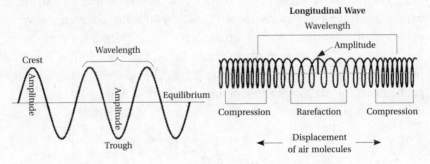

Fig. 9.3: Wavelength and amplitude in transverse and longitudinal waves

TIME PERIOD

It is the time for one wave to pass a given point. It is denoted by T. The period is measured in seconds.

FREQUENCY

The frequency of the wave is the number of waves passing a given point in a unit of time. It is denoted by ν, the Greek letter nu. Sometimes it is also denoted by f. Frequency is measured in cycles per second or the SI unit of hertz (Hz) with the dimensions of s^{-1}. The frequency is the reciprocal of time period T. Thus:

$$f = \frac{1}{T}$$

SPEED

It is a measure of the distance a wave travels in an amount of time. It is denoted by v. The speed of a wave is determined by the type of wave and the nature of the medium. The speed of a wave is related to the frequency and wavelength:

$$v = f\lambda$$

SOUND WAVES

Sound is a kind of longitudinal wave in which the particles oscillate to and fro in the same direction of wave propagation. Sound waves cannot be transmitted through vacuum. The transmission of sound requires at least a medium, which can be solid, liquid or gas. Sound waves propagate through compression and rarefaction of the medium.

Characteristics of Sound

A sound can be characterized by the following three quantities:

Pitch
Pitch depends on the frequency of the sound. A high frequency gives rise to a high pitch note and a low frequency produces a low pitch note.

Quality
A sound of single frequency is called a tone; for example, the sound that is made by a tuning fork or an electronic signal generator. A sound that is produced when several frequencies are mixed is called a note. For example, a musical note has tones of various frequencies (sounds of different pitch) and amplitudes (loudness). A note has many component waves in it whereas a tone is represented by a single wave form.

The fundamental note has the greatest amplitude and is heard predominantly because it has a larger intensity. The other frequencies are called overtones or harmonics and they determine the quality of the sound.

Loudness

This is a physiological sensation. It depends mainly on sound pressure but also on the spectrum of the harmonics and the physical duration.

Speed of Sound in Different Media

The speed of sound is the distance travelled per unit time by any sound wave that can be measured. It refers to the distance travelled per unit time by a sound wave propagating through a medium. The speed of sound, when travelling through air at 20°C, is 343.2 m/s, which translates to 1,236 km/h.

The speed of sound in gases is proportional to the square root of the absolute temperature (measured in Kelvin) but it is independent of the frequency of the sound wave or the pressure and the density of the medium. But none of the gases we find in real life are ideal gases and this causes the properties to slightly change. The speed of sound in a solid is larger than in a gas. Similarly, the density of a liquid is greater than the density of a gas. Therefore the distances between molecules is more in liquids than in solids but is less than in gases. Hence, the speed of sound in liquids lies in between the speed of sound in solids and gases.

Factors that Affect the Speed of Sound

We have learnt that the speed of sound is 1,236 km/h. That is partially true. The reason for this is that the speed of sound changes and it depends on certain factors. Here are the factors that affect the speed of sound:

Temperature: Temperature has had a significant effect on the speed of sound. Lower temperatures will decrease the speed of sound while higher temperatures will increase the speed of sound, all other factors being constant. Empirically, the relationship is:

$$v \, \alpha \, \sqrt{T}$$

where T is the absolute temperature (in Kelvin) of the gas.

Pressure: Pressure has had a significant impact on the speed of sound.

The more pressure that is applied to the material or medium, the denser it becomes, making any interaction between particles slower. Therefore, the speed of sound decreases with increase in pressure.

Humidity: The more the humidity, the greater is the speed of sound. Therefore, in dry air, sound has less speed than in humid air.

Wind: Wind acts as a vector. When wind blows in the direction of propagation of sound, the speed of sound increases.

Reflection of Sound

The reflection of sound is similar to the reflection of light as it follows the laws of reflections. These laws are: (i) the angle of incidence is equal to the angle of reflection, and (ii) the incident sound, the reflected sound and the normal lie in the same plane.

Echo

We are familiar with this phenomenon: when we stand some distance away from a tall tower or the cliff of a mountain and make a sound, the sound comes back to our ears after a while. The sound heard after reflection from a rigid surface such as a cliff or a wall is called an echo. It creates a persistence of sound even after the source of sound has stopped vibrating. The phenomenon of echo is used by bats and dolphins to detect obstacles or navigate. In oceanographic studies, the principle of echo is used for detection and location of unseen underwater objects, such as a submerged submarine, sunken ships and icebergs. The depth of the seabed is also measured with the help of echo technique.

Reverberation

A reverberation is a series of the same sound or repetition of the same sound coming at a regular interval for a considerable time (depending on the initial energy of the sound), which is created when a sound or signal is reflected, causing a large number of reflections to build up and then decay as the sound is absorbed by the surfaces of objects in the vicinity. Very often it is found that the source of the sound has stopped producing any sound, but the reflections continue. In every reflection the amplitude of sound decreases, eventually to reach zero amplitude when it is heard no more. Example of reverberation is the thundering of cloud.

Sometimes reverberation is added to the sound of musical instruments or of singers to make a melodious effect in the music.

DOPPLER EFFECT

When a car or train passes by, the frequency of the sound that you hear varies from a higher pitch as it approaches to a lower pitch as it goes away from you. This is called the Doppler effect, and is a common experience in everyday life when there is a relative motion between a source of sound and an observer. There are really two different causes for the effect. When the source of the sound is moving, the sound waves are compressed in front of the source and expanded behind. But the sound still travels with respect to the air at the speed of sound. So an observer in front of the source hears a higher frequency than the source is emitting, since the wave fronts arrive closer together than if the sources were not moving, whereas an observer behind the moving source hears a lower frequency.

If the source is stationary but the observer is moving, a similar effect occurs for a different reason. The wavefronts spread out from the source uniformly. But if the observer is moving towards the source, he or she encounters wavefronts more often, hence hears a higher frequency. If the observer is moving away from the source, the wavefronts arrive less often, hence there is a lower frequency.

THE RANGE OF HUMAN HEARING

There are a variety of sounds in our environment. Those which we can hear, we know of. Those sounds which we can never hear are not even known to the human ear. Therefore, the human ear can hear sounds only within a certain range. This human hearing range is called the audible range.

Pitch and Loudness

The human hearing range depends on both the pitch and the loudness of the sound. Pitch is measured in Hertz (Hz) and loudness is measured in decibels (dB). For a person with normal hearing, with respect to pitch, the human hearing range starts at as low as about 20 Hz and the highest possible frequency heard without discomfort is 20,000 Hz. While 20 Hz to 20 kHz form the absolute borders of the human hearing range, our hearing is most sensitive in the 2000–5000 Hz frequency range. Regarding loudness, humans can typically hear between 0–85 dB. Sounds that are more than 85 dB can be dangerous for our hearing if there is prolonged exposure to very loud sounds of this nature.

ULTRASOUND AND INFRASOUND

Ultrasound waves have a frequency above the normal range of human hearing. Infrasound has a frequency below normal hearing range. Although the normal range of human hearing is between 20 Hz and 20 kHz, the range becomes lesser as we get older. Sounds with frequencies above about 20 kHz are called ultrasound.

Uses of Ultrasound and Infrasound

Ultrasound: With advanced engineering techniques, images can be formed of objects that reflect ultrasound waves when passed through them. A detector placed near the source of the ultrasound waves is able to detect the reflected waves. It can measure the time between an ultrasound wave after leaving the source to reach the detector. Using this principle and with improved imaging technique in biomedical engineering, scientists have developed ultrasound scanning machines of unborn babies in their mothers' wombs. This has enabled early detection of the baby's health condition and helped in studying stages of development of the human embryo.

Ultrasound can also be used in industries for checking damages and defects in manufactured objects, such as railway tracks and oil pipelines, etc.

Another use of ultrasound is in SONAR, which is an acronym for Sound Navigation and Ranging, a technique that uses sound propagation (usually underwater, as in submarine navigation) to navigate, communicate with or detect objects on or under the surface of the water, such as other vessels.

Infrasound: This helps in detection of herds of wild animals like elephants and giraffes. Animals use infrasound to communicate between herds over long distances. Scientists can now use microphones to track the herds even if they are hidden in dense forests. This helps with the conservation and protection of these animals.

Another use of infrasound is to detect volcanic eruptions. As a volcano erupts, it produces infrasound, which can be detected even if the volcano is in a remote location a long way off. Scientists also use infrasound to track the passage of meteors through the atmosphere.

PRINCIPLE OF SUPERPOSITION OF WAVES

Most of us are familiar with the phenomenon of the superposition of waves. Imagine you are travelling by boat and can hear the siren of a ship. In such a case, you'll receive sound waves directly from the source, that is the ship siren, as well as the sound wave that gets reflected by the sea water. The principle of superposition of waves describes how individual waveforms can be algebraically added to determine the net waveform. The principle of superposition is expressed by affirming that overlapping waves add algebraically to create a resultant wave.

The superposition of waves can lead to the following three effects.

Case I

Whenever two waves having the same frequency travel with the same speed along the same direction in a specific medium, they superpose and create an effect termed the interference of waves. Consider two waves that are in phase with each other. They have the same amplitude, same angular frequency and same angular wave number.

If Wave 1 is represented by $y_1(x, t) = a \sin(kx - \omega t)$,

Wave 2 is also represented by $y_2(x, t) = a \sin(kx - \omega t)$

By the principle of superposition, the resultant wave $[2a \sin(kx - \omega t)]$ will also be in phase with both the individual waves but the amplitude of the resultant wave will be more.

Case II

In a situation where two waves having similar frequencies move with the same speed along opposite directions in a specific medium, they superpose to produce stationary waves.

Consider when the two waves are completely out of phase, i.e., $\phi = \pi$

If Wave 1 is represented by $y_1(x, t) = a \sin(kx - \omega t)$,

Wave 2 is represented by $y_2(x, t) = a \sin(kx - \omega t + \pi)$.

$y_2 = a \sin (\pi - (- kx + \omega t)$

$y_2 = - a \sin (kx - \omega t)$

Therefore, by superposition principle, $y = y_1 + y_2 = 0$.

Case III

Finally, when two waves having slightly varying frequencies travel with the same speed along the same direction in a specific medium, they superpose to produce beats.

Consider when the two waves are partially out of phase $\phi > 0$; $\phi < \pi$

If Wave 1 is represented by $y_1 (x, t) = a \sin (kx - \omega t)$,

Wave 2 is represented by $y_2 (x, t) = a \sin (kx - \omega t + \phi)$.

Therefore by the principle of superposition of waves, $y = y_1 + y_2$

$= a [\sin (kx - \omega t) + \sin (kx - \omega t) + \phi]$

$Y = 2a \cos (\phi/2) \sin (kx - \omega t + (\phi/2))$

(By using the formula $\sin A + \sin B = 2 \sin (A + B)/2 \cos (A - B)/2$)

Amplitude $= 2a \cos (\phi/2)$ and Phase will be determined by $(\phi/2)$.

OPTICS

INTRODUCTION

The human eye can detect the visible range of the electromagnetic waves. Electromagnetic radiation belonging to this region of the spectrum (wavelength of about 400 nm to 750 nm) is called light. We see the world around us through light and when there is no light, we cannot see. We can see an object when light falls on it and gets reflected from it. Light travels at a speed of c = 2.99792458 × 10^8 m s^{-1} in vacuum which, for all practical purposes, equals c = 3 × 10^8 m s^{-1}.

In this chapter, we will consider the phenomena of reflection, refraction and dispersion of light, using the ray picture of light. Using the basic laws of reflection and refraction, we shall study the image formation by plane and spherical reflecting and refracting surfaces. We will then go on to describe the construction and working of some important optical instruments, including the human eye.

COMMON TYPES OF MIRRORS

The three most common types of mirrors are:

Plane Mirror
These are flat mirrors that reflect images in their normal proportions, reversed from left to right.

Concave Mirror
Concave mirrors are spherical mirrors whose reflecting surfaces curve inward. They create the impression of largeness.

Convex Mirror

Convex mirrors are also another type of spherical mirror. However, their reflecting surface bulges out and makes the reflected image look smaller.

COMMON TYPES OF LENSES

Convex Lens: A convex lens is thicker in the middle than at its outside edges. Light travelling through a convex lens converges into a single point. Parallel rays of light join at a single point beyond the lens.

Concave Lens: A concave lens is thicker at the ends and thinner in the middle. It diverts light rays away from a focal point.

REFLECTION OF LIGHT

When light falls on a smooth surface, a part of it changes its direction of travel and returns to the medium from which it originated. This phenomenon is called the reflection of light. There are two laws of reflection:

a) The angle of reflection (i.e., the angle between the reflected ray and the normal to the reflecting surface or the mirror) equals the angle of incidence (angle between the incident ray and the normal).

b) The incident ray, reflected ray and the normal to the reflecting surface at the point of incidence lie in the same plane. These laws are shown in Figure 10.1 in the form of a ray diagram.

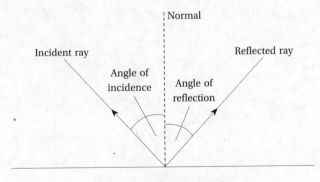

Fig. 10.1: Reflection of light

The two laws are valid at each point on any reflecting surface, whether plane or curved. Now, we direct our attention to the special case of curved surfaces, that is, spherical surfaces. The normal in this case is taken as normal to the tangent to surface at the point of incidence. That is, the normal is along the radius, the line joining the centre of curvature of the mirror to the point of incidence.

The geometric centre of a spherical mirror is called its pole while that of a spherical lens is called its optical centre. The line joining the pole and the centre of curvature of the spherical mirror is known as the principal axis. In the case of spherical lenses, the principal axis is the line joining the optical centre with its principal focus.

SIGN CONVENTION FOR SPHERICAL SURFACE

A sign convention for measuring distances in case of reflection by spherical mirrors and refraction by spherical lenses is needed. This is as described below:

➤ All distances are measured from the pole of the mirror or the optical centre of the lens.
➤ The distances measured in the same direction as the incident light are taken as positive and those measured in the direction opposite to the direction of incident light are taken as negative.
➤ The heights measured upwards with respect to the x-axis and normal to the principal axis (x-axis) of the mirror/lens are taken as positive whereas the heights measured downwards are taken as negative.

Figure 10.2 summarises the sign convention.

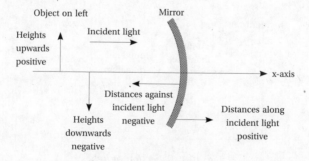

Fig. 10.2: Sign convention

PHYSICS

RELATIONSHIP BETWEEN RADIUS OF CURVATURE AND FOCAL LENGTH

When a parallel beam of light is incident on a concave mirror, the reflected rays converge at a point F on the principal axis. When a parallel beam of light is incident on a convex mirror, the reflected rays appear to diverge from a point F on its principal axis. This point F is called the principal focus of the mirror. If the parallel paraxial beam of light were incident, making some angle with the principal axis, the reflected rays would converge (or appear to diverge) from a point in a plane through F normal to the principal axis. This is called the focal plane of the mirror. These cases are explained in the ray diagram in Figure 10.3.

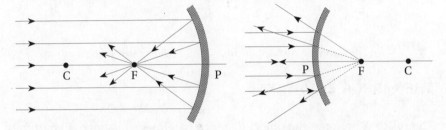

Fig. 10.3: Focal point of concave mirror.   *Focal point of convex mirror.*

The distance between the focus F and the pole P of the mirror is called the focal length of the mirror, denoted by f. The relationship between focal length (f) and radius of curvature (R) is:

$$f = \frac{R}{2}$$

HOW TO DRAW A RAY DIAGRAM FOR CURVED MIRRORS AND LENSES

If rays emerging from a point after reflection and/or refraction actually meet at another point, that point where they meet is called the image of the first point. The image is real if the rays actually converge at the point; however, it is virtual if the rays do not actually meet but appear to diverge from the point when produced backwards.

While drawing a ray diagram in case of spherical mirrors, we generally choose the following two rays and trace their path:

(i) The ray from the point which is parallel to the principal axis. The reflected ray goes through the focus of the mirror.

(ii) The ray incident at any angle at the pole. The reflected ray follows laws of reflection.

The ray diagrams for concave and convex mirrors are shown in Figure 10.4.

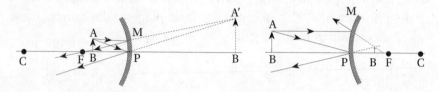

Fig. 10.4: Ray diagram for concave mirror   Ray diagram for convex mirror

THE MIRROR EQUATION

The relation between the object distance (u), image distance (v) and the focal length (f) is called the mirror equation. The equation is:

$$\frac{1}{v} + \frac{1}{u} = \frac{1}{f}$$

The size of the image relative to the size of the object is called linear magnification (m), and is defined as the ratio of the height of the image (h') to the height of the object (h). In terms of the image distance (v) and object distance (u), this relationship can be expressed as:

$$m = \frac{v}{u}$$

REFRACTION

When a beam of light travels from one medium to another, a part of light gets reflected back into the first medium, while the rest enters the second medium. The direction of propagation of an obliquely incident

PHYSICS

ray of light changes in the second medium at the interface of the two media. This phenomenon is called refraction of light.

The following two laws are called the laws of refraction:

(i) The incident ray, the refracted ray and the normal to the interface at the point of incidence, all lie in the same plane.

(ii) The ratio of the sine of the angle of incidence (i) to the sine of the angle of refraction (r), which are the angles that the incident and its refracted ray make with the normal, respectively, is constant.

$$\mu_{21} = \frac{\sin i}{\sin r}$$

where μ_{21} is called the refractive index of the second medium 2 with respect to the first medium 1. This equation is known as Snell's law of refraction.

If μ_{21} is the refractive index of medium 2 with respect to medium 1 and μ_{12} the refractive index of medium 1 with respect to medium 2, then

$$\mu_{21} = \frac{1}{\mu_{12}}$$

TOTAL INTERNAL REFLECTION

When a light ray strikes a medium boundary such that no refraction takes place at the second medium at the boundary, but the entire light comes back reflected at the first medium itself, the phenomenon is called total internal reflection. It occurs when the angle of incidence is larger than a particular critical angle with respect to the normal to the surface. The critical angle is the angle of incidence for which the angle of refraction is 90°.

One of the most interesting natural phenomena that occurs due to total internal reflection is called a mirage. It is a common phenomenon in hot deserts. This is nothing but an optical illusion. We have experienced mirages while driving through long stretches of road on hot and sunny days. Some distance away from us water appears to be there on the road. However, as we reach there, water appears now to be still at some distance and as we continue to drive towards that direction, actual water is never found, but the appearance of water on the road continues some distance away. This is called a mirage. On hot summer days, the air near the ground is hotter than the air at higher altitudes. Hotter air is less dense, and has a smaller refractive index than cooler air. If the air is not blowing at high speed, that is, if it is almost still, the optical density at different layers of air increases with height. As a result, light from a tall object, such as a tree, passes through a medium whose refractive index decreases towards the ground. Thus, a ray of light from such an object successively bends away from the normal and undergoes total internal reflection if the angle of incidence for the air near the ground exceeds the critical angle. To a distant observer, the light appears to be coming from somewhere below the ground. The observer naturally assumes that light is being reflected from the ground, say, by a pool of water near the tall object. Such inverted images of distant tall objects cause an optical illusion for the observer.

DISPERSION

When a beam of sunlight passes through a glass prism, the emergent light consists of seven colours. These are in this sequence: violet, indigo, blue, green, yellow, orange and red (the acronym VIBGYOR stands for the seven colours). The red light bends the least, while the violet light bends the most. This phenomenon of splitting of light into its component colours is known as dispersion. Newton showed that if the colours produced by dispersion of light from the first prism are passed through another inverted prism made of the same material and exactly of the same shape as the first but only inverted, the resulting emergent beam is again white light. The explanation is clear, that is, the first prism splits the white light into its component colours, while the inverted prism recombines them to give white light. Thus, white light itself consists of light of different colours, which are separated by the prism.

We now know that different colours are associated with different wavelengths of light. In the visible spectrum, red light is at the long wavelength end (~700 nm) while violet light is at the short wavelength end (~400 nm). Dispersion takes place because the refractive index of medium for different wavelengths (colours) is different. For example, the bending of the red component of white light is least, while it is most for violet. Red light travels faster than violet light in a glass prism.

11

ELECTROSTATICS

INTRODUCTION

All of us have experienced lightning in the sky during thunderstorms. When we take off our woollen clothes in dry winter we see sparks if we are in a dark room or hear crackling sounds. These are our common daily life experiences. You might have been told that this is due to generation of static electricity. In this chapter we will study about static electricity. Electrostatics deals with the study of forces, fields and potentials arising from static charges.

ELECTRIC CHARGE

Electric charge was discovered from observations that when amber was rubbed with wool or silk cloth, it developed the power to attract light objects like small piece of papers, etc. It was observed around 600 BC. The name electricity was derived from the Greek word 'elektron' meaning 'amber'.

After careful and detailed study of these observations, scientists concluded that there are two types of charges—positive and negative. Although the origin of charges in a body or why a body develops charge on rubbing with a piece of silk cloth was not known at that time, the two types of charges, positive and negative, were termed by the American scientist Benjamin Franklin. It was also concluded that (i) like charges repel and (ii) unlike charges attract each other. Since the underlying reason for the charges was not known or any concluding experiment to establish the type of charge was lacking at that time, by convention, the charge on a glass rod or cat's fur is called positive and that on a plastic rod or silk is termed negative. If an object possesses an electric charge, it is said to be electrified or charged. When it has no charge it is said to be neutral.

A simple apparatus to detect charge on a body was discovered and designed much later, and is called the gold leaf electroscope. Figure 11.1 shows a gold leaf electroscope.

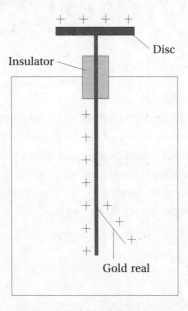

Fig. 11.1: Gold leaf electroscope

It consists of a vertical metal rod enclosed in a box, with two thin gold leaves attached to its bottom end. When a charged object touches the metal knob at the top of the rod, charge flows on to the leaves and they diverge. The degree of divergence is an indicator of the amount of charge.

To electrify a neutral body, we need to add or remove one kind of charge. When we say that a body is charged, we always refer to this excess charge or deficit of charge. In solids, some of the electrons, being less tightly bound in the atom, are the charges that are transferred from one body to the other. A body can thus be charged positively by losing some of its electrons. Similarly, a body can be charged negatively by gaining electrons. When we rub a glass rod with silk, some of the electrons from the rod are transferred to the silk cloth. Thus the rod gets positively charged and the silk gets negatively charged. No new charge is created in

PHYSICS

the process of rubbing. Also, the number of electrons that are transferred is a very small fraction of the total number of electrons in the material body. Moreover, only the less tightly bound electrons in a material body can be transferred from it to another by rubbing. Therefore, when a body is rubbed with another, the bodies get charged and that is why we have to stick to certain pairs of materials to notice charging on rubbing the bodies.

CONDUCTORS AND INSULATORS

There are certain materials that are easily charged while there are others that cannot be charged. Also, those materials that can be charged conduct electricity whereas those that cannot be charged do not conduct electricity. Suppose we connect one end of a copper wire to a neutral pith ball and the other end to a negatively charged plastic rod. We will find that the pith ball acquires a negative charge. If a similar experiment is repeated with a nylon thread or a rubber band, no transfer of charge will take place from the plastic rod to the pith ball. Substances that readily allow passage of electricity through them are called conductors. Substances that do not allow passage of electricity through them are called insulators. Metals, human and animal bodies and earth are conductors. Most of the non-metals like glass, porcelain, plastic, nylon, wood, etc. offer high resistance to the passage of electricity through them, and are insulators.

CHARGING A BODY

We have already learnt that when a glass rod or amber is rubbed with silk or a woollen cloth, it gets charged. A charged body can charge another conducting material in two ways. These are: (i) charging by contact and (ii) charging by induction.

In case of charging by contact, that part of the second body which is in direct contact with the first body develops the same charge as the first body from which it receives charge by direct contact.

If the charging of the second body does not happen through direct contact but by placing it in the immediate vicinity of the first charged body, then the process of charging is called charging by induction. In this case two opposite charges are developed.

BASIC PROPERTIES OF ELECTRIC CHARGE

Addition of Charge

A point charge is a charged body whose dimension is negligibly small and hence is considered to be a point. Let q_1, q_2, q_3...qn be point charges in a system. Then the total charge of the system is:

$$q = q_1 + q_2 + q_3 + ... + q_n$$

Since charge can either be positive or negative, proper signs have to be considered while adding the charges in a system.

Conservation of Charge

When bodies are charged by rubbing, there is transfer of electrons from one body to the other; no new charges are created or destroyed. When we rub two bodies, what one body gains in charge, the other loses.

Within an isolated system consisting of many charged bodies, charges may get redistributed, but it is found that the total charge of the isolated system is always conserved. This is called conservation of charges.

Amount of Charge

Experimentally it is established that all free charges are integral multiples of a basic unit of charge denoted by e. Thus charge q on a body is always given by:

$$q = ne$$

where n is any integer, positive or negative. This basic unit of charge is the charge that an electron or proton carries. By convention, the charge on an electron is taken to be negative; therefore charge on an electron is written as -e and that on a proton as +e.

The fact that electric charge is always an integral multiple of e is termed as quantization of charge. In the International System of Units (SI system), a unit of charge is called a coulomb and is denoted by the symbol C. One coulomb is the charge flowing through a wire in 1s if the current is 1A (ampere).

In this system, the value of the basic unit of charge is

$$e = 1.602192 \times 10^{-19} \text{ C}$$

For all practical purposes of calculation, this value is take to be $e = 1.6 \times 10^{-19}$ C. Thus, there are about 6×10^{18} electrons in a charge of

-1 C. Sometimes we use smaller units 1 μC (micro coulomb) = 10^{-6} C or 1 mC (milli coulomb) = 10^{-3} C.

COULOMB'S LAW

When two charges are in the vicinity of each other, they interact with each other. In fact, the interaction is even existent when they are separated from each other by a long distance. Coulomb's law deals with the force of interaction between two point charges. The force varies inversely as the square of the distance between the charges and is directly proportional to the product of the magnitude of the two charges and acts along the line joining the two charges. Thus, if two point charges q_1 and q_2 are separated by a distance r in vacuum, the magnitude of the force (F) between them is given by:

$$F = k\, \frac{|q_1 q_2|}{r^2}$$

In the relation, k is constant and is taken to be k = $1/4\pi\varepsilon_0$ where ε_0 is called the permittivity of free space. The value of ε_0 in SI units is:

$$\varepsilon 0 = 8.854 \times 10^{-12} C^2 N^{-1} m^{-2}$$

ELECTRIC FIELD

Like charges repel each other. Therefore, if a unit positive charge is placed near a positive charge, the unit positive charge will experience a repulsive force, due to which the unit positive charge will move away from the said charge. The imaginary line through which the unit positive charge moves is known as the line of force. Similarly, if a unit positive charge is placed in the field of negative electric charge, the unit positive charge will experience an attractive force, due to which the unit positive charge will come closer to the said negative charge. In that case, the line through which the positive unit charge moves is also known as the line of force. Hence, we can say that if a charge is a positive charge, then the lines of force come out of this charge. But for a negative charge, these lines of force come into this charge.

When a charged particle enters the electric field of another charged particle, it experiences a force as per Coulomb's law. In other word, the electric field is the region around a charged particle where the lines of force can be felt by another charge by getting repulsed or attracted as per their sign of charge.

The electric field due to a charge Q is numerically equal to the force exerted by it. Thus, the electric field due to a charge Q at a point in space may be defined as the force that a unit positive charge would experience if placed at that point. The charge Q, which is producing the electric field, is called a source charge and the charge q, which tests the effect of a source charge, is called a test charge.

ELECTRIC DIPOLE

An electric dipole is a pair of equal and opposite point charges q and -q, separated by a distance 2a. The line connecting the two charges defines a direction in space. By convention, the direction from -q to q is said to be the direction of the dipole. The midpoint of locations of - q and q is called the centre of the dipole. The total charge of the electric dipole is obviously zero. This does not mean that the field of the electric dipole is zero. Since the charges q and -q are separated by some distance, the electric fields due to them, when added, do not exactly cancel out.

In most molecules, the centres of positive charges and negative charges lie at the same place. Therefore, their dipole moment is zero. $CO2$ and $CH4$ are the two examples of this type of molecules. However, they develop a dipole moment when an electric field is applied. But in some molecules, the centres of negative charges and positive charges do not coincide. Therefore they have a permanent electric dipole moment, even in the absence of an electric field. Such molecules are called polar molecules. The water molecule H_2O is an example of this.

GAUSS'S LAW

Gauss's law states that the net flux of an electric field through a closed surface is proportional to the enclosed electric charge. It relates the electric fields at points on a closed surface (known as a 'Gaussian surface') and the net charge enclosed by that surface. The electric flux is defined as the electric field passing through a given area multiplied by the area of the surface in a plane perpendicular to the field. Another statement of Gauss's law is that the net flux of an electric field through a surface divided by the enclosed charge is equal to a constant.

Electric flux through a closed surface S = q/ε_0

q = total charge enclosed by S

The law implies that the total electric flux through a closed surface is zero if no charge is enclosed by the surface.

ELECTRIC POTENTIAL

An electric potential, also known as electrostatic potential, is the amount of work needed to move a unit positive charge from infinity to a specific point inside the field without producing any acceleration. For all practical purposes, infinity means any point beyond the influence of the electric field charge.

The unit of electrostatic potential is the volt (V), and 1 V = 1 J/C = 1 Nm/C.

Capacitance and Capacitor

A capacitor is a device or electrical component that has the ability to store energy in the form of an electrical charge producing a potential difference across its plates. In its basic form, a capacitor consists of two or more parallel conductive (metal) plates that are not connected or touching each other but are electrically separated either by air or by some form of a good insulating material such as waxed paper, mica, ceramic, plastic or some form of a liquid gel as used in electrolytic capacitors. The insulating layer between capacitor plates is commonly called the dielectric.

The property of a capacitor to store charge on its plates in the form of an electrostatic field is called the capacitance of the capacitor. Capacitance is the electrical property of a capacitor and is the measure of a capacitor's ability to store an electrical charge onto its two plates, with the unit of capacitance being the farad (abbreviated to F). A capacitor has the capacitance of 1 farad when a charge of 1 coulomb is stored on the plates by a voltage of 1 volt.

12

CURRENT ELECTRICITY

INTRODUCTION

All of us have the experience of current electricity. When we switch on the light, the fan starts, the light bulb glows, the electric motor or the air conditioner starts. This is due to electric current. When potential difference is applied across two terminals, charge flows, resulting in electric current. In this chapter we will study about electric current and its various aspects.

ELECTRIC CURRENT

Imagine a small area held normal to the direction of flow of charges. Let the net amount of charge flowing across the area in the forward direction in the time interval t be q, then the amount of current is the flow of charge in unit time, that is:

$$i = \frac{q}{t}$$

Currents are, however, not always steady, and hence more generally, we define the current as follows. Let ΔQ be the net charge flowing across a cross section of a conductor during the time interval Δt [i.e., between times t and $(t + \Delta t)$]. Then, the current at time t across the cross section of the conductor is defined as the value of the ratio of ΔQ to Δt in the limit of Δt tending to zero:

$$i = \lim_{\Delta t \to 0} \frac{\Delta Q}{\Delta t} = \frac{dQ}{dt}$$

In SI units, the unit of current is ampere.

OHM'S LAW

Imagine a conductor through which a current I is flowing and let V be the potential difference between the ends of the conductor. Then Ohm's law states that:

$$V \alpha I$$
$$\text{or, } V = RI$$

where the constant of proportionality R is called the resistance of the conductor. The SI unit of resistance is ohm, and is denoted by the symbol Ω.

The resistance R not only depends on the material of the conductor but also on the dimensions of the conductor. The relationship is:

$$R = \rho \frac{l}{A}$$

where ρ depends on the material of the conductor but not on its dimensions. ρ is called resistivity.

Limitations of Ohm's Law

There are certain cases where the proportionality between V and I does not hold good, hence Ohm's law fails. Materials and devices not obeying Ohm's law are actually widely used in electronic circuits. The deviations, broadly, are one or more of the following types:

(a) V is not proportional to I

(b) The relation between V and I depends on the sign of V. In other words, if I is the current for a certain V, then reversing the direction of V, keeping its magnitude fixed, does not produce a current of the same magnitude as I in the opposite direction.

(c) The relation between V and I is not unique, i.e., there is more than one value of V for the same current I. A material exhibiting such behaviour is gallium arsenide (GaAs).

ELECTRICAL ENERGY AND POWER

Consider a conductor with end points A and B, in which a current I is flowing from A to B. The electric potential at A and B are denoted by V(A) and V(B), respectively. Since current is flowing from A to B, V(A) > V(B) and the potential difference across AB is V = V(A) – V(B) > 0. In a time interval Δt, an amount of charge $\Delta Q = I \, \Delta t$ travels from A to B.

The energy dissipated per unit time is the power dissipated.

$P = \Delta W/\Delta t$ and we have,

$P = IV$

Using Ohm's law V = IR, we get

$P = I^2R = V^2/R$

COMBINATION OF RESISTANCES IN SERIES AND PARALLEL

Combination of Resistors in Series Connection

Consider three resistors R_1, R_2 and R_3 which are connected in series as shown in Figure 12.1. Here the charge first flows through R_1 and enters R_2 and finally reaches R_3.

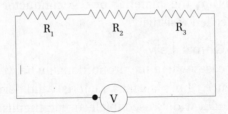

Fig. 12.1: Resistors in series

By Ohm's law, the potential difference across $R_1 = V_1 = IR_1$

The potential difference across $R_2 = V_2 = IR_2$.

The potential difference across $R_3 = V_3 = IR_3$.

Thus, the potential difference V across this series connection of resistors is:

$V = V_1 + V_2 + V_3$

$= IR_1 + IR_2 + IR_3$

$= I\,(R_1 + R_2 + R_3)$

Thus, in case of a series connection, the equivalent resistance, $R_{eq} = (R_1 + R_2 + R_3)$.

For n number of resistors connected in series, the equivalent resistance $R_{eq} = R_1 + R_2 + R_3 \ldots + R_n$

Combination of Resistors in Parallel Connection

Consider three resistors R1, R2 and R3 which are connected in parallel. The charge splits into three and flows through R1, R2 and R3.

Combination of Three Resistors in Parallel

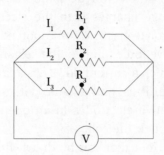

Fig. 12.2: Resistors in parallel

Current $I = I_1 + I_2 + I_3$.

The potential difference applied to $R_1 = V = I_1 R_1$

The potential difference across $R_2 = V = I_2 R_2$

The potential difference across $R_3 = V = I_3 R_3$

Since the total current in the circuit, $I = I_1 + I_2 + I_3$

$= V/R_1 + V/R_2 + V/R_3$

$= V (1/R_1 + 1/R_2 + 1/R_3)$

In other words, if this parallel combination is replaced by an equivalent resistance, R_{eq},

then $I = V/R_{eq}$

Hence,

$1/R_{eq} = 1/R_1 + 1/R_2 + 1/R_3$

Thus, for n number of resistors in parallel,

$$\frac{1}{R_{eq}} = \frac{1}{R_1} + \frac{1}{R_2} + \frac{1}{R_3} + ... \frac{1}{R_n}$$

So, in a parallel connection, the total resistance of a circuit is determined by adding the reciprocal of the resistance of each individual resistor.

CELLS, EMF, INTERNAL RESISTANCE

A cell is a simple device to maintain a steady current in an electric circuit and has two electrodes, called the positive and the negative electrodes. They are immersed in an electrolytic solution. Dipped in the solution, the electrodes exchange charges with the electrolyte. When there is no current, the electrolyte has the same potential throughout. This is called the electromotive force (emf) of the cell and is denoted by e. The electrolyte through which a current flows has a finite resistance, r, called the internal resistance. Thus, emf e is the potential difference between the positive and negative electrodes in an open circuit, i.e., when no current is flowing through the cell.

The maximum current that can be drawn from a cell is R = 0 and it is I_{max} = e/r. However, in most cells the maximum allowed current is much lower than this to prevent permanent damage to the cell.

The energy given by the cell in the flow of unit charge in a specific part of electrical circuit (external part) is called potential difference. Its unit is also volt. The voltage across the terminals of a cell when it is supplying current to external resistance is called potential difference or terminal voltage. Potential difference is equal to the product of current and resistance of that given part, i.e. V = iR.

Internal resistance (r): In case of a cell the opposition of electrolyte to the flow of current through it is called internal resistance of the cell. The internal resistance of a cell depends on the distance between electrodes, area of electrodes and the nature, concentration and temperature of the electrolyte. Internal resistance is different for different types of cells and even for a given type of cell it varies from cell to cell.

KIRCHHOFF'S RULES

(a) **Junction rule:** At any junction, the sum of the currents entering the junction is equal to the sum of currents leaving the junction. This applies equally well if instead of a junction of several lines, we consider a point in a line.

(b) **Loop rule:** The algebraic sum of changes in potential around any closed loop involving resistors and cells in the loop is zero. Thus

PHYSICS

starting with any point if we come back to the same point, the total change must be zero. In a closed loop, we do come back to the starting point, hence the rule.

ALTERNATING CURRENT AND DIRECT CURRENT

Alternating Current (AC)

Alternating current describes the flow of charge that changes direction periodically. As a result, the voltage also reverses along with the current. AC is used to deliver power to houses, office buildings, etc. AC can come in a number of forms, as long as the voltage and current are alternating. If we connect an oscilloscope to a circuit with AC and plot its voltage over time, we might see a number of different wave forms. The most common type of AC is the sine wave. The AC in most homes and offices has an oscillating voltage that produces a sine wave.

Applications

Home and office outlets are almost always AC. This is because generating and transporting AC across long distances is relatively easy. At high voltages (over 110kV), less energy is lost in electrical power transmission. Higher voltages mean lower currents, and lower currents mean less heat generated in the power line due to resistance. AC can be converted to and from high voltages easily using transformers.

AC is also capable of powering electric motors. Motors and generators are almost exactly the same device, but motors convert electrical energy into mechanical energy, while generators produce electrical energy.

Direct Current (DC)

Rather than oscillating back and forth, DC provides a constant voltage or current. It can be generated in a number of ways. Batteries provide DC, which is generated from a chemical reaction inside the battery.

DC is the unidirectional flow of current; current only flows in one direction. Voltage and current can vary over time so long as the direction of flow does not change. What does this mean? It means that we can count on most DC sources to provide a constant voltage over time. In reality, a battery will slowly lose its charge, meaning that the voltage will drop as the battery is used. For most purposes, we can assume that the voltage is constant.

Applications

Everything that runs on a battery is using DC. We use an AC adapter to convert AC to DC.

13

MAGNETIC EFFECTS OF CURRENT AND MAGNETISM

INTRODUCTION

Current passing through a conductor gives rise to magnetic fields. In other words, a moving charge gives rise to a magnetic field. If a free magnetic needle is brought in the vicinity of a current-carrying conductor, it shows deflection, indicating that the electric field influences the magnetic field. In this chapter, we shall study the magnetic effects of electric current.

PROPERTIES OF A MAGNET

➤ A free suspended magnet always points towards the north and south directions.
➤ The pole of a magnet which points toward the north is called the north pole, or north-seeking pole. The actual scientific expression, 'north-seeking pole', is simplified into 'north pole'.
➤ The pole of a magnet that points toward the south is called the south pole or south-seeking pole.
➤ Like poles of magnets repel each other while unlike poles of magnets attract each other.

Similar to other effects, electric current also produces a magnetic effect. The magnetic effect of electric current is known as the electromagnetic effect. It is observed that when a compass is brought near a current-carrying conductor, the needle of the compass gets deflected because of the flow of electricity. This shows that electric current produces a magnetic effect.

MAGNETIC FIELD AND MAGNETIC LINES OF FORCE

The influence of force surrounding a magnet is called the magnetic field. In the magnetic field, the force exerted by a magnet can be detected using a compass or any other magnet.

The imaginary lines of a magnetic field around a magnet are called field lines or lines of force of the magnet. When iron fillings are allowed to settle around a bar magnet, they get arranged in a pattern that shows the magnetic field lines. The field line of a magnet can also be detected using a compass. Magnetic field is a vector quantity, i.e., it has both direction and magnitude.

Direction of Field Line

Outside the magnet, the direction of magnetic field line is taken from the North Pole to the South Pole. Inside the magnet, the direction of magnetic field line is taken from the South Pole to the North Pole. Figure 13.1 shows the magnetic lines of force.

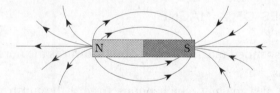

Fig. 13.1: Magnetic lines of force or field lines

Strength of Magnetic Field

The closeness of field lines shows the relative strength of the magnetic field, i.e., closer lines show a stronger magnetic field, and vice versa. Crowded field lines near the poles of a magnet show more strength.

MAGNETIC FIELD DUE TO A CURRENT-CARRYING CONDUCTOR

Magnetic Field Due to Current through a Straight Conductor

A current through a straight conductor has a magnetic field in the form of concentric circles around it. A magnetic field of current carrying a straight conductor can be shown by magnetic field lines.

The direction of magnetic field through a current-carrying conductor depends upon the direction of flow of electric current. The direction of magnetic field gets reversed in case of a change in the direction of electric current.

Let a current-carrying conductor be suspended vertically and the electric current flow from south to north. In this case, the direction of magnetic field will be anticlockwise. If the current is flowing from north to south, the direction of magnetic field will be clockwise.

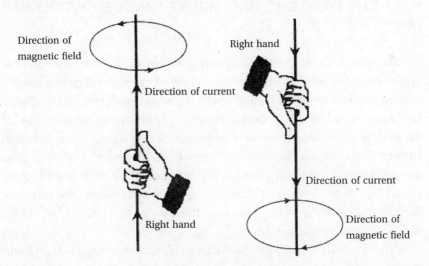

Fig. 13.2: Right hand thumb rule

The direction of magnetic field, in relation to the direction of electric current through a straight conductor, can be depicted by using the right hand thumb rule. It is shown in Figure 13.2. This is the thumb rule: If a current-carrying conductor is held by the right hand, keeping the thumb straight, and if the direction of electric current is in the direction of the thumb, then the direction of wrapping of other fingers will show the direction of the magnetic field.

PROPERTIES OF A MAGNETIC FIELD

› The magnitude of magnetic field increases with increase in electric current and decreases with decrease in electric current
› The magnitude of magnetic field produced by electric current decreases with increase in distance, and vice versa
› The size of concentric circles of magnetic field lines increases with distance from the conductor, which shows that the magnetic field decreases with distance
› Magnetic field lines are always parallel to each other
› No two field lines cross each other

MAGNETIC FIELD DUE TO CURRENT THROUGH A CIRCULAR LOOP

In case of a circular current-carrying conductor, the magnetic field is produced in the same manner as it is in case of a straight current-carrying conductor. In case of a circular current-carrying conductor, the magnetic field lines would be in the form of concentric circles around every part of the periphery of the conductor. Since magnetic field lines tend to remain closer when near a conductor, the magnetic field would be stronger near the periphery of the loop. On the other hand, the magnetic field lines would be distant from each other when we move towards the centre of the current-carrying loop. Finally, at the centre, the arcs of big circles would appear as straight lines.

The direction of magnetic field can be identified using the right hand thumb rule. Let us assume that the current is moving in an anticlockwise direction in the loop. In that case, the magnetic field would be in the clockwise direction; at the top of the loop. Therefore, it would be in an anticlockwise direction at the bottom of the loop.

Figure 13.3 shows the direction of the magnetic field when the current flows in a circular loop.

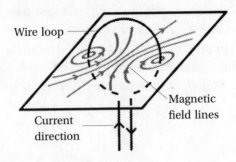

Wire loop

Magnetic
field lines

Current
direction

Fig. 13.3: Magnetic field lines due to current in a loop

MAGNETIC FIELD DUE TO A CURRENT IN A SOLENOID

Solenoid is the coil with many circular turns of insulated copper wire wrapped closely in the shape of a cylinder.

A current-carrying solenoid produces a similar pattern of magnetic field as a bar magnet. One end of a solenoid behaves as the north pole and another end behaves as the south pole. Magnetic field lines are parallel inside the solenoid; similar to a bar magnet, which shows that the magnetic field is the same at all points inside the solenoid.

By producing a strong magnetic field inside the solenoid, magnetic materials can be magnetized. A magnet formed by producing a magnetic field inside a solenoid is called an electromagnet.

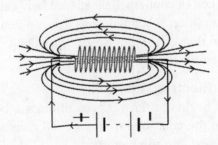

Fig. 13.4: Magnetic field lines due to current in a solenoid

FORCE ACTING ON A CURRENT-CARRYING CONDUCTOR

An electric current flowing through a conductor produces a magnetic field. This field will exert a force on a magnet placed in the proximity of the conductor. This means that the magnet also will exert an equal and opposite force on the current-carrying conductor.

The direction of this force is given by the left hand thumb rule. Stretch the thumb, forefinger and middle finger of your left hand such that they are mutually perpendicular to each other. This is shown in Figure 13.5.

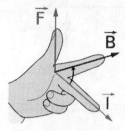

Fig. 13.5: Left hand thumb rule

If the middle finger points in the direction of the current in the conductor, the forefinger points in the direction of the magnetic field and the thumb points in the direction of the force acting on the conductor.

ELECTRIC MOTOR

An electric motor is a device that converts electrical energy to mechanical energy. It has the following parts.

A rectangular coil of copper wire is placed between the two poles of a magnet. Two disjointed C-shaped rings act as a commutator and are placed on the axle that can rotate freely. The outside of the split rings are connected to conducting brushes.

Working of An Electric Motor
When the current begins to flow, it goes through a brush, then to the commuter, then to the coil, then to the second commuter, and then to the second brush and into the battery.

Applying Fleming's left hand thumb rule to the wire, the current is along the wire, the magnetic field is along north to south and the motion of the coil is downwards. Now applying Fleming's left hand thumb rule to the other part of the wire, the current is along that wire, the magnetic field is along north to south and the motion of the wire is upwards. The rectangular coil begins to move in the anti-clockwise direction. The same thing keeps repeating and the reversal of current in the coil results in the continuous rotation of the coil. The reversal of current is achieved by the commutator rings.

EARTH'S MAGNETISM

A bar magnet, when suspended freely, points in the north-south direction. It is due to the earth's giant magnetic field. Electric currents circulating from the earth's core to space give rise to the earth's magnetic field. The SI unit of the earth's magnetic field is given by tesla.

Different Aspect of Earth's Magnetism

A hypothetical giant magnetic dipole is supposed to be located at the centre of the earth. It does not coincide with the axis of the earth. The dipole is tilted by 11.3° with respect to the earth's axis. If we observe carefully the magnetic field lines of the earth carefully, we will find that they lines enter the north pole and leave the south pole, unlike a bar magnet, where the magnetic field lines enter the south pole and leave the north pole. This is because the magnetic north pole of a bar magnet actually behaves like the south pole, and vice versa. It was named magnetic north because the magnetic needle (north pole) of the bar magnet pointed in this direction.

Components of Earth's Magnetic Field

The components that are responsible for the magnitude as well as the direction of the earth's magnetic field at a particular place are:

- Magnetic declination
- Horizontal component of Earth's magnetic field
- Angle of dip or magnetic inclination

Magnetic Declination

When a magnetic needle is suspended freely in the air, it always points in the north-south direction. This direction in which a magnetic needle points freely in a particular direction free from all other attracting forces is known as the magnetic meridian. Magnetic declination is defined as the angle made by the magnetic meridian with the geographic meridian.

Here the geographic meridian is defined as the plane passing through the north and south poles of the earth. The angle θ is known as the magnetic declination.

Angle of Dip or Magnetic Inclination

Take a magnetic needle and suspend it freely so that it can rotate about a horizontal axis. The angle that the north pole of the needle makes with the horizontal axis is known as the angle of dip or magnetic inclination.

Horizontal Component of Earth's Magnetic Field

The magnetic intensity of the earth's magnetic field makes an angle known as angle of dip (δ) with the horizontal axis. The intensity of the earth's magnetic field can be resolved into two components:

- Horizontal component (H)
- Vertical component (V)

These three elements of the earth's magnetic field give us sufficient knowledge about the magnitude and direction of the earth's magnetic field. However, these elements sometimes undergo regular or irregular changes at times at all places on Earth.

14

NUCLEAR PHYSICS AND RADIOACTIVITY

INTRODUCTION

The nucleus of an atom consists of neutrons and protons. Most of the elements that we find around us are stable. However, there are a number of elements whose nucleus is not stable and which emit radiations. In this process they give rise to new elements. The subject of nuclear physics deals with the stability of a nucleus and the changes that occur due to an unstable nucleus. This branch of physics is a very important subject of study for various reasons. It has direct application in nuclear energy, in the medicinal use of radioactivity, industrial use of radioactivity, defence, etc.

NUCLEAR STABILITY

The nucleus of an atom contains protons and neutrons. An atom has as many extra-nuclear electrons as protons. It is found that for those elements whose neutron to proton ratio n:p is close to 1, their nucleus shows stability. For those cases n:p > 1 or n:p < 1, the nucleus has a tendency to show unstability. The greater of the two numbers of particles (either proton or neutron) breaks down to achieve stability by attaining n:p = 1. In this process radioactivity is shown by these elements.

MASS-ENERGY

Einstein showed that mass is another form of energy and one can convert mass into energy and vice versa. These two are related by a mass-energy equivalence relation.

$$E = mc^2$$

Here the energy equivalent of mass m is related by the above equation and c is the velocity of light in vacuum and is approximately equal to $3 \times 10^8 ms^{-1}$.

NUCLEAR BINDING ENERGY

Since an atomic nucleus is made of neutrons and protons, it may be expected that the mass of the nucleus is equal to the total mass of its individual protons and neutrons. However, the nuclear mass m is found to be always less than this. For example, let us consider $^{16}O_8$, a nucleus that has eight neutrons and eight protons. We calculate the total mass of nuclear particles as below:

Mass of 8 neutrons = 8 × 1.00866 u

Mass of 8 protons = 8 × 1.00727 u

Therefore the expected mass of $^{16}O_8$ nucleus = 8 × 2.01593 u = 16.12744 u

The atomic mass of $^{16}O_8$ found from mass spectroscopy experiments is seen to be 15.99493 u. Subtracting the mass of eight electrons (8 × 0.00055 u) from this, we get the experimental mass of this nucleus to be 15.99053 u. Thus, we find that the mass of the nucleus is less than the total mass of its constituents by 0.13691 u. The difference in mass of a nucleus and its constituents is called the mass defect.

What is the significance of the mass defect? According to Einstein's mass-energy equivalence relationship, the equivalent energy of the oxygen nucleus is less than that of the sum of the equivalent energies of its constituents. If one wants to break the oxygen nucleus into eight protons and eight neutrons, this extra energy has to be supplied. This energy required E_b is related to the mass defect by:

$$E_b = \Delta Mc^2$$

and is known as the binding energy. A more useful measure of the binding between the constituents of the nucleus is the binding energy per nucleon, E_{bn}, which is the ratio of the binding energy E_b of a nucleus to the number of the nucleons, A, in that nucleus:

$$E_{bn} = E_b/A$$

PHYSICS

NUCLEAR FORCE

For nuclei of average mass the binding energy per nucleon is approximately 8 MeV, which is much larger than the binding energy in atoms. Therefore, to bind a nucleus together, there must be a strong attractive force of a totally different kind. It must be strong enough to overcome the repulsion between the (positively charged) protons and bind both protons and neutrons into the tiny nuclear volume. We have already seen that the constancy of binding energy per nucleon can be understood in terms of its short-range nature. Many features of the nuclear binding force are given below.

(i) The nuclear force is much stronger than the Coulomb force acting between charges or the gravitational forces between masses. The nuclear binding force has to dominate over the Coulomb repulsive force between protons inside the nucleus. This happens only because the nuclear force is much stronger than the Coulomb force.

(ii) The nuclear force between two nucleons falls rapidly to zero as their distance is more than a few femtometres. This leads to saturation of forces in a medium or large-sized nucleus, which is the reason for the constancy of the binding energy per nucleon.

(iii) The nuclear force between neutron-neutron, proton-neutron and proton-proton is approximately the same. The nuclear force does not depend on the electric charge. Unlike Coulomb's law or Newton's law of gravitation there is no simple mathematical form of the nuclear force.

RADIOACTIVITY

Radioactivity is a nuclear phenomenon in which an unstable nucleus undergoes decay. This is referred to as radioactive decay. Three types of radioactive decay occur in nature:

(i) Alpha decay or α-decay in which a helium nucleus $^4He_2$ is emitted

(ii) Beta decay or β-decay in which electrons or positrons (particles with the same mass as electrons, but with a charge exactly opposite to that of electrons) are emitted

(iii) Gamma decay or γ-decay in which high energy (hundreds of keV or more) photons are emitted

LAW OF RADIOACTIVE DECAY

In any radioactive sample which undergoes α, β or γ-decay, it is found that the number of nuclei undergoing the decay per unit time is proportional to the total number of nuclei in the sample. If N is the number of nuclei in the sample and ΔN undergo decay in time Δt then

$$\Delta N / \Delta t \; \alpha \; N$$
$$\text{or, } \Delta N / \Delta t = \lambda N$$

where λ is called the radioactive decay constant or disintegration constant.

Further simplifying the equation, we get:

$$\ln \frac{N}{N_0} = -\lambda t$$

which gives

$$N = N_0 e^{-\lambda t}$$

Here N_0 is the number of radioactive nuclei in the sample at some arbitrary time $t = 0$ and N is the number of radioactive nuclei at any subsequent time t.

Alpha Decay

Decay of uranium $^{238}U_{92}$ to thorium $^{234}Th_{90}$ with the emission of a helium nucleus $^4He_2$ is an example of alpha decay. In alpha decay the mass number of the resulting nucleus decreases by 4 units and the atomic number by 2 units and the new element shifts two groups left to the parent element in the periodic table.

$$^{238}U_{92} \quad \rightarrow \quad ^{234}Th_{90} + {}^4He_2 \quad (\alpha - \text{decay})$$

Beta Decay

In beta decay, a nucleus spontaneously emits an electron (β - decay) or a positron (β + decay). A common example of β - decay is:

$$^{32}P_{15} \quad \rightarrow \quad ^{32}S_{16} + e^- + \bar{v}$$

and that of β + decay is:

$$^{22}\text{Na}_{11} \quad \rightarrow \quad ^{22}\text{Ne}_{10} + e^+ + \nu$$

In both β - and β + decay, the mass number A remains unchanged. In β - decay, the atomic number Z of the nucleus goes up by 1, while in β + decay Z goes down by 1. The basic nuclear process underlying β - decay is the conversion of neutron to proton:

$$n \rightarrow p + e^- + \nu^-$$

while for β + decay, it is the conversion of proton into neutron:

$$p \rightarrow n + e^+ + \nu$$

Gamma Decay

When a nucleus in an excited state spontaneously decays to its ground state (or to a lower energy state), a photon is emitted with energy equal to the difference in the two energy levels of the nucleus. This is the case of gamma decay. The energy (MeV) corresponds to radiation of extremely short wavelength. Typically, a gamma ray is emitted when an α or β decay results in a daughter nucleus in an excited state. This then returns to the ground state by a single photon transition or successive transitions involving more than one photon.

NUCLEAR FISSION

The process of breaking a heavier nucleus into two smaller nuclei with the release of a vast amount of energy along with more bombarding particles, when bombarded by a particle like a proton, a neutron or an α-particle, is called nuclear fission. An example of fission is when a uranium isotope $^{235}\text{U}_{92}$ bombarded with a neutron breaks into two intermediate mass nuclear fragments.

$$^{1}_{0}\text{N} + ^{235}_{92}\text{U} \rightarrow ^{236}_{92}\text{U} \rightarrow ^{144}_{56}\text{Ba} + ^{89}_{36}\text{Kr} + 3\,^{1}_{0}\text{n}$$

The energy released in the fission reaction of nuclei like uranium is of the order of 200 MeV per fissioning nucleus. The disintegration energy in fission events first appears as the kinetic energy of the fragments and neutrons. Eventually it is transferred to the surrounding matter appearing as heat. The source of energy in nuclear reactors, which produce electricity, is nuclear fission. The enormous energy released in an atom bomb comes from uncontrolled nuclear fission because every three neutrons produced bombard another three atoms of uranium, resulting in the release of a vast amount of energy, and very soon the reaction goes out of control unless carried out in a controlled environment. This is the crux of use of a nuclear fission reaction behind an atom bomb where the reaction multiples very soon because of the chain reactions involved.

NUCLEAR FUSION

Nuclear fusion is a reaction in which two or more atomic nuclei coalesce to form one or more different heavier atomic nuclei and subatomic particles (neutrons or protons). The difference in mass between the reactants and products is manifested as the release of large amounts of energy. This difference in mass arises due to the difference in atomic binding energy between the atomic nuclei before and after the reaction. Fusion is the process that powers active or main sequence stars, or other high magnitude stars.

The sun is a main-sequence star, and thus generates its energy by nuclear fusion of hydrogen nuclei into helium. In its core, the sun fuses 620 million metric tons of hydrogen each second.

Controlled Thermonuclear Fusion

The main challenge in nuclear fusion is to control the tremendous amount of energy released in it and the reaction. The natural thermonuclear fusion process in a star is replicated in a thermonuclear fusion device. In controlled fusion reactors, the aim is to generate steady power by heating the nuclear fuel to a temperature in the range of 108 K. At these temperatures, the fuel is a mixture of positive ions and electrons (plasma). The challenge is to confine this plasma, since no container can stand such a high temperature. Several countries around the world, including India, are developing techniques in this connection. If successful, fusion reactors will hopefully supply almost unlimited power to humanity.

15

SEMICONDUCTORS AND DIODES

INTRODUCTION

Before the discovery and use of transistors, electronic devices were made of valves. Those were not very efficient, but that was the beginning of the era of electronics. Even transistors later gave way to integrated circuits and chips, but that's a separate matter altogether. In the early days of electronics, vacuum tubes were used. In a vacuum tube, the electrons are supplied by a heated cathode and the controlled flow of these electrons in vacuum is obtained by varying the voltage between its different electrodes. In these devices the electrons can flow only from the cathode to the anode (i.e., only in one direction). Therefore, such devices are generally referred to as valves.

In this chapter we will learn about the physics of semiconductors and some semiconductor devices.

CLASSIFICATION OF SOLIDS

Solids can be classified into metals, insulators and semiconductors. This can either be done on the basis of the relative values of electrical conductivity (σ) or resistivity ($\rho = 1/\sigma$) or on the basis of the energy gap between the valence band and the conduction band.

On the basis of the relative values of electrical conductivity (σ) or resistivity ($\rho = 1/\sigma$), solids are broadly classified as:

(i) **Metals:** They possess very low resistivity (or high conductivity).
(ii) **Semiconductors:** They have resistivity or conductivity intermediate to metals and insulators.

(iii) **Insulators:** They have high resistivity (or low conductivity).

Table 15.1: The values of conductivity and resistivity of three types of solids

Type of solid	Conductivity (σ) (S m^{-1})	Resistivity (ρ = 1/σ) (Ω m)	Conclusion
Metals	$10^2 - 10^8$	$10^{-2} - 10^{-8}$	Low resistivity, high conductivity
Semiconductors	$10^5 - 10^{-6}$	$10^{-5} - 10^6$	Resistivity and conductivity both intermediate to metals and insulators
Insulators	$10^{-11} - 10^{-19}$	$10^{11} - 10^{19}$	High resistivity and low conductivity

In this chapter we are interested in semiconductors only. The types of semiconductors that are used these days are as given below.

(i) Elemental semiconductors: silicon (Si) and germanium (Ge)
(ii) Compound semiconductors:
  • Inorganic: CdS, GaAs, CdSe, InP, etc.
  • Organic: anthracene, doped pthalocyanines, etc.
  • Organic polymers: polypyrrole, polyaniline, polythiophene, etc.

Most of the currently available semiconductor devices are based on elemental semiconductors, Si or Ge, and compound inorganic semiconductors. However, we will restrict ourselves to the study of inorganic semiconductors, particularly elemental semiconductors Si and Ge.

BAND THEORY OF SOLIDS

The nature of electron motion in a solid is very different from that in an isolated atom. This is because in an isolated atom the energy of any of its electrons is decided by the orbit in which it revolves. But when the atoms come together to form a solid, they are close to each other. So the outer orbits of electrons from neighbouring atoms come very close, or could even overlap.

Inside a solid each electron will have a different energy level. These different energy levels with continuous energy variation form energy bands. The energy band which includes the energy levels of the valence electrons is called the valence band. The energy band above the valence band is called the conduction band. With no external energy, all the valence electrons will reside in the valence band. If the lowest level in the conduction band happens to be lower than the highest level of the valence band, the electrons from the valence band can easily move into the conduction band. Normally the conduction band is empty. But when it overlaps with the valence band, electrons can move freely into it. This is the case with metallic conductors.

If there is some gap between the conduction band and the valence band, electrons in the valence band all remain bound and no free electrons are available in the conduction band. This makes the material an insulator. But some of the electrons from the valence band may gain external energy to cross the gap between the conduction band and the valence band. Then these electrons will move into the conduction band. At the same time they will create vacant energy levels in the valence band where other valence electrons can move. Thus the process creates the possibility of conduction due to electrons in a conduction band as well as due to vacancies in the valence band.

Let us consider what happens in the case of Si or Ge crystal containing N atoms. For Si, the outermost orbit is the third orbit ($n = 3$), while for Ge it is the fourth orbit ($n = 4$). The number of electrons in the outermost orbit is four (two s electrons and two p electrons). Hence the total number of outer electrons in the crystal is 4N. The maximum possible number of electrons in the outer orbit is eight (two s + six p electrons). So, for the 4N valence electrons there are 8N available energy states. These 8N discrete energy levels can either form a continuous band or they may be grouped in different bands, depending upon the distance between the atoms in the crystal.

At the distance between the atoms in the crystal lattices of Si and Ge, the energy band of these 8N states is split apart into two, which are separated by an energy gap E_g. The lower band which is completely occupied by the 4N valence electrons at a temperature of absolute zero is the valence band. The other band consisting of 4N energy states, called the conduction band, is completely empty at absolute zero.

The lowest energy level in the conduction band is E_C and highest energy level in the valence band is E_V. Above E_C and below E_V there are a large number of closely spaced energy levels.

The gap between the top of the valence band and bottom of the conduction band is called the energy band gap (energy gap E_g). It may be large, small or zero, depending upon the material. These different situations are discussed below:

Case I: This refers to a situation, as shown in Figure 14.2 (a). One can have a metal either when the conduction band is partially filled and the balanced band is partially empty or when the conduction and valence bands overlap. When there is an overlap, electrons from a valence band can easily move into the conduction band. This situation makes a large number of electrons available for electrical conduction. When the valence band is partially empty, electrons from its lower level can move to a higher level, making conduction possible. Therefore, the resistance of such materials is low, or the conductivity is high.

Case II: In this case, a large band gap E_g exists ($E_g > 3$ eV). There are no electrons in the conduction band, and therefore no electrical conduction is possible. Note that the energy gap is so large that electrons cannot be excited from the valence band to the conduction band by thermal excitation. This is the case of insulators.

Case III: Here a finite but small band gap ($E_g < 3$ eV) exists. Because of the small band gap, at room temperature some electrons from a valence band can acquire enough energy to cross the energy gap and enter the conduction band. These electrons (though small in number) can move in the conduction band. Hence, the resistance of semiconductors is not as high as that of insulators.

INTRINSIC SEMICONDUCTOR

Pure semiconductors are called intrinsic semiconductors. Silicon and germanium are the most common examples of intrinsic semiconductors. An intrinsic semiconductor is also called an undoped semiconductor or I-type semiconductor. In an intrinsic semiconductor, the number of electrons in the conduction band is equal to the number of holes in the valence band. Therefore, the overall electric charge of an atom is zero and the atom is neutral.

Atomic Structures of Silicon and Germanium

The atomic number of silicon is 14, i.e., it has fourteen protons and its atom has fourteen electrons (two electrons in the first orbit, eight electrons in the second orbit, and four electrons in the outermost orbit).

The atomic number of germanium is 32, i.e. there are thirty-two protons in the nucleus and thirty-two electrons outside the nucleus (two electrons in the first orbit, eight electrons in the second orbit, eighteen electrons in the third orbit and four electrons in the outermost orbit).

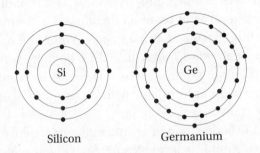

Silicon   Germanium

Fig. 15.1: Atomic structure of silicon and germanium

A silicon atom forms four covalent bonds with the four neighbouring atoms. In covalent bonding each valence electron is shared by two atoms. Similarly, in germanium also, four electrons are shared in forming covalent bonds. In its crystalline structure, every Si or Ge atom tends to share one of its four valence electrons with each of its four nearest neighbour atoms, and also to take share of one electron from each such neighbour. These shared electron pairs are referred to as forming a covalent bond, or simply a valence bond. The two shared electrons can be assumed to shuttle back and forth between the associated atoms, holding them together strongly.

At low temperatures no bonds are broken (all bonds are intact). As the temperature increases, some of these electrons may break away (becoming free electrons contributing to conduction). The thermal energy effectively ionizes only a few atoms in the crystalline lattice and creates a vacancy in the bond. The neighbourhood, from which the free electron (with charge - q) has come out, leaves a vacancy with an effective charge (+ q). This vacancy with the effective positive electronic charge is called a hole. The hole behaves as an apparent free particle with effective positive charge. In intrinsic semiconductors, the number of free electrons is equal to the number of holes.

In conductors current is caused only by the motion of electrons but in semiconductors current is caused by both electrons in a conduction band and holes in a valence band. Current that is caused by electron motion is called electron current and current that is caused by hole motion is called hole current. Electron is a negative charge carrier whereas a hole is a positive charge carrier.

At absolute zero temperature an intrinsic semiconductor behaves as an insulator. However, at room temperature the electrons present in the outermost orbit absorb thermal energy. When the outermost orbit electrons get enough energy, they break the bonding with the nucleus of an atom and jump into the conduction band. The electrons present in a conduction band are not attached to the nucleus of an atom, so they are free to move.

The process of conduction in an intrinsic semiconductor is shown in the figure below. An intrinsic semiconductor is connected to a battery. Here, the positive terminal of the battery is connected to one side and the negative terminal is connected to the other side. As we know, like charges repel and opposite charges attract each other. In a similar way, negative charge carriers (electrons) are attracted towards the positive terminal of a battery and positive charge carriers (holes) are attracted towards the negative terminal of the battery.

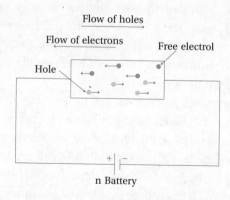

Fig. 15.2: Movement of electrons and holes in intrinsic semiconductor

The total current in an intrinsic semiconductor is the sum of hole and electron current.

Total current = Electron current + Hole current

$I = I_{hole} + I_{electron}$

EXTRINSIC SEMICONDUCTOR

The conductivity of an intrinsic semiconductor depends on its temperature, but at room temperature its conductivity is very low. Hence there is a necessity of improving their conductivity. This can be done by making use of impurities. When a small amount, say, a few parts per million (ppm), of a suitable impurity is added to the pure semiconductor, the conductivity of the semiconductor is increased manifold. Such materials are known as extrinsic semiconductors or impurity semiconductors. The deliberate addition of a desirable impurity is called doping and the impurity atoms are called dopants. Such a material is also called a doped semiconductor.

There are two types of dopants used in doping; the tetravalent Si or Ge:

(i) Pentavalent (valency 5); like arsenic (as), antimony (sb), phosphorous (p), etc.

(ii) Trivalent (valency 3); like indium (in), boron (B), aluminium (al), etc.

There are two types of extrinsic semiconductors, depending on the type of dopant added.

N-type Semiconductor

Suppose we dope Si or Ge with a pentavalent element. When an atom of valency 5 occupies the position of an atom in the crystal lattice of Si, four of its electrons bond with the four silicon neighbours while the fifth remains very weakly bound to its parent atom. This is because the four electrons participating in bonding are seen as part of the effective core of the atom by the fifth electron. As a result the ionization energy required to set this electron free is very small and even at room temperature it will be free to move in the lattice of the semiconductor. On the other hand, the number of free electrons (with an equal number of holes) generated by Si atoms increases weakly with temperature. In a doped semiconductor the total number of conduction electrons n_e is due to the electrons contributed by donors and those generated intrinsically, while the total number of holes n_h is only due to the holes from the intrinsic source. But the rate of recombination of holes would increase due to the increase in the number of electrons. As a result, the number of holes would get reduced further.

Thus, with proper level of doping the number of conduction electrons can be made much larger than the number of holes. Hence, in an extrinsic semiconductor doped with pentavalent impurity, electrons become the majority carriers and holes the minority carriers. These semiconductors are, therefore, known as n-type semiconductors. For n-type semiconductors, we have:

$$n_e >> n_h$$

P-type Semiconductor

This is obtained when Si or Ge is doped with a trivalent impurity like Al, B, In, etc. The dopant has one valence electron less than Si or Ge and, therefore, this atom can form covalent bonds with the neighbouring three Si atoms but does not have any electron to offer to the fourth Si atom. So the bond between the fourth neighbour and the trivalent atom has a vacancy or hole. Since the neighbouring Si atom in the lattice wants an electron in place of a hole, an electron in the outer orbit of an atom in the neighbourhood may jump to fill this vacancy, leaving a vacancy or hole at its own site. Thus the hole is available for conduction. Note that the trivalent foreign atom becomes effectively negatively charged when it shares the fourth electron with the neighbouring Si atom. Therefore, the dopant atom of p-type material can be treated as the core of one negative charge along with its associated hole. It is obvious that one acceptor atom gives one hole. These holes are in addition to the intrinsically generated holes while the source of conduction electrons is only intrinsic generation. Thus, for such a material, the holes are the majority carriers and electrons are minority carriers. Therefore, extrinsic semiconductors doped with trivalent impurity are called p-type semiconductors. We have, for p-type semiconductors:

$$n_h >> n_e$$

P-N Junction

A p-n junction diode is a two-terminal or two-electrode semiconductor device that allows electric current in only one direction while blocking the electric current in the opposite or reverse direction.

We know that in an n-type semiconductor, the concentration of electrons (number of electrons per unit volume) is more compared to the concentration of holes. Similarly, in a p-type semiconductor, the concentration of holes is more than the concentration of electrons. During the formation of the p-n junction, and due to the concentration gradient across p- and n-sides, holes diffuse from p-side to n-side (p → n) and electrons diffuse from n-side to p-side (n → p). This motion of charge carried gives rise to diffusion current across the junction.

When an electron diffuses from n → p, it leaves behind an ionized donor on the n-side. This ionized donor (positive charge) is immobile as it is bonded to the surrounding atoms. As the electrons continue to diffuse from n → p, a layer of positive charge (or positive space-charge region) on the n-side of the junction is developed.

Similarly, when a hole diffuses from p → n due to the concentration gradient, it leaves behind an ionized acceptor (negative charge), which is immobile. As the holes continue to diffuse, a layer of negative charge (or negative space-charge region) on the p-side of the junction is developed.

Semiconductor Diode

A semiconductor diode is basically a p-n junction with metallic contacts provided at the ends for the application of an external voltage. It is a two-terminal device. The direction of arrow indicates the conventional direction of current (when the diode is under forward bias). The equilibrium barrier potential can be altered by applying an external voltage V across the diode.

In n-type semiconductors, free electrons are the majority charge carriers whereas in p-type semiconductors, holes are the majority charge carriers. When the n-type semiconductor is joined with the p-type semiconductor, a p-n junction is formed. The p-n junction, which is formed when the p-type and n-type semiconductors are joined, is called a p-n junction diode.

The p-n junction diode is made from semiconductor materials such as silicon, germanium and gallium arsenide. For designing the diodes, silicon is more preferred over germanium. The p-n junction diodes made from silicon semiconductors work at a higher temperature when compared with the p-n junction diodes made from germanium semiconductors.

The basic symbol of a p-n junction diode under forward bias and reverse bias is shown in Fig 15.3.

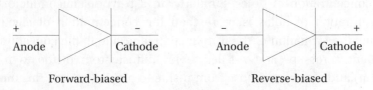

Forward-biased   Reverse-biased

Fig. 15.3: P-n junction diode

In Figure 15.3, the arrowhead of a diode indicates the conventional direction of electric current when the diode is forward-biased (from positive terminal to the negative terminal). The holes move from the positive terminal (anode) to the negative terminal (cathode) in the conventional direction of current. The free electrons moving from the negative terminal (cathode) to the positive terminal (anode) actually carry the electric current. However, due to the convention we have to assume that the current direction is from the positive terminal to the negative terminal.

Biasing of p-n Junction Semiconductor Diode

The process of applying the external voltage to a p-n junction semiconductor diode is called biasing. External voltage to the p-n junction diode is applied in any of the two methods: forward-biasing or reverse-biasing.

If the p-n junction diode is forward-biased, it allows the electric current flow. Under the forward-biased condition, the p-type semiconductor is connected to the positive terminal of the battery, whereas the n-type semiconductor is connected to the negative terminal of the battery.

If the p-n junction diode is reverse-biased, it blocks the electric current flow. Under the reverse-biased condition, the p-type semiconductor is connected to the negative terminal of the battery, whereas the n-type semiconductor is connected to the positive terminal of the battery.

Advantages of p-n Junction Diode

➤ The p-n junction diode is the simplest form of all the semiconductor devices. However, diodes play a major role in many electronic devices.

➤ A p-n junction diode can be used to convert the alternating current (AC) to the direct current (DC). These diodes are used in power supply devices.

➤ If the diode is forward-biased, it allows the current flow. On the other hand, if it is reverse-biased, it blocks the current flow. In other words, the p-n junction diode becomes turned on when it is forward- biased whereas the p-n junction diode becomes turned off when it is reverse-biased (i.e., it acts as a switch). Thus, the p-n junction diode is used as an electronic switch in digital logic circuits.

SECTION II

CHEMISTRY

1

BASIC CONCEPTS OF CHEMISTRY

INTRODUCTION

Chemistry is the study of matter and energy. It is also about how matter and energy interact primarily at the level of atoms and molecules. Chemistry can help us understand the world around us. Everything we touch, taste or smell is made of chemicals. Furthermore, study of chemical reactions helps us understand the formation of many new chemical compounds. The study of chemistry also explains how food cooks, why detergent cleans our clothes, and why a specific medicine cures a disease. When we better understand chemical principles, it becomes possible to design and synthesize new materials having specific properties, to use for specific purposes. Therefore, it can be concluded that chemistry is one of the most fundamental subjects that any student of science has to read, and understand its concepts well.

In this chapter we will develop and understand the basic concepts used in chemistry. The topics of this chapter are:

- Units and measurement
- SI units
- Uncertainty in measurements
- Accuracy and precision
- Significant figures
- Laws of chemical combination
- Dalton's atomic theory
- A few terms related to mass
- The mole concept

UNITS AND MEASUREMENT

Measurement is a fundamental operation in the study of science. When we carry out scientific experiments, we measure certain parameters and report the results of the experiments. In order to report any scientific measurement, we write a number followed by the unit in which it is measured. Without a unit, the number is meaningless. For example, if the length of a room is stated as 10, it is meaningless and nobody will be able to understand the result of this measurement. However, if we say the length is 10 metre, it gives everybody an idea of the dimension of the room. If we know the length 1 metre as the unit of measurement, we understand that the length of the room is 10 times the length of 1 metre. Thus, a unit is a standard of measurement.

SIGNIFICANT FIGURES

The uncertainty in the experimental or calculated values is indicated by mentioning the number of significant figures. In a measurement, significant figures are meaningful digits that are known with certainty. The uncertainty is indicated by writing the certain digits and the last uncertain digit. Thus, if we write a result as 11.2 mL, we say the 11 is certain and 2 is uncertain and the uncertainty would be +1 in the last digit. Unless otherwise stated, an uncertainty of +1 in the last digit is always understood.

There are certain rules for determining the number of significant figures. These are stated below:

- All non-zero digits are significant
  For example:
  123. (3 significant figures)
- Zeroes between non-zero digits are significant
  For example:
  12.507 (5 significant figures)
- Zeroes to the left of the first non-zero digit are not significant
  For example:
  1.02 (3 significant figures)
  0.12 (2 significant figures)

0.012 (2 significant figures)

- If a number ends in zeroes to the right of the decimal point, those zeroes are significant.
  For example:
  2.0 (2 significant figures)
  2.00 (3 significant figures)
- If a number ends in zeroes to the left of the decimal point, those zeroes may or may not be significant.
  For example:
  If we make a statement that the weight of an object is 120 g, how do we convey our knowledge of whether the balance was accurate to ± 1 g or ± 10 g?

The ambiguity can be removed by using exponential notation.

The weight can be expressed as $12. \times 10^1$ g or 1.2×10^2 g if we wish to quote unambiguously to two significant figures, and 12.0×10^1 g or 1.20×10^2 g if we have a confidence level extending to three significant figures. In numbers written in scientific notation, all digits are significant, e.g., 4.01×10^2 has three significant figures, and 8.256×10^{-3} has four significant figures.

- These rules apply to measured quantities that are non-exact. If you are told that a number is exact, then there is no uncertainty; i.e., the number is good to an infinite number of significant figures. Exact integers fall in this category.

An important example of an exact quantity is the coefficient of a reagent in a chemical reaction. This number, called the stoichiometric coefficient, expresses the specific number of molecules of reagent A which undergo reaction with a specific number of molecules of reagent B. The stoichiometric coefficients are exact.

$$2 \text{ H}_2 + \text{O}_2 \longrightarrow 2 \text{ H}_2\text{O}$$

The result of addition or subtraction or multiplication or division involving significant digits cannot have more digits to the right of the decimal point than either of the original numbers. In order to do so, sometimes the result obtained needs to be rounded off for limiting the result to the required number of significant figures. The following are the rules for rounding off:

1. If the rightmost digit to be removed is more than 5, the preceding number is increased by one. For example, if we have to reduce the number 1.576 to three significant digits, we have to remove 6; hence we have to round it off to 1.58.
2. If the rightmost digit to be removed is less than 5, the preceding number is not changed. For example, 4.234, rounded off to three significant figures, becomes 4.23.
3. If the rightmost digit to be removed is 5, then the preceding number is not changed if it is an even number but it is increased by one if it is an odd number. For example, if 6.35 is rounded off by removing 5, we have to increase 3 to 4, making it 6.4. However, if 6.25 is to be rounded off, it is rounded off to 6.2.

LAWS OF CHEMICAL COMBINATION

When chemical elements combine to form compounds, they do so following certain principles and rules, which are known as the laws of chemical combination. These are described below:

Law of Conservation of Mass

This law states that matter can neither be created nor destroyed. In a chemical reaction the net change in mass of the reactants and products before and after a chemical reaction is zero. In other words, the total mass in a chemical reaction remains constant.

This law was put forth by Antoine Lavoisier in 1789.

Law of Constant Proportion

The law of constant proportion states that when a compound is broken, the masses of the constituent elements remain in the same proportion. In other words, in a chemical compound, the elements are always present in definite proportions by mass. This means each compound has the same elements in the same proportions, regardless of where the compound was obtained, who prepared it or its mass. It is also known as the law of definite proportions.

This law was formulated and proven by Joseph Louis Proust in 1799.

Law of Multiple Proportions

According to this law, if two elements can combine to form more than one compound, the masses of one element that combine with a fixed mass of the other element are in the ratio of small whole numbers.

Let us understand this law with the help of an example. Carbon combines with oxygen to form two different compounds (under different circumstances). One is the most common gas CO_2 and the other is CO. We know that the mass of carbon is 12 u and the mass of oxygen is 16 u.

So, we can say that 12 g of carbon combines with 32 g of oxygen to form CO_2.

Similarly, 12 g of carbon combines with 16 g of oxygen to form CO.

So, the ratio of oxygen in the first and second compound is 32:16, that is, 2:1, which is a whole number.

This law was proposed by Dalton in 1803.

Law of Reciprocal Proportions

The law of reciprocal proportions states that when two different elements combine with the same quantity of the third element, the ratio in which they will do so will be the same, or a multiple of the proportion in which they combine with each other.

This law was proposed by Jeremias Richter in 1792.

Oxygen and sulfur react with copper to create copper oxide and copper sulfide, respectively. Sulfur and oxygen also react with each other to form sulfur dioxide. Therefore,

In CuS, Cu:S = 63.5:32

In CuO, Cu:O = 63.5:16

Thus, S:O = 32:16 = 2:1

Now in SO_2 we have S:O = 32:16 = 2:1

This establishes the law of reciprocal proportions.

Gay Lussac's Law of Gaseous Volumes

When gases combine or are produced in a chemical reaction, they do so in a simple ratio by volume provided all gases are at the same temperature and pressure.

For example, in the following reaction, the ratio of volumes of hydrogen, chlorine and hydrogen chloride is 1:1:2 (a simple ratio):

$$H_2 + Cl_2 \longrightarrow 2\ HCl$$
$$\text{1 vol} \qquad \text{1 vol} \qquad\qquad \text{2 vol}$$

Avogadro's Law

The law states that under the same conditions of temperature and pressure, equal volumes of different gases contain an equal number of molecules. The specific number of molecules in one gram-mole of a substance, defined as the molecular weight in grams, is $6.022140857 \times 10^{23}$, a quantity called Avogadro's number, or the Avogadro constant. For example, the molecular weight of oxygen is 32.00; so one gram-mole of oxygen has a mass of 32.00 grams and it contains $6.022140857 \times 10^{23}$ molecules. For the sake of convenience, this number is sometimes written in its simpler (shorter) form as 6.022×10^{23}. The volume occupied by one gram-mole of gas is about 22.4 L (0.791 cubic foot) at standard temperature and pressure (0°C, 1 atm) and is the same for all gases, according to Avogadro's law.

DALTON'S ATOMIC THEORY

John Dalton, a British school teacher, published his theory about atoms in 1808. The postulates of his theory are as follows:

- Matter consists of indivisible particles called atoms.
- Atoms of the same element are similar in shape and mass, but they differ from the atoms of other elements.
- Atoms cannot be created or destroyed.
- Atoms of different elements may combine with each other in fixed, simple and whole number ratios to form compound atoms.
- Atoms of the same element can combine in more than one ratio to form two or more compounds.
- The atom is the smallest unit of matter that can take part in a chemical reaction.

A FEW TERMS RELATED TO MASS

Atomic Mass

Although today we have sophisticated techniques, e.g., mass spectrometry, for determining the atomic masses fairly accurately, earlier scientists used to determine the mass of one atom relative to another by experimental means. The comparison used to be with hydrogen which was arbitrarily assigned a mass of 1 (without any units). However, the present system of atomic masses is based on carbon-12 as the standard and has been agreed upon in 1961. Here carbon-12 is one of the isotopes of carbon and can be represented as ^{12}C. In this system, ^{12}C is assigned a mass of exactly 12 atomic mass unit (amu) and masses of all other atoms are given relative to this standard. One atomic mass unit is defined as a mass exactly equal to one-twelfth the mass of one carbon-12 atom. And 1 amu = 1.66056×10^{-24} g. Today, 'amu' has been replaced by 'u', which is known as unified mass, and sometimes the unit dalton (Da) is also used.

Average Atomic Mass

When we use atomic masses of elements in chemical calculations, we use masses that have decimal numbers. These are mostly not whole numbers. The reason for this is that we actually use average atomic masses of elements. While we find out the average atomic mass of an element, we consider its various isotopes and their abundance in nature. We now know that many naturally-occurring elements exist as more than one isotope. Let us understand this with the following example. Carbon has the following three isotopes with their relative abundances and masses, as shown.

Table 1.1: Isotopes and their atomic mass

Isotope	Abundance (%)	Atomic mass (u)
^{12}C	98.892	12
^{13}C	1.108	13.00335
^{14}C	2×10^{-10}	14.00317

From the above data, the average atomic mass of carbon can be calculated as:

$(0.98892) \times (12$ u$) + (0.01108) \times (13.00335$ u$) + (2 \times 10^{-12}) \times (14.00317$ u$)$
= 12.011 u

In a similar way we can find out the average atomic mass of other elements, provided we know their isotopes, the relative abundance of the isotopes and the atomic mass of each isotope.

Molecular Mass

Like atomic mass, we also need to compute molecular mass in chemical calculations. Molecular mass is the sum of atomic masses of the elements present in a molecule. It is obtained by multiplying the atomic mass of each element by the number of its atoms and adding them together. For example, the molecular mass of carbon dioxide which contains one carbon atom and two oxygen atoms can be obtained as follows:

$$CO_2 = (12.011 \text{ u}) + 2\ (16.00 \text{ u})$$
$$= 44.011 \text{ u}$$

Similarly, molecular mass of ethyl alcohol, C_2H_5OH, is obtained as:

$$C_2H_5OH = 2(12.011 \text{ u}) + 5(1.008 \text{ u}) + (16.00 \text{ u}) + (1.008 \text{ u})$$
$$= 24.022 \text{ u} + 5.040 \text{ u} + 16.00 \text{ u} + 1.008 \text{ u}$$
$$= 46.07 \text{ u}$$

Equivalent Mass

The equivalent mass (also loosely called equivalent weight) of a substance is calculated by dividing its molecular mass by its valency.

$$\text{Equivalent mass} = \frac{\text{Molecular mass}}{\text{Valency}}$$

THE MOLE CONCEPT

Atomic mass of an element is a very small number as we have now understood. In other words, even in a small quantity of a substance, a large number of its atoms are present. In order to define such a large number of atoms, the concept of the mole is introduced. The mole is the base quantity of measurement of the amount of a substance in the SI system. One mole is the amount of a substance that contains as many particles or entities as there are atoms in exactly 12 g (or 0.012 kg) of the ^{12}C isotope. It may be noted here that one mole of a substance always contains the same number of entities, and it does not depend on what the substance is. Let us now see what this number is which is contained in 12 g of ^{12}C. The mass of a carbon-12 atom, as determined by a mass spectrometer, is 1.992648×10^{-23} g. As one mole of carbon weighs 12 g, the number of atoms in it is given by:

$$\frac{12 \text{ g/mol } C^{12}}{1.992648 \times 10^{-23} \text{ g/ } C^{12} \text{ atom}} = 6.0221367 \times 10^{23} \text{ atoms/mol}$$

This number 6.0221367×10^{23} is called the Avogadro number (N_A) in honour of the scientist Amedeo Avogadro. The amount of any substance that contains Avogadro number of particles in it is called one mole. The mass of one mole of a substance in grams is called its molar mass. The molar mass in grams is numerically equal to atomic/molecular/formula mass in u. The amount of a gas which occupies 22.4 L at STP (Standard Temperature and Pressure) is also called one mole.

For example,

Molar mass of water = 18.02 g mol^{-1}

Molar mass of hydrogen chloride = 36.51 g mol^{-1}

The following relationship is important from the chemical calculations perspective:

$$\text{Number of moles} = \frac{\text{Amount of substance in g}}{\text{Molecular weight (or atomic weight) of the substance in g}}$$

$$\text{Number of moles} = \frac{\text{Volume of a gas at STP in L}}{22.4}$$

$$\text{Number of moles} = \frac{\text{Number of particles at STP}}{\text{Avogadro number}}$$

2

MATTER AND ITS DIFFERENT STATES

INTRODUCTION

If we look around us, we find a lot of objects of various shapes, sizes and states. All of these objects are made of matter. Anything that has mass and occupies some space is called matter. Air, water, sugar, sand, hydrogen, oxygen, etc. are all matter.

Ancient Indian philosophers said that all matter, living or non-living, was made up of five basic elements: air, earth, fire, sky and water. However, modern-day scientists classify matter on the basis of its physical and chemical properties.

On the basis of physical properties, matter can be classified as solids, liquids and gases. These are also called the three states of matter.

On the basis of chemical properties, matter can be classified as elements, compounds and mixtures.

In this chapter we will learn about:

- Different states of matter
- Interconversion of different states of matter
- Classification of matter on the basis of composition
- Particles of matter
- Methods of separation of substances in a mixture

DIFFERENT STATES OF MATTER

Matter can commonly exist in three different states: solid, liquid and gas. The three states differ in the arrangement and behaviour of constituent particles of the substance, as shown in Figure 2.1.

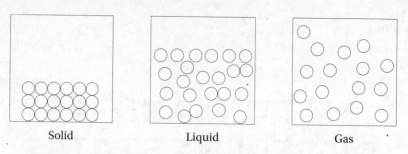

| Solid | Liquid | Gas |

Fig. 2.1: Arrangement of constituting particles in solid, liquid and gas

Comparison of characteristics of matter in the three states is given in Table 2.1.

Table 2.1: Comparison of solid, liquid and gaseous states

Solid	Liquid	Gas
Particles in a solid are tightly packed, usually in a regular pattern.	Particles in a liquid are close together; however, there is no regular arrangement of particles.	Particles in a gas are separated from each other and there is no arrangement of particles in a gas.
Particles in a solid vibrate along their mean position, but do not move from place to place.	Particles in a liquid vibrate along their mean position, move about and slide past each other.	Particles in a gas vibrate and move freely at high speed. They move almost independent of each other with practically no one influencing the other.
Solids are rigid and retain a fixed volume and shape.	Liquids take the shape of the container in which they are kept.	Gases take the shape and volume of the container in which they are kept.
Solids are very less compressible.	Liquids can be compressed, although with difficulty. The compressibility is because of the space between the particles.	Gases are compressible.

In addition to the three states as mentioned above as commonly occurring, there are two more states of matter.

Plasma: Plasma state, which is called the fourth state of matter, is made of ionized gaseous particles, meaning there are positively charged ions and free negatively charged electrons. Plasmas may have a net charge of zero over their whole volume. However, at the level of individual particles, there are positively charged ions and negatively charged electrons. That makes the electrostatic forces between the particles in the plasma, as well as the effect of magnetic fields, significant. Matter in the plasma state, therefore, has high kinetic energy.

Bose-Einstein condensate: In 1995, using a combination of lasers and magnets, Eric Cornell and Carl Weiman were able to cool a sample of rubidium to within a few degrees of absolute zero. At this extremely low temperature there is almost no kinetic energy transfer happening from one atom to another. Thus, atoms begin to clump together, forming what is now called a super atom.

Solid State

A solid state is characterized by the following properties:

- Particles are tightly or closely packed
- The gaps between the particles are very small
- It is tough to compress solids
- Solids have fixed shape and volume
- Particles can only vibrate about their mean position and cannot move
- The rate of diffusion in solids is very low

Therefore, when we talk about solids, we consider the positions of the constituent atoms, molecules or ions essentially fixed in space. The constituents of a solid can be arranged in two ways: they can form a regular repeating three-dimensional structure called a crystal lattice, thus producing a crystalline solid, or they can cluster in no particular order, in which case they form an amorphous solid. Examples of crystalline solid are sodium chloride, diamond, etc. Examples of amorphous solids are glass, rubber, etc.

Liquid State

A liquid state is characterized by the following properties:

- Particles are less tightly packed as compared to solids
- Liquids take the shape of the container in which they are kept
- Liquids are difficult to compress as particles have less space

between them to move
- Liquids have fixed volume but no fixed shape
- The rate of diffusion in liquids is higher than that of solids

Gaseous State

A gaseous state is characterized by the following properties:

- Particles are far apart from each other
- Particles attract each other with negligible force and they can move freely
- Gases have neither fixed volume nor fixed shape
- The gaseous state has the highest compressibility as compared to solids and liquids
- The rate of diffusion is higher than solids and liquids
- The kinetic energy of particles is higher than solids and liquids

INTERCONVERSION OF STATES OF MATTER

> **Melting**: The process by which a solid is converted into a liquid is referred to as melting or fusion. It is done by heating the solid.
> **Freezing**: The reverse of melting is called freezing. A liquid is converted into a solid by the process of freezing, in which temperature is lowered.
> **Boiling**: The process of conversion of a liquid into vapour or gas is known as boiling. It is done by increasing the temperature of the liquid.
> **Condensation:** It is the reverse of boiling. Gas can be converted into liquid form by lowering the temperature.
> **Sublimation**: The process by which solids can be directly converted into vapour upon heating is called sublimation.
> **Deposition**: The reverse of sublimation is deposition. Vapours are directly converted to solid by this process.

Figure 2.2 schematically represents the interconnectivity between the three processes and how the conversion from one state to the other is achieved.

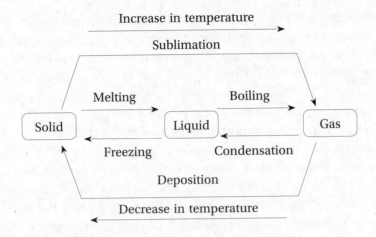

Increase in temperature

Sublimation

Melting → Boiling →

Solid | Liquid | Gas

← Freezing | Condensation ←

Deposition

← Decrease in temperature

Fig. 2.2: Conversion of one state of matter into another

CLASSIFICATION OF MATTER

Depending on the composition, matter can be classified into pure substances or mixtures. A mixture contains two or more different types of matter mixed together. A mixture can further be classified into homogeneous and heterogeneous, depending on whether the mixing of constituent particles is uniform or non-uniform, respectively. Some of the common examples of a mixture are: sugar solution, salt solution, alcohol and water mixture, and air. These are also examples of homogeneous mixtures. Consider, on the contrary, a mixture of sand and pebbles, or a mixture of sand and sugar. These are examples of heterogeneous mixtures because in these examples the different components can be observed. It may be mentioned here that suitable methods can be adopted to separate the components of a mixture. Some of the physical methods employed to separate components of a mixture are hand-picking, filtration, crystallization, distillation, etc.

Pure substances can be classified into elements and compounds, depending on whether they are made of one type of particle only or more than one type of particle. In case of elements, it is one type of particle, whereas in case of compounds, more than one element is involved. One very important difference between a pure substance and a mixture is that the composition of a pure substance remains the same, irrespective of the source it is taken from. For example, sodium, potassium, water and carbon dioxide are pure substances and their composition does not depend on how they are formed or from which source they are collected. Particles that constitute a pure substance may either be atoms or molecules. Carbon, hydrogen, oxygen, nitrogen, sulfur, sodium, etc. are some examples of elements. Each one of them is made up of atoms of one type. However, atoms of different elements are different in nature. In some cases a single atom is the smallest particle of that substance, viz. carbon, sodium, boron, sulfur, etc. In some other cases two or more atoms of the same kind combine together to form the smallest unit of these elements. These smallest units are called molecules. For example, an oxygen molecule contains two atoms of oxygen, a nitrogen molecule contains two atoms of nitrogen, a hydrogen molecule has two atoms of hydrogen, whereas an ozone molecule has three atoms of oxygen. When two or more atoms of different elements combine, the molecule of a compound is obtained. When an atom of oxygen combines with two atoms of hydrogen, a water molecule is formed. A molecule of carbon dioxide has a carbon atom and two oxygen atoms; a sodium chloride molecule has a sodium atom and a chlorine atom. Figure 2.3 shows the classification of matter.

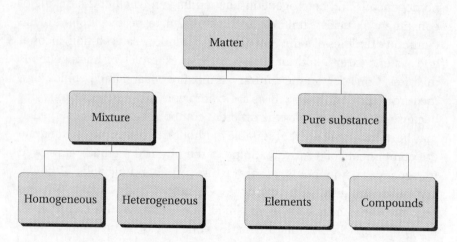

Fig. 2.3: Classification of matter

PARTICLES OF MATTER

All matter is composed of a basic component that is the smallest particle having the same chemical or physical properties of that matter. It cannot be broken down any further in which the properties are retained. An **atom** is the smallest particle of an element. Although modern science has established that it can further be broken down into sub-atomic particles, it is the smallest particle of an element since it retains all the properties of that element. For example, carbon atoms make a diamond, and also graphite. Pure gold is composed of only one type of atom, a gold atom. Therefore, it can be said that atoms are the smallest particles into which an element can be divided. Ancient Greek philosophers developed the concept of the atom, although they considered it a fundamental particle that could not be broken down.

A molecule consists of two or more atoms combined in a definite proportion, which are bonded together by means of a chemical bond. A molecule is the smallest particle of a compound and is capable of independent existence, showing properties same as that of the compound. Contrary to atoms, molecules do not take part in a chemical reaction.

A molecule may have two or more atoms of the same type. This is called a homomolecule. For example, an oxygen molecule consists of two atoms of oxygen and an ozone molecule consists of three atoms of oxygen. Similarly, a hydrogen molecule is made of two atoms of hydrogen. On the other hand, a heteromolecule consists of two or more different types of atoms combined in a definite proportion. For example, a molecule of water is made of two atoms of hydrogen and one atom of oxygen; a molecule of carbon dioxide consists of one atom of carbon and two atoms of oxygen, whereas a molecule of carbon monoxide has one atom each of carbon and oxygen.

METHODS OF SEPARATION OF COMPONENTS IN A MIXTURE

As discussed earlier, a mixture is made of two or more different types of matter mixed together. Sometimes it is necessary to isolate different components from their mixture. Components of a heterogeneous mixture can be separated by easy methods like hand-picking, sieving, etc. However, special techniques are required to separate the components in case of a homogeneous mixture. Studies of biochemical systems, environmental analysis, pharmaceutical research, etc. are some of the areas of study that require reliable separation methods.

Here are a few common separation techniques:

Chromatography

Chromatography is the method of separating components of a mixture by passing the mixture in solution or suspension or as a vapour (as in gas chromatography) through a medium, in which the components move at different rates. Thin-layer chromatography is a special type of chromatography used for separating and identifying mixtures that are or can be coloured, especially pigments.

Distillation

Distillation is a process of purification, and separation of components, where the components of a liquid mixture are vaporized and then condensed and isolated. The method is very effective to separate mixtures of two or more pure liquids. There are various types of distillation. In simple distillation, a mixture is heated and the most volatile component vaporizes at the lowest temperature. The vapour passes through a cooled tube (a condenser), where it condenses back into its liquid state. The condensate that is collected is called the distillate. Similar to simple distillation, fractional distillation is best for separating a solution of two miscible liquids. (Miscible liquids are liquids that dissolve in each other.) The fractional method takes advantage of the different boiling points of the two liquids. The one with lower boiling point distils first.

Separating Funnel

A separating funnel is used to separate two immiscible liquids by making use of their property of unequal density. A mixture of oil and water, for example, can be separated by using a separating funnel. The liquid mixture is allowed to settle so that two different liquids remain together but one remains above the other. The lighter of the two will float over the heavier one. Thus, by opening the stopper of the separating funnel and allowing one liquid to flow out without disturbing the overall condition, the two liquids can be separated from each other.

Filtration

Filtration is a commonly used method of separating an insoluble solid from a liquid. An example of such a mixture is sand and water. Filtration is used in water treatment plants, where insoluble impurities are filtered to remove solid particles from the water.

Evaporation

Evaporation is a good technique for separating a mixture of a soluble solid and a solvent. The process involves heating the solution until the solvent evaporates (turns into gas), leaving behind the solid residue. The rate of evaporation increases with temperature. So heating makes the evaporation process faster. Table salt is prepared by evaporation of sea water.

Magnetic Separation

Magnetic separation is ideal for separating a mixture of two solids with one part having magnetic properties. Some metals like iron, nickel and cobalt have magnetic properties while gold, silver and aluminum do not. Magnetic elements are attracted to a magnet. So, in a mixture of magnetic and non-magnetic substances, a magnet separates magnetic substances from its non-magnetic counterpart.

3

ATOMIC STRUCTURE

INTRODUCTION

What constitutes matter has always been a subject of intensive scientific study. However, when it became known that matter is made of small particles called atoms, the focus of the scientific community shifted to the investigation, regarding whether the atom was the smallest part of matter and whether it could be further subdivided. The prevalent concept until the nineteenth century that atoms were the smallest particles started changing with the results of some of the experiments carried out around the late nineteenth century and early twentieth century by Thomson, Rutherford, Bohr, Chadwick, Moseley and the likes, and this started revealing the presence of sub-atomic particles making up an atom.

DALTON'S ATOMIC THEORY

Let us recapitulate the concepts of Dalton's atomic theory. The points made there are:

- Matter consists of indivisible particles called atoms.
- Atoms of the same element are similar in shape and mass, but they differ from the atoms of other elements.
- Atoms cannot be created or destroyed.
- Atoms of different elements may combine with each other in fixed, simple and whole number ratios to form compound atoms.
- Atoms of the same element can combine in more than one ratio to form two or more compounds.
- The atom is the smallest unit of matter that can take part in a chemical reaction.

Dalton's atomic theory could explain the laws of chemical combination.

EXPERIMENTS LEADING TO DISCOVERY OF SUB-ATOMIC PARTICLES

Cathode Ray Discharge Experiment

A gas is kept at very low pressure inside a closed tube, fitted with two electrodes. When high voltage is passed through the gas at very low pressure, as low as 10^{-6}atm, a stream of particles starts flowing from the negative electrode or cathode. These are called **cathode rays**. These particles were later proved to be negatively charged electrons.

Properties of Cathode Rays

1. Cathode rays are made up of negatively charged particles.
2. Cathode rays travel in straight lines. However, they get deflected towards the positively charged plate (anode) when subjected to an electrical field. Cathode rays also get deflected when subjected to a strong magnetic field.
3. Cathode rays travel with speed nearly equal to that of light.
4. Cathode rays consist of matter particles. Therefore, they cast the shadow of any solid object placed in their path.
5. Cathode rays set a paddle wheel into motion when it is placed in the path of these.
6. Cathode rays heat an object on which they fall.
7. Cathode rays can penetrate through thin metallic sheets.
8. The charge to mass ratio (e/m) of these particles is 1.758820×10^8 C/g or 1.758820×10^{11} C/kg. Here e is the charge of the electron in C and m is its mass in g (or kg).
9. Cathode rays ionize the gases through which they travel.
10. When cathode rays fall on certain metals such as copper, X-rays are produced. The X-rays are not deflected by electrical or magnetic fields. X-rays pass through opaque materials such as black paper, but are stopped by solid objects such as bones.

Charge and Mass of an Electron

The charge of an electron was determined by R.S. Millikan by his famous oil drop experiment. The detail of the experiment is outside the purview of this book. However, for the sake of continuity, the charge of an electron as determined by Millikan, and subsequently verified by other experiments, is -1.6022×10^{-19} C. Based on this value and Thomson's e/m ratio, the mass of an electron is computed to be 9.1094×10^{-31} kg.

Discovery of Proton and Neutron

E. Goldstein, in his canal rays experiment, proposed the presence of positively charged particles. However, it was not until the experiment by Rutherford that the name proton was coined. Rutherford, in 1919, concluded the presence of particles of the same charge as electrons in an atom. This explained the concept of electro-neutrality of atoms and at the same time explained some of the phenomena observed in different but similar experiments. The charge of a proton is, therefore, $+1.6022 \times 10^{-19}$C (same as that of an electron, only the sign reversed), and its mass is 1.6727×10^{-27} kg.

James Chadwick, in 1932, while explaining the findings of his experiment of bombardment of a thin sheet of beryllium by alpha particles felt the presence of another particle in an atom. However, these particles have to be electrically neutral. These electrically neutral particles were found to have mass slightly more than that of protons, and were named neutrons. The mass of a neutron is 1.6750×10^{-27} kg and its charge is zero.

EARLY ATOMIC MODELS

Thomson's Plum Pudding Model

Thomson proposed that an atom is a sphere of positive charges in which negatively charged electrons are embedded.

However, Thomson's model could not explain the results of Rutherford's alpha particle scattering experiment.

Rutherford's Nuclear Atom or Planetary Model of an Atom

Rutherford's model of an atom is based on the alpha-particle scattering experiment. In this experiment, a very thin gold foil was bombarded by alpha particles. Most of the alpha particles passed through undeviated, implying that most of the space in an atom is empty. Some alpha particles were deflected slightly, suggesting interactions with other charged particles within the atom. Still other alpha particles were scattered at large angles, while a very few even bounced back toward the source. This would not have been possible with the plum pudding model proposed by Sir J.J. Thomson. Hence he disapproved Thomson's model.

The sole postulates of Rutherford's model were:

(a) An atom has a tiny, dense, positively charged core called a nucleus, in which nearly all the mass is concentrated. Since the neutron had not been discovered till then, Rutherford's model considered the nucleus to be consisting only of protons.

(b) Around the nucleus, the light, negative constituents called electrons circulate at some distance, much like planets revolving around the sun.

(c) Most of the space in an atom is empty, with the nucleus occupying only a very small part of the atom.

Drawbacks of Rutherford's Model

1. According to classical electrodynamics, an electron revolving around the nucleus should get accelerated towards the nucleus. Furthermore, according to the electromagnetic theory, an accelerating charged particle must emit radiation continuously, and thereby lose energy. As a result of this loss of energy, the electron should slow down, and because of the attraction from the nucleus the electron should follow a spiral path and ultimately fall into the nucleus, resulting in a collapse of the atom. But contrarily, atoms are found to be very stable.

2. Rutherford's model of the atom does not say anything about the arrangement of electrons in an atom.

Bohr's Model of an Atom

The postulates of Rutherford could not stand the test of established scientific principles hitherto known. Particularly the fact that an atom, according to this model, is not stable, led to the conclusion that Rutherford's model suffered from serious drawbacks, hence could not be correct. Niels Bohr modified Rutherford's model about an atom and proposed a new model. According to him, an atom is a tiny, spherical body that is made of a nucleus at the centre and negatively charged particles (electrons) revolving around the nucleus in a certain path known as the orbit. Electrons cannot revolve around the nucleus in any path; only certain paths are permissible for that; this was the hallmark of Bohr's theory. He proposed some new postulate with same basic concepts of Rutherford's theory.

The postulates of Bohr's atomic model are:

1. In an atom, the electrons revolve around the nucleus in certain definite circular paths or concentric circles, called **orbits**, or **shells**.

2. Each shell or orbit corresponds to a definite energy. Therefore, these circular orbits are also known as energy levels or energy shells.

3. The orbits or energy levels are characterized by an integer n, where n has values 1, 2, 3, 4... It (n = 1, 2, 3...) is called the **quantum number** of the respective orbit. These orbits are designated as K,L,M,N...etc., corresponding to the value of n equals 1, 2, 3, 4...etc., where K stands for the first orbit closest to the nucleus, and L, M, N, etc. are the orbits that occur as one goes outward and away from the nucleus. The K shell has the lowest energy and the electron in the lowest energy state is said to be in the ground state. Since each orbit has a certain defined energy, electrons in an atom can have only certain permissible energies. The energy of an electron in a certain orbit remains constant. As long as it remains in that orbit, it neither emits nor absorbs energy. These are termed stationary states or main energy states.

4. The electrostatic force of attraction of an electron by the nucleus is balanced by the centripetal force of the moving electron.

5. The angular momentum of an electron is quantized. Thus, an electron can be in those orbits only where its angular momentum is an integral multiple of $h/2\pi$, where h is the Planck's constant.

    Therefore, $mvr = nh/2\pi$, where m is the mass of the electron, v is the velocity of the electron in the orbit, r is the radius of that orbit, and n is a simple integer having values 1, 2, 3....

6. An electron can jump from a lower energy level (E_{lower}) to a higher energy level (E_{higher}) by absorbing the appropriate amount of energy. That means if the appropriate amount of energy is

CHEMISTRY

supplied to an electron, it may go to an excited state (higher energy level of an electron is known as its excited state). Similarly, an electron can jump from a higher energy level (E_{higher}) to a lower energy level (E_{lower}) by losing the appropriate amount of energy. The energy absorbed or lost equals the difference between the two energy levels, i.e.,

$$\Delta E = E_{higher} - E_{lower}$$

In this process a photon of energy $h\nu$ is emitted (or absorbed, as the case may be), which is the same as the difference between the two energy layers. That is,

$\Delta E = h\nu = hc/\lambda$ where c is the velocity of light, λ is the wavelength of the emitted (or absorbed) photon and h is the Planck's constant.

Drawbacks of Bohr's Model of an Atom

1. This model could not explain the spectrum of atoms other than hydrogen.
2. The theory does not give any information regarding the distribution and arrangement of electrons in an atom.
3. Bohr's theory could not explain the fine structure of spectral lines observed in a high-resolution spectrum of a hydrogen atom. The spectral lines of a hydrogen atom are found to be made of a fine structure of spectral lines when examined by spectrometers having high-resolution power.
4. Hydrogen atom spectral lines are found to further split when an electric or a magnetic field is applied to the atom. Bohr's theory could not explain these effects of splitting of spectral lines in the electric field (known as Stark effect) or magnetic field (known as Zeeman effect).

ELECTRONIC CONFIGURATION OF AN ATOM

Shells and Subshells

According to Bohr's theory, electrons orbit the nucleus of an atom at different energy levels, called shells. Each energy level is given a number called the principal quantum number, n. The shell closest to the nucleus has a value of n = 1. The next outward shell has a value of n = 2, etc. These numbers correspond to K, L, M, N, etc. shells. The maximum number of electrons possible in an orbit is given by the formula $2n^2$.

The maximum number of electrons in the first four energy levels are (calculated based on the $2n^2$ formula):

Table 3.1: Atom shells and number of electrons in each shell

Value of n	Name of the shell	Maximum number of electrons in the shell ($2n^2$)
1	K	2
2	L	8
3	M	18
4	N	32

Each shell is further subdivided into orbitals. For the shell whose principal quantum number value is n, there are n number of subshells and they correspond to values 0, 1...n-1. The values of subshells corresponding to 0, 1, 2, etc., are called s, p, d, etc. The following table shows how the maximum number of electrons in different subshells adds up to the maximum number of electrons in shells.

Table 3.2: The number of electrons in different subshells adds up to the number of electrons in the shell

Value of n	Name of shell	Subshell	Orbitals	Number of electrons in orbitals	Number of electrons in shell by addition of electrons in subshells	Number of electrons in a shell as per $2n^2$ formula
1	K	s	1s	2	2	2
2	L	s	2s	2	2 + 6 = 8	8
		p	2p	6		
3	M	s	3s	2	2 + 6 + 10 = 18	18
		p	3p	6		
		d	3d	10		
4	N	s	4s	2	2 + 6 + 10 + 14 = 32	32
		p	4p	6		
		d	4d	10		
		f	4f	14		

Further advanced studies (which is beyond the scope of this book) in atomic structure revealed that electrons show a wave-like nature. The subject that deals with the nature of electrons at an advanced level and studies is called quantum mechanics. Rather than an exact location of an electron, quantum mechanics talks about the probability of finding an electron around the nucleus. The maximum probability density in a region around the nucleus is called an orbital. These are three-dimensional spaces and are called the orbital. The s-orbital is spherical in shape, the p-orbital dumbbell-shaped, the d-orbital double-dumbbell-shaped, and so on. Higher orbitals have complicated three-dimensional shapes that are beyond the scope of this book.

Filling up of Orbitals with Electrons

Electrons fill up orbitals in the manner in which the energy of the atom is minimized. Electrons fill in the increasing order of the energy of the orbital, that is 1s, 2s, 2p, etc. What it means is that the lowest energy orbital is filled up first and only then the next higher energy orbital is filled. The sequence in which orbitals are filled in by electrons is called the **aufbau principle**. According to this principle the arrangement of orbitals is like this:

1s 2s 2p 3s 3p 4s 3d 4p 5s 4d 5p 6s 4f 5d 6p 7s

The simplest way to remember this sequence is to write 1s in one row, 2s and 2p in the second row, 3s, 3p and 3d in the third row, and so on, and cut arrows through them in the way shown in Figure 3.1 and read them in the sequence as arrows cut them across from the tail towards the tip.

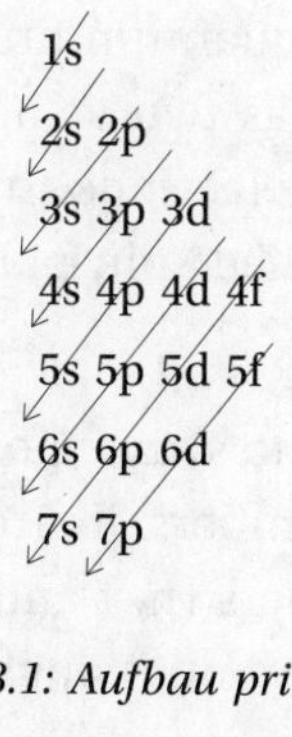

1s
2s 2p
3s 3p 3d
4s 4p 4d 4f
5s 5p 5d 5f
6s 6p 6d
7s 7p

Fig. 3.1: Aufbau principle

The electronic configuration of an atom is written as nl^x where x is the number of electrons and the nl combination stands for 1s, 2s, 2p, etc. orbitals. Thus the electronic configuration of hydrogen will be $1s^1$ because it has only one electron. The electronic configuration of helium will be $1s^2$ because it has two electrons. The next electron goes in the 2s orbital, and the electronic configuration of Li is $1s^2 2s^1$. Sometimes a shorthand notation is used as $[He]2s^1$ for Li. The symbol in square brackets refers to the electronic configuration of that atom. And for Li, it is called the helium core $2s^1$. Be has electronic configuration $1s^2 2s^2$, and B has electronic configuration $1s^2 2s^2 2p^1$.

SOME ADVANCED CONCEPTS OF ELECTRONIC STRUCTURE OF AN ATOM

Advanced study of electronic structure of an atom has established the requirement of four quantum numbers to explain the energy levels, stability, spectrum, chemical reactions and many more concepts. Although the details of such study cannot be covered in this chapter, for the sake of brevity and basic level of understanding the concept is introduced here in a brief outline of the subject. These four quantum numbers are principal quantum number (n) azimuthal quantum number (l), magnetic quantum number (m) and spin quantum number (s). While the azimuthal quantum number is associated with the angular momentum of an electron, the magnetic quantum number determines the orientation of orbitals in space. In other words, the magnetic quantum number determines the direction of an orbital in space in the presence of a magnetic field. The spin quantum number determines the spin of an electron in an orbital. It has two values, +1/2 and -1/2. An orbital can hold a maximum of two electrons that have opposite spin. These two electrons are therefore called spin-paired.

Pauli's Exclusion Principle
Pauli Exclusion Principle states that no two electrons can have the same set of four quantum numbers. Therefore, for an electron, even if the first three quantum numbers (n, l and m) are the same, the fourth quantum number must be different. A single orbital can hold a maximum of two electrons, which must have opposing spins; otherwise they would

have the same four quantum numbers, which is forbidden. One electron would spin up ($s = +1/2$) and the other would spin down ($s = -1/2$). This explains why each subshell has twice the electrons per orbital. For example, it is now clear that the s-subshell has one orbital that can hold up to two electrons, the p-subshell has three orbitals that can contain upto six electrons, the d-subshell has five orbitals that contain up to ten electrons, and the f-subshell has seven orbitals with fourteen electrons.

Hund's Rule

When assigning electrons in orbitals, if orbitals with the same energy (which are called degenerate orbitals) are available, each electron will first fill all the degenerate orbitals before starting to spin-pair with another electron.

ATOMIC NUMBER AND MASS NUMBER OF AN ATOM

An atom has negatively charged electrons (except hydrogen which has one electron) and positively charged protons. The latter is a component of the nucleus, and carries positive charge. An atom being electrically neutral, it must have the same number of electrons as protons. The number of protons or electrons in an atom is called its atomic number (represented by uppercase Z).

A few examples: a hydrogen atom contains one proton and therefore has atomic number 1; a carbon atom contains six protons and has atomic number 6; an oxygen atom contains eight protons and thus its atomic number is 8. The atomic number of an element remains the same all the time. It means that the number of protons in the nucleus of every atom (hence the number of electrons outside the nucleus) in an element is always the same.

The mass number of an atom is the number of protons and neutrons together in the nucleus. It is represented by uppercase A.

A few examples: An atom of carbon has six protons and six neutrons. Thus, its mass number is 12; there are eight protons and eight neutrons in the nucleus of an oxygen atom, hence its mass number is 16; similarly the mass number of nitrogen ($Z = 7$) is 14.

An atom with its atomic number and mass number is represented as $_{Z}^{A}X$ where X represents the symbol of an atom. Thus, a carbon atom is written as $^{12}_{6}C$ and an oxygen atom will be represented as $^{16}_{8}O$.

Isotopes, Isobars and Isotones

Sometimes we find an atom with different mass numbers. For example, $^{13}_{6}C$ and $^{14}_{6}C$; $^{2}_{1}H$ and $^{3}_{1}H$; $^{35}_{17}Cl$ and $^{37}_{17}Cl$, etc. Quite obviously the atomic number will remain the same always for an element. Therefore it is always 6 for carbon, 8 for oxygen, 11 for sodium, etc. However, different mass numbers mean different number of neutrons, because the number of neutrons is given by mass number minus atomic number. Atoms having the same atomic number but different atomic mass numbers are called **isotopes**.

The number of neutrons in $^{12}_{6}C$ = 6

The number of neutrons in $^{13}_{6}C$ = 7

The number of neutrons in $^{14}_{6}C$ = 8

However, two different atoms may have same mass number despite their atomic number being different. Nuclides having the same mass number but different number of protons, that is, different atomic number, are called **isobars**. For example, $^{40}_{18}Ar$ and $^{40}_{20}Ca$ are isobars. In this example, the number of neutrons is twenty-two (that is, 40 – 18) in case of Ar and twenty (that is, 40 – 20) in case of Ca.

Atoms of different elements having different mass number and different atomic number but same neutron number are called isotones. Examples of isotones are $^{12}_{5}B$ and $^{13}_{6}O$. They have seven neutrons each.

4

CHEMICAL BONDING AND MOLECULAR STRUCTURE

INTRODUCTION

A chemical bond is a force that holds the atoms of various elements or ions of various elements together to form compounds. There may be a huge number of possibilities of combinations of the elements, and thereby creation of a large number of compounds. While in principle that may be correct, how atoms will interact with each other to form a chemical bond and hence a chemical compound between them is governed by certain principles and factors. Not all possibilities are allowed. At the end of this chapter you will have a fair idea about the types of bonds and the type of interaction that is required to create those bonds, so that you can understand the chemistry behind bond formation. There are many theories that have been put forward from time to time to explain chemical bond formation between two (or more) constituting entities. These are the Kössel-Lewis approach, the Valence Shell Electron Pair Repulsion (VSEPR) theory, the Valence Bond (VB) theory and the Molecular Orbital (MO) Theory. While all of these theories have contributed to developing the understanding of chemical bond formation, the last one, namely the MO theory, is widely accepted to be the latest and most successful theory of chemical bond formation. Bonding takes place when lowering of energy of the system takes place to attain stability. In other words, the sum total of energy of the isolated system before bonding is more than the same after bonding has taken place. It is under this condition that bonding will take place.

VALENCE ELECTRONS AND VALENCY OF AN ELEMENT

The reactivity of an atom or its tendency to form a bond with another atom depends on the number of electrons present in the outer shell of the elements. **Valence electrons** are the electrons that are present in the outermost orbit of an atom, and that orbit (shell) is called the **valence shell**. When an atom wants to make a bond with another atom, these valence electrons make that happen. Here is an example of a valence shell:

Oxygen has atomic number 8 and its electronic configuration is $1s^2 2s^2 2p^4$. In its inner shell (closer to the nucleus), K, it has two electrons. There are six electrons in the L shell. This outermost orbit is called the valence shell. Since according to Hund's rule one of the 2p orbitals will have two electrons and the remaining two 2p orbitals will have one electron each, out of the six valence electrons four will come in pairs of two and they are called the lone pair. This leaves an oxygen atom with two electrons which are in single occupancy in the two 2p orbitals. These electrons will participate in bonding. In the Lewis electron dot diagram, these lone pairs are drawn as two dots together and single electrons are drawn as one dot around the symbol of the atom. Therefore, the Lewis electron dot structure of oxygen is:

Fig. 4.1: Electron dot structure of oxygen

Similarly, the electron dot structure of carbon (atomic number 6) is:

Fig. 4.2: Electron dot structure of carbon

Noble gases have outer shells filled with eight electrons (except helium, which has two electrons). The Lewis structure of neon is shown below:

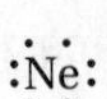

Fig. 4.3: Electron dot structure of neon

Valency of an element is the number of electrons lost or gained in the process of a chemical bond formation. We will illustrate valency when we discuss the formation of a chemical bond in accordance with various theories proposed.

TYPES OF CHEMICAL BONDS

Ionic Bond

Ionic bonds are formed by the transfer of electrons from one atom to another. Because of complete transfer of electron or electrons, oppositely charged ions are formed. The atom that donates an electron becomes a positive ion and the atom that accepts that electron becomes a negative ion. These two ions of opposite charge attract each other because of the electrostatic force of attraction.

Characteristics of Ionic Compounds

➤ Ionic bonds are formed between metals and non-metals. Metals tend to lose electrons and become positive ions while non-metals become negative ions by gaining electrons.
➤ Ionic compounds dissolve in water as well as other polar solvents.
➤ Solutions of ionic compounds and their aqueous solutions can conduct electricity.
➤ Ionic compounds have higher melting points. It means that these bonds can remain stable for a greater temperature range.

Covalent Bond

A covalent bond is formed between two atoms when they share an electron pair. Since this involves sharing, the nature of both the atoms involved in this type of bonding should ideally be the same. This type of bond is formed between two non-metal atoms.

Characteristics of Covalent Compounds

➤ A covalent bond is directional in nature. Due to this, molecules of covalent compounds have a definite shape. For example, the methane molecule, CH_4, has regular tetrahedral shape, and the ammonia molecule, NH_3, has pyramidal shape, with definite bond angles.
➤ When a covalent bond is formed between atoms of different elements with different electronegativity values, the bond tends to have a

certain amount of polar or ionic characteristic. For example, the covalent HCl molecule seems to have partial ionic character due to the difference in electronegativity between the hydrogen and chlorine atoms.

➤ Covalent compounds are by and large liquid and gaseous. There are some exceptions like diamond, silica, etc. They are solid.

➤ Covalent compounds have low melting and boiling points because covalent molecules are held by weak forces.

➤ Covalent compounds do not conduct electricity.

➤ Covalent compounds are in general soluble in non-polar solvents like benzene, toluene, etc., but are insoluble in polar solvents like water.

Coordinate Covalent Bond

A coordinate covalent bond is formed when both the shared electrons are donated by one atom only. Unlike a covalent bond in which both the atoms contribute the shared electrons, one each, a coordinate covalent bond is a special type of covalent bond because both the electrons come from one atom. The atom that donates the electron pair is called the donor atom and the atom that receives it is called the acceptor atom. The bond is written as an arrow with the arrowhead pointing to the acceptor atom. A coordinate covalent bond can be seen in the formation of an ammonium ion. Nitrogen donates its lone pair of electrons to the hydrogen ion which has no electron in its shell because it is formed by the loss of an electron from a hydrogen atom. Figure 4.4 shows the coordinate covalent bond in ammonium ion.

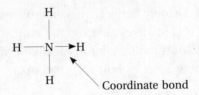

Fig. 4.4: Coordinate covalent bond in ammonium ion

Characteristics of Coordinate Covalent Bond

➤ Compounds having coordinate covalent bonds have lower melting point and boiling point than covalent compounds.

➤ These compounds are found in all the three states of matter.

CHEMISTRY

> Reactions involving coordinate covalent compounds occur at a slow rate.

LEWIS' THEORY OF CHEMICAL BONDING

According to Lewis, the nucleus and the inner shell electrons of an atom constitute the 'kernel' that does not take part in bonding. The outer shell that can accommodate a maximum of eight electrons takes part in bonding. He further assumed that these eight electrons or octet signifies a stable electronic arrangement. Lewis then postulated that atoms form a chemical bond to achieve the stable octet.

Formation of Sodium Chloride

The atomic number (Z) of sodium is 11. Its electronic configuration is $1s^2 2s^2 2p^6 3s^1$. The number of valence electrons is 1. Chlorine (Z = 17) has electronic configuration $1s^2 2s^2 2p^6 3s^2 3p^5$. It has seven electrons in its valence shell. Sodium can transfer its valence electron to a chlorine atom to attain a stable octet arrangement. The electronic configuration of the ion thus formed, Na^+, is $1s^2 2s^2 2p^6$. Thus, chlorine also attains a stable octet by gaining one electron, in which case the electronic structure of the ion, Cl^-, becomes $1s^2 2s^2 2p^6 3s^2 3p^6$. In the case of sodium chloride, because of oppositely charged ions, Na^+ and Cl^-, ions are bound together by an electrostatic force of attraction. Such a bond is called an **ionic bond**.

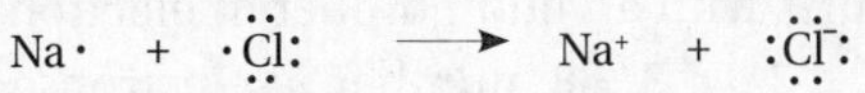

$$Na\cdot \quad + \quad \cdot \ddot{\underset{\cdot\cdot}{Cl}}: \quad \longrightarrow \quad Na^+ \quad + \quad :\ddot{\underset{\cdot\cdot}{Cl}}:^-$$

Fig. 4.4: Ionic bond

Formation of Chlorine Molecule

In the case of formation of chlorine molecule (Cl_2), each chlorine atom has an electronic configuration, $1s^2 2s^2 2p^6 3s^2 3p^5$. In order to fulfil the octet, both atoms can share one electron with each other, thereby making two electrons common to both chlorine atoms. Thus, the bond formed between the two chlorine atoms in a chlorine molecule is due to sharing of electrons. Such a bond is called a **covalent bond**.

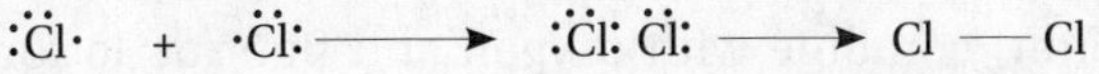

$$:\ddot{\underset{\cdot\cdot}{Cl}}\cdot \quad + \quad \cdot \ddot{\underset{\cdot\cdot}{Cl}}: \longrightarrow \quad :\ddot{\underset{\cdot\cdot}{Cl}}:\ddot{\underset{\cdot\cdot}{Cl}}: \longrightarrow \quad Cl - Cl$$

4.5: Ionic bond

Formation of Water Molecule

Hydrogen (Z = 1) has one electron and oxygen (Z = 8) has six valence shell electrons. Each hydrogen atom can share one electron with oxygen and thereby achieve the stable duplet of helium configuration. Oxygen also achieves its octet by sharing its two valence shell electrons with hydrogen. Thus, two covalent bonds are formed, one each with the two hydrogen atoms. The electron sharing between the oxygen atom and the two hydrogen atoms in water is shown in Figure 4.6.

$$H \colon \overset{\cdot\cdot}{\underset{\cdot\cdot}{O}} \colon H$$

Fig. 4.6: Electron sharing in water

LIMITATIONS OF OCTET RULE

Octet rule is very useful for understanding the structures of a majority of compounds. However, the rule is not universal and there are a number of limitations. Three types of exceptions to the octet rule are generally known.

a) The incomplete octet of the central atom: In some compounds, the number of electrons surrounding the central atom is less than eight. This is especially the case with elements having less than four valence electrons. Examples are LiCl, BeH_2 and BCl_3.

b) In molecules with an odd number of electrons, like nitric oxide, NO (N, Z = 7; O, Z = 8; number of electrons = 15) and nitrogen dioxide, NO_2 (number of electrons = 23), the octet rule is not satisfied for all the atoms.

c) This rule applies mainly to the second period elements of the periodic table. In a number of compounds of the third period, there are more than eight valence electrons around the central atom. This is termed as the expanded octet. Obviously the octet rule does not apply in such cases. Examples of such compounds are PF_5, SF_6, H_2SO_4, etc.

d) As per the octet rule, noble gases are inert and should not form bonds. However, some noble gases (viz. xenon and krypton) combine with oxygen and fluorine to form a number of compounds, like XeF_2, KrF_2, $XeOF_2$, etc.

VALENCE SHELL ELECTRON PAIR REPULSION (VSEPR) THEORY

The valence shell electron pair repulsion theory had been put forward by Sidgwick and Powell and later modified and presented by Nyholm and Gillespie. The shape of a molecule depends on how the valence shell electrons (both bonded and non-bonded) of the central atom are available. These electrons overlap with electrons from other constituent atoms of the compound. The key concept behind the VSEPR theory is that pairs of electrons that surround the central atom of a molecule or ion are arranged as far apart as possible to minimize electron-electron repulsion and hence require the lowest energy. The electron-electron repulsion decreases in the order: lone pair-lone pair (lp-lp), lone pair-bond pair and bond pair-bond pair.

The working principle of the VSEPR theory can be stated in the following four steps:

(a) Identify the central atom in a molecule. In case it is not clear which will be the central atom, consider the least electronegative atom for this purpose.

(b) Count the number of valence (outer shell) electrons on the central atom.

(c) Count the electrons used by the outer atoms to make bonds with the central atom.

(d) In order to find out the number of pairs of valence shell electron, find the sum of (b) + (c) and divide it by two.

The predicted geometry of the molecule is based on the number of valence shell electron pairs. The following table gives the connection between the number of valence shell electron pairs and the geometry of the molecule.

A detailed treatise of the VSEPR theory is beyond the scope of this book. Presence of lone pairs, charged ions, multiple bonds and how these affect the shape of molecules will be taught in higher standards.

Table 4.1: Connection between the number of valence shell electron pairs and the geometry of the molecule

Number of valence shell electron pairs	Shape of the molecule	Examples
2	Linear	BeF_2
3	Trigonal planar	BF_3
4	Tetrahedral	CH_4
5	Trigonal bipyramidal	PF_5
6	Octahedral	SF_6

VALENCE BOND THEORY

The fundamental principle behind the valence bond theory is the overlap between two atomic orbitals to form a covalent bond. It should be kept in mind that while two atomic orbitals overlap, a chemical bond is formed when the energy of the system is the minimum. Consider two isolated atoms A and B. When B approaches A from infinity, the potential energy drops. The net energy at any position of separation of the two atoms will not only be a function of the following components but also a complex combination of them. These are: attraction of nucleus of A and electron cloud of B, attraction of electron cloud of A and nucleus of B, repulsion between nucleus of A and nucleus of B, and repulsion of electron cloud of A and that of B. At a distance when the energy is the lowest, bond formation takes place.

Consider, for example, the formation of hydrogen. At the distance between the two hydrogen atoms when the energy of the system is the minimum, the two atoms are so near that their atomic orbitals overlap, resulting in the pairing of electrons. The strength of a covalent bond is determined by the extent of overlap. In general, the greater the overlap, the stronger is the bond formed between two atoms. Therefore, according to the orbital overlap concept, the formation of a covalent bond between two atoms results due to the pairing of electrons having opposite spins present in the valence shell. A direct overlap of half-filled atomic orbitals results in a sigma bond and sideways overlap results in a pi bond.

MOLECULAR ORBITAL (MO) THEORY

The molecular orbital (MO) theory, developed by Hund and Mulliken, states that just as in an atom electrons are present in atomic orbitals, the electrons in a molecule are present in various molecular orbitals. The atomic orbitals whose energies are somewhat similar and which have correct symmetry combine to form molecular orbitals. The combination is known as linear combination of atomic orbitals (LCAO). The number of MOs formed by LCAO is equal to the number of combining atomic orbitals. Therefore, when two atomic orbitals overlap, two molecular orbitals are formed. One MO is called the bonding orbital and the other the antibonding orbital. The bonding molecular orbital will have lower energy. Thus it will have more stability than the corresponding antibonding molecular orbital. The molecular orbitals so formed are filled in accordance with the aufbau principle obeying Pauli's exclusion principle and Hund's rule. What it means is that electrons start getting filled into the available bonding MOs. Molecular orbitals of diatomic molecules are designated as σ (sigma), π (pi), δ (delta), etc. In this nomenclature, the sigma (σ) molecular orbitals are symmetrical around the bond-axis while pi (π) molecular orbitals are not symmetrical.

Although the mathematical treatise of MO theory is beyond the scope of this book, the similarity and dissimilarity between the VB and the MO theories are very important. MO theory is one of the most modern theories of chemical bonding between various constituent atoms.

5

GASEOUS STATE

INTRODUCTION

The gaseous state, one of the three states of matter, is characterized by the following properties:

- Gas takes the shape and volume of the container in which it is kept
- Gases are compressible
- Particles in a gas are separated from each other and they do not follow any arrangement
- Particles in a gas vibrate and move freely at high speed
- They move almost independent of each other with practically no one influencing the other

Many properties arise from the large intermolecular distance between gaseous particles and very feeble intermolecular forces between particles. Temperature and pressure also play an important role. In this chapter, the effect of pressure and temperature on the volume of a given amount of gas will be discussed. Based on various experiments carried out by different scientists from time to time, who studied the above aspect of gaseous properties, the following gas laws, namely Boyle's law, Charles's law, Gay Lussac's law and Avogadro's law will be discussed here. Dalton's law of partial pressure and Graham's law of diffusion will also form the subject matter of this chapter.

GAS LAWS

The variables describing the macroscopic properties of a gas are pressure (P), volume (V), temperature (T) and the number of moles (n) that decides the amount of gas. The relationship between these variables under different conditions constitutes various gas laws.

Boyle's Law

For different gases, Robert Boyle, in 1662, studied the effect of pressure on the volume of gas for a given amount of the gas at constant temperature. He observed that if the volume of the gas is doubled, the pressure is halved, and vice versa. In other words, at constant temperature, the pressure and volume of a gas maintain an inverse relation between them. Boyle's law states that at constant temperature, the volume of a given amount of a gas is inversely proportional to its pressure.

$$p \propto \frac{1}{V} \text{ (at constant T and n)}$$

Or, $pV = k$ (constant)

For two gases at temperature T, where subscripts 1 and 2 stand for gas 1 and gas 2 respectively,

$$p_1 V_1 = p_2 V_2$$

The plot of p versus V, p versus 1/V and pV versus p for a certain amount of gas (n constant) and at a particular temperature (T constant) are shown in Figure 5.1 (a), Figure 5.1 (b) and Figure 5.1 (c) respectively.

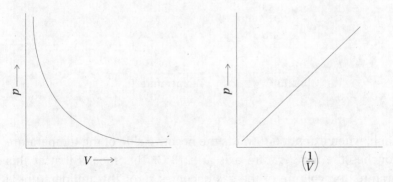

Fig. 5.1 (a) and (b): p vs V and p vs 1/V

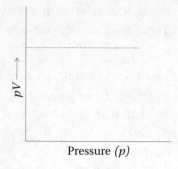

Pressure *(p)*

Fig. 5.1: (c) pV vs p

Charles' Law

Charles' law observed that the volume of a gas increases as its absolute temperature increases; whereas if its absolute temperature is lowered, its volume decreases. Charles' law states that at a constant pressure, the volume of a given amount of gas is directly proportional to the absolute temperature of the gas.

Mathematically, this is expressed as $V \propto T$

Or, $V = Constant.T$

The plot of V (in the y-axis) versus T (in the x-axis) at constant p and for a certain amount of gas (n constant) is a straight line as shown in Figure 5.2.

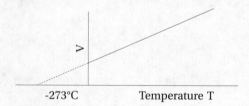

-273°C   Temperature T

Fig. 5.2: V vs T

The graph, when extended towards the negative side of the temperature axis, touches the temperature axis at -273°C. This means that at this temperature, the volume of the gas becomes zero. This temperature is called absolute zero because at this temperature the volume of any gas should be zero. In other words, the gas hypothetically ceases to exist at absolute zero.

This has given rise to a new scale of temperature, called the kelvin scale (K). If a temperature is t in °C, in kelvin its value will be:

$$T (K) = t (°C) + 273$$

Gay Lussac's Law

As discussed before in this book, the effect of temperature on pressure at a constant volume for a given mass of gas is the same as in a volume-temperature relationship in Charles' law. This law states that the pressure of a given amount of gas at constant volume is directly proportional to its temperature in kelvin:

$$P \alpha T$$

Avogadro's Law

As stated in the first chapter of chemistry, Amadeo Avogadro was the first to propose a relationship between the volume of a gas and the number of molecules present in it. This is known as Avogadro's Law and it states that equal volumes of all gases at the same temperature and pressure contain equal number of molecules.

Mathematically, Avogadro's Law is expressed as:

$V \alpha N$ (at constant temperature and pressure)

where V and N are volume and number of molecules, respectively.

At STP, 1 mole of gas occupies 22.4 L.

The number of molecules in 1 mole of a gas is 6.022×10^{23}. This is called Avogadro's number.

Combined Gas Laws

If we combine Boyle's Law, Charles' Law and Avogadro's Law, we get the combined gas laws equation. If the temperature, volume and pressure of a fixed amount of gas change from T_1, V_1 and P_1 to T_2, V_2 and P_2, then, according to the combined gas law:

$$\frac{P_1 V_1}{T_1} = \frac{P_2 V_2}{T_2}$$

Dalton's Law of Partial Pressures

Dalton's law of partial pressures states that in a mixture of non-reacting gases, the total pressure exerted is equal to the sum of the partial pressures of the individual gases. In other words, if there are non-reacting gases A, B, C, etc. in a mixture of theirs, then mathematically:

$$P = p_A + p_B + p_C + ...$$

Partial pressure of a gas is defined as the pressure the gas would have exerted on the walls of the container if it was alone in the container.

If n_A, n_B, n_C...are the number of moles of A, B and C respectively, in the mixture, then the mol-fraction of a component is defined as:

$$x_A = \frac{n_A}{n_A + n_B + n_C + ...} = \frac{n_A}{n} \text{ where n is the total number of moles.}$$

From the above expression it follows that each pressure in Dalton's law of partial pressures is expressed as:

$p_A = x_A P$

$p_B = x_B P$

$p_C = x_C P$

$p_A + p_B + p_C = x_A P + x_B P + x_C P$

or, $p_A + p_B + p_C = P (x_A + x_B + x_C) = P$

because $x_A + x_B + x_C = \frac{1}{n}(n_A + n_B + n_C) = \frac{n}{n} = 1$

Graham's Law of Diffusion

When a bottle of perfume is kept open in one corner of a room we can smell the fragrance of the perfume in the other corner of the room, in fact all over the room. The phenomenon by which the smell of perfume spreads from one point of the room to the other by mixing with air is known as diffusion. Diffusion occurs in liquids and gases.

Graham formulated the following law regarding the rate at which gases diffuse. According to him, at constant temperature and pressure, the rate of diffusion of a gas is inversely proportional to the square root of its density.

Mathematically, if r is the rate and d is the density of a gas, then:

$$r \, \alpha \frac{1}{\sqrt{d}}$$

For two gases with density d_1 and d_2 respectively, if their rates of diffusion are r_1 and r_2 respectively, then:

$$\frac{r_1}{r_2} = \sqrt{\frac{d_2}{d_1}}$$

Since molar mass, M, is twice the density, that is:

$$M = 2d$$

$$\text{Or, } d = \frac{M}{2}$$

then:
$$\frac{r_1}{r_2} = \sqrt{\frac{M_2}{M_1}}$$

IDEAL GAS

So far we have learnt about various gas laws which scientists have formulated from time to time based on their experiments with different gases under various circumstances. Some of the concepts were also derived theoretically, for example, the absolute temperature, by extrapolating the straight line obtained from Charles' law. However, in all these experiments, the underlying assumptions were that the molecules of a gas are point masses, which means they do not occupy any space because of their own dimension. Secondly, there are no intermolecular forces. In other words, molecules are free to travel in the space of the container without any influence from other molecules. A gas which satisfies these two above conditions is called an ideal gas. In an ideal gas all collisions between atoms or molecules are perfectly elastic, that is, there is no loss of energy due to collision.

Ideal Gas Equation

An ideal gas can be characterized by three variables: absolute pressure (P), volume (V) and absolute temperature (T). The relationship between them is obtained by combining the gas laws.

According to Boyle's law: $V \alpha \frac{1}{p}$ (at constant T and n)

According to Charles' law: $V \alpha T$ (at constant P and n)

According to Avogadro's law: $V \alpha n$ (at constant p and T)

Combining the above three relationships:

$$V \alpha \frac{nT}{p}$$

Or, $pV \alpha nT$

Or, $pV = \text{constant.} nT$

The constant in this case is called the universal gas constant or molar gas constant and is represented by R.

Thus the ideal gas equation is:

pV = nRT

and for one mole, the equation is: pV = RT

The value of R in different units is:

R = 0.082057 L atm K^{-1}mol^{-1} (for calculation purpose the value is taken as 0.0821 L atm K^{-1}mol^{-1})

R = 8.314 × 10^7 erg K^{-1}mol^{-1}

R = 8.314 J K^{-1}mol^{-1}

R = 1.987 cal K^{-1}mol^{-1}.

Pressure of an Ideal Gas

Based on the postulates of kinetic theory of gases, the following relationship between pressure, volume and velocity of gas molecules can be derived:

$$pV = \frac{1}{3}mNc^2$$

where p is the pressure, V is the volume, m is the mass of a gas molecule, N is the total number of molecules and c is the root mean square velocity of gas molecules.

Root Mean Square Velocity

Root mean square velocity is defined as the square root of the square of average velocities of the molecules in a gas. Mathematically it is written as:

$$v_{rms} = \sqrt{\frac{3RT}{M}}$$

where v_{rms} is the root mean square velocity (speed) in metre per second, M is the molar mass of the gas in kg per mole, R is the universal gas constant and T is the temperature in kelvin.

KINETIC THEORY OF GASES

The kinetic theory of gases explains the behaviour of an ideal gas. The essence of this theory is that gases are made up of tiny particles that are always in random, straight line motion. They move continuously and make collisions, both with each other and with the walls of the container in which they are kept. This was the first theory to describe gas pressure in terms of collisions with the walls of the container, rather than from static forces that push the molecules apart. Kinetic theory also explains how the different sizes of the particles in a gas can give them different, individual speeds.

Postulates of Kinetic Theory

Gases consist of particles that are in constant, random motion. They move continually in a straight line until they collide with something. There are two types of collision possible. Particles of a gas usually collide with each other and with the walls of their container.

Particles of a gas are point masses with no volume. The particles are so small that their volume is negligible compared to the space between them, and we consider the entire space available for their movement.

There is no intermolecular attraction or repulsion between the particles of a gas.

The pressure of the gas is due to the collision of molecules with the walls of the container. These collisions are perfectly elastic.

The time it takes for two particles to collide is negligible compared with the time between collisions.

The kinetic energy of a gas is a measure of its absolute temperature. Individual gas molecules have different speeds, but the temperature and kinetic energy of the gas correspond to the average of these speeds. An increase in temperature increases the speed of the gas molecules.

REAL GASES

The postulates of the kinetic theory of gases stated that molecules are point masses and that there is no interaction between molecules. When scientists tried to establish the gas laws and apply the ideal gas equation based on the postulates of kinetic theory of gases, they found that there was difference between the value of pressure and volume obtained from experiments and theory. It did not take long to establish that the difference in value is because of the flaws in the assumptions of the kinetic theory. Obviously real gas particles cannot be point masses whose dimensions are negligibly small. They do occupy space and attract each other. These properties become apparent at low temperatures or high pressures. At high temperatures usually the particles have enough kinetic energy so that they brush past each other, neither affecting others nor letting themselves be influenced. However, at low temperatures the molecules have little kinetic energy and therefore the mutual attraction is much more prominent, resulting in change in pressure. Similarly, at very high pressures, the molecules of a gas become tightly packed. Therefore, their volume becomes significant and cannot be neglected. It is with these two corrections, known as pressure correction and volume correction, respectively, that scientists were able to explain the difference between the theoretically predicted result of pressure and volume and experimentally obtained results. This gave rise to the study of real gases, the details of which are beyond the scope of this book. It is also worth noting that before a gas ever reaches absolute zero, it will condense into a liquid. Therefore the theoretical presence of absolute zero from Charles' law also requires further study in the light of new revelations about real gases.

6

CHEMICAL KINETICS

INTRODUCTION

Ever since we learnt about chemical reactions and to form new products by chemical reactions, there are two basic questions that we have sought answers for:

1. Will the reaction happen?
2. If the reaction happens, how fast will it happen?

While the first question is the subject matter of chemical thermodynamics, the second question is dealt with in chemical kinetics. At what speed will a reaction happen? What if the conditions of a reaction are changed? Systematic scientific investigation about these questions gave rise to the branch that is known as chemical kinetics. Chemical kinetics is that branch of physical chemistry where the measurement of how quickly reactions occur is studied. More elaborately, chemical kinetics is the study of chemical reactions for reaction rates, effect of various factors, formation of intermediates, etc.

The study of chemical kinetics has had huge practical implications. For example, in the industry, if kinetic study of a reaction is properly done, it will help us understand and hence improve every aspect of product formation, appropriate conditions for optimum results, etc. By understanding how a reaction takes place, many processes can be improved.

Kinetic studies are also important for understanding biological processes and their mechanisms. Early studies on enzyme-catalysed reactions helped us understand a lot about these reactions and consequently led to some important work on medicinal compounds and how they play an important role in our body.

Work done in chemical kinetics has enabled scientists to conclude that some chemical reactions occur in a single step. These reactions are known as elementary reactions. A vast number of other reactions, however, take place in more than one step. These are composite or complex reactions.

TYPES OF CHEMICAL REACTIONS ON THE BASIS OF REACTION SPEED

Chemical reactions are classified as fast, slow or moderate, based on the speed of reaction.

A fast reaction goes to completion in almost no time or instantaneously. An example of such a reaction is ionic reaction.

A slow reaction takes much longer to complete than a fast reaction. These reactions may sometimes take years to complete. Rusting of iron is an example of slow reaction.

On the other hand, there are chemical reactions that take place neither very fast nor very slow. These reactions take place at a moderate speed. An example of such a reaction is hydrolysis of starch.

RATE OF A REACTION

The rate of a reaction is measured in terms of the rate with which the products of the reaction are formed or the reactants of the reaction are consumed. In chemical reactions involving reactants and products, it is usual to deal with the concentrations of substances. The rate of a reaction can therefore be defined as the increase in concentration of a product in unit time or the decrease in concentration of reactants in unit time.

$$\text{Rate of a reaction} = \frac{\text{Increase in concentration of product}}{\text{Time taken}}$$

or,

$$\text{Rate of a reaction} = \frac{\text{Decrease in concentration of reactant}}{\text{Time taken}}$$

If we express concentration in mol L^{-1} and time in sec, the unit of rate of a reaction is mol $L^{-1}sec^{-1}$. When the reactants and products are gaseous, we measure their partial pressure as the concentration, and therefore express the same in atm. In such a case, the unit of rate of reaction will be atm sec^{-1}.

Factors Influencing Rate of Reaction

The rate of a chemical reaction depends on various factors: reactant concentrations, temperature, physical states and surface areas of reactants, solvent properties and catalyst properties if either are present, and light (in some cases). By studying the kinetics of a reaction, chemists learn how to control various reaction conditions to achieve an expected outcome.

Effect of Concentration

The more the reactant particles collide per unit time, the more are the chances of reaction between them, because collision between reacting particles is a prerequisite for a chemical reaction. With increase in concentration of reactants, more particles become available for collision. Therefore, the rate of a reaction usually increases with increase in the concentration of the reactants.

Effect of Temperature

The kinetic energy of reactant molecules increases with increase in the temperature of a system. This increase in kinetic energy results in the faster movement of particles and more number of collisions per unit time. Furthermore, when they collide, they already possess greater energy. Therefore, the rate of a reaction increases with increasing temperature. This happens virtually for all reactions. On the other hand, the rate of reaction of virtually all reactions decreases with decreasing temperature.

Effect of Surface Area

The greater the surface area of reactants, the more is the rate of a chemical reaction. It is because of this reason that if a reactant is solid, it is crushed before reaction, as crushing to powder form increases the surface area and hence the reaction rate.

Effect of Solvent

If the solvent interacts with reactants, say by making hydrogen bonds with the reactants, then the reaction rate reduces considerably, because with hydrogen bonding, the number of sites available for the reaction to take place reduces to a large extent. However, that not being the case, the more the solvent viscosity is, the less will be the reaction rate. This is because in highly viscous solvents, dissolved particles diffuse much more slowly than in less viscous solvents and can collide less frequently per unit time. Thus the reaction rates of most reactions decrease rapidly with increasing solvent viscosity.

Effect of Catalyst

A catalyst is a substance that takes part in a chemical reaction but itself does not undergo any change after the reaction. A catalyst increases the rate of a reaction by choosing an alternative path of reaction whose activation energy is less.

Effect of Light

The rate of some chemical reactions increases in the presence of light. Therefore, in order to ensure a slow rate, these reactions are carried out away from a light source or the reactants are kept away from light.

ORDER OF A REACTION

The order is defined as the sum of the exponents of the concentration terms of reactants on which the rate of a reaction actually depends, as observed experimentally. In other words, the order of a reaction with respect to a given substance is the exponent (or index or power) to which its concentration term in the rate equation is raised. As an example, consider the following expression for the rate of a reaction:

$$Rate = k.[A]^n[B]^m$$

Here [A] is the concentration of species A and [B] is the concentration of species B. The reaction is said to be of order n with respect to A and m with respect to B, and the overall order of the reaction is n + m.

Order of a reaction can be integers (1, 2, 3, etc.), 0, even fractional. Zero order means that the rate is independent of the concentration of a particular reactant.

MOLECULARITY OF A REACTION

A chemical reaction may occur in one step or in more than one step. If a chemical reaction takes place in more than one step, its overall rate is determined by the slowest step, which is the rate-determining step. The molecularity of a reaction is defined as the number of molecules or ions that participate in the rate-determining step. Depending on whether one molecule is involved in the rate-determining step, or two molecules or three, the molecularity of the reaction will be one, two or three, respectively.

ACTIVATION ENERGY

Activation energy is the minimum amount of energy required to initiate a reaction. Consider Figure 6.1.

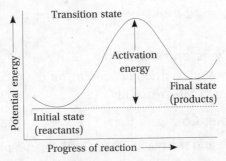

Fig. 6.1: Potential energy of reactants and energy required to initiate a reaction

It is the difference between the potential energy of the reactants and that of the transition state. In other words, the reactants must overcome this energy barrier for products. Activation energy is denoted by E_a and typically has units of kilojoules per mole (kJmol⁻¹) or kilocalories per mole (kcalmol⁻¹).

CATALYSIS

A substance that does not take part in a chemical reaction despite being one of the components of the reaction is called a catalyst. After the reaction is over, the catalyst remains in the same form as at the beginning of the reaction. Advanced studies, however, have proved that a catalyst does take part in the reaction by altering the path of the reaction and providing a lower energy barrier path for the reaction. In other words, a catalyst lowers the activation energy of a chemical reaction. Basically, a catalyst acts by modifying the transition state of a reaction. Figure 6.2 shows how a catalyst lowers the activation energy of a reaction.

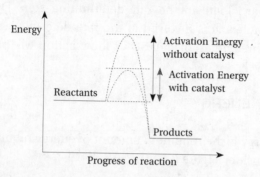

Fig. 6.2: A catalyst lowering the activation energy of a reaction

Types of Catalysis and Catalysts

There are two types of catalysis, depending on the phase of the catalyst compared with that of the reactants.

a) Homogeneous Catalysis

When the catalyst and the reactants are in the same phase, the process is called homogeneous catalysis. Example of homogeneous catalysis is hydrolysis of sugar:

$$C_{12}H_{22}O_{11} \text{ (l)} + H_2O \text{ (l)} \xrightarrow{H_2SO_4(l)} C_6H_{12}O_6 \text{ (l)} + C_6H_{12}O_6 \text{ (l)}$$

b) Heterogeneous Catalysis

When the catalyst and the reactants are in different phases, the process is called homogeneous catalysis. Example of homogeneous catalysis is hydrogenation of ethylene:

$$CH_2 = CH_2 + H_2 \xrightarrow{Ni} CH_3 - CH_3$$

Depending on the nature of catalysis, catalysts can be classified into the following types.

Positive catalysts: These are substances that increase the rate of reaction.

Negative catalysts: These are substances that reduce the rate of a reaction.

Auto-catalysts: When the product itself acts as a catalyst in a chemical reaction, it is known as an auto-catalyst.

Induced catalysts: When the product of one reaction acts as a catalyst for another reaction, it is called an induced catalyst. The second reaction generally follows the first reaction in such cases.

7

CHEMICAL EQUILIBRIUM

INTRODUCTION

At the start of a chemical reaction when only reactants are present, the chemical reaction goes in the direction in which products are formed. But as the reaction proceeds and the concentration of products increases, they also start to react with each other and form the products back, which increase the concentration of reactants once again. This process continues until a stage is reached when the rate at which products are formed becomes the same at which reactants are formed back. This is, therefore, a state of dynamism in the chemical reaction when the rate of forward reaction is the same as that of the backward reaction, and is called the chemical equilibrium. In a chemical reaction, chemical equilibrium is the state in which the concentration of both the reactants and products show no further tendency to change with time.

LAW OF CHEMICAL EQUILIBRIUM AND EQUILIBRIUM CONSTANT

Let us consider a general reaction:

$$aA + bB \rightleftharpoons cC + dD$$

As the reaction proceeds, the rate of forward reaction decreases and that of the backward reaction increases. This continues up to the stage when both the rates become equal. A plot of concentration with time shows the nature as shown in Figure 7.1.

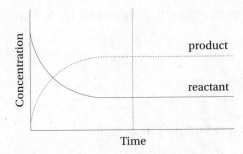

Fig. 7.1: Graph of concentration with time

The region right of the vertical dotted line is the equilibrium region and the left is the non-equilibrium region.

For the reaction in solution

$$aA + bB \rightleftharpoons cC + dD$$

the concentrations in an equilibrium mixture are related by the following equilibrium equation:

$$K_c = \frac{[C]^c \times [D]^d}{[A]^a \times [B]^b}$$

where K_c is called the equilibrium constant, and [A], [B], [C] and [D] are the equilibrium concentrations of the reactants and products. The expression on the right side is called the equilibrium constant expression.

At a given temperature, the product of concentrations of the reaction products raised to the respective stoichiometric coefficient in the balanced chemical equation divided by the product of concentrations of the reactants raised to their individual stoichiometric coefficients has a constant value. This is known as the Equilibrium Law or the Law of Chemical Equilibrium.

It is important here to understand a few relationships between the equilibrium constant and the reaction involved.
a) The equilibrium constant for the reverse reaction is the inverse of the equilibrium constant for the forward reaction.

This is clear from the following discussion. Suppose the forward reaction is:

$$aA + bB \rightleftharpoons cC + dD$$

The expression for equilibrium constant Kc for this reaction is:

$$K_c = \frac{[C]^c \times [D]^d}{[A]^a \times [B]^b}$$

The reverse of this reaction is:

$$cC + dD \leftrightharpoons aA + bB$$

The equilibrium constant for this reaction is:

$$K_c' = \frac{[A]^a \times [B]^b}{[C]^c \times [D]^d} = \frac{1}{\dfrac{[C]^c \times [D]^d}{[A]^a \times [B]^b}} = \frac{1}{K^c}$$

Therefore,

$$K_c' = \frac{1}{K^c}$$

b) The stoichiometric equation is multiplied by a factor n (all the terms on both sides have to be multiplied by the same factor). For example, the equilibrium constant for the reaction

naA + nbB $\leftrightharpoons$ ncC + ndD, that is, n (aA + bB) $\leftrightharpoons$ n (cC + dD)

would be:

$$K_c'' = (K_c)^n$$

It is clear from the above expression that the equilibrium constant value depends on the stoichiometric equation written. Therefore, while reporting an equilibrium constant value, it is necessary to also mention the corresponding equation.

For the reaction in gaseous medium, aA (g) + bB (g) $\leftrightharpoons$ cC (g) + dD (g), the equilibrium constant is denoted by K_p since in case of gas we deal with partial pressures. Therefore:

$$K_p = \frac{p_C^c \times p_D^d}{p_A^a \times p_B^b}$$

Applying the ideal gas equation:

$$pV = nRT$$

or, p = (n/V) RT = cRT, where c is the concentration.

And replacing the p terms in the expression for K_p, we get

$$K_p = \frac{[C]^c \times [D]^d}{[A]^a \times [B]^b} \times \frac{[RT]^c \times [RT]^d}{[RT]^a \times [RT]^b}$$

$$K_p = K_c \times \frac{[RT]^c \times [RT]^d}{[RT]^a \times [RT]^b}$$

$$K_p = K_c \times (RT)^{(c+d)-(a+b)}$$

$$K_p = K_c \times (RT)^{\Delta n}$$

where $\Delta n = (c + d) - (a + b)$

UNITS OF EQUILIBRIUM CONSTANT

The equilibrium constant expression involves the concentrations (K_c) or partial pressures (K_p) of the reactants and products. The unit of equilibrium constant, K, therefore, will depend on the number of moles of reactants and products.

This can be discussed as the following two cases:

Case 1: When the total number of moles of products is equal to the total number of moles of reactants

For example:

N_2 (g) + O_2 (g) $\rightleftharpoons$ 2NO (g)

$K = [NO]^2/[N_2] [O_2]$

If the concentrations are expressed in terms of $molL^{-1}$, then

$(molL^{-1})^2/(molL^{-1}) (molL^{-1})$

= no units

Therefore, equilibrium constant K has no unit when the total number of moles of products is equal to the total number of moles of reactants.

Case 2: When the total number of moles of products is different from the total number of moles of reactants

For example:

N_2 (g) + $3H_2$ (g) $\rightleftharpoons$ $2NH_3$ (g)

Equilibrium constant K will be given as:

$K = [NH3]^2/[N2] [H2]^3$

The units of K will be

$K = [(molL^{-1})^2]/[(molL^{-1}) (molL^{-1})^3]$

$= (molL^{-1})^2$

Note: In the above case if partial pressures are taken for gases, the result will follow accordingly, but it will show that the equilibrium constant has a unit.

Therefore, if the total number of moles of products is different from the total number of moles of reactants, then K has specific units.

CHARACTERISTICS OF EQUILIBRIUM CONSTANT

The important characteristics of equilibrium constant are mentioned below:

- Equilibrium constant has a definite value for every reaction at a particular temperature.
- The value of equilibrium constant is independent of the original concentration of reactants.
- The value of equilibrium constant tells the extent to which a reaction proceeds in the forward or reverse direction. The large value of K signifies that the equilibrium concentration of the components in the numerator of the equilibrium constant expression is higher than the denominator. Hence the forward reaction must have proceeded more than the components on the left hand side of the reaction. The reverse of this is also true; that means if the value of equilibrium constant is small, the backward reaction is more dominant than the forward reaction.
- The equilibrium constant is independent of the presence of a catalyst. This is because the catalyst affects the rate of forward reaction and backward reaction equally.
- For a reversible reaction, the equilibrium constant for the forward reaction is the inverse of the equilibrium constant for the backward reaction, i.e.,

$$K_c' = \frac{1}{K^c}$$

- Equilibrium constant is dependent on temperature. (The expression for temperature dependence of equilibrium constant is the subject matter of advanced studies in chemical thermodynamics.)

APPLICATIONS OF EQUILIBRIUM CONSTANT

Equilibrium constant can be applied to:

(a) Predict the extent of a reaction on the basis of its magnitude
(b) Predict the direction of the reaction
(c) Calculate equilibrium concentrations

Let us discuss these applications one by one.

Prediction of the Extent of a Reaction

The large value of K signifies that the equilibrium concentration of the components in the numerator of the equilibrium constant expression is higher than the denominator. Hence the forward reaction must have proceeded more than the components on the left hand side of the reaction. The reverse of this is also true; that means if the value of the equilibrium constant is small, the backward reaction is more dominant than the forward reaction.

Although no numerical value can be associated with the equilibrium constant with certainty to predict the extent of completion of a reaction, the following table gives an observation which has been concluded after studying a large number of reactions:

Table 7.1: Prediction of the extent of a reaction

K_c value	Extent of reaction
Greater than 10^3	Forward reaction nearly to completion
Between 10^{-3} and 10^3	Both reactants and products are present at equilibrium
Less than 10^{-3}	Reaction has hardly proceeded in the forward direction

Prediction of Direction of a Reaction

Equilibrium constant can be used to find the direction in which a reaction proceeds. For this, we have to calculate the reaction quotient Q (with molar concentrations it gives Q_c, and with partial pressures it gives Q_p).

The reaction quotient Q is the ratio of the product of concentrations of the products to that of the reactants.

Consider the following reaction:

$$A + B \rightleftharpoons X + Y$$

The reaction quotient, $Q = [X] [Y]/[A] [B]$

In other words the reaction quotient is defined in the same way as the equilibrium constant with molar concentrations (Q_c) or partial pressures (Q_p) as:

$aA + bB \rightleftharpoons cC + dD$

$Q_c = [C]^c [D]^d/[A]^a [B]^b$

$Q_p = p_C^c p_D^d/p_A^a p_B^b$

The following table gives a generalized observation about direction of a reaction based on comparison of values between reaction quotient and equilibrium constant.

Table 7.2: Prediction of the direction of a reaction

Comparison between Q_c and K_c (or Q_p and K_p)	Direction of reaction
$Q_c < K_c$	The reaction will proceed in the forward direction, i.e., in the direction of products.
$Q_c > K_c$	The reaction will proceed in the reverse direction, i.e., in the direction of reactants.
$Q_c = K_c$	The reaction will not proceed as the reaction is already in equilibrium. Hence, no net reaction.

Calculation of Equilibrium Concentrations

To calculate equilibrium concentration of reactants and products from an equilibrium constant, you must keep in mind that equilibrium is a state of dynamic balance where the ratio of the concentrations of product to that of reactants is constant. This ratio of the concentrations of the products to the concentrations of the reactants at equilibrium is the equilibrium constant.

In order to find out the concentrations of reactants and products at equilibrium, we need to know the initial concentrations of the reactants (the initial concentration of products being zero) and the equilibrium constant. The following steps (1–4) are carried out:

Step 1: Write the balanced equation for the reaction.

Step 2: Under the balanced equation, make an ICE table (see below

CHEMISTRY

for the acronym of ICE) that lists the following three things for each substance involved in the reaction:

(a) the initial (I) concentration
(b) the change (C) in concentration on going to equilibrium
(c) the equilibrium (E) concentration

In constructing the table, define x as the concentration (mol/L) of one of the substances that reacts on going to equilibrium, then use the stoichiometry of the reaction to determine the concentrations of the other substances in terms of x.

Step 3: Substitute the equilibrium concentrations into the equilibrium equation for the reaction and solve for x. If it involves more than one value of x, choose the mathematical solution that makes chemical sense.

Step 4: Calculate the equilibrium concentrations from the calculated value of x.

Step 5: Check your results by substituting them into the equilibrium equation.

We will elaborate the above steps with an example.

Question:

Calculate the equilibrium concentration for reactants and the product at equilibrium for hydrogenation of ethylene. Given, Kc = 0.88, initial concentration of ethylene 0.32 mol L^{-1}, and that of hydrogen 0.52 mol L^{-1}.

Solution:

Step 1:

$C_2H_4 + H_2 \rightleftharpoons C_2H_6$
$K_c = [C_2H_6]/[C_2H_4][H_2]$

Step 2:

ICE	C_2H_4	H_2	C_2H_6
Initial concentration	0.32	0.52	0
Change in concentration	x	x	x
Equilibrium concentration	0.32 - x	0.52 - x	x

Step 3:

0.88 = x/(0.32 - x)(0.52 - x)

Solving this, we get two values of x. These are:

$$x = 1.89 \text{ and } x = 0.09$$

If we substitute the value of x as 1.89, we get the equilibrium concentration of C_2H_4 as 0.32 – 1.89, which is equal to – 1.57. But the equilibrium concentration of a reactant cannot be negative. Hence, the value of x as 1.89 is rejected and x = 0.09 is accepted.

Step 4:

Thus the equilibrium concentration of the three components is as follows:

C_2H_4 = 0.32 – 0.09 = 0.23 mol L^{-1}
H_2 = 0.52 – 0.09 = 0.43 mol L^{-1}
C_2H_6 = 0.09 mol L^{-1}

8

ELECTROCHEMISTRY

INTRODUCTION

Electrochemistry is the study of generation of electricity due to chemical reactions and also chemical reactions that are caused by electricity. In other words, electrochemistry is that branch of physical chemistry that deals with chemical processes that cause electrons to move. At the heart of the electron movement from one element to another is a reaction (or a couple of reactions) known as oxidation–reduction reaction, together known as redox reaction.

REDOX REACTIONS

A redox reaction is a reaction that involves oxidation and reduction. Oxidation is a process by which electron (s) is (are) lost. Reduction is a process by which electron (s) is (are) gained. It also effects a change in the state of oxidation of the substances undergoing oxidation and reduction. When a substance loses an electron, its oxidation state increases; thus, it is oxidized. In other words, increase in oxidation number means oxidation. When a substance gains an electron, its oxidation state decreases; thus it is reduced. Therefore, decrease in oxidation state means reduction.

Consider for example the reaction:

$$H_2 + I_2 \longrightarrow 2HI$$

The above reaction can be rewritten as two separate equations:

Oxidation reaction

$$H_2 \longrightarrow 2H^+ + 2e^-$$

Reduction reaction:

$$I_2 + 2e^- \longrightarrow 2I^-$$

Overall reaction:

$$H_2 + I_2 \longrightarrow 2H^+ + 2I^-$$

Oxidation is associated with the loss of electrons, whereas reduction is associated with the gain of or acquisition of electrons. The species being oxidized is also known as the reducing agent or reductant, and the species being reduced is called the oxidizing agent or oxidant. In this case, H_2 is being oxidized (and is the reducing agent), while I2 is being reduced (and is the oxidizing agent).

ANODE AND CATHODE

An anode is an electrode where oxidation takes place. A cathode is an electrode where reduction takes place.

ELECTROLYTE

An electrolyte is a compound that can conduct electricity in molten or aqueous state. Since these substances are capable of carrying electricity in the molten or aqueous state, they occur as ions. Depending on the degree of dissociation, electrolytes can be classified into two types.

Strong Electrolytes
These substances dissociate completely in the molten or aqueous state. For example, NaCl, KCl, etc. remain dissociated almost completely.

Weak Electrolytes
These substances dissociate only partially and their degree of dissociation varies under different conditions. For example, acetic acid, CH_3COOH, is a weak electrolyte.

ELECTROCHEMICAL CELLS

An electrochemical cell is a device that generates electricity due to chemical reaction occurring in it. The chemical reaction that takes place in an electrochemical cell is a redox reaction. It contains two electrodes that are connected externally by a conducting wire. Each electrode is dipped in an electrolyte. The setup of an electrode dipped in an electrolyte in a container is called a half-cell. The electrolytes of the two half-cells are connected by a salt bridge.

Galvanic Cells or Voltaic Cells

These are cells that can produce electricity due to chemical reactions. Therefore these are electrochemical cells. The name voltaic cell is in honour of Alessandro Volta who, in 1793, discovered that electricity could be produced by placing different metals on the opposite sides of a wet paper or cloth. A voltaic cell consists of two compartments called half-cells. The half-cell where oxidation occurs is called the anode. The other half-cell, where reduction occurs, is called the cathode. The electrons in voltaic cells flow from the negative electrode to the positive electrode—from the anode to the cathode. Figure 8.1 shows a Danielle cell.

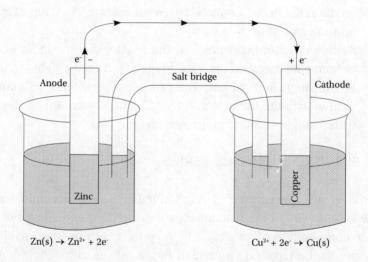

Fig. 8.1: Danielle cell

The figure shows that Zn(s) is oxidized, producing aqueous Zn^{2+}:

$$Zn(s) \longrightarrow Zn^{2+}(aq) + 2e^-$$

In the cathode, Cu^{2+} is reduced and deposits on the copper electrode:

$$Cu^{2+}(aq) + 2e^- \longrightarrow Cu(s)$$

A shorthand notation is adopted to represent the construction of an electrochemical cell. For the cell described above, the cell diagram in shorthand notation is as follows:

$$Zn(s)|Zn^{2+}(aq)||Cu^{2+}(aq)|Cu(s)$$

The following points are important about the shorthand notation of a cell:

- Two half-cells are written with a double vertical line (||) between them to separate the anode half reaction from the cathode half reaction. This double vertical line represents the salt bridge.
- The anode (where oxidation occurs) is written on the left side of the ||.
- The cathode (where reduction occurs) is placed on the right side of the ||.
- A single vertical line (|) is used to separate different states of matter on the same side. A comma is used to separate like states of matter on the same side.
- Since oxidation takes place at the anode, the anode half-cell is written with metal on the left and metal ion on the right separated by the single vertical line. The cathode representing reduction is written with the metal ion on the left and metal atom on the right with a single vertical line separating the two.

THE ELECTROCHEMICAL SERIES

When electrodes are connected as described in the above section, subject to the spontaneity of the reactions involved, cell potential is generated. In fact, combination of an electrode in contact with its ions in solution gives rise to the electrode potential. Based on the electrode potential, electrodes are arranged in order of their standard electrode potentials (redox potentials). The most negative E° values are placed at the top of the electrochemical series, and the most positive at the bottom. Hydrogen has been arbitrarily assigned the electrode potential zero and it therefore comes in between negative and positive electrode potentials. Lithium has the highest negative reduction potential of -3.05 V while fluorine has the highest positive reduction potential of +2.87 V.

Characteristics of Electrochemical Series

➤ The negative sign of standard reduction potential signifies that an electrode, when joined with a standard hydrogen electrode (SHE), acts as the anode and oxidation occurs on this electrode. For example, standard reduction potential of zinc is -0.76 volt; when the zinc electrode is joined with SHE, it acts as the anode (-ve electrode) i.e., oxidation occurs on this electrode. Similarly, the +ve sign of standard reduction potential indicates that the electrode, when joined with SHE, acts as the cathode and reduction occurs on this electrode.

➤ Substances that are stronger reducing agents than hydrogen are placed above hydrogen in the series and have negative values of standard reduction potentials. All those substances that have positive values of reduction potentials and placed below hydrogen in the series are weaker reducing agents than hydrogen.

➤ The metals on the top (having high negative value of standard reduction potentials) have the tendency to lose electrons readily. These are active metals. The activity of metals decreases from top to bottom, whereas the activity of non-metals increases from top to bottom.

ELECTROLYSIS

Electrolysis is the process of carrying out a chemical reaction by passing electric current through it. Therefore, it means carrying out a non-spontaneous reaction by passing electric current through the substance. The substance that is undergoing electrolysis, called the electrolyte, is in molten or aqueous state. The site where electrolysis occurs is an electrolytic cell. An electrolytic cell is an apparatus having two electrodes held apart and dipped into a solution of positive and negative ions. The cell is fitted with an external source of electric current, like a battery. Two electrodes of the electrolytic cell are connected to the two terminals of the battery. The electrode that is connected with the positive terminal of the battery is positively charged and called the anode, and the electrode that is connected with the negative terminal of the battery has negative polarity and is called the cathode. A typical electrolytic cell is shown in Figure 8.2.

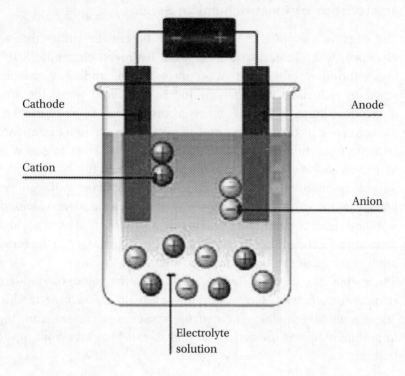

Cathode

Anode

Cation

Anion

Electrolyte
solution

Fig. 8.2: Electrolytic cell

Faraday's Laws of Electrolysis

Faraday's First Law of Electrolysis

Faraday's first law of electrolysis states that the chemical deposition due to flow of current through an electrolyte is directly proportional to the quantity of electricity (coulombs) passed through it; i.e., mass of chemical deposition:

$M \alpha Q$

Or, $m = ZQ$

where Z is a constant of proportionality and is known as the electro-chemical equivalent of the substance.

If we put Q = 1 coulombs in the above equation, we will get Z = m, which implies that the electro-chemical equivalent of any substance is the amount of the substance deposited on the passing of 1 coulomb through its solution. This constant of passing of electro-chemical equivalent is generally expressed in terms of mg per coulomb or kilogram per coulomb.

Faraday's Second Law of Electrolysis

Faraday's second law of electrolysis states that when the same quantity of electricity is passed through several electrolytes, the mass of the substances deposited are proportional to their respective chemical equivalent or equivalent weight.

Equivalent weight is defined as atomic mass of the metal divided by its valency or the atomic mass of the metal divided by the number of electrons required to reduce the metal ion.

If W1, W2 and W3 are the amount of deposited substances when the same amount of electricity is passed through three substances, 1, 2 and 3, respectively, whose chemical equivalent weights are E1, E2 and E3 respectively, then:

$$\frac{W_1}{W_2} = \frac{E_1}{E_2}$$

and

$$\frac{W_2}{W_3} = \frac{E_2}{E_3}$$

or

$$z \propto E$$

Applications of Electrolysis

Electrolysis finds a large number of applications in industries. Some of the important applications are given below:

- Production of hydrogen by electrolysis of water
- Manufacture of heavy water
- A few metals like K, Mg, Al, etc., are obtained by electrolysis; this process is called electrometallurgy
- A few non-metals like H, F, Cl, etc. are obtained by electrolysis
- Electroplating on ornaments is done by electrolysis
- Compounds like NaOH, KOH, etc. are synthesized by electrolysis, which is called electrosynthesis

SOLUTIONS AND COLLOIDS

INTRODUCTION

A solution is a homogeneous mixture of two or more substances. One component in such a mixture is called a solute, which is the substance dissolved in another substance; and the second substance in which solute is mixed is known as the solvent. Commonly solute is in smaller quantity than the amount of solvent in which it is mixed.

CONCENTRATION OF A SOLUTION

As a solution is prepared by mixing of solute in a solvent, the amount of solute mixed and the amount of solvent taken both determine the concentration of the solution. There are many ways to express the concentration of the solution. These are discussed here.

Per Cent Composition (by mass)
Per cent by mass (or weight per cent, as it is loosely but commonly called) in two ways:

(a) The parts of solute per 100 parts of solution. Note here that the word 'parts' is used as a general term and whatever is the unit of the solute, the same unit has to be used for the solution. For example, if the solute is in grams, the solution should also be in grams.
(b) The fraction of a solute in a solution multiplied by 100.

Therefore, we need the following two pieces of information to calculate the per cent by mass of a solute in a solution:

- The mass of the solute in the solution
- The mass of the solution

The following equation is used to calculate per cent by mass:

$$\text{Per cent by mass} = \frac{\text{Mass of solute}}{\text{Mass of solution}} \times 100$$

Molarity

Molarity is the number of moles of solute in exactly one litre of a solution. Molarity is represented by uppercase M. (Note the word 'solution' in the definition.)

We need the following two pieces of information to calculate the molarity of a solute in a solution:

- The moles of solute present in the solution
- The volume of solution (in litres) containing the solute

The following equation is used to calculate molarity of a solution:

$$\text{Molarity} = \frac{\text{Number of moles of solute}}{\text{Volume of solution in L}}$$

Molality

Molality is defined as the number of moles of solute dissolved in exactly one kg of solvent. Molality is represented by lowercase m. (Note the word 'solvent' in the definition.)

In order to calculate the molality of a solute in a solution, we need the following two pieces of information:

- The moles of solute present in the solution
- The mass of solvent (in kg)

The following equation is used to calculate molality of a solution:

$$\text{Molality} = \frac{\text{Number of moles of solute}}{\text{Mass of solvent in kg}}$$

Mole Fraction

The mole fraction of a component in a solution is defined as the ratio of the number of moles of that component to the total number of moles of all the components in the solution. Mole fraction is represented by x.

We can calculate mole fraction if we have the number of moles of each component present in the solution.

Suppose a solution consists of components A, B, C,..... Suppose n_A moles of A, n_B moles of B, n_C moles of C...constitute the solution. The mole fraction of A, written as x_A, in the solution will be calculated using the equation:

$$x_A = \frac{n_A}{n_A + n_B + n_C}$$

Similarly, the mole fraction for B and C, x_B and x_C are, respectively:

$$x_B = \frac{n_B}{n_A + n_B + n_C}$$

$$x_C = \frac{n_C}{n_A + n_B + n_C}$$

Therefore, $x_A + x_B + x_C = 1$

TYPES OF SOLUTIONS

Solutions can be classified based on different considerations. In the following section some of the classifications are discussed.

Classification Based on Amount of Solute

Depending on the amount of solute present in a given amount of solvent, a solution can be classified as a dilute solution if the amount of solution is very small compared to the amount of solvent, and a concentrated solution if the amount of solute is large.

Alternatively, based on the amount of solute, a solution can be classified as:

Unsaturated solution: A solution in which more solute can be dissolved in a given quantity of solvent at a particular temperature.

Saturated solution: A solution in which no more solute can be dissolved in a given quantity of solvent at a particular temperature and the maximum possible quantity has been dissolved at that temperature.

Supersaturated solution: If the temperature of a saturated solution is increased, more solute goes into the solution. Such a solution is called a supersaturated solution which has dissolved more solid than its capacity at a given temperature.

Classification Based on Solute and Solvent

Table 9.1: Classification of solutions

Type of solution	Solute	Solvent
Gaseous solution	Gas	Gas
	Liquid	Gas
	Solid	Gas
Liquid solution	Gas	Liquid
	Liquid	Liquid
	Solid	Liquid
Solid solution	Gas	Solid
	Liquid	Solid
	Solid	Solid

SOLUBILITY

The maximum quantity of solute that can dissolve in a given quantity of solvent (generally 100 g) at a given temperature or pressure is called the solubility of the solute.

Effect of Temperature on Solubility

There are three distinct cases under this category:

Case I: If the dissolution of the solute in the solvent is endothermic. In this case, solubility increases with temperature.

Case II: If the dissolution of the solute in the solvent is exothermic. In this case, solubility decreases with temperature.

Case III: Solubility of a gas in a liquid decreases with increase in temperature.

Effect of Pressure on Solubility

Solubility of solids and liquids remains almost unchanged with changes in pressure. But solubility of gases depends on the pressure of the system. The concentration of a solute gas in a solution is directly proportional to the partial pressure of that gas above the solution. This statement, known as Henry's law, suggests that with increase in pressure, the solubility of a gas increases in a solution.

COLLOIDAL SOLUTION

A colloidal solution, occasionally identified as a colloidal suspension, is a heterogeneous mixture in which the substances are regularly suspended in a fluid. The two phases are known as the dispersed phase (solute) and the dispersion medium (solvent). The distinguishing feature between a true solution and a colloidal solution is fundamentally the dimensions of the constituent particles. In a colloidal solution, particle sizes vary between 1 nm and 1,000 nm.

Classification of Colloids

Table 9.2: Classification of colloids based on physical state

Dispersed phase	Dispersion medium	Name	Examples
Solid	Liquid	Sol	Mud, paints
Solid	Solid	Solid sol	Gemstones
Solid	Gas	Aerosol	Smoke
Liquid	Solid	Gel	Jelly
Liquid	Liquid	Emulsion	Milk
Liquid	Gas	Liquid aerosol	Cloud, fog
Gas	Solid	Solid foam	Sponge, pumice stone
Gas	Liquid	Foam	Shaving foam, froth

Classification of Colloids Based on Nature of Interaction Between Dispersed Phase and Dispersion Medium

Lyophilic sols: The term lyophilic means liquid-loving (i.e., solvent-loving). Certain substances have an affinity for certain liquids and readily form colloidal dispersions with them. When water is used as the dispersion medium, such colloids are termed as hydrophilic colloids and their colloidal dispersion in water is known as hydrophilic sols. Starch is an example of lyophilic colloid.

Lyophilic sols are stable and they do not require any stabilizing agent to preserve them. An important characteristic of these sols is that if the dispersed phase is separated from the dispersion medium (say by evaporation), the dispersed phase can again be brought in the sol state simply by mixing it with the dispersion medium. This is why hydrophilic sols are also known as reversible sols.

Lyophobic sols: The term lyophilic means liquid-hating (i.e., solvent-hating). Substances that do not possess much affinity for the dispersion medium and do not readily pass into the sol state when mixed with the medium are called lyophobic colloids. Gold sol is an example of lyophobic sol.

Lyophobic sols are relatively less stable as compared to lyophilic sols. They are easily precipitated (or coagulated) by the addition of small amounts of electrolytes, by heating or agitation. Moreover, the precipitated dispersed phase cannot be brought back into the sol state by simply mixing it with the dispersion medium. This is why lyophobic sols are also known as irreversible sols. Lyophobic sols need stabilizing agents to keep them in the sol form for a long time.

Properties of Colloidal Solutions

All the properties of colloidal solutions can be grouped under three heads:

Physical Properties

> **Heterogeneity:** Colloidal solutions are heterogeneous in nature.
> **Visibility of dispersed particles:** Although colloidal solutions are heterogeneous in nature, the dispersed particles present in them are not visible to the naked eye and they appear homogenous. This is because colloidal particles are too small to be visible to the naked eye.
> **Filterability:** Due to very small size, the colloidal particles pass through an ordinary filter paper.
> **Stability:** Lyophilic sols in general and lyophobic sols in the absence of substantial concentrations of electrolytes are quite stable and the dispersed particles present in them do not settle down even on keeping.

> **Colour:** The colour of a colloidal solution depends upon the size of colloidal particles present in it. Larger particles absorb the light of longer wavelength and transmit light of shorter wavelength.
> **Homogenous appearance:** Even though colloids have suspended particles and are heterogeneous in nature, they appear as if they form a homogenous solution. This is because the suspended particles are so tiny that they are not visible to the naked eye.

Mechanical Properties

Brownian movement: Pollen grains in aqueous suspensions were observed by Robert Brown to be in constant motion. A similar phenomenon was also found in case of a colloidal solution, when observed through the ultra microscope. This continuous and rapid zigzag motion of the colloidal particles is called the Brownian movement. This motion is independent of the nature of the colloidal particles. It is more rapid when the size of the particles is small and the solution is less viscous.

Optical Properties

Tyndall effect: Tyndall (1869) observed that when a strong beam of light is focused on a colloidal solution, the path of the beam becomes visible, and when viewed through a microscope placed at a right angle to the path of light (ultramicroscopically), the colloidal particles appear as pin points of light moving against a dark background in a colloidal solution. This phenomenon is known as the Tyndall effect.

Electrical Properties

Electrophoresis: Colloidal particles are electrically charged (+ or -) with respect to the dispersion medium. Therefore, when electric current is passed through a colloidal solution, the charged particles move towards oppositely charged electrodes and get discharged to give a precipitate. This migration of colloidal particles under the influence of the electric field is called electrophoresis.

Electro-osmosis: When electrophoresis of dispersed particles in a colloidal system is prevented by some suitable means, the dispersion medium itself begins to move in an electric field. This phenomenon is known as electro-osmosis.

Coagulation: Stability of the colloidal solution is due to mutual repulsion between similarly charged colloidal particles. When the charge on the colloidal particles is neutralized by the addition of an electrolyte or oppositely charged sol, precipitation takes place. This process of precipitating a colloidal solution is known as coagulation or flocculation.

10

ACIDS, BASES AND SALTS

INTRODUCTION

Acids, bases and salts are part of our daily life and we find them in a variety of things we handle daily. For example, we come across acids in citrus fruits that give them their sour taste. Bases such as washing soda are found in many types of cleaners. The commonest example of a salt is very well known to all of us in the form of table salt or sodium chloride. The subject matter of acids, bases and salts is very interesting and lot of scientific study has been done on them, and in this chapter we will learn about the basics of acids, bases and salts.

ACID

Definition

An acid is a compound that has sour taste and that turns blue litmus paper red. According to the early definition of acid proposed by Arrhenius, an acid is a compound that can furnish hydrogen ions (H^+). A more generalized definition of acids was proposed later by Brønsted and Lowry. According to them, an acid is a compound that is a proton (hydrogen ion) donor. A much broader definition that takes into account all the deficiencies that the earlier two definitions suffered from was proposed by Lewis later and this has now been widely accepted as the definition of an acid. This definition does not contradict the earlier definitions proposed, but only widens and strengthens the concept of acids. According to Lewis's definition, an acid is a compound that accepts a pair of electrons.

Classification of Acids

Acids can be classified in many ways; for example, according to its source, strength, basicity, etc. In the following section these classifications have been discussed.

According to the Degree of Ionization

Strong acids: Acids that are completely ionized in water at all concentrations are called strong acids. Their aqueous solution conducts electric current. Examples: hydrochloric acid (HCl), sulphuric acid (H_2SO_4), etc.

Weak acids: Acids that are partially ionized in water are called weak acids. Examples: acetic acid (CH_3COOH), formic acid (HCOOH), etc.

According to Source

Organic acids: Acids that have an organic origin (plant or animal) are called organic acids. They are weak acids. Examples: lactic acid, acetic acid, citric acid, etc.

Inorganic acids: Acids that have no organic origin are called inorganic acids. They are also called mineral acids. Some of them are strong acids and others are weak. Examples: hydrochloric acid (HCl), phosphoric acid (H_3PO_4), nitric acid (HNO_3), etc.

According to Basicity

Basicity of an acid is defined as the number of hydrogen ions (H^+) one molecule of the acid can produce when dissolved in water. Acids are classified according to the basicity into monobasic acids, dibasic acids and tribasic acids, depending on the number of hydrogen ions one molecule of the acid can produce as one, two or three, respectively. Examples: monobasic acid – hydrochloric acid; dibasic acid – sulphuric acid; tribasic acid – phosphoric acid.

Properties of Acids

Properties of acids can be discussed under the heads of physical properties and chemical properties.

Physical Properties

> Acids taste sour.

- Acids turn the colour of blue litmus to red.
- Acids are electrolytes and ionize in aqueous solutions moderately to strongly.
- Acids are corrosive in nature and can damage skin if they come in direct contact with the skin, especially in case of strong acids. They cause burns on the skin.

Chemical Properties

Neutralization

When an acid reacts with a base, salt and water are produced. This reaction is called neutralization:

$$HCl + NaOH \rightarrow NaCl + H_2O$$

Reaction with carbonates

Acid reacts with metal carbonates to produce salt, water and carbon dioxide:

$$MgCO_3 + 2HCl \rightarrow MgCl_2 + CO_2 + H_2O$$

Reaction with bicarbonates

Acid reacts with metal bicarbonates to produce salt, water and carbon dioxide:

$$NaHCO_3 + HCl \rightarrow NaCl + CO_2 + H_2O$$

Reaction with metal

With zinc: $Zn + 2HCl \rightarrow ZnCl_2 + H_2$
With aluminum: $2Al + 6HCl \rightarrow 2AlCl_3 + 3H_2$

Reaction with metal oxide

$$6HCl + Fe_2O_3 \rightarrow 2FeCl_3 + 3H_2O$$

BASE

Definition

A base is a compound that has bitter taste and that turns red litmus blue. According to the early definition proposed by Arrhenius, a base is a compound that can furnish hydroxyl ions (OH^-) in the molten state or in an aqueous solution. A more generalized definition of bases was proposed later by Brønsted and Lowry. According to them, a base is a compound that is a proton (hydrogen ion) acceptor. A much broader definition that takes into account all the deficiencies that the earlier two definitions suffered from was proposed by Lewis later and this has now been widely accepted as the definition of a base. This definition does not contradict the earlier definitions proposed, but only widens and strengthens the concept of bases. According to Lewis's definition, a base is a compound that gives a pair of electrons, that is, bases are electron pair donors.

Classification of Bases

According to the Degree of Dissociation

Based on the degree of dissociation in water, bases can be classified into two types.

Strong base: These are bases that dissociate completely in water. Example: sodium hydroxide (NaOH), calcium hydroxide $Ca(OH)_2$, etc.

Weak base: These are bases that dissociate feebly in water. Example: ammonium hydroxide.

According to the Chemical Composition

Bases are classified according to their chemical composition into:

- Metal oxides such as iron oxide (FeO) and magnesium oxide (MgO).
- Metal hydroxides such as calcium hydroxide [$Ca(OH)_2$], sodium hydroxide (NaOH)
- Metal carbonates such as potassium carbonate (K_2CO_3) and sodium carbonate (Na_2CO_3)
- Metal bicarbonates such as potassium bicarbonate ($KHCO_3$) and sodium bicarbonate ($NaHCO_3$)

Properties of Bases

Properties of bases can be discussed under the heads of physical properties and chemical properties.

Physical Properties

➤ Bases are bitter in taste
➤ When touched, they feel slippery

> They are electrically conducting in nature
> Bases turn the colour of red litmus to blue

Chemical Properties

Reaction with acids
Bases react with acids to form salt and water:
$$KOH + HCl \rightarrow KCl + H_2O$$

Reaction with salts
$FeCl_3 + 3NaOH \rightarrow Fe(OH)_3 + 3NaCl$

Reaction with metals
Bases react with metals to form salt, and hydrogen gas is liberated:
$$2Al + 2NaOH + 2H_2O \rightarrow 2NaAlO_2 + 3H_2$$

SALTS

A salt is compounds formed by reaction between an acid and a base. The other product formed in a neutralization reaction is water. Therefore, a salt is formed by replacement of the hydrogen ion of an acid by the metal ion of a base.

Classification of Salts
Salts are classified as follows:

Simple salt or normal salt: These are formed by complete replacement of hydrogen from acid. For example, $NaCl$ (by replacing H of HCl), Na_2SO_4 (by replacing both the Hs of H_2SO_4), etc.

Acidic salt: These are formed by partial replacement of hydrogen from an acid. For example, $NaHSO_4$ from H_2SO_4.

Basic salt: These are formed by partial replacement of the OH group from a base. For example, $Mg(OH)C$, etc.

Double salt: It is a mixture of two salts. For example, alum [K_2SO_4. $Al_2(SO_4)_3.24H_2O$].

Complex salt: These are complex compounds and contain ligands. For example, potassium ferrocyanide {$K_4[Fe(CN)_6]$}.

pH SCALE

How strong a solution is acidic is given by the concentration of hydrogen ions in the solution. Similarly, the strength of a basic solution is given by the concentration of hydroxyl ions in the solution. When an acid reacts with a base, the hydrogen ions of the former react with the hydroxyl ions of the latter, resulting in a neutral solution. A neutral solution is neither acidic nor basic. A scale has been proposed, which measures the hydrogen ion concentration of a solution. This scale is called the pH scale.

pH is defined as the negative of logarithm of hydrogen ion concentration.

$$pH = -\log [H^+] = \log (1/[H^+])$$

The pH scale lies between 0 and 14. The pH of water (neutral) is 7. A pH value less than 7 indicates acidic character and more than 7 indicates basic character. A pH of 7 is neutral. Acidic nature decreases with ascending pH value between 0 and 7 and basic nature of a solution increases from 7 to 14.

INDICATORS

An indicator is a substance that changes its colour in acidic and basic medium. In other words, with change of pH value from acidic to basic or from basic to acidic, an indicator shows colour change, indicating the change in pH. They are usually weak acids or bases, which, when dissolved in water, dissociate slightly and form ions. Consider an indicator that is a weak acid, with the formula HIn.

$$HIn + H_2O \rightarrow H_3O^+ + In^-$$

The compound HIn shows acidic colour and In^- shows basic colour.

In the table below some indicators and their colour in acidic and basic medium is given.

Table 10.1: Indicators and their colours

Indicator	Colour	
	Acid	Base
Thymol blue – 1st change	red	yellow
Methyl orange	red	yellow
Bromocresol green	yellow	blue
Methyl red	yellow	red
Bromothymol blue	yellow	blue
Phenol red	yellow	red
Thymol blue – 2nd change	yellow	blue
Phenolphthalein	colourless	pink

BUFFER SOLUTION

A buffer is a substance that resists change in pH when a small quantity of acid or base is added to it. It is a very important substance in chemistry and biochemistry. A buffer is made by mixing a weak acid with its salt or a weak base and its salt.

Types of Buffer Solutions
There are two types of buffer solutions.

Acidic buffer: An acidic buffer is commonly made from a weak acid and one of its salts is often a sodium salt. It is a solution that has a pH less than 7. A common example of acidic buffer is a mixture of acetic acid and sodium acetate in solution.

Basic buffer: An alkaline buffer solution is commonly made from a weak base and one of its salts. An alkaline buffer solution has a pH greater than 7. A common example of a basic buffer is a mixture of ammonium hydroxide and ammonium chloride solution.

HYDROLYSIS OF SALTS

Hydrolysis of a salt is defined as a reaction in which the cation or anion (or both) of a salt react with water to produce acidity or alkalinity. Water dissociates into H^+ and OH^- ions. Neutral water has as many H^+ as OH^-

ions. However, if by any chance, $[H^+] > [OH^-]$, the water becomes acidic and when $[H^+] < [OH^-]$, the water acquires basic nature. This is exactly the change that occurs during the phenomenon of salt hydrolysis.

Four distinct cases of salt hydrolysis can be discussed.

(a) **Salt of strong acid and strong base:** Example: sodium chloride (NaCl). It ionizes in the solution but does not produce any excess H^+ or OH^- ions. Hence its solution remains neutral.

$$NaCl + H_2O \rightarrow Na^+ + Cl^- + H_2O$$

(b) **Salt of strong acid and weak base:** Example: NH_4Cl. It is a salt of strong acid HCl and weak base NH_3. On dissolution, the following reaction happens.

$$NH_4Cl + H_2O \rightarrow NH_4OH + H^+ + Cl^-$$

HCl being a strong acid will dissociate into H^+ and Cl^-, making the solution acidic. Therefore, hydrolysis of salts of a strong acid and a weak base makes the solution acidic.

(c) **Salt of weak acid and strong base:** Example: sodium acetate (NaAc). When it is dissolved in water, the following reaction happens.

$$NaAc + H_2O \rightarrow Na^+ + OH^- + HAc$$

NaOH being a strong base will dissociate in water to produce OH^- ions. Hence the solution will be basic. Therefore, hydrolysis of salts of a weak acid and a strong base will make the solution basic.

(d) **Salt of weak acid and weak base:** Example: ammonium acetate $(NH_4CH_3CO_2)$. This salt on hydrolysis may render the solution acidic or basic or neutral.

11

CLASSIFICATION OF ELEMENTS

INTRODUCTION

With more and more elements discovered with time and as more and more properties of elements came to be known, chemists had started facing a unique crisis—how to remember so much information about elements. It is not only about this much information of elements; the amount of information itself was also increasing with every discovery and the result of investigation of their properties, etc. It was this unique crisis that led chemists to look for ways of arranging the elements to reflect the similarities between their properties. This gave rise to the concept of periodicity of properties and hence a periodic arrangement of elements. The modern periodic table, as we know today, lists the elements in order of increasing atomic number (the number of protons in the nucleus of an atom). Historically, however, relative atomic masses were used by scientists in trying to organize the elements. In this chapter we will learn about the periodic classification of elements.

HISTORY OF PERIODIC CLASSIFICATION OF ELEMENTS

Among early attempts to classify elements, one of the first organized scientific studies dates back to 1829. At that time only 31 elements were known. Johann Döbereiner, a German chemist, had identified groups of three elements, each showing similar behaviour. These groups were known as Döbereiner's Triads. A few of these triads were:

1. Lithium (Li), Sodium (Na), Potassium (K)

2. Calcium (Ca), Strontium (Sr), Barium (Ba)
3. Chlorine (Cl), Bromine (Br), Iodine (I)

The Law of Triads for this classification observed that the atomic weight of the middle element in each triad is roughly the average of the other two and the properties of the middle element are the intermediate of the first and last element.

This method failed because all the elements known even until that point in time couldn't be made into triads and the observations were largely considered coincidental.

A French geologist, A.E.B de Chancurtois, came up with a cylindrical table of elements in 1862, in which elements were arranged in the increasing order of their atomic weights. This model too didn't earn much recognition because it could not be widely applicable for elements known even at that point in time.

The next notable classification was propounded in 1865 by John Alexander Newlands, an English chemist. He propounded the Law of Octaves, which states that when elements are arranged in the increasing order of their atomic weights, every eighth element shows properties similar to the first element. The work of Newlands too threw light on periodic repetition of properties as de Chancourtois, but could be applied to elements up to calcium (Ca) only.

The independent works of Russian chemist Dmitri Mendeleev and German chemist Lothar Meyer in the latter half of the 1800s led to the formulation of the periodic law, which states that properties of elements are a periodic function of their atomic weights. Both Mendeleev and Lothar Meyer arranged the elements in the form of rows and columns, keeping similar elements in the same column. But Mendeleev studied the compounds formed by the elements of a group and even went on to change the order of atomic weights in a few cases; so that elements in each group exhibit similar properties. He even left gaps in his table and predicted the properties of elements that would fill the gaps.

The modern periodic table, developed by an English physicist, Henry Moseley, is based on the studies through X-ray diffraction, which revealed that atomic number—an indicator of the number of protons in the nucleus, which is unique for any element—is the fundamental criteria and not atomic mass. He stated the modern periodic law as properties of elements are a periodic function of their atomic numbers. Keeping the atomic number as the base also enables us to predict how many more elements are yet to be found out in between the two known elements in the modern periodic table. Later, when noble gases were invented, they could be easily accommodated in the table.

Mendeleev's Periodic Table

Mendeleev's periodic law: The physical and chemical properties of elements are a periodic function of their atomic weights. If the elements are arranged in order of their increasing atomic weights, after a regular interval, elements with similar properties are repeated. On the basis of his law, Mendeleev proposed a periodic table for classification of elements, known as Mendeleev's periodic table.

The table is divided into nine vertical columns called groups and seven horizontal rows called periods.

Advantages of Mendeleev's Periodic Table

Study of elements: For the first time all known elements were classified in a group according to their similar properties. So, the study of the properties of elements became easier.

Predicting new elements: It gave encouragement to the discovery of new elements, as some gaps were left in it. Sc, Ge and Tc were the elements for whom position and properties were defined by Mendeleev even before their discoveries, and he left blank spaces for them in his table.

A blank space at atomic weight 72 in Si group was called Eka silicon and the element discovered later was named germanium. Some other elements for which Mendeleev left space in his periodic table and in which elements were discovered and placed later are:

- Eka Aluminium: Gallium
- Eka Boron: Scandium
- Eka Manganese: Technetium

Demerits of Mendeleev's Periodic Table

Position of hydrogen: Hydrogen resembles both, the alkali metals (1A) and halogens (VII A) in properties, so Mendeleev could not decide where to place it.

Position of isotopes: As atomic weights of isotopes differ, they should have been placed in different positions in Mendeleev's periodic table. But there were no such positions for isotopes in Mendeleev's periodic table.

Anomalous pairs of elements: There were some pairs of elements that did not follow the increasing order of atomic weights. For example, Ar and Co were placed before K and Ni respectively in the table but have higher atomic weights.

Like elements were placed in different groups: Pt and Ag, which have similar properties, were placed in group VIII and group IB respectively.

Modern Periodic Table

Modern periodic law: It states that properties of elements are the periodic function to their atomic numbers. In other words, the periodicity in properties is due to repetition of similar outer shell electronic configuration at certain regular intervals.

In the modern periodic table, which is based on the modern periodic law, the elements are arranged in rows and columns. These rows are known as periods and columns as groups. The table consists of 7 periods and 18 groups. In Figure 11.1, the modern periodic table is shown.

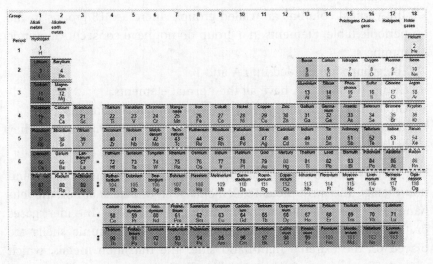

Fig. 11.1: Modern periodic table

A period in the periodic table indicates the value of 'n' (principal quantum number) for the outermost or valence shell. However, in a group, the outer electronic configuration of the elements remains the same; only the electron goes into the next principal quantum number.

Characteristics of Periodic Table

▶ The first period is the shortest period and consists of just two elements, H and He.

▶ The second and the third periods have eight elements each and are called short periods.

▶ The fourth and the fifth periods are long periods and have eighteen elements each.

▶ The sixth period has thirty-two elements. The period has a fifteen-element series called the lanthanide series, separated from the table. The lanthanide series are rare earth elements that show similar properties.

▶ The seventh period contains all the rest of the elements. It is incomplete. This period also has a fifteen-element series called the actinide series, separated from the table. The actinide series has a separate identity and contains uranium and most of the known transuranic elements.

▶ The vertical columns are called groups. There are 18 groups in the periodic table. Elements in a group do not have consecutive atomic numbers.

▶ The groups are divided into A and B.

▶ Group 1 A to VIII A have all the normal elements.

▶ Group 1 B to VIII B hold all the transition metal elements.

▶ The other two groups are the lanthanide and the actinide series. They are also known as inner transition elements.

The modern periodic table is approximately divided into metals and non-metals. The most metallic elements such as alkalis are on the left-hand side. The non-metals are on the right-hand side. The inert gases or the noble gases with their completely filled electronic shells are placed on the extreme right-hand side. The transition metals, which are a bridge between highly metallic alkali elements and non-metals, lie in the centre of the table. Lanthanide and actinide series (or the inner transition elements), which have metal-like behaviour, are kept separately, as their outermost electronic configurations differ from the transition metal elements.

Classification of elements

The periodic table can be considered as consisting of s-, p-, d-, and f-block elements on the basis of electronic configuration, as shown in Figure 11.2.

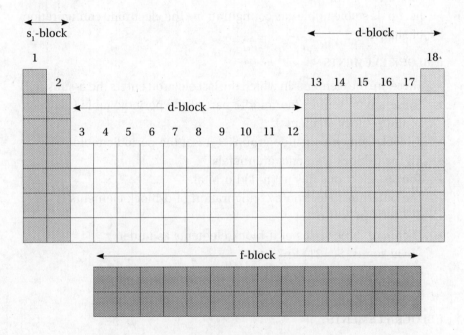

Fig. 11.2: Periodic table elements

s-BLOCK ELEMENTS

> These are the elements in which the last electron enters the s-subshell.
> These elements are placed in the left part of the periodic table.
> These include group 1 and 2 elements.
> All the s-block elements are metals.
> The general electronic configuration of valence shell for s-block elements is ns^{1-2} (n = 1 to 7).

p-BLOCK ELEMENTS

➤ These are the elements in which the last electron enters the p-subshell.

➤ These are placed in the right part of the periodic table.

➤ These include groups 13–18 of the periodic table.

➤ Most of the p-block elements are metalloids and non-metals but some of them are metals also.

➤ The general electronic configuration of the valence shell is ns^2np^{1-6} (n = 2 to 7).

➤ $ns^2\,np^6$ is stable noble gas configuration. The electronic configuration of He is Is^2.

d-BLOCK ELEMENTS

➤ These are the elements in which the last electron enters the d-subshell.

➤ These are present in the middle part of the periodic table (between s- and p-block elements).

➤ d-block elements include groups 3–12 of the periodic table.

➤ All the d-block elements are metals.

➤ The last electrons fills in $(n-1)d$ orbital.

➤ The outermost electronic configuration of d-block elements is $(n-1)d^{1-10}ns^{1-2}$ (n = 4 to 7)

➤ There are three series of d-block elements as under
  • 3d series: Sc (21) to Zn (30)
  • 4d series: Y (39) to Cd (48)
  • 5d series: La (57), Hf (72) to Hg (80)

f-BLOCK ELEMENTS

➤ These are placed separately below the main periodic table.

➤ These are mainly related to III B i.e. group 3 of the periodic table.

➤ There are two series of f-block elements as under
  • 4f series – Lanthanides – 14 elements, i.e., Ce (58) to Lu (71)
  • 5f series – Actinides – 14 elements, i.e., Th (90) to Lw (103)

➤ The last electron fills in $(n-2)$ f-orbital.

➤ Their general outermost electronic configuration is $(n-2)f^{1-14}(n-1)s^2(n-1)p^6(n-1)d^{0-1}ns^2$ (n = 6 and 7).

TRENDS IN PROPERTIES OF ELEMENTS IN PERIODIC TABLE

The modern periodic table is based on the modern periodic law which predicts repetition of electronic configuration after a certain number of elements. In other words, elements in a group have the same outer electronic configuration. Since properties of elements are a function of their electronic structure, periodic trends can be seen among elements in the periodic table. Properties in which the periodic trend can be seen include electronegativity, ionization energy, electron affinity, atomic radius, melting point and metallic character. Periodic trends provide chemists with an invaluable tool to quickly predict an element's properties.

Periodic Trend in Electronegativity

Electronegativity can be understood as a chemical property describing an atom's ability to attract and bind with electrons. Elements on the left side of the periodic table generally lose electrons when forming bonds. Conversely, elements on the right side of the periodic table tend to gain electrons to complete the octet. From left to right across a period of elements, electronegativity increases. From top to bottom down a group, electronegativity decreases. Important exceptions of the above rules include the noble gases, lanthanides and actinides. The noble gases possess a complete valence shell and do not usually attract electrons. The lanthanides and actinides possess more complicated chemistry that does not generally follow any trends. Therefore, noble gases, lanthanides and actinides do not have electronegativity values. As for the transition metals, although they have electronegativity values, there is little variance among them across the period and up and down a group. This is because their metallic properties affect their ability to attract electrons as easily as the other elements.

Periodic Trend in Ionization Energy

Ionization energy is the energy required to remove an electron from a neutral atom in its gaseous phase. Generally, elements on the right side of the periodic table have higher ionization energy because their valence shell is nearly filled. Elements on the left side of the periodic table have low ionization energies because of their willingness to lose electrons and become cations. Thus, ionization energy increases from left to right on the periodic table. The ionization energy of the elements within a group generally decreases from top to bottom. This is due to electron shielding. The noble gases possess very high ionization energies because of their full valence.

Periodic Trend in Electron Affinity

Electron affinity is the ability of an atom to accept an electron. It is a quantitative measure of the energy change that occurs when an electron is added to a neutral gaseous atom. Electron affinity generally decreases down a group of elements in the periodic table. Moving from left to right across a period, the electron affinity increases.

Periodic Trend in Atomic Radius

The atomic radius is considered to be half of the distance between the nuclei of two atoms. Atomic size gradually decreases from left to right across a period of elements. This is because of the following reason. Across a period, all electrons are added to the same shell. At the same time, protons are being added to the nucleus. Therefore attraction between nucleus and electrons increases. As a result, the atomic radius decreases. Down a group, atomic radius increases. This is because the valence electrons are added in shells corresponding to a higher quantum number (n). As a result, the valence electrons are further away from the nucleus. Electron shielding prevents these outer electrons from being attracted to the nucleus, and the resulting atomic radius is large.

Periodic Trends in Metallic Character

The metallic character of an element can be defined as how readily an atom can lose an electron. Metallic character decreases from left to right across a period. Metallic character increases down a group.

12

HYDROGEN AND ITS COMPOUNDS

INTRODUCTION

In the world of chemistry, hydrogen is unique in many senses. It is the simplest of all elements with one electron and one proton with n neutron; it is the first element in the periodic table; it is the most abundant element in the universe and the third-most abundant element on the surface of the earth. It exists as a diatomic molecule, i.e., H_2 in its elemental form. Hydrogen is a matter of big interest to researchers because of its potential power to become a source of energy—clean energy, green energy.

ISOTOPES OF HYDROGEN

Hydrogen has three isotopes: protium or simple hydrogen, $^1H_1$, or H; deuterium, also known as heavy hydrogen, $^2H_1$, or D; and Tritium, $^3H_1$, or T. These differ from each other in respect of the number of neutrons present in the nucleus. Protium does not have any neutron; deuterium contains one neutron, while the number of neutrons in the nucleus of tritium is two. Tritium is a radioactive isotope of hydrogen.

POSITION OF HYDROGEN IN THE PERIODIC TABLE

The position of hydrogen in the periodic table has been a subject of much discussion and study for the past several decades due to its similarities with both halogens and alkali metals, although it is more or less settled today that hydrogen is placed in group 1 as the first element of the periodic table; but the question is still open. A proper position could not be assigned to hydrogen either in Mendeleev's periodic table or the modern periodic table because of the following reason: in some properties, it resembles alkali metals and in some properties it resembles halogens. So hydrogen can be placed both in group 1 and group 17, with alkali metals and halogens, respectively. Let us see some of the similarities with alkali metals and halogens.

RESEMBLANCE WITH ALKALI METALS

1. **Electronic configuration:** Hydrogen contains one electron in the valence shell like the alkali metals in the first group.

Table 12.1: Elements and their electronic configurations

Element	Electronic configuration
H	$1s^1$
Li	$[He]2s^1$
Na	$[Ne]3s^1$
K	$[Ar]4s^1$
Rb	$[Kr]5s^1$
Cs	$[Xe]6s^1$
Fr	$[Rn]7s^1$

2. **Electropositive character:** Like alkali metals, hydrogen also loses its only electron to form hydrogen ion, i.e., H^+.
3. **Oxidation state:** Like alkali metals, hydrogen exhibits an oxidation state of +1 in its compounds.
4. **Reducing agent:** Alkali metals act as reducing agents because of their tendency to lose valence electrons. Hydrogen is also a very good reducing agent.
5. **Combination with electronegative elements:** Just like alkali metals, hydrogen combines with electronegative elements, such as halogen, oxygen, sulphur, etc., to form compounds with similar formula.

DIFFERENCE FROM ALKALI METALS

1. **Enthalpy of ionization:** Enthalpy of ionization of hydrogen (1312 kJ mol^{-1}) is high compared to the enthalpy of ionization of alkali metals.

2. **Existence of H⁻:** Although the existence of hydride ion has been established, its alkali earth metals counterpart is not known.
3. **Difference in halides:** Hydrogen halides are different from the alkali metals, halides, although they have similar molecular formulae. For example:
   (i) Pure HCl is a covalent compound while NaCl is an ionic compound.
   (ii) HCl is a gaseous compound while NaCl is a solid at ordinary temperature.
4. **Existence as a free atom:** Hydrogen does not exist as a free atom, while alkali metals do.

Resemblance with Halogens

1. **Electronic configuration:** Just like halogens, hydrogen needs one electron to attain the configuration of the nearest noble gas.
2. **Atomicity:** Like halogens, hydrogen also exists in a diatomic state. The atomicity of hydrogen as well as halogens is two.
3. **Electrochemical nature:** During electrolysis of LiH, CaH_2, etc., in a molten state, hydrogen evolves at the anode, indicating its electronegative nature. In this respect, hydrogen shows resemblance with halogens which are also liberated at the anode during electrolysis.
4. **Oxidation state:** Just like halogens, hydrogen also exhibits a state of -1 in some of its compounds such as metal hydrides.
5. **Combination with alkali metals:** Just like halogen, hydrogen also combines with alkali metals to form salts with similar formula.
6. **Combination with non-metals:** Just like halogens, hydrogen also reacts with non-metals such as carbon, silicon, germanium, etc., to form covalent compounds.

From the above discussion, it is clear that there is a marked resemblance in the properties of hydrogen with alkali metals as well as with halogens. Therefore, it is still a matter of further scientific study to conclusively provide hydrogen a unique position in the periodic table.

PREPARATION OF DIHYDROGEN
Some of the common methods of preparing dihydrogen from metals and metal hydrides are given here.

Laboratory Preparation of Hydrogen Gas

(a) By the reaction of granulated zinc with dilute sulphuric acid.

$$Zn + H_2SO_4 \rightarrow ZnSO_4 + H_2$$

(b) By the reaction of zinc with aqueous alkali.

$$Zn + 2NaOH \rightarrow Na_2ZnO_2 + H_2$$

COMMERCIAL PRODUCTION OF HYDROGEN GAS

The commonly used processes for commercially preparing hydrogen are stated below.

(a) Electrolysis of acidified water using platinum electrodes gives hydrogen.

$$H_2O \rightarrow H^+ + OH^-$$

At anode: $4OH^- \rightarrow 2H_2O + O_2 + 4e^-$

At cathode: $2H^+ + 2e^- \rightarrow H_2$

(b) It is obtained as a byproduct in the manufacture of sodium hydroxide and chlorine by the electrolysis of brine solution (aqueous sodium chloride). The reactions that take place in electrolysis are:

At anode: $2Cl^-(aq) \rightarrow Cl_2(g) + 2e^-$

At cathode: $2H_2O \, (l) + 2e^- \rightarrow H_2(g) + 2OH^-$

PHYSICAL PROPERTIES OF HYDROGEN

> Hydrogen is the smallest chemical element.
> It has only one proton in its nucleus and one electron outside.
> Its symbol is H, and its atomic number is 1.
> It has an average atomic weight of 1.0079 amu.
> The melting point of hydrogen is -259.14°C.
> The boiling point of hydrogen is -252.87°C.
> Hydrogen has a density of 0.08988 g/L.
> It has two distinct oxidation states, (+1, -1), which make it able to act as both an oxidizing and a reducing agent.
> Its covalent radius is 31.5 pm.

CHEMICAL PROPERTIES OF HYDROGEN

Hydrogen gas (H_2) is highly flammable and burns in air with a blue flame at a very wide range of concentrations between 4 per cent and 75 per cent by volume. The enthalpy of combustion for hydrogen is -286 kJ/mol, and is described by the equation:

$$2H_2(g) + O_2(g) \rightarrow 2H_2O(l) + 572kJ \; (286kJ/mol \; H_2)$$

This reaction between hydrogen and oxygen is called a combination reaction. Also, oxygen oxidizes hydrogen—this reaction is called an oxidation reaction. In ordinary conditions, without heating, the reaction takes place slowly. But at a temperature of above 550°C there is an explosion (so-called detonation gas forms).

Chlorine reacts with hydrogen to form hydrogen chloride. The reaction takes place only in the presence of light and heat.

$$H_2 + Cl_2 \rightarrow 2HCl$$

The interaction of nitrogen and hydrogen to form ammonia takes place at high temperature and in the presence of a catalyst.

$$3H_2 + N_2 \rightarrow 2NH_3$$

Hydrogen reacts with sulphur to form hydrogen sulfide that can be identified easily by its characteristic smell of rotten eggs.

$$H_2 + S \rightarrow H_2S$$

Hydrogen forms hydrides with metals.

$$2Na + H_2 \rightarrow 2NaH$$

Hydrogen reduces copper oxide. The reaction takes place on heating.

$$CuO + H_2 \rightarrow Cu + H_2O$$

Hydrogen also reacts with several other metal oxides, such as HgO, PbO, etc., reducing the metal oxide.

HARD AND SOFT WATER

Water that does not readily form lather with soap is called hard water. Soft water readily forms lather with soap. Hard water contains dissolved compounds that are usually calcium or magnesium compounds. For example, limestone contains calcium carbonate, $CaCO_3$. Carbonic acid in rainwater, which is formed by reaction of aerial carbon dioxide with water, reacts with calcium carbonate to produce soluble calcium hydrogen carbonate.

$$H_2CO_3(aq) + CaCO_3(s) \rightarrow Ca(HCO_3)_2(aq)$$

The presence of calcium ions and magnesium ions in the water makes it hard. The dissolved calcium ions and magnesium ions in hard water react with soap to form scum, so more soap is needed. There are varying degrees of hardness in water—from slightly hard to very hard.

Types of Hardness

Hardness of water is of two types—temporary and permanent. Temporary hardness is that type of hardness which can be removed easily and even by domestic processes. Permanent hardness requires more complex treatment of water.

Permanent hard water stays hard, even when water is boiled.

Temporary hardness of water is caused by dissolved hydrogen carbonate ions, HCO_3^-. Temporary hard water can be softened by boiling it. When boiled, these ions decompose (break down) to form carbonate ions, CO_3^{2-}. The carbonate ions in the boiled water react with dissolved calcium and magnesium ions to form insoluble precipitates (calcium carbonate and magnesium carbonate).

Permanent hardness of water is caused by dissolved sulphate ions, SO_4^{2-}. These do not decompose when heated. They remain dissolved and do not react with calcium and magnesium ions. Therefore, the water remains hard even when boiled.

There are two methods for softening hard water: (a) adding sodium carbonate to the water; (b) using ion exchange columns.

Adding Sodium Carbonate

Sodium carbonate, Na_2CO_3, also known as washing soda, can remove temporary and permanent hardness from water. Sodium carbonate is soluble but calcium carbonate and magnesium carbonate are insoluble. The carbonate ions from sodium carbonate react with the calcium and magnesium ions in the water to produce insoluble precipitates. The water is softened because it no longer contains dissolved calcium and magnesium ions.

CHEMISTRY

$$Ca^{2+}(aq) + Na_2CO_3(aq) \rightarrow CaCO_3(s) + 2Na^+(aq)$$

Ion Exchange Columns

Commercial water softeners often use ion exchange resins, which are usually made into beads and packed into cylinders called ion exchange columns. The resin beads have sodium ions attached to them. As the hard water passes through the column, the calcium and magnesium ions swap places with the sodium ions. The calcium and magnesium ions are left attached to the beads, while the water leaving the column contains more sodium ions. The hard water is softened because it no longer contains calcium or magnesium ions. Once the resin beads in ion exchange columns become saturated with calcium and magnesium ions, they must be regenerated by adding sodium chloride (common salt). The sodium ions it contains replace the calcium and magnesium ions on the beads. Sodium chloride is cheap and widely available, making this a convenient and cost-effective system.

13

EXTRACTION OF METALS

INTRODUCTION

The journey through which an ore turns into a pure metal is the process of extraction of metal. In other words, an ore passes through various steps of physical phenomena and chemical reactions to finally turn into a metal. In this chapter we will learn about those processes whose selection in extracting a metal from its ore not only depends on the viability of a chemical reaction or a physical phenomenon, but also on the consideration of profitability. The treatment adopted for an ore also depends upon the nature of the ore, the impurities and the metal. We will also learn the general principles of metal extraction in this chapter.

WHAT IS AN ORE?

An ore is a naturally-occurring source of a metal from which the metal can be economically extracted.

Some of the metals and their ores are given in the table below.

Table 13.1: Metals and their ores

Metal	Ores	Chemical formula
Sodium (Na)	Chile saltpetre	$NaNO_3$
	Trona	$Na_2Co_3, 2NaHCO_3.3H_2O$
	Borax	$Na_2B_4O_7.10H_2O$
	Common salt	$NaCl$

Metal	Ores	Chemical formula
Aluminium (Al)	Bauxite	$Al_2O_3.2H_2O$
	Corundum	Al_2O_3
	Felspar	$KAlSi_3O_8$
	Cryolite	Na_3AlF_6
	Alunite	$K_2SO_4.Al_2(SO_4)_3.4Al(OH)_3$
	Kaolin	$3Al_2O_3.6SiO_2.2H_2O$
Potassium (K)	Nitre (saltpetre)	KNO_3
	Carnalite	$KCl.MgCl_2.6\ H_2O$
Magnesium (Mg)	Magnesite	$MgCO_3$
	Dolomite	$MgCO_3.CaCO_3$
	Epsom salt	$MgSO_4.7H_2O$
	Kieserite	$MgSO_4.H_2O$
	Carnalite	$KCl.MgCl_2.6H_2O$

From the above table, we see that ores are commonly oxides, sulfides, etc.

STEPS OF METALLURGICAL PROCESS

Metallurgy consists of three general steps: (1) mining the ore, (2) separating and concentrating the metal or the metal-containing compound, (3) reducing the ore to the metal, and (4) refining the crude metal. Additional processes are sometimes required to improve the mechanical properties of the metal or increase its purity. Many ores contain relatively low concentrations of the desired metal; for example, copper ores that contain even 1 per cent Cu by mass are considered commercially useful. Here we will not discuss the mining process, hence we will discuss the following three steps.

- Concentration or benefaction of the ore
- Extraction of crude metal from the concentrated ore
- Refining of the crude metal

(1) CONCENTRATION OR BENEFACTION OF THE ORE

This is an important step in metallurgy. The ore is obtained from the earth and it usually contains various impurities such as dust, stone, quartz and other foreign materials. These impurities are known as gangue or matrix. The process of separation of gangue from the ore is known as concentration. Some of the important processes of concentration are:

- Crushing and grinding of the ore
- Gravity separation
- Hydraulic classifier
- Magnetic separation: If the ore is attracted by the magnet then it is separated from non-magnetic impurities by the means of a magnetic separator
- Froth floatation process
- Liquation
- Leaching: It is a chemical process in which the powder ore is treated with a suitable reagent

  $Al_2O_3.2H_2O + 2NaOH \rightarrow 2NaAlO_2 + 3H_2O$

  $NaAlO_2 + 2H_2O \rightarrow Al(OH)_3\downarrow + NaOH$

  $2Al(OH)_3 \rightarrow Al_2O_3 + 3H_2O$

(2) EXTRACTION OF CRUDE METAL FROM THE CONCENTRATED ORE

The extraction of crude metal from the concentrated ore involves the following steps:

Calcination

The concentrated ore is heated in the absence of air to a temperature below the melting points of metal.

$$Al_2O_3.2H_2O \text{ (bauxite)} \xrightarrow{Calcination} Al_2O_3 + 2H_2O\uparrow$$

$$Fe_2O_3.3H_2O \text{ (limonite)} \xrightarrow{Calcination} Fe_2O_3 + 3H_2O\uparrow$$

Carbonate ores are decomposed to their oxides:

$$ZnCO_3 \text{ (zincite)} \xrightarrow{Calcination} ZnO + CO_2\uparrow$$

$$MgCO_3 \text{ (magnesite)} \xrightarrow{Calcination} MgO + CO_2\uparrow$$

$$CaCO3 \text{ (limestone)} \xrightarrow{Calcination} CaO + CO_2\uparrow$$

Roasting

In this process the ore is heated alone or mixed with other materials under regular supply of air at a temperature below the melting point of the metal. Roasting is usually applied to sulfide ore.

$$2Zns + 3O_2 \rightarrow 2ZnO + 2SO_2\uparrow$$

$$4FeS_2 + 11O_2 \rightarrow 2Fe_2O_3 + 8SO_2\uparrow$$
$$2HgS + 3O_2 \rightarrow 2HgO + 2SO_2\uparrow$$

Sometimes the ore is mixed with suitable material and then subjected to roasting in the absence of air:

$$Ag_2S + 2NaCl \rightarrow 2AgCl + Na_2S$$

Reduction of Metals

There are three main methods of extracting metals from their ore.

- Reduction of the ore with carbon
- Reduction of the molten ore by electrolysis
- Reduction of the ore with a more reactive metal

Extraction Using Carbon

Metals such as zinc, iron and copper are present in ores as their oxides. Each of these oxides is heated with carbon to obtain the metal. The metal oxide loses oxygen, and is therefore reduced. The carbon gains oxygen, and is therefore oxidized.

Electrolysis

Ionic substances can be broken down into the elements they are made from by electricity, in a process called electrolysis. For electrolysis to work, the ions must be free to move. When an ionic compound is dissolved in water or it melts, the ions break free from the ionic lattice. These ions are then free to move. The solution or molten ionic compound is called an electrolyte.

What happens during electrolysis? Positively charged ions move to the negative electrode. Metal ions are positively charged, so metals are produced at the negative electrode (cathode). Negatively charged ions move to the positive electrode. Non-metal ions, such as oxide ions and chloride ions, are negatively charged, so gases such as oxygen or chlorine are produced at the positive electrode (anode).

Reduction of Metal Halides with Metals

In many cases, carbon cannot be used to reduce the metal oxide to the metal as the metal reacts with carbon to form the carbide instead. It is possible to avoid this problem by first converting the ore to the chloride, and then reducing the chloride with a more reactive metal such as magnesium or sodium. This is the method used to extract titanium.

(3) REFINING OF CRUDE METALS

Metals are seldom pure, hence need further purification. The choice of the purification method depends on the nature of metals and the impurities present. Some purification methods are discussed below.

Oxidative refining

In this method, the impure metal is heated to a high temperature and then exposed to air when the impurities are oxidized to their volatile oxides which escape along with outgoing gases.

Distillation

This is the process of separating the components or substances from a liquid mixture by using selective boiling and condensation.

Liquation

The impure metal is heated on the sloping hearth of a furnace when the molten metal flows away from the infusible impurities.

Electrolytic refining

In this method, the cathode is made of pure metal and impure metal is used as the anode.

14

CHEMISTRY OF METALS

INTRODUCTION

All elements except hydrogen which form positive ions by losing electrons during chemical reactions are called metals. Thus metals are electropositive elements. In this chapter we will learn about metals and their chemistry. Metals are found at many places in the periodic table. Figure 14.1 explains the places in the periodic table where metals are found.

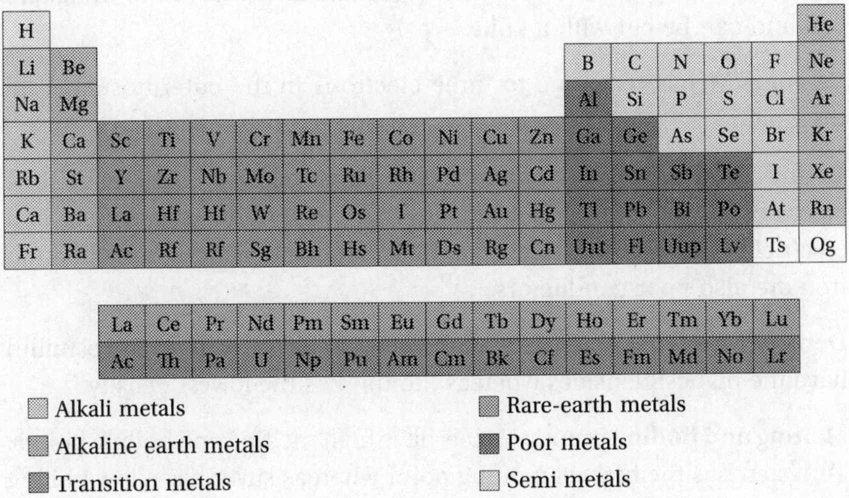

H																	He
Li	Be											B	C	N	O	F	Ne
Na	Mg											Al	Si	P	S	Cl	Ar
K	Ca	Sc	Ti	V	Cr	Mn	Fe	Co	Ni	Cu	Zn	Ga	Ge	As	Se	Br	Kr
Rb	St	Y	Zr	Nb	Mo	Tc	Ru	Rh	Pd	Ag	Cd	In	Sn	Sb	Te	I	Xe
Ca	Ba	La	Hf	Hf	W	Re	Os	I	Pt	Au	Hg	Tl	Pb	Bi	Po	At	Rn
Fr	Ra	Ac	Rf	Rf	Sg	Bh	Hs	Mt	Ds	Rg	Cn	Uut	Fl	Uup	Lv	Ts	Og

La	Ce	Pr	Nd	Pm	Sm	Eu	Gd	Tb	Dy	Ho	Er	Tm	Yb	Lu
Ac	Th	Pa	U	Np	Pu	Am	Cm	Bk	Cf	Es	Fm	Md	No	Lr

☐ Alkali metals   ☐ Rare-earth metals
☐ Alkaline earth metals   ☐ Poor metals
☐ Transition metals   ☐ Semi metals

Fig. 14.1: Location of metals in the periodic table

PHYSICAL PROPERTIES OF METALS

Metals are characterized by bright lustre, hardness, ability to resonate sound and their property to conduct heat and electricity. They are malleable and ductile. Metals are solids at room temperature except mercury.

Some of the properties of metals are as given below.

State: Metals are solids at room temperature with the exception of mercury, which is liquid at room temperature (gallium is liquid on hot days).

Lustre: Metals have the quality of reflecting light from their surface and can be polished e.g., gold, silver and copper.

Malleability: Metals have the ability to withstand hammering and can be made into thin sheets known as foils (a sugar cube chunk of gold can be pounded into a thin sheet which will cover a football field).

Ductility: Metals can be drawn into wires. 100 gm of silver can be drawn into a thin wire about 200 m long.

Hardness: All metals are hard except sodium and potassium, which are soft and can be cut with a knife.

Valency: Metals have one to three electrons in the outermost shell of their atoms.

Conduction: Metals are good conductors because they have free electrons. Silver and copper are the two best conductors of heat and electricity. Lead is the poorest conductor of heat. Bismuth, mercury and iron are also poor conductors.

Density: Metals have high density and are very heavy. Iridium and osmium have the highest densities whereas lithium has the lowest density.

Melting and boiling points: Metals have high melting and boiling points. Tungsten has the highest melting point whereas silver has a low boiling point. Sodium and potassium have low melting points.

GENERAL PROPERTIES OF METALS

A metal can refer to an element, compound or alloy that is a good conductor of both electricity and heat.

Metals typically consist of closely-packed atoms, meaning that the atoms are arranged like closely-packed spheres. In a metal, atoms readily lose electrons to form positive ions (cations). Those ions are surrounded by de-localized electrons, which are responsible for the conductivity. The solid produced is held together by electrostatic interactions between the ions and the electron cloud, which are called metallic bonds.

Metals are shiny and lustrous with a high density. They have very high melting and boiling points because metallic bonding is very strong, so the atoms are reluctant to break apart into a liquid or a gas.

Sodium is soft enough to be cut with a plastic knife.

Metals in general are conductive, with high electrical and thermal conductivity. Typically they are malleable and ductile, deforming under stress without cleaving. For example, hitting a metal with a hammer will 'dent' the metal, not shatter it into pieces.

The electrical and thermal conductivities of metals originate from the fact that their outer electrons are delocalized. This means the electrons are not locked into any one atom but can move freely throughout the metal. Metals can be viewed as a collection of atoms embedded in a sea of electrons, which are highly mobile. This is very instrumental in the conductivity of the metal.

Metals are usually inclined to form cations through electron loss. An example is the reaction with oxygen in the air to form oxides over various timescales (iron rusts over years, while potassium burns in seconds). The transition metals (such as iron, copper, zinc and nickel) are slower to oxidize because they form a passivating layer of oxide that protects the interior. Others, like palladium, platinum and gold do not react with the atmosphere at all. Some metals form a barrier layer of oxide on their surface, which cannot be penetrated by further oxygen molecules. As a result, they retain their shiny appearance and good conductivity for many decades (like aluminium, magnesium, some steels and titanium). Metallic properties tend to decrease across a period and increase down a periodic group.

When two elements are joined in a chemical bond, the element that attracts the shared electrons more strongly has more electronegativity. Elements with low electronegativity tend to have more metallic properties. So, the metallic properties of elements tend to decrease across a period and increase down a group. The fact that the metallic elements are found on the left side of the periodic table offers an important clue to the nature of how they bond together to form solids. These elements all possess low electronegativities and readily form positive ions.

CHEMICAL PROPERTIES OF METALS

Metals are electropositive elements that generally form basic or amphoteric oxides with oxygen. Some of the chemical properties of metals are as given below.

Electropositive character: Metals tend to have low ionization energies, and typically lose electrons (i.e., they are oxidized) when they undergo chemical reactions. They normally do not accept electrons.

$$Na \rightarrow Na^+ + e^-$$
$$Mg \rightarrow Mg^{2+} + 2e^-$$
$$Al \rightarrow Al^{3+} + 3e^-$$

- Alkali metal ions always carry 1+ (lose the electron in s-subshell)
- Alkaline earth metal ions always carry 2+ (lose both electrons in s-subshell)
- Transition metal ions do not follow an obvious pattern; 2+ is common and 1+ and 3+ are also observed

Compounds of metals with non-metals tend to be ionic in nature. Most metal oxides are basic oxides and dissolve in water to form metal hydroxides:

Metal oxide + water → metal hydroxide
$$Na_2O(s) + H_2O(l) \rightarrow 2NaOH(aq)$$
$$CaO(s) + H_2O(l) \rightarrow Ca(OH)_2(aq)$$

Metal oxides exhibit their basic chemical nature by reacting with acids to form salts and water.

Metal oxide + acid → salt + water
$$MgO(s) + HCl(aq) \rightarrow MgCl_2(aq) + H_2O(l)$$
$$NiO(s) + H_2SO_4(aq) \rightarrow NiSO_4(aq) + H_2O(l)$$

15

CHEMISTRY OF NON-METALS

INTRODUCTION

Chemistry of non-metals is the chemistry of p-block elements. The elements in the p-block are non-metals and metalloids. There are six groups of p-block elements in the periodic table numbering from 13 to 18. Boron, carbon, nitrogen, oxygen, fluorine and helium head the groups, although He, among these elements, occurs in the first period while the others are in the second period. The elements in these respective groups are: in the boron group–boron, aluminum, gallium, indium and thallium; in the carbon group–carbon, silicon, germanium, tin and lead; in the nitrogen group–nitrogen, phosphorous, arsenic, antimony, bismuth; in the oxygen group–oxygen, sulfur, selenium, tellurium, polonium; in the fluorine group–fluorine, chlorine, bromine, iodine, astatine; and in the helium group–helium, neon, argon, krypton and xenon.

GENERAL CONCEPTS

When non-metals react with metals, they usually produce ionic compounds. Ionic compounds are typically hard solids at room temperature and can conduct electricity when dissolved in water or are in the molten state. On the other hand, compounds formed between non-metals are usually molecular compounds and are frequently gases, liquids or low-melting solids at room temperature.

Members of the second row (Li–F) differ in some ways from the members of the rows below it. This is because they are smaller and have higher electronegativities. Furthermore, they have no accessible low energy d-orbitals. Therefore, these elements are limited to a maximum of four bonds each. They cannot have sp^3d and sp^3d^2 hybridized orbitals, hence cannot form five or six bonds. This is the reason why oxygen forms only one compound with fluorine (OF_2), while sulfur forms three (SF_2, SF_4 and SF_6).

Second-row elements frequently form multiple bonds (e.g., $HC\equiv CH$, $H_2C=CH_2$, $N\equiv N$, and $O=O$), while those of the lower rows do so rarely, or not at all.

We have studied the details of hydrogen chemistry in another chapter, so we will not study about hydrogen here, although we have seen in that chapter that hydrogen can be classified as a non-metal, and that is why it can be placed with the halogens.

GROUP 18: NOBLE GASES

Group 8A elements are helium, neon, argon, krypton, xenon and radon. All Group 8A elements are gases at ambient temperature. With a few exceptions, they are completely chemically inert.

Although helium is the most chemically inert of the elements, it is interesting in a number of other ways. Xenon forms compounds with oxygen and fluorine. They include XeF_2, XeF_4, XeF_6, XeO_3 and XeO_4; krypton forms KrF_2, among others. Although a lot of study has unravelled the chemistry of noble gases, they are still called inert gases because of historical reasons.

GROUP 17: HALOGENS

There are six elements in Group 8A. They are called halogens. They are diatomic molecules; F_2, Cl_2, Br_2, I_2 and At_2, although the metallic character increases down the group. They all form negatively charged ions: F^-, Cl^-, Br^-, I^- and At^-.

None of the halogens can be found in nature in their elemental form. They are invariably found as salts of the halide ions (F^-, Cl^-, Br^- and I^-). Fluoride ions are found in minerals such as fluorite (CaF_2) and cryolite (Na_3AlF_6). Chloride ions are found in rock salt (NaCl), the oceans. Both bromide and iodide ions are found at low concentration in the oceans.

Fluorine (F_2) is a highly reactive substance; in fact, the most reactive element known; it is a toxic, colourless gas. It is so reactive it even forms compounds with Kr, Xe and Rn. Fluorine is so reactive that it is difficult to find a container in which it can be stored. Fluorine is a very powerful oxidizing agent that can bring out unusually high oxidation numbers in other elements.

Fluorine is used in the manufacture of certain polymeric compounds with carbon, like Teflon or poly (tetrafluoroethylene), which are used in non-stick cookware. Chlorofluorocarbons or simply freons (such as CCl_2F_2) are used in refrigerators, air conditioners, etc.

Chlorine (Cl_2), the next member in the group after fluorine, is a highly toxic gas with a pale yellow-green colour. Chlorine is also a very strong oxidizing agent, which is used commercially as a bleaching agent and as a disinfectant. The other places where chlorine is used in large quantities are in the making of solvents like carbon tetrachloride (CCl_4), chloroform ($CHCl_3$), dichloroethylene ($C_2H_2Cl_2$) and trichloroethylene (C_2HCl_3).

Bromine (Br_2) is a reddish-orange liquid with an unpleasant, choking odour. Bromine vapours are bad for health.

Iodine is an intensely coloured solid with an almost metallic lustre. This solid is relatively volatile, and it sublimes when heated to form a violet-coloured gas. Iodine has been used for many years as a disinfectant in 'tincture of iodine'. Iodide is added to salt to protect against goiter, an iodine-deficiency disease characterized by a swelling of the thyroid gland.

There is a regular increase in the melting point, boiling point, the radius of the corresponding halide ion and the density of the element as we go down the group. On the other hand, the first ionization energy decreases in the group. Therefore, regular decrease in the oxidizing strength of the halogens from fluorine to iodine can be observed.

Methods of Preparation of Halogens from their Halides

Halogens can be made by reaction of a solution of the halide ion with any substance that is a stronger oxidizing agent. Iodine, for example, can be made by making the iodide ion with either bromine or chlorine:

$$2I^-(aq) + Br_2(aq) \rightarrow I_2(aq) + 2Br^-(aq)$$

To prepare Cl_2, we need a particularly strong oxidizing agent, such as manganese dioxide (MnO_2).

$$2\ Cl^-(aq) + MnO_2(aq) + 4\ H^+(aq) \rightarrow Cl_2\ (aq) + Mn^{2+}(aq) + 2\ H_2O(l)$$

Attempts to prepare fluorine by electrolysis were initially unsuccessful. However, Henri Moissan successfully isolated F_2 gas from the electrolysis of a mixed salt of KF. Electrolysis of KHF_2 is still used to prepare fluorine today.

$$2\ KHF_2(s) \rightarrow H_2(g) + F_2(g) + 2\ KF(s)$$

GROUP 16: OXYGEN FAMILY

Oxygen is the most abundant element in the earth's crust and hydrosphere. It ranks second in the atmosphere. Oxygen has two naturally occurring allotropes (O_2 and O_3). Oxygen has a high electron affinity, electronegativity and ionization energy. It tends to form compounds in the -2 oxidation state, although -1, -½ and +2 compounds exist (e.g., H_2O_2, KO_2 and OF_2 respectively). O_2 is an odourless, colourless and tasteless gas at room temperature. Oxygen is obtained by the fractional distillation of air. Ozone is a pale blue gas with an irritating odour. It is a stronger oxidizing agent than dioxygen.

The other elements in Group 6A are S, Se, Te and Po. These elements differ from oxygen in a few notable ways. First, they are far less electronegative and the electronegativity decreases down the group. This is reflected in the positive oxidation states (+2, +4, +6) for these elements as opposed to oxygen, which does so only with fluorine (OF_2). Among the elements other than O in this group, there are non-metals (S, Se), a metalloid (Te) and a metal (Po). Of these elements, only sulfur occurs widespread in nature as the free element.

Oxygen does not react with itself, nitrogen or water under normal conditions. Oxygen does, however, dissolve in water at 20°C and 1 atm. Oxygen also does not normally react with bases or acids. Group 1 metals (alkaline metals) are very reactive with oxygen and must be stored away from oxygen in order to prevent them from becoming oxidized. The metals at the bottom of the group are more reactive than those at the top. Group 2 metals (alkaline earth metals) react with oxygen through the process of burning to form metal oxides, but there are a few exceptions. Beryllium is very difficult to burn because it has a layer of beryllium oxide on its surface which prevents further interaction with oxygen. Strontium and barium react with oxygen to form peroxides. Group 13 reacts with oxygen in order to form oxides and hydroxides. Group 14 elements react with oxygen to form oxides. The oxides formed at the top of the group are more acidic than those at the bottom of the group. Oxygen reacts with silicon and carbon to form silicon dioxide and carbon dioxide. Carbon is also able to react with oxygen to form carbon monoxide, which is slightly acidic. Germanium, tin and lead react with oxygen to form monoxides and dioxides that are amphoteric, which means that they react both with acids and bases. Group 15 elements react with oxygen to form oxides. Group 16 elements react with oxygen to form various oxides. Group 17 elements (halogens) fluorine, chlorine, bromine and iodine react with oxygen to form oxides. Fluorine forms two oxides with oxygen which are F_2O and F_2O_2. Both fluorine oxides are called oxygen fluorides because fluorine is the more electronegative element. Among Group 18 elements, xenon does react with oxygen to form XeO_3 and XeO_4. Transition metals react with oxygen to form metal oxides. However, gold, silver and platinum do not react with oxygen.

GROUP 15: NITROGEN FAMILY

Nitrogen is incredibly abundant in the atmosphere. Only $NaNO_3$ and KNO_3 are found in significant amounts as mineral deposits. Compounds of nitrogen occur in all oxidation states from -3 to +5. In this property, nitrogen differs from all other second-row elements except carbon which has very limited number of accessible oxidation states. Nitrogen is obtained in large quantities from the fractional distillation of air (just like oxygen). Molecular nitrogen is quite inert and considerable interest exists in developing compounds that will break the triple bond at low temperatures and pressures.

Ammonia is one of the world's most important feedstock chemicals. Although one may purchase household cleaning ammonia, almost all of the ammonia produced is used in the preparation of other chemicals, with the majority of ammonia eventually converted into fertilizer.

Nitrogen has four valence orbitals (one 2s and three 2p), so it can participate in at most four electron-pair bonds by using sp^3 hybrid orbitals. Unlike carbon, however, nitrogen does not form long chains.

These interactions become important at the shorter internuclear distances encountered with the smaller, second-period elements of groups 15, 16 and 17.

Few binary molecular compounds of nitrogen are formed by direct reaction of the elements. At elevated temperatures, N_2 reacts with H_2 to form ammonia, with O_2 to form a mixture of NO and NO_2, and with carbon to form cyanogen (N≡C–C≡N); elemental nitrogen does not react with the halogens or the other chalcogens.

At elevated temperatures, nitrogen reacts with highly electropositive metals to form ionic nitrides, such as Li_3N and Ca_3N_2. Nitrogen also reacts with semi-metals at very high temperatures to produce covalent nitrides, such as Si_3N_4 and BN, which are solids with extended covalent network structures similar to those of graphite or diamond. Consequently, they usually have a high melting point and are chemically inert materials.

GROUP 14: CARBON FAMILY

Members of this group are carbon, silicon, germanium, tin and lead. Carbon exists as two crystalline allotropes known since antiquity: diamond and graphite. Another allotrope of carbon has been discovered a few years ago: buckminsterfullerene. Diamond is the hardest naturally occurring substance. Graphite is a very soft, black material that is quite slippery and is a good conductor of electricity. The third allotrope, buckminsterfullerene, C_{60}, has the shape of a soccer ball if one imagines a carbon atom at each intersection point of the hexagons and pentagons that line its surface.

Carbon has the unique property to form strong bonds with itself. This property is called catenation. Carbon forms single, double and triple bonds with carbon. Carbon forms a large number of organic compounds in which the other two major elements are hydrogen and oxygen. In addition, nitrogen, sulphur, phosphorous and other elements are also found in organic compounds. Compounds of carbon and hydrogen are known as hydrocarbons.

Oxides of Carbon
Carbon monoxide is a colourless, odourless, tasteless gas with a relatively low boiling point. It is formed due to incomplete combustion of carbon

or hydrocarbons or when carbon or hydrocarbons burn in a deficiency of oxygen.

$$2 C(s) + O_2 (g) \rightarrow 2 CO (g)$$

It is toxic in either high doses or after prolonged exposure even in low doses. The toxicity is due to the fact that haemoglobin has a bigger affinity for carbon monoxide than oxygen. Death can occur even when a patient is given pure oxygen because the oxygen only slowly displaces the CO and only too little oxygen makes it to the body cells and they die.

Like carbon monoxide, carbon dioxide, CO_2, is colourless, odourless and tasteless. It is much less toxic than CO, but will induce unconsciousness and death at very high concentrations even if it is not inhaled! It is an unusual substance in that it converts directly from the gaseous to the solid state (deposits) at atmospheric pressure. Solid CO_2 is frequently called 'dry ice' because it sublimes directly to the gaseous state without passing through a liquid form.

Silicon differs from carbon in two distinct features:

1) It has a very low tendency to bond with itself and form chains.
2) It interacts with oxygen using only σ-bonds and these bonds are so strong, they dominate the chemistry of this element.

Elemental silicon is a semi-conductor and a very pure material (99.9999 per cent) and is used in the production of computer chips. Moderately pure silicon is prepared by the reduction of silicon dioxide by carbon.

Although silicon, germanium, tin and lead in their +4 oxidation states often form binary compounds with the same stoichiometry as carbon, the structures and properties of these compounds are usually significantly different from those of the carbon analogues. Silicon and germanium are both semi-conductors with structures analogous to diamond. Tin has two common allotropes: white (β) tin has a metallic lattice and metallic properties, whereas gray (α) tin has a diamond-like structure and is a semi-conductor. The metallic β form is stable above 13.2°C, and the non-metallic α form is stable below 13.2°C. Lead is the only group 14 element that is metallic in both structure and properties under all conditions.

The group 14 elements show the greatest diversity in chemical behaviour of any group; covalent bond strengths decrease with increasing atomic size and ionization energies are greater than expected, increasing from C to Pb. The tendency to form multiple bonds and to catenate decreases as the atomic number increases. Consistent with periodic trends, metallic behaviour increases down the group. Silicon has a tremendous affinity for oxygen because of partial Si–O π bonding. Dioxides of the group 14 elements become increasingly basic down the group and their metallic character increases. Silicates contain anions that consist of only silicon and oxygen. Aluminosilicates are formed by replacing some of the Si atoms in silicates by Al atoms; aluminosilicates with three-dimensional framework structures are called zeolites. Nitrides formed by reacting silicon or germanium with nitrogen are strong, hard and chemically inert. The hydrides become thermodynamically less stable down the group. Moreover, as atomic size increases, multiple bonds between or to the group 14 elements become weaker. Silicones, which contain an Si–O backbone and Si–C bonds, are high-molecular-mass polymers whose properties depend on their compositions.

GROUP 13: BORON FAMILY

Except for the first element of this group, which is boron, the group 13 elements are all relatively electropositive; that is, they tend to lose electrons in chemical reactions rather than gain them. The group includes aluminum, which is the most abundant metal on the earth.

Elemental boron is a semi-metal that is remarkably unreactive; in contrast, the other group 13 elements all exhibit metallic properties and reactivity. We therefore consider the reactions and compounds of boron separately from those of other elements in the group. All group 13 elements have fewer valence electrons than valence orbitals, which generally results in delocalized, metallic bonding. With its high ionization energy, low electron affinity, low electronegativity and small size, however, boron does not form a metallic lattice with delocalized valence electrons. Instead, boron forms unique and intricate structures that contain multicentre bonds, in which a pair of electrons holds together three or more atoms.

All four of the heavier group 13 elements (Al, Ga, In and Tl) react readily with the halogens. Of the halides, only the fluorides exhibit behaviour typical of an ionic compound: they have high melting points (> 950°C) and low solubility in non-polar solvents. In contrast, the trichorides, tribromides and triiodides of aluminum, gallium and indium, as well as $TlCl_3$ and $TlBr_3$, are more covalent in character and are halogen-bridged. Although the structure of these dimers is similar to that of diborane (B_2H_6), the bonding can be described in terms of electron-pair bonds rather than the delocalized electron-deficient bonding found in diborane.

In water, the halides of the group 13 metals hydrolyse to produce the metal hydroxide $M(OH)_3$:

$$MX_3(s) + 3H_2O(l) \rightarrow M(OH)_3(s) + 3HX(aq)$$

Of the group 13 halides, only the fluorides behave as typical ionic compounds.

Like boron, all the heavier group 13 elements react with excess oxygen at elevated temperatures to give the trivalent oxide (M_2O_3), although Tl_2O_3 is not stable.

All group 13 oxides dissolve in dilute acid, but Al_2O_3 and Ga_2O_3 are amphoteric.

Unlike boron, the heavier group 13 elements do not react directly with hydrogen. Only the aluminum and gallium hydrides are known, but they must be prepared indirectly; AlH_3 is an insoluble, polymeric solid that is rapidly decomposed by water, whereas GaH_3 is unstable at room temperature.

16

BASIC CONCEPTS OF ORGANIC CHEMISTRY

INTRODUCTION

By virtue of its unique property of catenation, carbon can form a covalent bond with carbon, which is single, double and triple type. It also forms covalent bonds with atoms of other elements such as hydrogen, oxygen, nitrogen, sulphur, phosphorus, halogens and other metal atoms. The branch of chemistry in which compounds of carbon which have historically been extracted from organic matter are studied is called organic chemistry. Organic chemistry is basically the study of compounds of primarily carbon, hydrogen and oxygen, and other elements.

HISTORY OF ORGANIC COMPOUNDS

Leaving aside the earlier unstructured classification and attempts to define organic chemistry, it was first defined as a branch of modern science in the early 1800s by Jon Jacob Berzelius. According to him, chemical compounds can be classified into two main groups: organic, if they originated in living or once-living matter, and inorganic, if they came from mineral or non-living matter. Scientists continued to hold on to this classification of separate branches as organic and inorganic chemistry until the discovery by a student of Berzelius's, which blurred the line separating the two branches of chemistry or which compelled people to think that the separation was more of a pragmatic concept than scientific. In 1828, Frederich Wöhler discovered that urea—a hitherto known organic compound—could be made in the laboratory by heating ammonium cyanate (an inorganic compound). Wöhler mixed silver cyanate and ammonium chloride to produce solid silver chloride and aqueous ammonium cyanate. Thus began a new era in the study of chemistry where traditional concepts of two branches of chemistry appeared to be vague. Further studies led to the pioneering synthesis of acetic acid by Kolbe (1845) and that of methane by Berthelot (1856), which showed conclusively that organic compounds could be synthesized from inorganic sources in a laboratory. However, due to the historical reason, we still call those compounds which come from living matter organic compounds and their study organic chemistry.

QUADRAVALENCY OF CARBON AND SHAPES OF ORGANIC COMPOUNDS

In order to understand the shapes of carbon compounds that are at the heart of the study of organic chemistry, the knowledge of fundamental concepts of valency and molecular structure is very important.

The electronic configuration of carbon (Z = 6) is $1s^2 2s^2 2p^2$. In other words, carbon has two unpaired valence shell electrons. This is not sufficient for carbon to show valency of four, which is the case encountered in organic chemistry. In the environment of compound formation, the two 2s electrons get unpaired and one of them is promoted to the 2p orbital. Also, mixing or hybridization of 2s and 2p orbitals takes place, giving rise to four sp^3 hybrid orbitals directed along four corners of a regular tetrahedron, each containing one unpaired electron. When four such sp^3 hybridized orbitals overlap with 1s orbital of each of the four hydrogen atoms, four single covalent bonds are formed with four hydrogen atoms. Thus, the compound so formed, methane, CH4, is tetrahedral in shape, with each HCH bond angle equalling 109°28' (or approximately 109.5°).

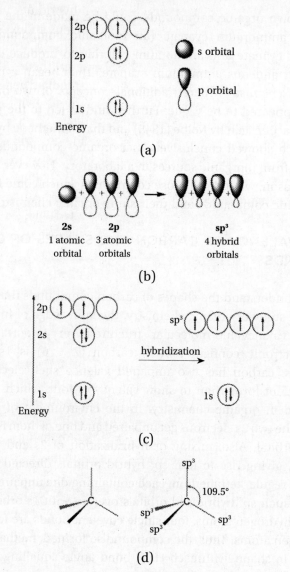

Fig. 16.1: *(a) atomic orbitals of C atom; (b) overlap of 2s and 2p orbitals to form four sp³ hybrid orbitals; (c) distribution of electrons in hybrid orbitals; (d) shape of sp³ hybridized carbon compound and the measure of bond angles*

The hybridization in ethene (C_2H_4) is sp^2 and the shape of the compound is plane triangular with one carbon-carbon double bond between the two carbon atoms. Ethyne (C_2H_2) has a linear structure with sp hybridization and it has a carbon-carbon triple bond. The sp hybrid orbital contains more s characters and hence it is closer to its nucleus and forms shorter and stronger bonds than the sp^3 hybrid orbital. The sp^2 hybrid orbital is intermediate in s character between sp and sp^3, hence, the length and enthalpy of the bonds it forms are also intermediate between them. The change in hybridization affects the electronegativity of carbon. The greater the s character of the hybrid orbitals, the greater is the electronegativity. Thus, a carbon atom having an sp hybrid orbital with 50 per cent s character is more electronegative than those possessing sp^2 or sp^3 hybridized orbitals. In case of sp^2 hybridization, one of the bonds is a π bond and in case of sp, there are two π bonds. A rotation of one CH_2 fragment with respect to the other is restricted due to the π bond. And in case of sp hybrid, it is also restricted because of two π bonds. In general, π bonds provide the most reactive centres in the molecules containing multiple bonds.

Structures of organic compounds are represented in several ways. However, the most widely used representation is the one in which the single covalent bond between two atoms is shown by a straight line joining the two atoms. This is called the Lewis structure or dot structure, dash structure or condensed structure. Just as a single dash represents a single bond, a double dash is used for a double bond and a triple dash represents a triple bond. Lone pairs of electrons on heteroatoms (e.g., oxygen, nitrogen, sulphur, halogens, etc.) may or may not be shown. Thus, ethane (C_2H_6), ethene (C_2H_4), ethyne (C_2H_2) and methanol (CH_3OH) can be represented by the following structural formulas.

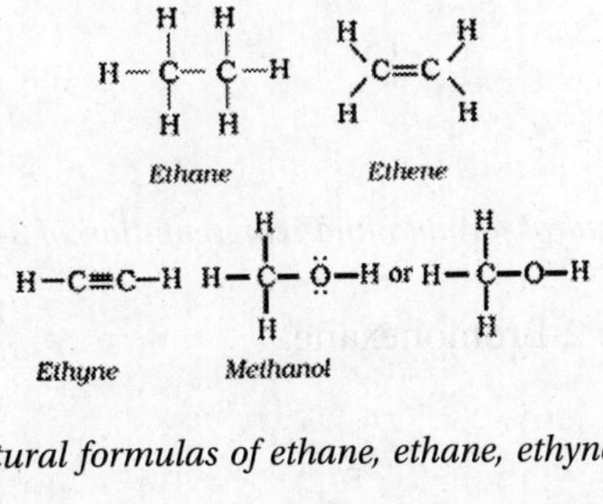

Fig. 16.2: Structural formulas of ethane, ethane, ethyne and methanol

Sometimes quick structures are required to be drawn, in which we generally omit drawing single bonds. Thus the above four compounds in quick shorthand structure can be drawn as:

CH_3CH_3 $H_2C=CH_2$ $HC≡CH$ CH_3OH
Ethane   Ethene   Ethyne   Methanol

Sometimes we use an even shorter and quicker way of writing the formula of an organic compound. For example, the compound $CH_3CH_2CH_2CH_2CH_2CH_2CH_2CH_2CH_2CH_2CH_2CH_2CH_2CH3$ can be written in condensed form as $CH_3(CH_2)_{12}CH_3$.

Another widely adopted way of representing the structures is the representation of bonds (represented by lines—a single line representing a single bond, double and triple lines representing double and triple bonds, respectively). Carbon and hydrogen atoms are not shown and the lines representing carbon-carbon bonds are drawn in a zig zag fashion. Occurrence of atoms like oxygen, sulphur, phosphorous, chlorine, nitrogen, etc. is shown by the use of their symbols in the structural diagram. The terminals denote methyl ($-CH_3$) groups (unless indicated otherwise by a functional group), while the line junctions denote carbon atoms bonded to appropriate number of hydrogens required to satisfy the valency of the carbon atoms. Let us try to illustrate with an example.

3-Methylheptane can be represented in various forms as:

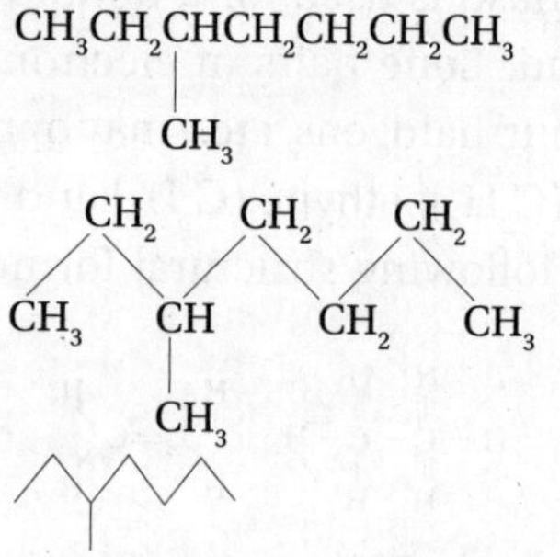

$$CH_3CH_2CHCH_2CH_2CH_2CH_3$$
$$|$$
$$CH_3$$

Fig. 16.3: Structural formula and representation of 3-Methylheptane

Another example is 2-Bromohexane:

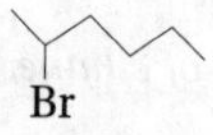

Fig. 16.4: 2-Bromohexame

In case of cyclic compounds, we write it the following way.

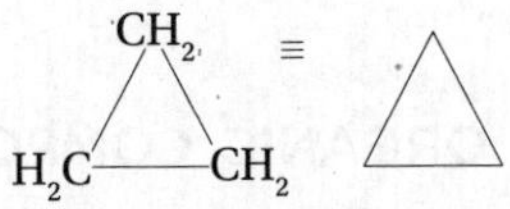

Cyclopropane

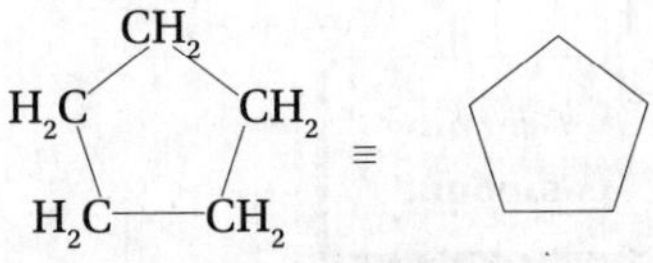

Cyclopentane

Fig. 16.5: Structural representation of cyclic compounds

We have learnt about the tetrahedral structure of sp³ hybridized carbon. In order to understand the three-dimensional shape of an organic compound, their reactions, mechanism for reaction, etc., sometimes three-dimensional structures, are required to be shown. However, it is not easy to show the three-dimensional structure on a two-dimensional paper. Special techniques and certain conventions are therefore adopted for this purpose. For example, by using solid (◤━━◣) and dashed (◖▥▥▥) wedge formula, the 3-D image of a molecule from a two-dimensional picture can be perceived. In these formulas, the solid wedge is used to indicate a bond projecting out of the plane of paper, towards the observer. The dashed wedge is used to depict the bond projecting out of the plane of the paper and away from the observer. The bonds lying in the plane of the paper are depicted by using a normal line (—). Such a 3-D representation of a hypothetical molecule is shown in the figure below.

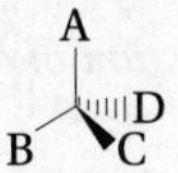

Fig. 16.6: Three-dimensional structure and its representation

Sometimes drawing a three-dimensional structure on a two-dimensional piece of paper is not only cumbersome, but understanding it correctly also becomes difficult. It is with this view that scientists propounded the idea of a projection formula of a compound. Two such projections are very popular and important. These are Fischer projection and Newman projection.

CLASSIFICATION OF ORGANIC COMPOUNDS

Organic compounds are broadly classified as follows:

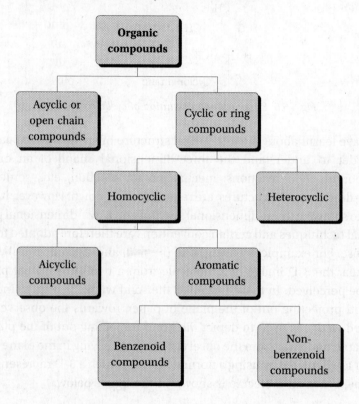

Fig. 16.7: Classification of organic compounds

Acyclic or open chain compounds: These compounds are also called aliphatic compounds. These are either straight or branched chain compounds. Examples of these compounds are methane, ethane, ethyne, methanol, etc.

Cyclic or closed chain or ring compounds: Alicyclic (the word is formed from aliphatic cyclic) compounds contain carbon atoms joined in the form of a ring.

Homocyclic and heterocyclic compounds are the two types of cyclic compounds. Examples of homocyclic compounds: cyclopropane, cyclobutane, cyclohexane, etc. Sometimes atoms other than carbon are also present in the ring. These are called heterocyclic compounds. Example of this type (heterocyclic) of compound is: tetrahydrofuran (contains O as the heteroelement in the ring), pyridine (contains N), thiophene (contains S), etc.

Aromatic compounds are special types of compounds that show aromaticity. These compounds have alternate double and single bonds and are cyclic or have a ring structure. Aromatic compounds include benzene and other related ring compounds (benzenoid). Examples of benzenoid aromatic compounds are: benzene, aniline, benzoic acid, naphthalene, etc. Aromatic compounds may also have hetero atoms in the ring. Examples: furan (contains O), thiophene (contains S), pyridine (contains N), etc. An example of a non-bezenoid aromatic compound is tropolone.

FUNCTIONAL GROUPS

A functional group is an atom or a group of atoms joined in a specific manner giving rise to the characteristic chemical properties of the organic compounds. Examples of a functional group are hydroxyl group (–OH), aldehyde group (–CHO), carboxylic acid group (–COOH), nitro group (–NO_2), amino group (–NH_2), etc.

Organic molecules are often organized by functional groups, which are a characteristic arrangement of atoms that define many of the physical and chemical properties of a class of organic compounds.

- The simplest of the functional groups are the hydrocarbons, which include the alkanes, alkenes, alkynes and aromatic hydrocarbons.
- Many functional groups contain oxygen atoms, such as alcohols, ethers, aldehydes, ketones, carboxylic acids and esters.
- Some other functional groups contain nitrogen atoms, such as the amines and amides.
- Molecules with the same functional group tend to share similar chemical and physical properties.

Some organic compounds and the functional groups they contain are given in the table below:

Class	Functional group	Example of expanded structural formula	Example of condensed structural formula	IUPAC/Common name
Alkane	None	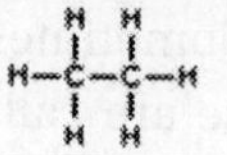 H-C-C-H (with H's)	CH_3CH_3	ethane
Alkene	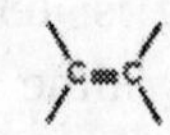 C=C	 H₂C=CH₂ (expanded)	$H_2C = CH_2$	ethene (ethylene)
Alkyne	 —C≡C—	 H—C≡C—H	$HC \equiv CH$	ethyne (acetylene)
Aromatic	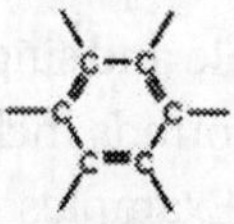 (benzene ring)	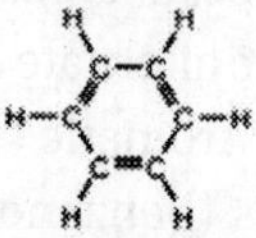 (benzene ring with H)	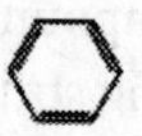 (hexagon)	benzene
Alcohol	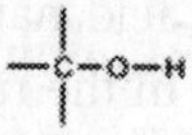 —C—O—H	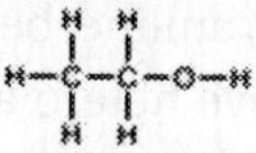 H-C-C-O-H	CH_3CH_2OH	ethyl alcohol
Ether	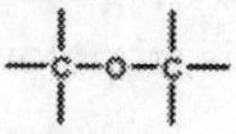 —C—O—C—	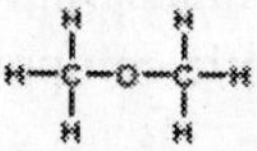 H-C-O-C-H	CH_3OCH_3	methoxymethane (dimethyl ether)
Aldehyde	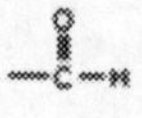 —C=O, H	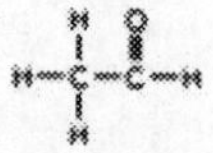 H-C-C=O, H	CH_3CHO	ethanal (acetaldehyde)
Ketone	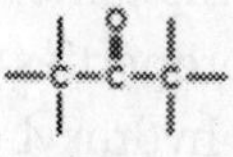 —C—C(=O)—C—	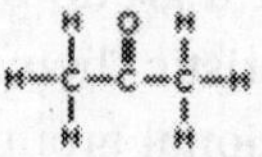 H-C-C(=O)-C-H	CH_3COCH_3	2-propanone (acetone)
Carboxylic acid	 —C(=O)—O—H	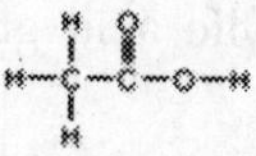 H-C-C(=O)-O-H	CH_3COOH	ethanoic acid (acetic acid)
Ester	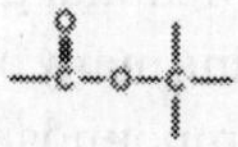 —C(=O)—O—C—	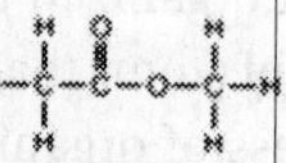 H-C-C(=O)-O-C-H	CH_3COOCH_3	methyl ethanoate (methyl acetate)
Amine	 —N—H	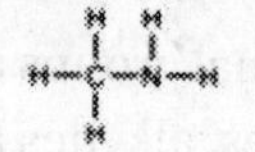 H-C-N-H	CH_3NH_2	metahylamine
Amide	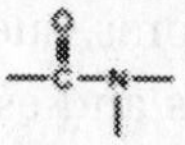 —C(=O)—N—	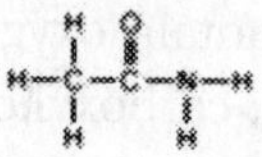 H-C-C(=O)-N-H	CH_3CONH_2	ethanamide (acetamide)

Fig. 16.8: Organic compounds and their functional groups

HOMOLOGOUS SERIES

A series of organic compounds, each containing the characteristic functional group the same as the other, forms a homologous series when the successive members in the series differ from each other in a molecular formula by a $-CH_2$ unit. The members of a homologous series are called homologues. Some of the homologous series commonly known are alkanes, alkenes, alkynes, haloalkanes, alkanols, alkanals, alkanones, alkanoic acids, amines, etc.

IUPAC NOMENCLATURE OF COMMON ORGANIC COMPOUNDS

Fundamental principle: IUPAC nomenclature is based on naming a molecule's longest chain of carbons connected by single bonds, whether in a continuous chain or in a ring. All deviations, either multiple bonds or atoms other than carbon and hydrogen, are indicated by prefixes or suffixes, according to a specific set of priorities.

IUPAC Name of a Compound

The IUPAC name of a compound is made of four parts:

- Prefix
- Word root
- Primary suffix
- Secondary suffix

Prefix

Prefix denotes the substituent group, if any, present in the organic compound. For example, some prefixes are shown in the table below.

Table 16.1: Substituent group present in the organic compound

Substituent group	Prefix
$-F$	fluoro
$-Cl$	chloro
$-Br$	bromo
$-I$	iodo
$-CH_3$	methyl
$-C_2H_5$	ethyl
$-C_3H_7$	propyl
$-NO_2$	nitro

Word root

It indicates the number of carbon atoms in the longest possible chain.

Table 16.2: Number of carbon atom in the longest chain

Number of carbon atoms	Word root	Name of the saturated hydrocarbon
1	meth	methane
2	eth	ethane
3	prop	propane
4	but	butane
5	pent	pentane
6	hex	hexane
7	hept	heptane
8	oct	octane
9	non	nonane
10	de	decane
11	undec	undecane
12	dodec	dodecane

Primary Suffix

Primary suffix denotes the nature of carbon-carbon bond in the organic compounds.

    ane: carbon-carbon single bond
    ene: carbon-carbon double bond
    yne: carbon-carbon triple bond

Secondary Suffix

It represents the functional group if present in an organic molecule and is attached to the primary suffix while writing the IUPAC name.

Table 16.3: Functional compounds

Class of functional compounds	Secondary group	Suffix
Alcohol	–OH	–ol
Aldehydes	–CHO	–al
Ketones	>C=O	–one
Carboxylic acids	–COOH	–oic acid
Esters	–COOR	–ate
Amines	–NH$_2$	–amine

The following basic rule will come in handy for writing the IUPAC name of an aliphatic compound:

IUPAC = prefix (es) + word root + primary suffix + secondary suffix

There are three parts in the name of an organic compound according to the IUPAC nomenclature system. These are: the base part which reflects the number of carbons in the parent chain, the suffix of the name that reflects the type(s) of functional group(s) present on (or within) the parent chain, and other groups called substituents that are attached to the parent chain.

Here are some examples:

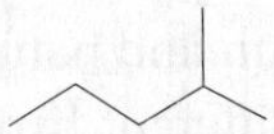

2-methylpentane

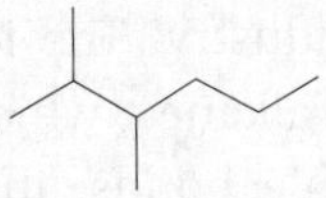

2, 3-dimethylhexane

17

COMMON ORGANIC COMPOUNDS

INTRODUCTION

Organic compounds are an essential part of life. What had earlier been thought about these compounds as of organic origin could be synthesized in the laboratory only later, hence the thin line between organic compounds and inorganic compounds was blurred. Approximately one-third of the compounds produced industrially are organic compounds. All living organisms are composed of organic compounds, as are most foods, medicines, clothing fibres and plastics. The simplest class of organic compounds is the hydrocarbon, which consists entirely of carbon and hydrogen. Petroleum and natural gas are complex, naturally-occurring mixtures of many different hydrocarbons that furnish raw materials for the chemical industry. The four major classes of hydrocarbons are the following: the alkanes, which contain only carbon-hydrogen and carbon-carbon single bonds; the alkenes, which contain at least one carbon-carbon double bond; the alkynes, which contain at least one carbon-carbon triple bond and the aromatic hydrocarbons, which usually contain rings of six carbon atoms that can be drawn with alternating single and double bonds. Other than these hydrocarbons, some other types of common organic compounds are alcohols, carboxylic acids, aldehydes, ketones, ethers, esters, amines, etc. Apart from these compounds, there are polymers that are made up of repeating small units, known as monomers.

In this chapter we will learn about some common organic compounds.

METHANE (CH$_4$)

The simplest alkane is methane (CH$_4$), a colourless, odourless gas that is the major component of natural gas. In larger alkanes whose carbon atoms are joined in an unbranched chain (straight-chain alkanes), each carbon atom is bonded to at the most two other carbon atoms. The names of all alkanes end in -ane, and their boiling points increase as the number of carbon atoms increases.

Methane is a tetrahedral molecule with four equivalent C–H bonds. At room temperature and standard pressure, methane is a colourless, odourless gas. Methane has a boiling point of -164°C at a pressure of 1 atm.

Methods of Preparation of Methane

Catalytic Reduction of Methyl Iodide

$$CH_3\text{-}I + H_2 \rightarrow CH_4 + HI$$

Hydrolysis of Aluminium Carbide

In the laboratory, methane can be prepared by boiling aluminium carbide with water:

$$Al_4C_3 + 12H_2O \rightarrow 3CH_4 + Al(OH)_3$$

Chemical Reactions of Methane

Combustion Reaction

Combustion of methane is an exothermic reaction in which a large amount of energy is liberated. Due to this property, methane is used as a domestic and industrial fuel.

$$CH_4 + 2O_2 \rightarrow CO_2 + 2H_2O$$

Halogenation

Replacement of halogen atom with H-atom of an organic compound is called halogenation. It is a substitution reaction. This reaction occurs in the presence of sunlight. The reaction will continue till the replacement of all four hydrogen atoms of methane with chlorine.

Chlorination

$$CH_4 + Cl_2 \rightarrow CH_3Cl \text{ (chloro methane)} + HCl$$

$CH_3Cl + Cl_2 \rightarrow CH_2Cl_2$ (dichloro methane) + HCl
$CH_2Cl_2 + Cl_2 \rightarrow CHCl_3$ (chloroform) + HCl
$CHCl_3 + Cl_2 \rightarrow CCl_4$ (carbon tetrachloride) + HCl

Uses of Methane

> Domestic and industrial fuel
> Shoe polish
> Printing ink
> Tyre manufacturing
> Manufacture of methyl alcohol

ETHANE (C$_2$H$_6$)

Methods of Preparation

From the Wurtz Reaction

$$2CH_3I + 2Na \rightarrow C_2H_6 + 2NaI$$

From Grignard's Reagent

Ethane may be obtained by the hydrolysis of ethyl magnesium iodide:

$$C_2H_5\text{-}Mg\text{-}I + H\text{-}OH \rightarrow C_2H_6 + Mg\text{-}OH\text{-}I$$

Catalytic Reduction of Ethyl Iodide

$$C_2H_5\text{-}I + H_2 \rightarrow C_2H_6 + HI$$

Chemical Reactions of Ethane

Combustion Reaction

Ethane burns in air or oxygen with a non-luminous flame to produce carbon dioxide and water. It is an exothermic reaction:

$$2C_2H_6 + 7O_2 \rightarrow 4CO_2 + 6H_2O + heat$$

Halogenation

Replacement of halogen with H-atom of an organic compound is called halogenation. It is a substitution reaction.

Chlorination

$C_2H_6 + Cl_2 \rightarrow C_2H_5Cl$
$C_2H_5Cl + Cl_2 \rightarrow C_2H_4Cl_2$

ETHENE (C_2H_4)

Bond Length:
C=C bond length 1.34Å
C-H bond length 1.09Å

Methods of Preparation

From Vicinal Dihalide

When vicinal dihalide (halogen atoms in the adjacent carbon atoms) is heated with zinc dust, two halide atoms are removed from the compound and ethene is formed.

$$CH_2Cl\text{-}CH_2Cl + Zn \rightarrow CH_2{=}CH_2 + ZnCl_2$$

Reduction of Ethyne

Under control conditions ethyne adds two H-atoms to form ethene in the presence of Nickel (Ni) at 200°C.

$$C_2H_2 + H_2 \rightarrow H_2C{=}CH_2$$

Dehydrohalogenation of Alkyl Halide

When alkyl halide (ethyl chloride) is treated with alcoholic KOH, ethane is obtained.

$$CH_3\text{-}CH_2Cl + KOH \text{ (alc)} \rightarrow CH_2{=}CH_2 + KCl + H_2O$$

Dehydration of Alcohol

When ethyl alcohol is heated with concentreated $H2SO_4$ at 170°C, dehydration of alcohol takes place and ethene is formed.

$$C_2H_5OH \rightarrow C_2H_4 + H_2O$$

Ethyl alcohol may also be converted into ethene by passing vapours of ethyl alcohol over a catalyst ($Al_2O_3, H_3PO_4/Al_2O_3$).

$$C_2H_5OH \rightarrow C_2H_4 + H_2O$$

Chemical Reactions of Ethene

Addition Reactions of Ethene

Addition of chlorine:

$$CH_2{=}CH_2 + Cl_2 \rightarrow CH_2Cl\text{-}CH_2Cl \text{ (1,2-dichloroethane)}$$

Addition of bromine:

$$CH_2=CH_2 + Br_2 \rightarrow CH_2Br\text{-}CH_2Br \text{ (1,2-dibromoethane)}$$

Addition of iodine:

$$CH_2= CH_2 + I_2 \rightarrow CH_2I\text{-}CH_2I \text{ (1,2-diiodoethane)}$$

Order of reactivity:

$$Cl_2 > Br_2 > I_2$$

Addition of hydrogen:

$$CH_2 = CH_2 + H_2 \rightarrow CH_3\text{-}CH_3$$

Addition of H$_2$SO$_4$:

$$CH_2 = CH_2 + H_2SO_4 \rightarrow CH_3\text{-}CH_2HSO_4$$

Addition of H$_2$O:

$$CH_2 = CH_2 + HOH \rightarrow CH_3\text{-}CH_2OH$$

Addition of HCl:

$$CH_2= CH_2 + HCl \rightarrow CH_3\text{-}CH_2Cl$$

Addition of HBr:

$$CH_2= CH_2 + HBr \rightarrow CH_3\text{-}CH_2Br$$

Addition of HI:

$$CH_2= CH_2 + HI \rightarrow CH_3\text{-}CH_2I$$

Combustion Reaction:

$$CH_2= CH_2 + 3O_2 \rightarrow 2CO_2 + 2H_2O$$

Oxidation Reaction

When ethene is treated with acidified $KMnO_4$ solution, purple colour of $KMnO_4$ disappears due to formation of colourless ethylene glycol.

$$CH_2 = CH_2 + H_2O + [O] \rightarrow HOCH_2\text{-}CH_2OH$$

Polymerization

$$n(CH2=CH2) \rightarrow n(\text{-}CH2\text{-}CH2\text{-})$$

ETHYNE OR ACETYLENE (C_2H_2)

Bond Length:

The C-H bond length is 1.09Å and the C-C one is 1.2Å

Bond Angle:

H-C-C bond angle one is 180°

Methods of Preparation

Hydrolysis of Calcium Carbide

$$CaC_2 + 2H_2O \rightarrow C_2H_2 + Ca(OH)_2$$

From tetra chloroethane:

$$Cl_2CH\text{-}CHCl_2 + 2Zn \rightarrow C_2H_2 + 2ZnCl_2$$

HBr elimination from 1,2-dibromoethane:

$$Br\text{-}CH_2\text{-}CH_2\text{-}Br + KOH \text{ (alc)} \rightarrow C_2H_2 + 2KBr + 2H_2O$$

Chemical Reactions of Ethyne

Combustion Reaction

$$2C_2H_2 + 5O_2 \rightarrow 4CO_2 + 2H_2O + heat$$

Addition Reactions

Addition of hydrogen:

$$C_2H_2 + H_2 \rightarrow CH_2=CH_2$$
$$CH_2=CH_2 + H_2 \rightarrow C_2H_6$$

Addition of halogen:

$$C_2H_2 + Cl_2 \rightarrow Cl\text{-}CH=CH\text{-}Cl$$
$$Cl\text{-}CH=CH\text{-}Cl + Cl_2 \rightarrow Cl_2CH\text{-}CHCl_2$$

Addition of hydrogen halide:

$$C_2H_2 + HBr \rightarrow CH_2=CH\text{-}Br$$
$$CH_2=CH\text{-}Br + HBr \rightarrow CH_3\text{-}CHBr_2$$

Addition of HCN:

$$C_2H_2 + HCN \rightarrow CN\text{-}CH=CH_2$$

Addition of water:

$$C_2H_2 + HOH \rightarrow CH_2=CH\text{-}OH \rightarrow \text{(After rearrangement) } CH_3CHO \text{ (ethanal)}$$

Oxidation of Ethyne

In Cold Solution

$$C_2H_2 + HOH + 3[O] \rightarrow 2HCOOH \text{ (Formic acid)}$$

In Hot Solution

$$C_2H_2 + 4[O] \rightarrow (COOH)2 \text{ (Oxalic acid)}$$

METHANOL (CH_3OH)

Industrial Preparation of Methanol

Methanol is prepared from a mixture of carbon monoxide and hydrogen. The gaseous mixture at a pressure of 200 atm is passed over a heated catalyst mixture of ZnO and Cr_2O_3 kept at 400°C to 450°C. This reaction results in the formation of methanol vapours that are then condensed to the liquid state.

$$CO + 2H_2 \rightarrow CH_3OH$$

Physical Properties of Methanol

1. It is a colourless liquid.
2. It is highly volatile and less viscous.
3. Its boiling point is 64°C.
4. It is a poisonous liquid.
5. It is miscible in water.

Chemical Reactions of Methanol

Ester Formation

$$CH3\text{-}OH + CH3COOH \rightarrow CH_3\text{-}CO\text{-}O\text{-}CH_3 + H_2O$$

Reaction with halogen acid (in the presence of $ZnCl_2$):

$$CH_3\text{-}OH + HCl \rightarrow CH_3\text{-}Cl + H_2O$$

Oxidation

In the presence of potassium dichromate ($K_2Cr_2O_7$) in acidic medium, on heating, methanol is oxidized to formaldehyde.

$$CH_3\text{-}OH + [O] \rightarrow HCHO + H_2O$$

FORMIC ACID OR METHANOIC ACID (HCOOH)

Formic acid, whose IUPAC name is methanoic acid, is the simplest carboxylic acid. It is found in the body of some insects and ants. The word 'formic' comes from the Latin word for ant, formica, referring to its early detection and isolation by the distillation of ant bodies.

Methods of Preparation of Formic Acid

When methanol and carbon monoxide are combined in the presence of a strong base and heated at 80°C under 40 atm pressure, methyl formate is formed.

$$CH_3OH + CO \rightarrow HCOOCH_3$$

Hydrolysis of the methyl formate produces formic acid:

$$HCOOCH_3 + H_2O \rightarrow HCOOH + CH_3OH$$

Sometimes methyl formate is heated with ammonia to give formamide, which is then hydrolyzed with sulfuric acid:

$$HCOOCH_3 + NH_3 \rightarrow HCONH_2 + CH_3OH$$
$$2\ HCONH_2 + 2H_2O + H_2SO_4 \rightarrow 2HCOOH + (NH_4)_2SO_4$$

Hydrogenation of Carbon Dioxide

Catalytic hydrogenation of CO_2 to formic acid is another way of producing formic acid.

$$CO_2 + H_2 \rightarrow HCOOH$$

Laboratory method:

In the laboratory, formic acid is obtained by heating oxalic acid in glycerol and extraction by steam distillation. Glycerol acts as a catalyst, as the reaction proceeds through a glyceryl oxalate intermediary. If the reaction mixture is heated to higher temperatures, allyl alcohol is formed.

$$(COOH)_2 \rightarrow HCOOH + CO_2$$

Chemical Reactions of Formic Acid

Decomposition

Heat and especially acids cause formic acid to decompose to carbon monoxide (CO) and water (dehydration). Treatment of formic acid with sulfuric acid is a convenient laboratory source of CO.

$$HCOOH \rightarrow CO + H_2O$$

In the presence of platinum, formic acid, however, decomposes to form hydrogen and carbon dioxide.

$$HCOOH \rightarrow H_2 + CO_2$$

Esterification

Formic acid reacts with alcohol to form ester. The reaction can take place even in the absence of any inorganic acid.

$$HCOOH + R\text{-}OH \rightarrow HCOOR + H_2O$$

Addition to Alkenes

Formic acid is unique among the carboxylic acids in its ability to participate in additional reactions with alkenes. Formic acids and alkenes readily react to form formate esters. The reaction takes place in accordance with Markovnikov's rule.

$$HCOOH + C_2H_4 \rightarrow H_3C\text{-}CH_2\text{-}OCOH$$

In the presence of certain acids, including sulfuric and hydrofluoric acids, however, a variant of the Koch reaction occurs instead, and formic acid adds to the alkene to produce a larger carboxylic acid.

ACETIC ACID OR ETHANOIC ACID (CH_3COOH)

Acetic acid is the next higher carboxylic acid after formic acid which has a single carboxylic acid functional group.

Methods of Preparation of Acetic Acid

Carbonylation of Methanol

Most acetic acid is produced by carbonylation of methanol. In this process, methanol and carbon monoxide react to produce acetic acid.

$$CH_3OH + CO \rightarrow CH_3COOH$$

HI acts as a catalyst in this reaction.

$$CH_3OH + HI \rightarrow CH_3I + H_2O$$
$$CH_3I + CO \rightarrow CH_3COI$$
$$CH_3COI + H_2O \rightarrow CH_3COOH + HI$$

Acetaldehyde Oxidation

Acetic acid can be produced by oxidation of acetaldehyde.

CHEMISTRY

$$2CH_3CHO + O_2 \rightarrow 2CH_3COOH$$

Acidified potassium dichromate is a good agent for this reaction.

Ethylene Oxidation

Acetaldehyde may be prepared from ethylene by oxidizing it.

$$C_2H_4 + O_2 \rightarrow CH_3COOH$$

Oxidative Fermentation or Aerobic Fermentation

Ethyl alcohol can be fermented by acetic acid bacteria of the genus Acetobacter, in the form of vinegar. Commonly used feedstock for ethyl alcohol include apple cider, wine and fermented grain, malt, rice or mashed potatoes.

$$C_2H_5OH + O_2 \rightarrow CH_3COOH + H_2O$$

Anaerobic Fermentation

Species of anaerobic bacteria, including members of the genus Clostridium or Acetobacterium, can convert sugars to acetic acid directly. No intermediate product is formed in this case.

$$C_6H_{12}O_6 \rightarrow 3\ CH_3COOH$$

Chemical Reactions of Acetic Acid

Esterification Reaction

When carboxylic acid and alcohol react, the product formed is known as an ester. When acetic acid reacts with ethanol in the presence of a trace amount of acid, ethyl acetate is formed.

$$CH_3COOH + CH_3CH_2OH \rightarrow CH_3COOCH_2CH_3$$

Reaction with a Base

Ethanoic acid reacts with a base to give salt and water, just like other mineral acids.

Reaction with Carbonates and Hydrogen Carbonates

Carbon dioxide, salt and water are produced when ethanoic acid reacts with carbonates and hydrogen carbonates. Sodium acetate is usually produced as a salt when ethanoic acid reacts with sodium bicarbonate.

$$CH_3COOH + NaHCO_3 \rightarrow CH_3COONa + H_2O + CO_2$$

18

BIOMOLECULES

INTRODUCTION

Biochemistry is that branch of chemistry which deals with the study of chemical processes taking place in living organisms. Chemical compounds that are involved in biochemical processes are called biomolecules. Some of the examples of biomolecules are carbohydrates, proteins, lipids, vitamins, enzymes, hormones, etc. Although the subject of biochemistry and biomolecules is very vast, our attention will be to the latter, that too, the study of food chemistry. Although the six essential nutrients are carbohydrates, proteins, fats, vitamins, minerals and water, we will confine ourselves to the study of the first three components, and the last two are essentially inorganic in nature.

CARBOHYDRATES

Carbohydrates are an important class of naturally-occurring organic compounds constituting one of the main components of our food. Carbohydrates can be defined as the polyhydroxy aldehydes or polyhydroxy ketones or the compounds which, on hydrolysis, can produce such compounds. Most of them have a general formula, $C_x(H_2O)_y$, and were considered hydrates of carbon from where the name carbohydrate was derived. Glucose ($C_6H_{12}O_6$), fructose ($C_6H_{12}O_6$), sucrose ($C_{12}H_{22}O_{11}$), galactose, starch, cellulose, etc. are examples of carbohydrates.

Classification of Carbohydrates

According to Taste

On the basis of taste, carbohydrates can be divided into two categories:

1. **Sugars**: Carbohydrates which are sweet in taste are known as sugars. They are water-soluble. Glucose, sucrose and fructose are examples of sugars.

There are two classes of sugars.

Reducing sugars: The sugars that can reduce Tollen's Reagent and Fehling's Solution are known as reducing sugars. They contain free aldehyde (-CHO) or ketone (=CO) group along with hydroxyl (-OH) group on the carbon adjacent to these groups. All monosaccharides such as glucose, fructose and all oligosaccharides except sucrose are examples of reducing sugars.

Non-reducing sugars: Sugars that do not reduce Tollen's Reagent and Fehling's Solution are known as non-reducing sugars. They do not contain free aldehyde or ketone group with adjacent hydroxyl group. Sucrose and all polysaccharides are examples of non-reducing sugars.

2. **Non-sugar**: Carbohydrates which are tasteless are known as non-sugars. They are insoluble in water. Examples are starch, cellulose, etc.

Classification of Carbohydrates According to Molecular Structure

According to the number of C-atoms or the number of simple sugar units present in the molecule, carbohydrates are divided into three major classes:

- Monosaccharides
- Oligosaccharides
- Polysaccharides

Monosaccharides

Carbohydrates that cannot be divided into simpler carbohydrate units by hydrolysis are known as monosaccharides. Generally they contain 3 to 10 carbon atoms. Monosaccharides containing aldehyde group are called aldoses and those containing ketone group are called ketoses.

Oligosaccharides

Carbohydrates that, on hydrolysis, produce 2 to 10 monosaccharide units are known as oligosaccharide. Example: sucrose, maltose, lactose.

Polysaccharides

Carbohydrates that produce more than 10 monosaccharide units on hydrolysis are known as polysaccharide. Example: glycogen, starch, amylase, amylopectin, cellulose.

Types of polysaccharides: According to their origin, polysaccharides are divided into two classes.

1. Animal polysaccharides: found in animals; for example, glycogen (stored in muscles and liver)
2. Plant polysaccharides: found in plants; for example, starch, cellulose

GLUCOSE

Glucose occurs freely in nature as well as in combined form. It is present in sweet fruits and honey. Ripe grapes also contain glucose in large amounts.

Preparation of Glucose

1. From sucrose (cane sugar): If sucrose is boiled with dilute HCl or H_2SO_4 in an alcoholic solution, sucrose hydrolyses into glucose and fructose.

$$C_{12}H_{22}O_{11} + H_2O \rightarrow C_6H_{12}O_6 + C_6H_{12}O_6$$

2. From starch: Commercially glucose is obtained by hydrolysis of starch by boiling it with dilute H_2SO_4 at 393 K under pressure.

$$(C_6H_{10}O_5)_n + nH_2O \rightarrow nC_6H_{12}O_6$$

Reactions of Glucose

a) With HI/P it undergoes reduction to form n-hexane while with sodium amalgam it forms sorbitol:

$$C_6H_{12}O_6 + HI/P \rightarrow CH_3\text{-}(CH_2)_4\text{-}CH_3$$
$$C_6H_{12}O_6 + Na/Hg \rightarrow CH_2OH\text{-}(CHOH)_4\text{-}CH_2OH$$

b) With hydroxylamine (NH_2OH), it forms glucose oxime:

$$C_6H_{12}O_6 + NH_2OH \rightarrow HC\text{=}NOH\text{-}(CHOH)_4\text{-}CH_2OH$$

c) With HCN, it forms an additional product, cyanohydrin:

$$C_6H_{12}O_6 + HCN \rightarrow NC\text{-}(CHOH)_5\text{-}CH_2OH$$

d) With Tollen's reagent and Fehling's solution, glucose forms silver mirror and red precipitate of Cu_2O respectively.

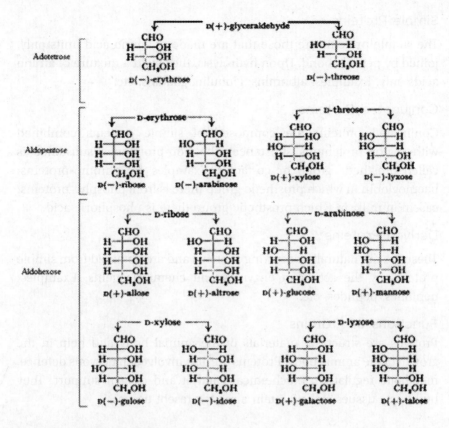

Fig. 18.1: Structure of carbohydrates

PROTEINS

Proteins are one of the most important constituents in our body. They are primary constituents of our body parts such as muscles, skin, hair and nails. In addition to that, proteins carry out all vital life processes in the human system. The simplest form of proteins is amino acid.

Classification of Proteins

Proteins are divided into three main classes:

1. Simple proteins
2. Conjugated proteins
3. Derived proteins

Simple Proteins

The simple proteins are those that are made of amino acid units only, joined by peptide bond. Upon hydrolysis, they yield a mixture of amino acids only. Examples: albumins, globulin, gliadins, etc.

Conjugated Proteins

Conjugated proteins are composed of simple proteins combined with a non-proteinous substance. The non-proteinous substance is called prosthetic group or co-factor. Examples are chromo-proteins: haemoglobin in which prosthetic group there is iron; phospho-proteins: casein in milk, in which prosthetic group there is phosphoric acid.

Derived Proteins

These are not naturally-occurring proteins and are obtained from simple proteins by the action of enzymes and chemical agents. Examples: peptones, peptides, etc.

Functions of Proteins

Proteins are structural materials of the animal body and help in the growth of the animal body. Proteins are also involved in nervous defence, metabolic regulation, biochemical catalyst and oxygen support. They build new tissues and maintain already-present tissues.

AMINO ACIDS

Amino acids are compounds containing both carboxylic acid group (-COOH) and basic amino group (-NH2). Hence the name amino acid. They are building blocks of proteins. They are linked together by a peptide bond.

$$\overset{\displaystyle H}{\underset{\displaystyle NH_2}{R-C-COOH}}$$

Amino acid

The peptide bond is formed between two amino acid molecules when the amino group of one amino acid is linked with the carboxylic group to the other amino acid molecule by the elimination of a water molecule.

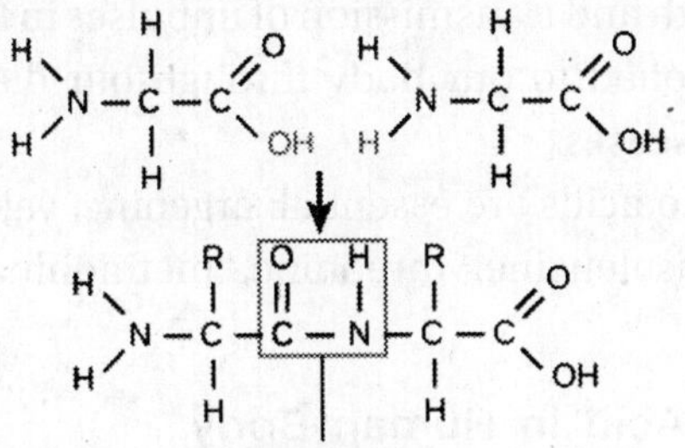

Peptide Bond

Fig. 18.2: Peptide bond

Types of Amino Acids

According to Structure

According to molecular structure, amino acids can be divided into three classes:

Alpha-Amino Acid: Amino acids having ($-NH_2$) group attached to the alpha carbon atom are called α-Amino acids.

$$NH_2-\overset{\alpha}{C}H-COOH$$
$$\underset{CH_2}{|}$$

α-Amino acid

Beta-Amino Acid: Amino acids having (-NH2) group attached to the beta carbon atom are called β-Amino acids.

$$NH_2-\overset{\beta}{C}H_2-\overset{\alpha}{C}H_2-COOH$$

β-Amino acid

Gamma-Amino Acid: Amino acids having (-NH2) group attached to the gamma carbon atom are called γ-Amino acids.

$$NH_2-\overset{\gamma}{C}H_2-\overset{\beta}{C}H_2-\overset{\alpha}{C}H_2-COOH$$

γ-Amino acid

Essential Amino Acids

Amino acids that cannot be synthesized by our body but are needed for normal functioning are known as essential amino acids. They are necessary for growth and transmission of impulses in the nervous system. They must be supplied to our body through our diet. Their deficiency results in many diseases.

About 10 amino acids are essential: argenine, valine, lysine, phenyl-alanine, leucine, isoleucine, threonine, methionine, tryptophan and histadine.

Role of Amino Acid in Human Body

> Amino acids have a very vital role in our body. When we eat protein-rich food, many enzymes act on protein and hydrolyze it into amino acids. The blood receives it by absorption through the walls of the intestine and carries them to cells where one of the following reactions takes place.
> The amino acid may be converted into body protein.
> Oxidation may take place to provide energy.
> If our diet is low in carbohydrates or fats, body proteins may be transformed into either of these or used to make hormones and other requirements.

LIPIDS

Lipids are organic compounds that are soluble in non-polar solvents. Non-polar solvents are typically hydrocarbons. The main biological functions of lipids include storing energy, signalling and acting as structural components of cell membranes.

Types of Lipids
There are three classes of lipids:

1. Simple lipids
2. Compound lipids
3. Steroids

Simple Lipids

Naturally occurring oils, fats and waxes are collectively known as simple lipids. Simple lipids are the esters of long-chain fatty acids with alcohols.

Fats and oils
Natural fats and oils are the esters of glycerol with long- chain carboxylic

acid (12 to 20 carbon atoms). These are known as triglycerides or triacylglycerols.

Waxes

They are chemically inert for they do not have double bonds in their hydrocarbon chains and are highly insoluble in water. Plant wax occurs in the cuticle on the leaf surface.

Fatty Acids

Fatty acids are carboxylic acids (or organic acid), often with long aliphatic tails (long chains), either saturated or unsaturated.

(a) Saturated

(b) Unsaturated

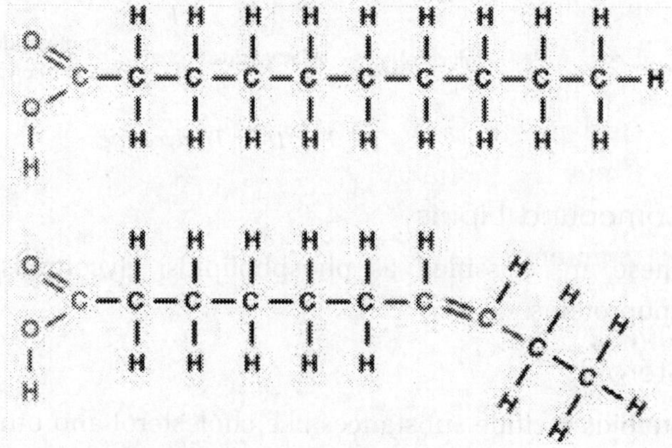

Fig. 18.3: Saturated and unsaturated fatty acids

SATURATED FATTY ACIDS

When a fatty acid is saturated, it is an indication that there are no carbon-carbon double bonds. The saturated acids have higher melting points than unsaturated acids of the corresponding size.

UNSATURATED FATTY ACIDS

If a fatty acid has at least one carbon-carbon double bond then this is an indication that it is an unsaturated fatty acid. Saturated fatty acids have higher melting points due to their ability to pack their molecules together, thus leading to a straight rod-like shape. Unsaturated fatty acids, on the other hand, have cis-double bonds that create a kink in their structure which doesn't allow them to group their molecules in a straight rod-like shape.

Triglyceride

In mammals, triglycerides are found in the cytoplasm of adipose cells which are specialized for the synthesis and storage of triglycerides. Animal triglycerides contain a higher proportion of long-chained saturated fatty acids.

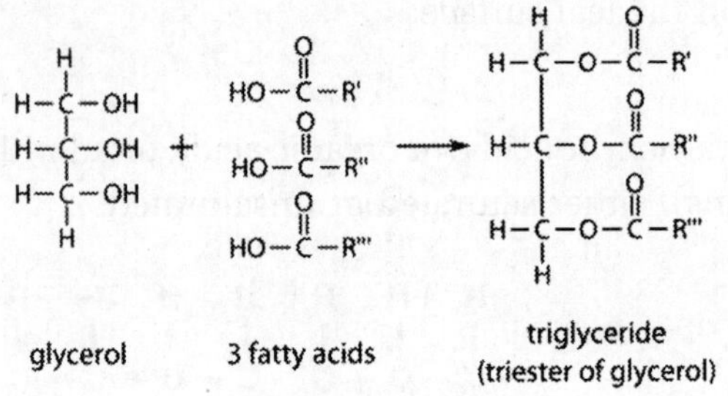

glycerol   3 fatty acids   triglyceride (triester of glycerol)

Fig. 18.4: Triglyceride

Compound Lipids

These are classified as phospholipids, glycolipids, gangliosides and lipoproteins.

Steroids

Steroids include substances like cholesterol and other sterols.

Cholesterol

Cholesterol is an important lipid found in the cell membrane. It is a sterol, which means that cholesterol is a combination of a steroid and an alcohol. It is an important component of cell membranes and is also the basis for the synthesis of other steroids, including the sex hormones estradiol and testosterone, as well as other steroids such as cortisone and vitamin D. In the cell membrane, the steroid ring structure of cholesterol provides a rigid hydrophobic structure that helps boost the rigidity of the cell membrane. Without cholesterol, the cell membrane would be too fluid. In the human body, cholesterol is synthesized in the liver.

SECTION III

BIOLOGY

1

DIVERSITY IN THE LIVING WORLD

INTRODUCTION

The branch of science in which we study about life and living processes is known as biology (bios – living, logos – study). Biological sciences is an exciting and rapidly developing subject. From the study of living things, biology has undergone tremendous expansion in recent years. Many new areas of study and research within biology have emerged, and it is ever-expanding its boundary. Some of these topics are cell biology, neuroscience, evolutionary biology and ecology. On the other hand, biology is blurring its boundary to interface and partially merge with other disciplines, giving rise to new areas of study, such as biophysics, biochemistry, biotechnology, etc. In this chapter we will learn about diversity that exists in the living world.

THE LIVING WORLD

A huge variety of living creatures can be seen on this planet. Their systematic study requires classifying and categorizing them into different groups, depending on their similarities and dissimilarities. Living organisms show a great biodiversity and are classified into different kingdoms—monera, protista, fungi, plantae and animalia.

CHARACTERISTICS OF LIVING ORGANISMS

While it is not easy to define life or to pinpoint a set of characteristics to enable or help one to identify whether a certain thing is living or non-living, scientists have nevertheless been able to come to a consensus about a set of characteristics that define living organisms. These are the following:

- Living things are made of cells
- Living things produce, obtain and use energy
- Living things grow and develop
- Living things reproduce
- Living things respond to their surrounding environment and stimuli
- Living things adapt to their environment

CLASSIFICATION OF LIVING THINGS

All living organisms are classified into groups based on very basic, shared characteristics. From very broad-level similarities to the most detailed similarities, organisms are put into further smaller groups within a bigger group. This specialized grouping system is called the classification of living things. The classification of living things includes seven levels: kingdom, phylum, classes, order, families, genus and species.

Kingdom is the most basic classification of living things. Currently there are five kingdoms.

The **phylum** is the next level following kingdom in the classification of living things. It is an attempt to find some kind of physical similarities among organisms within a kingdom.

Classes are the next level, a way to further divide organisms of a phylum.

Organisms in each class are further broken down into **orders**.

Orders are divided into **families**. Organisms within a family have more in common than with organisms in any classification level above it.

Genus is the sixth level in the classification of living things. It constitutes one of the parts in the taxonomy to describe the generic name for an organism.

Species are at the lowest level in the classification system. Thus the species gives the most detailed information about an organism. The species of an organism determines the second part of its two-part name. A species is therefore the unit of classification.

BINOMIAL SYSTEM OF NOMENCLATURE

Scientists throughout the world use the binomial nomenclature system. In this system two words are used to name an organism. The first of these two words is what represents its generic name and the second one is the specific name. Scientific names consist of two terms—the genus name, followed by the species name. The genus name always starts with an uppercase letter and the species name always starts with a lowercase letter. This process of naming organisms scientifically is known as **taxonomy**, first developed by a Swedish scientist, Carl Linnaeus.

THE FIVE KINGDOMS

Scientists have developed kingdoms to categorize all living things. Kingdoms, being the topmost classification level, give the broadest similar characteristics. It essentially means these divisions are based on what living things have in common and how they differ. There are five kingdoms in which all living things are divided: kingdom monera, kingdom protista, kingdom fungi, kingdom plantae and kingdom animalia.

Kingdom Monera: Kingdom monera consists of organisms that are made up of one cell. These organisms are called unicellular. These unicellular organisms are made of a very simple cell that often lacks many cell parts, such as a nucleus, that are commonly found in other cells. Bacteria are a type of monera.

Kingdom Protista: Kingdom protista is unicellular and hence is similar to monera in that respect. However, in protista, the nucleus is also present. They also have moving parts and can move around within their environment.

Kingdom Fungi: Fungi are eukaryotic in nature. Fungi cannot make their own food. Mushrooms are a type of fungi.

Kingdom Plantae: The kingdom plantae or plant kingdom has all the plants in its scope. They all share the common characteristic of being able to make their own food using water and sunlight.

Kingdom Animalia: Organisms in the animal kingdom (kingdom animalia) are multicellular and rely on other organisms for food. This kingdom is by far the largest of all the kingdoms.

KINGDOM MONERA

Characteristics

> Organisms in this kingdom are unicellular, primitive and prokaryotic.
> They are present and can survive in both living and non-living environment—in harsh and extreme climatic conditions—like in hot springs, acidic soils, the seabed, etc.
> There is no membrane-bound nucleus.
> A rigid cell wall is present.
> They are found everywhere.
> They are autotrophs, which means they can prepare their own food; they can be heterotrophs also, which means they depend on others for food; they are saprophytes, meaning they feed on dead and decaying matter; they are parasitic, that is, they live on other host cells for survival and they are symbiotic, that is, they are in mutual relations with other organisms.
> Circulation takes place through diffusion.
> Movement takes place with the help of flagella.
> Reproduction is mostly asexual; however, sexual reproduction is also found. Asexual reproduction occurs by binary fission, whereas sexual reproduction occurs by conjugation, transformation and transduction.

Bacteria are examples of animals in kingdom monera.

Bacteria

Bacteria (singular bacterium) which belong to kingdom monera constitute a large domain of prokaryotic organisms. Typically a few micrometres in length, bacteria have a number of shapes, ranging from spheres to rods and spirals. Bacteria were among the first life forms to appear on Earth, and are present in most of its habitats. Bacteria inhabit soil, water, acidic hot springs, radioactive waste and the deep portions of Earth's crust.

Shape of Bacteria

Bacteria are found in a variety of shapes. Some are spherical—called cocci (singular coccus); some are rod-shaped—called bacilli (singular bacillus); some bacteria are shaped like slightly curved rods or are comma-shaped—called vibrio; some are spiral-shaped—called spirilla; some are tightly coiled—called spirochaetes; a small number of other unusual shapes have also been found, such as star-shaped bacteria.

Characteristics of bacteria

> Bacteria don't have a nucleus.
> They lack membrane-bound organelles, such as mitochondria or chloroplasts.
> Bacterial DNA is contained in one circular chromosome, located in the cytoplasm. Eukaryotes have several linear chromosomes.
> Bacteria also have two additional unique features: a cell wall and flagella. Flagella are tail-like structures. Flagella help bacteria move. Some bacteria also have a capsule outside the cell wall.
> Bacteria are autotrophic and heterotrophic.

Beneficial bacteria

> Although bacteria are often known as the cause of human and animal disease, certain bacteria, the actinomycetes, produce antibiotics such as streptomycin and nocardicin.
> Some other bacteria live symbiotically in the guts of animals (including humans) or elsewhere in their bodies.
> There are some bacteria residing in the roots of certain plants, converting nitrogen into a usable form.
> Bacteria are responsible for the tang in yogurt.
> Bacteria make the bread dough.
> Bacteria help to break down dead organic matter.
> Bacteria make up the base of the food web in many environments.

KINGDOM PROTISTA

Characteristics
> Organisms of kingdom protista are eukaryotic in nature; they have a membrane-bound nucleus and endomembrane systems.

- Most of the organisms are unicellular; some are colonial and some are multicellular, like algae.
- They have mitochondria for cellular respiration and some have chloroplasts for photosynthesis.
- The nuclei of protista contain multiple DNA strands; the number of nucleotides is significantly less than complex eukaryotes.
- They mostly live in water; some in moist soil; some even in human body and plants.
- Movement is often by flagella or cilia.
- Cellular respiration is primarily aerobic, but some living in the mud below ponds or in the digestive tracts of animals are anaerobes.
- They are found as either heterotrophic or autotrophic.
- Some species have a complex life cycle, involving multiple organisms; example: plasmodium; some reproduce sexually and others asexually.
- They form cysts in adverse conditions.
- Some protista are pathogens of both animals and plants; example: plasmodium falciparum causes malaria in humans.

KINGDOM FUNGI

Characteristics
- Fungi are eukaryotic organisms that reproduce by means of spores.
- Depending on the species and conditions, both sexual and asexual spores may be produced.
- The vegetative body of the fungi may be unicellular or composed of microscopic threads called hyphae.
- The fungi cell wall is composed of chitin.
- Fungi are heterotrophic organisms.
- Fungi store their food as starch.

KINGDOM PLANTAE

The kingdom plantae can be defined as multicellular, autotrophic, eukaryotes, which can carry out photosynthesis. All members of this kingdom possess a true nucleus and advanced membrane-bound organelles. This kingdom is very important not only because plants are the source of food for all other living creatures present on Earth, but also for their contribution to save the animal kingdom by providing a balance to atmospheric oxygen.

Characteristics
> Most of the plants are eukaryotic.
> They are organisms that contain chlorophyll.
> Cell walls are made of cellulose.
> Cells grow by cell division.
> Plants have both organs and organ systems.
> They carry out photosynthesis using solar energy.
> Reproduction is both sexual and asexual.

Classification of Kingdom Plantae
The plant kingdom is further classified as shown below.

Sub-kingdom Cryptogamae
These are plants that do not bear flowers or seeds. They form three divisions.

Thallophyta
> The plant body is not differentiated into stem, root and leaves but is in the form of an undivided thallus.
> Vascular tissues are absent.
> The reproductive organs are single-celled and there is no embryo formation after fertilization.

This division includes three sub-divisions: algae, fungi and lichens.

ALGAE
Algae (singular alga) are mostly aquatic photosynthetic organisms. These organisms can thrive in freshwater lakes or in saltwater oceans. They can also endure a range of temperatures, oxygen or carbon dioxide concentrations, acidity and turbidity. Algae are also able to survive on land. Some unexpected places where they grow are tree trunks, animal fur, snow banks, hot springs and the soil, including desert crusts. Depending on their photosynthetic pigments, algae are further classified as red, green and brown algae. Algae are capable of reproducing through asexual or vegetative methods and via sexual reproduction. Examples: spirogyra,

volvox, eurodivia, ulothrix, cladophora, ulva and chlamydomonas.

Bryophyta

Bryophyta are non-vascular land plants. The only prime feature of a bryophyte is that it does not have a true vascular tissue. Moss and liverwort belong to this variety of plants. These are the simplest forms of land plants. The plant body is flat and lacks true leaves and roots. The upper surface of the plant body produces a stalk which bears a capsule. The capsule contains spores.

- Plants in this category do not have roots but have crude stems and leaves.
- They have 'rhizoids' instead of roots that help the plant to anchor.
- These roots or rhizoids do not absorb nutrients like other usual plant roots.
- Mosses release spores from their leaves that travel by water and make new mosses in new locations.
- Water is very essential for mosses to grow and spread. They can entirely dry out and survive when there is no water. When in contact with water, they again revive and continue growing.
- Bryophytes have life cycles like all land plants (embryophytes) with alternation of generations.

Pteridophyta

Pteridophytes are vascular plants that reproduce and disperse via spores. These plants produce neither flowers nor seeds. Pteridophytes are the first true land plants. Example: fern.

- They are seedless, vascular cryptogams.
- Sporophytes have true roots, stems and leaves.
- They develop spores.

FERN

➤ The plant body is differentiated into stem, leaves and roots.
➤ A vascular system is present.
➤ Leaves usually have leaflets.
➤ Spores are borne on the undersurface of the leaf.
➤ They grow in damp cool shady places.

Sub-kingdom Phenerogamae

Gymnosperm

The gymnosperms are a group of seed-producing plants in which the seeds are not covered. The term gymnosperm is created from the Greek composite word gymnos, meaning naked, and sperma, meaning seed. Therefore gymnosperm literally means naked seeds. Since these plants bear uncovered seeds, hence the name gymnosperm. Gymnosperm seeds develop either on the surface of scales or leaves, which are often modified to form cones, or solitary.

Gymnosperms are known as the ancestors of flowering plants that were known to exist many million years ago. With the passage of time, flowering plants evolved with modifications in various organs, like flowers, leaves, stems, endosperm, etc. Thus angiosperm came to be later known as a separate category than gymnosperm.

Examples of gymnosperm are: redwood, fir, cypress, juniper, ephedra, ginkgo, spruce, conifers, pine, etc.

Angiosperm

Angiosperms are the most evolved plants and are fruit-bearing in nature. Their seeds remain covered in their ovaries. Their reproductive structures are flowers in which the ovules are enclosed in an ovary. Angiosperms are found in almost all habitats, from forests and grasslands to sea margins and deserts. Angiosperms display a huge variety of life forms including trees, herbs, submerged aquatics, bulbs and epiphytes. There are an estimated 3,52,000 species of flowering plants or angiosperms.

Angiosperms are classified as monocotyledons or simply, monocots, and dicotyledons or simply, dicots, depending on whether the seed has one cotyledon (leaf) or two cotyledons (leaves), respectively.

KINGDOM ANIMALIA

The kingdom animalia contains eukaryotes. All the members of this kingdom are multicellular, eukaryotes. They are heterotrophs—they depend on other organisms directly or indirectly for food. Most of the organisms are motile, which means they can move independently and spontaneously. There are around 9 to 10 million species of animals, and about 8,00,000 species are identified. Animals are divided further into various sub-groups.

Characteristics

> Animals are eukaryotic, multicellular and heterotrophic organisms.
> Members of kingdom animalia inhabit seas, fresh water and land.
> Bodies of animals are made of cells organized into tissues to perform specific functions. In most animals, tissues are further organized into complex organs, which form organ systems.
> Animal cells are much evolved and contain organelles like the nucleus, mitochondria, Golgi complex, ribosomes, endoplasmic reticulum, lysosomes, etc.
> Most of the animals are bilaterally symmetrical, while primitive animals are asymmetrical and cnidarians and echinoderms are radially symmetrical.
> Respiration takes place through organs like the lungs, gills, and in some animals, skin is also used.
> Animals have the nervous system to respond to stimuli, carry out activities, and for coordination of the organ systems.
> Distribution of nutrients, exchange of gases and removal of wastes are the main functions of the circulatory system.
> Removal of wastes from the body takes place through the excretory system.
> The skeletal system provides support and protection to the body and organs of the body; it also helps in movement and locomotion.
> Most animals reproduce sexually by the fusion of haploid cells like eggs and sperms.

Classification of Kingdom Animalia

Kingdom animalia is divided into two sub-kingdoms: protozoa and metazoa.

Sub-kingdom Protozoa

Protozoa are one-celled microscopic animals found in most habitats. Most species are free-living. Cysts form stages of their life cycle. Cysts occur with a protective membrane or thickened wall. Protozoan cysts can survive outside the host usually even under extreme circumstances and conditions.

Sub-kingdom Metazoa

The sub-kingdom metazoa is further divided into the following phylum.

Phylum Porifera

Phylum porifera includes organisms with holes in their bodies. They are primitive multicellular animals and have a cellular level of organization. They are attached to some solid support and cannot move on their own. They are commonly called sponges. They are generally marine and mostly asymmetric animals.

Sponges have a water transport or canal system. Water enters through minute pores (ostia) in the body wall into a central cavity, from where it goes out through the osculum. This pathway of water transport is helpful in food gathering, respiratory exchange and removal of waste. The body is supported by a skeleton made up of fibres.

They are hermaphrodite, i.e., eggs and sperms are produced by the same individual species. Sponges reproduce asexually by fragmentation and sexually by formation of gametes. Fertilization is internal.

Phylum coelenterata (cnidaria)

Coelenterates are aquatic with radially symmetrical bodies. They exhibit tissue level of organization, having a central gastro-vascular cavity with a single opening. They are diploblastic. Some of these species live in colonies (corals). Some of them live alone, like the hydra. Jellyfish and sea anemones are common examples. Digestion is both extracellular and intracellular.

Phylum ctenophora

Ctenophora are commonly known as sea walnuts or comb jellies. They are marine, radially symmetrical and diploblastic. They exhibit tissue level of organization. Digestion is both extracellular and intracellular. Bioluminescence (the property of a living organism to emit light) is well-marked in ctenophores. Sexes are not separate and reproduction takes place only by sexual means. Fertilization is external.

Phylum platyhelminthes

They have bilaterally symmetrical bodies. They are triploblastic. This allows outside and inside body linings as well as some organs to be made. They may be free-living or parasitic. Hooks and suckers are present in the parasitic forms. Example of free-living platyhelminthes is planarian. Sexes are not separate. Fertilization is internal and development is indirect. Examples of platyhelminthes are tapeworm, liver fluke, etc.

Phylum aschelminthes (nemotoda)

Aschelminthes (nemotoda) have cylindrical bodies that are bilaterally symmetrical. They have tissues, but no real organs. They are triploblastic. Body cavity is present. They are free-living, aquatic, terrestrial or parasitic in plants and animals. These are very familiar as parasitic worms causing diseases, such as the worms causing elephantiasis (filarial worms) or the worms in the intestines (roundworms or pinworms). The body is circular in cross section, hence the name roundworms. The alimentary canal is complete. An excretory tube removes body wastes from the body cavity through the excretory pore. Sexes are separate (dioecious), i.e., males and females are distinct. Often females are longer than males. Fertilization is internal and development may be direct (where the young ones resemble the adults), or indirect.

Phylum annelida

Annelida are aquatic (both marine and fresh water) or terrestrial, free-living, and sometimes parasitic. Their characteristic feature is that their body surfaces are distinctly marked out, hence, the phylum name annelida. They exhibit an organ-system level of body organization. They are bilaterally symmetric and triploblastic. They possess longitudinal and circular muscles which help in locomotion. A closed circulatory system is present. Nephridia (singular nephridium) help in osmoregulation and excretion. The neural system consists of paired ganglia (singular ganglion) connected by lateral nerves to a double ventral nerve cord. Sexes are separate, but earthworms and leeches are monoecious, that is, they have both the male and female reproductive organs in the same individual. Reproduction is sexual.

Phylum arthropoda

Arthropods have hard, external shells, segmented bodies and jointed legs. Insects, arachnids and crustaceans are members of this largest category of creatures on the planet. They exhibit organ-system level of organization. They have bilaterally symmetrical body, and are triploblastic. The coelomic cavity is blood-filled. The body consists of a head, a thorax and an abdomen. There is an open circulatory system. Respiratory organs are gills, book gills, book lungs and the tracheal system. Sensory organs like antennae, eyes (compound and simple), statocysts or balance organs are present. Excretion takes place through malpighian tubules. They are mostly dioecious. Fertilization is usually internal. They are mostly oviparous. Development may be direct or indirect. Some examples are prawns, butterflies, houseflies, spiders, scorpions, bees, wasps, beetles, mosquitoes, flies, grasshoppers, ants, lobsters, crayfish, shrimp and crabs.

Phylum mollusca

Mollusca are the second-largest animal phylum in the kingdom animalia. They are terrestrial or aquatic. They exhibit organ-system level of organization. They are bilaterally symmetrical, triploblastic, coelomate animals. They have an open circulatory system and kidney-like organs for excretion. The anterior head region has sensory tentacles. They are usually dioecious and oviparous with indirect development. The body is covered by a calcareous shell and is unsegmented, with a distinct head, muscular foot and visceral hump. A soft and spongy layer of skin forms a mantle over the visceral hump. Some examples are octopus, snails and mussels.

Phylum echinodermata

These animals have an endoskeleton of calcium carbonate. They are exclusively free-living marine animals with organ-system level of organization. They are triploblastic with a coelomic cavity. The adult echinoderms are radially symmetrical but larvae are bilaterally symmetrical. Their digestive system is complete. An excretory system is absent. The sexes are separate. Reproduction is sexual. Fertilization is usually external. Development is indirect with free-swimming larva. Some examples are starfish, sea urchin, sea lily, sea cucumber, etc.

Phylum hemichordata

This phylum consists of a small group of worm-like marine animals with organ-system level of organization. They have bilaterally symmetrical cylindrical bodies. They are triploblastic, coelomate animals. The circulatory system is of open type. Respiration takes place through gills. The excretory organ is present. Sexes are separate. Fertilization is external. Development is indirect. Some examples are balanoglossus and saccoglossus.

Phylum chordata

Animals belonging to the phylum chordata have bilaterally symmetrical bodies, are triploblastic, coelomate with organ-system level of organization. They possess a closed circulatory system.

Phylum chordata is divided into three subphyla: urochordata, cephalochordata and vertebrata.

Subphyla urochordata and cephalochordata are often referred to as protochordates and are exclusively marine.

In urochordata, notochord is present only in the larval tail, while in cephalochordata, it extends from the head to the tail region and is persistent through life.

Examples of urochordata: ascidia, salpa and doliolum

Example of cephalochordata: amphioxus or lancelet

VERTEBRATES

These animals have a true vertebral column and internal skeleton, allowing a completely different distribution of muscle attachment points to be used for movement. The members of subphylum vertebrata possess a notochord during the embryonic period. The notochord is replaced by a cartilaginous or bony vertebral column in the adult. Thus all vertebrates are chordates but all chordates are not vertebrates. Besides the basic chordate characters, vertebrates have a ventral muscular heart with two, three or four chambers, kidneys for excretion and osmoregulation and paired appendages which may be fins or limbs. Vertebrates have bilaterally symmetrical bodies, are triploblastic, coelomic and segmented, with complex differentiation of body tissues and organs.

Vertebrates are further classified into five classes. These are pisces, amphibia, reptilia, aves and mammalia.

Pisces are fish. Their skin is covered with scales. They lay eggs. They obtain oxygen dissolved in water by using gills. The body is streamlined, and a muscular tail is used for movement. They are cold-blooded and their hearts have only two chambers. Some fish skeletons are made entirely of cartilage, such as sharks, and some have a skeleton made of both bone and cartilage.

Amphibians spend part of their lives under water and part on land. Frogs, toads and salamanders are amphibians. All of them return to water in order to reproduce. They start life with gills, like fish, and later develop lungs to breathe in air.

The class **reptilia** includes turtles, snakes, lizards, alligators and other large reptiles. All of them have lungs to breathe with on land. They produce an amniotic egg which usually has a calcium carbonate-rich, hard shell that protects the embryo from drying out. This is an advantage over fish and amphibians because the amniotic egg can be laid on land where it is usually safer from predators than in water bodies like lakes, rivers and oceans.

The class **aves** includes all the birds. They also produce amniotic eggs but usually give them greater protection from predators by laying them in their nest high off the ground or in other relatively inaccessible locations. In the case of both reptiles and birds, the eggs are fertilized within the reproductive tract of females. There are other striking similarities between reptiles and birds in their anatomies and reproductive systems.

Dogs, cats, monkeys, humans, etc. are members of the vertebrate class **mammalia**. All mammals conceive their young ones within the reproductive tract of the mother and the young ones develop up to the phase of complete development of the embryo. Mammalian mothers, after birth, nourish them with milk produced by their mammary glands. Mammals are heterodonts with strong jaws. That is to say, they have a variety of specialized teeth (incisors, canines, premolars and molars). This allows them to chew their food into small pieces before swallowing it. Subsequently, they can eat plants of any size or animals. Many reptiles must swallow their prey whole, which limits them to hunting smaller game. Mammals are warm-blooded. They are able to maintain a relatively constant body temperature. Sweating helps to dissipate heat by evaporative cooling. Mammals have four-chambered hearts, complex nervous systems and large brains relative to the size of their bodies.

2

CELL—STRUCTURE AND FUNCTIONS

INTRODUCTION

Cells are the structural and functional unit of living organisms. Cells are called the building blocks of life because, as the smallest unit of organisms, cells can carry on all the processes of life. Every living thing, from the tiniest bacterium to the largest whale, is made of one or more cells. Prior to the seventeenth century no one knew about the existence of cells, since cells are too small to be seen with the naked eye. The invention of the microscope made it possible for Robert Hooke (1665) and Antoni van Leeuwenhoek (1675) to see and draw the first cells.

DIFFERENT TYPES OF CELLS

Although it is true that cells are the basic unit of life and cells do share many traits in common, there are differences as well. To put it in simple words, the cells that make a tree cannot be the same as the ones that make a human being. Even within the same organism, there are different types of cells. Since a group of cells perform a certain task, groups of cells will be different from one to another. For example, our skin cells are different from muscle cells, or bone cells, or blood cells. Like organisms, cells can be characterized by their traits. We will focus here on the structural aspect of a cell.

CELL SIZE

While cells are, in general, microscopic in size, that is, they can be seen with the help of a compound microscope only, a few types of cells are large enough to be seen by the unaided eye. The human egg (ovum) is the largest cell in the body, and can be seen without the aid of a microscope.

CELL SHAPE

Cells come in a variety of shapes, depending on their functions. For example, the neurons from our toes to our head are long and thin so that they can transmit 'information', while blood cells are rounded discs, so that they can flow smoothly.

CELL THEORY

Cell theory consists of three fundamental principles:

- All living things are composed of one or more cells.
- Cells are the basic units of structure and function in an organism.
- Cells come only from the replication of existing cells.

CELL STRUCTURE

Cells are of two types—prokaryotic and eukaryotic. Cells vary based on complexity and structure. Primitive cells are relatively simple in structure and complexity. With time, cells have evolved to having a more complex structure and they also perform complex functions. These primitive cells are called prokaryotic. Usually, prokaryotic cells carry out some form of anaerobic respiration. They have no nucleus or membrane-bound organelles. Their single loop of DNA is termed a nucleoid, but is not isolated from the cytoplasm by a membrane. Prokaryotic cells do have cell organelles like cytoplasm, ribosomes, cell walls, cell membranes, etc. The more complex type of cell is termed eukaryotic. These cells are larger in size and contain cell organelles. These cells can carry out anaerobic respiration, but most also carry out aerobic respiration due to the greater energy yield per molecule of glucose.

CELL ORGANELLES

The components or constituents of a cell are called cell organelles. An organelle is a membrane-bound structure found within a cell. Typically a cell will be filled with cytoplasm, a viscous liquid found within the cell membrane. Therefore, these organelles are found in the cytoplasm. The structure and function of these organelles are described below.

Cytoplasm

Cytoplasm is the fluid part of the cell. The cytoplasm contains dissolved ions and other materials. It allows for the movement of materials within the cell, and allows for the movement of organelles. All living cells have cytoplasm.

Nucleus

The largest organelle in a cell is its nucleus. It is round in shape and has a double membrane called the nuclear membrane that creates its boundary. The nucleus contains genetic information (DNA) on special strands called chromosomes. Due to the extra protection provided by the nuclear membrane, the DNA is a bit more secure from enzymes, pathogens and potentially harmful products of fat and protein metabolism.

Nucleolus

Within the nucleus there is a small space known as the nucleolus. It is not bound by any membrane. So, by definition, it is not an organelle. However, it performs an extremely important function in the cell. This space forms near the part of DNA with instructions for making ribosomes. Ribosomes are the molecules responsible for making proteins. Ribosomes are assembled in the nucleolus, and exit the nucleus through nuclear pores.

Endoplasmic Reticulum (ER)

The endoplasmic reticulum is a network of membranous canals filled with fluid. They carry materials throughout the cell. The ER therefore constitutes the transport system of the cell. There are two types of ER: rough ER and smooth ER. Rough endoplasmic reticulum is lined with ribosomes and is rough in appearance and smooth endoplasmic reticulum contains no ribosomes and is smooth in appearance. The rough endoplasmic reticulum is thus the site of protein production while the smooth endoplasmic reticulum is where lipids (fats) and steroids are made. These are fat-based molecules that are important in energy storage, membrane structure and communication (steroids can act as hormones). The smooth endoplasmic reticulum is also responsible for detoxifying the cell.

Golgi Apparatus (Golgi body)

Golgi bodies are flattened membranous stacks which temporarily store protein after it is synthesized. The Golgi body is responsible for packing proteins from the rough endoplasmic reticulum into membrane-bound vesicles, which then translocate to the cell membrane. At the cell membrane, the vesicles can fuse with the lipid bilayer of the cell membrane, causing the contents of the vesicle to either become part of the cell membrane or be released outside.

Lysosome

The lysosome is the cell's recycling centre. These are small sac-like structures surrounded by a single membrane and contain strong digestive enzymes which, when released, can break down worn-out organelles or food.

Mitochondria

The mitochondria are round-edged tube-like important cell organelles that are surrounded by a double membrane. The inner of the two membranes is highly folded. The mitochondria are often referred to as the powerhouse of the cell. ATP (adenosine triphosphate) is the energy currency of the cell, and is produced in a process known as cellular respiration. Though the process begins in the cytoplasm, the bulk of the energy produced comes from later steps that take place in the mitochondria.

Cell Membrane

This is the barrier between the living part of the cell and the non-living environment. It is a selective barrier; it allows some materials to pass through, but does not allow some others to pass. Water and small particles can slip through the phospholipid bilayer while larger and more complex materials must pass through one of the protein channels embedded in the membrane. All cells have membranes.

Plastids

Plastids are cell organelles that are bound by two membranes. Plants make and store food in plastids. Plastids are found in the cytoplasm. There are two main types: leucoplasts—colourless organelles which store starch or other plant nutrients, and chromoplasts—they contain different coloured pigments. The most important type of chromoplast is the chloroplast, which contains the green pigment chlorophyll. This is important in the process of photosynthesis.

DIFFERENCE BETWEEN PLANT CELL AND ANIMAL CELL

The difference between plant cell and animal cell are given in the table below.

Animal cell	Plant cell
In general, smaller than plant cells. 10 to 30 micrometres in length.	In general, larger than animal cells. 10 to 100 micrometres in length.
Does not have cell wall. The outermost boundary is the cell membrane.	Plant cells have a cellulosic cell wall as the outermost cell boundary.
Animal cells do not possess chloroplast.	Plant cells possess chloroplasts that take part in photosynthesis.
Centrioles which form spindles during cell division are present.	Centrioles are absent.
Vacuoles are small in size.	Plant cells possess large vacuoles. Plant cells have a large central vacuole that can occupy up to 90 per cent of the cell's volume.
Food is stored as glycogen.	Food is stored as starch.
Lysosome is present in animal cells	Lysosome is absent
Animal cells do not have plasmodesmata.	Plant cells have plasmodesmata, which are pores between plant cell walls that allow molecules and communication signals to pass between individual plant cells.
Chromosomes are small in size.	Chromosomes are large in size.

Plant Cell

Cross section of a typical plant cell is shown in Figure 2.1.

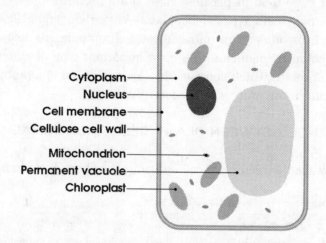

Cytoplasm
Nucleus
Cell membrane
Cellulose cell wall

Mitochondrion
Permanent vacuole
Chloroplast

Fig. 2.1: Cross section of a plant cell (Wikimedia commons)

Animal Cell

Cross section of a typical animal cell is shown in Figure 2.2.

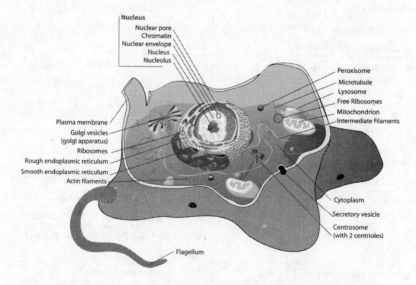

Nucleus
Nuclear pore
Chromatin
Nuclear envelope
Nucleus
Nucleolus

Peroxisome
Microtubule
Lysosome
Free Ribosomes
Mitochondrion
Intermediate Filaments

Plasma membrane
Golgi vesicles
(golgi apparatus)
Ribosomes
Rough endoplasmic reticulum
Smooth endoplasmic reticulum
Actin filaments

Cytoplasm
Secretory vesicle
Centrosome
(with 2 centrioles)

Flagellum

Fig. 2.2: Cross section of animal cell (Wikimedia commons)

3

CELL DIVISION

INTRODUCTION

In the simplest words, cell division is the process by which a cell divides into two or more cells. The cell which divides is called the parent cell, and the cells that result out of division of a parent cell are called the daughter cells. Division of a cell occurs due to various reasons and it usually constitutes part of a larger cell cycle. Living cells divide to form new cells for either of the following two reasons:

a) In order to repair worn-out or damaged tissues. This is a vegetative division, whereby each daughter cell is genetically identical to the parent cell—the process being called mitosis.

b) A reproductive cell division, whereby the number of chromosomes in the daughter cells is reduced by half to produce haploid gametes—the process being known as meiosis—is to enable the exchange of genetic material at the initial stage of the process of sexual reproduction.

For simple unicellular microorganisms such as the amoeba, cell division has a different meaning and consequence. In case of amoeba, one cell division is equivalent to reproduction—an entire new organism is created.

TYPES OF CELL DIVISION

The two types of cell division are generally called mitosis and meiosis, as mentioned earlier.

Mitosis is the type of cell division by which a single cell divides in such a way so as to produce two genetically identical daughter cells. By this method the body produces new cells for both growth and repair of ageing or damaged tissues in the body.

Meiosis, also known as reduction division, is the form of cell division in which a cell divides into four daughter cells, each of which has half of the number of chromosomes of the original cell. Meiosis occurs prior to the formation of sperm in males and ovum in females.

CELL CYCLE

In all somatic cells the cell cycle consists of two periods:

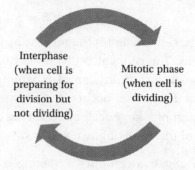

Interphase
(when cell is
preparing for
division but
not dividing)

Mitotic phase
(when cell is
dividing)

Fig. 3.1: Cell cycle

a) During **interphase** (also known as interkinesis), cells perform all the functions necessary for life, including the synthesis of DNA (deoxyribonucleic acid) so that both of the new cells formed by the mitotic phase will contain a complete copy of the original and hence have all the necessary information

b) **Mitotic** phase when the cell is dividing

The mitotic phase of the cell cycle consists of two stages, as depicted below:

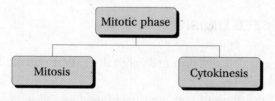

Fig. 3.2: Mitotic phase of a cell

- Mitosis

Mitosis is the division of the cell nucleus.

- Cytokinesis

It follows mitosis. Cytokinesis is the division of the cytoplasm of the cell into two daughter cells. Therefore, cell division is complete in cytokinesis, after which two identical daughter cells are born.

Mitosis

Mitosis (nuclear division) consists of the following phases.

Interphase

Although interphase is not part of mitosis, it is included here so that the reader is reminded that interphase precedes mitosis.

A brief introduction about chromatin is required to be given here. Chromatin is a material located in the nucleus of cells. It exists in the form that resembles a thread-like mass when the cell is not dividing. However, it forms chromosomes when the cell divides. Chromatin consists of DNA and protein.

Prophase

> Prophase is the first stage of division.
> The nuclear envelope is broken down.
> Long strands of chromatin condense to form chromosomes.
> The nucleolus disappears.
> Microtubules (referred to as the spindle and spindle fibres, associated with the alignment and separation of chromosomes, respectively) attach to the chromosomes at the kinetochores present in the centromere.
> Chromosomes are connected at the centromere.
> During this condensation and alignment period, homologous chromosomes may swap portions of their DNA in a process called crossing over.

Metaphase

> Metaphase is the stage in cell division when the chromosomes line up in the middle of the cell.
> The chromosomes are still condensing and are currently one step

away from being the most coiled and condensed they will be.

➤ Spindle and spindle fibres have already connected to the kinetochores.
➤ The chromosomes are ready to split into opposite poles of the cell towards the spindle to which they are connected.

Anaphase

➤ Anaphase is a very short stage of the cell division process.
➤ It occurs after the chromosomes align at the mitotic plate.
➤ After the chromosomes line up in the middle of the cell, the spindle fibres will pull them apart.
➤ The chromosomes are split apart as the sister chromatids move to opposite sides of the cell.

Telophase

➤ Telophase is the last stage of the cell cycle.
➤ Telophase begins after the chromosomal movement stops.
➤ The identical sets of chromosomes, which are by this stage at opposite poles of the cell, uncoil and revert to the long, thin, thread-like chromatin form.
➤ A new nuclear envelope forms around each chromatin mass.
➤ Nucleoli appear.
➤ Eventually the mitotic spindle breaks up.
➤ The cytoplasm begins to divide around the two new nuclei.

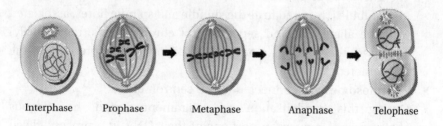

| Interphase | Prophase | Metaphase | Anaphase | Telophase |

Fig. 4.3: Phases of mitosis

Meiosis

Meiosis is the type of cell division used for the production of gametes or sex cells (sperm and eggs). This division takes us from a diploid cell, i.e., one with two sets of chromosomes, to haploid cells, i.e., ones with a single set of chromosomes. Therefore, we can say, the type of cell division that reduces the number of chromosomes by half and creates four haploid cells, each genetically distinct from the parent cell that gave rise to it, is called meiosis. In meiosis, DNA replication is followed by two rounds of cell division to produce four daughter cells, each with half the number of chromosomes as the original parent cell. In humans, the haploid cells made in meiosis are sperms and eggs. When a sperm and an egg join in fertilization, the two haploid sets of chromosomes form a complete diploid set again and a new genome is formed. The stages of meiosis are as given below.

PHASES OF MEIOSIS

Although meiosis is a lot like mitosis in many ways, the entire steps of the cell division process in meiosis are described in a two-step division process, called meiosis I and meiosis II. Homologue pairs separate during a first round of cell division. This happens in meiosis I. Sister chromatids separate during a second round. This is meiosis II. In each round of division, cells go through four stages: prophase, metaphase, anaphase and telophase.

Meiosis I

1. Interphase
> The DNA in the cell is copied, resulting in two identical full sets of chromosomes.
> There are two centrosomes outside the nucleus. Each centrosome contains a pair of centrioles.
> During interphase, microtubules extend from these centrosomes.

2. Prophase I
> The copied chromosomes change into x-shaped structures. Each chromosome consists of two sister chromatids containing identical genetic information.
> The chromosomes pair up in such a way that both copies of chromosome 1 are together, both copies of chromosome 2 are together, and so on.
> The pairs of chromosomes may then exchange bits of DNA in a process called recombination or crossing over.

> At the end of prophase I the membrane around the nucleus in the cell breaks, releasing the chromosomes.
> The meiotic spindle, consisting of microtubules and other proteins, extends across the cell between the centrioles.

3. Metaphase I
> The chromosome pairs line up next to each other along the centre (equator) of the cell.
> The centrioles are now at opposites poles of the cell with the meiotic spindles extending from them.
> The meiotic spindle fibres attach to one chromosome of each pair.

4. Anaphase I
> The pair of chromosomes is pulled apart by the meiotic spindle, which pulls one chromosome to one pole of the cell and the other chromosome to the opposite pole.
> In meiosis I the sister chromatids stay together.

5. Telophase I and cytokinesis
> The chromosomes complete their movement to the opposite poles of the cell.
> At each pole of the cell a full set of chromosomes gather together.
> A membrane forms around each set of chromosomes to create two new nuclei.
> The single cell then breaks in the middle to form two separate daughter cells, each containing a full set of chromosomes within a nucleus, the process being known as cytokinesis.

Meiosis II

1. Prophase II
> At the end of meiosis I, two daughter cells are formed, each with 23 chromosomes (23 pairs of chromatids).
> In each of the two daughter cells, the chromosomes condense again into visible x-shaped structures.
> The membrane around the nucleus in each daughter cell dissolves, releasing the chromosomes.
> The centrioles duplicate.
> The meiotic spindle forms again.

2. Metaphase II

> In each of the two daughter cells, the chromosomes (pair of sister chromatids) line up end to end along the equator of the cell.

> The centrioles are now at opposite poles in each of the daughter cells.

> Meiotic spindle fibres at each pole of the cell attach to each of the sister chromatids.

3. Anaphase II

> The sister chromatids are pulled to opposite poles in this phase. This happens due to the action of the meiotic spindle.

> The separated chromatids are now individual chromosomes.

4. Telophase II and cytokinesis

> The chromosomes complete their movement to the opposite poles of the cell.

> At each pole of the cell a full set of chromosomes comes together.

> A membrane forms around each set of chromosomes to create two new separate cell nuclei.

> Once cytokinesis is complete, there are four granddaughter cells, each with half a set of chromosomes (haploid): in males, these four cells are all sperm cells; in females, one of the cells is an egg cell while the other three are polar bodies (small cells that do not develop into eggs).

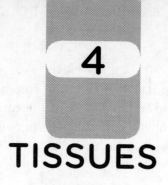

TISSUES

INTRODUCTION

A group of cells that are structurally similar and perform similar functions together is called a tissue. The branch of biology in which study of tissues is undertaken is called histology. A collection of tissues gives rise to an organ.

There are two types of tissues: plant tissues and animal tissues.

PLANT TISSUE

Plant tissues primarily take part in providing plants with support and structural strength. In addition to that, another vital function of plant tissues is transportation of water and minerals, and food. Plant tissues also have a role in photosynthesis and food storage.

Most of the plant tissues are dead, since dead cells can provide mechanical strength as easily as live ones, and need less maintenance.

Based on the dividing capacity of the tissues, various plant tissues can be classified as growing or meristematic tissue and permanent tissue. The following chart shows the categorization of plant tissues.

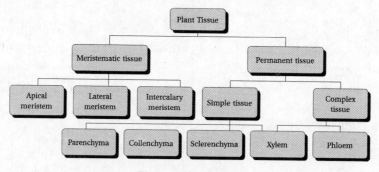

Fig. 4.1: Plant tissue

MERISTEMATIC TISSUE

Meristematic tissue, also known as the dividing tissue, is located only in certain specific regions of plants. Therefore, growth of plants occurs only in these regions. Depending on the region where they are present, meristematic tissues are classified as apical, lateral and intercalary.

Apical meristem is present at the growing tips of stems and roots and increases the length of the stem and the root.

The circumference of the stem or that of the root increases due to lateral meristem (cambium).

Intercalary meristem is the meristem at the base of the leaves or internodes (on either side of the node) on twigs.

PERMANENT TISSUE

Some of the meristematic tissues lose their ability to divide. Thus they become permanent. The process by which meristematic tissues turn into permanent tissues, taking up a permanent shape, size and function, is known as **differentiation**. These tissues can be classified into simple permanent tissue which is made up of only one type of cell, and complex permanent tissue which is made up of more than one type of cell.

Simple Permanent Tissue

Parenchyma

A few layers of cells form the basic packing tissue. It consists of relatively unspecialized cells with thin cell walls. They are usually loosely packed, so that large spaces between cells (intercellular spaces) are found in these tissues.

Collenchyma

The flexibility in plants is due to another permanent tissue, collenchyma. It allows easy bending in various parts of a plant (leaf, stem) without breaking. It also provides mechanical support to plants. We can find this tissue in leaf stalks below the epidermis. The cells of this tissue are living, elongated and irregularly thickened at the corners. There is very little intercellular space.

Sclerenchyma

Sclerenchyma is another type of permanent tissue. It is the tissue that makes the plant hard and stiff. Example, husk of a coconut is made of sclerenchyma tissue. The cells of this tissue are dead. They are long and narrow as the walls are thickened due to lignin (a chemical substance that acts like cement and hardens them). Often these walls are so thick that there is no internal space inside the cell. This tissue is present in stems, around vascular bundles, in the veins of leaves and in the hard covering of seeds and nuts. It provides strength to the plant parts.

Complex Permanent Tissue

Complex tissues are made of more than one type of cell. All these cells coordinate to perform a common function.

Xylem and phloem are examples of such complex tissues. They are both conducting tissues and constitute vascular bundles. Vascular or conductive tissue is a distinctive feature of the complex plants, one that has made possible their survival in the terrestrial environment.

Xylem

Xylem consists of tracheids, vessels, xylem parenchyma and xylem fibres. The cells have thick walls, and many of them are dead cells. Tracheids and vessels are tubular structures. This allows them to transport water and minerals vertically. The parenchyma stores food and helps in the sideways conduction of water. Fibres are mainly supportive in function.

Phloem

Phloem is made up of four types of elements: sieve tubes, companion cells, phloem fibres and the phloem parenchyma. Sieve tubes are tubular cells with perforated walls. Phloem is unlike xylem in that materials can move in both directions in it. Phloem transports food from leaves to other parts of the plant. Except for phloem fibres, phloem cells are living cells.

ANIMAL TISSUE

Animal tissues are more complex than plant tissues and perform more diverse functions than plant tissues. All complex animal tissues can be classified into four types: epithelial tissues, connective tissues, muscular tissues and neural tissues (nervous tissues).

EPITHELIAL TISSUE

Epithelial tissue covers various parts of the human body. Epithelial tissue forms the surface of skin, lining of various cavities and tubes of the body, and covering of the internal organs. Epithelial tissue is made of closely-packed cells arranged in flat sheets.

Functions of Epithelial Tissues

➤ Epithelial tissue forms boundaries between different environments, and nearly all substances must pass through the epithelium. The main functions of epithelial tissue are the roles it performs as an interface tissue, as given below.

➤ It protects the underlying tissues from external stimuli like radiation, exposure to toxins and physical trauma.

➤ It helps in absorption of substances in the digestive tract lining.

➤ It supports regulation and excretion of chemicals between the underlying tissues and the body cavity.

➤ Secretion of hormones into the blood vascular system; the secretion of sweat, mucus, enzymes and other products that are delivered by ducts come from the glandular epithelium.

➤ Epithelial tissues help in detection of sensation.

Types of Epithelial Tissue

Epithelial tissues are identified by both the number of layers and the shape of the cells in the upper layers. There are eight basic types of epithelium: six of them are identified based on both the number of cells and their shape; two of them are named by the type of cell (squamous) found in them. Epithelial tissue is classified based on the number of cells, the shape of those cells and the types of those cells.

The following table shows the location of various types of epithelial tissues and their functions.

Table 4.1: Epithelial tissues and their functions

Type of epithelial tissue	Location	Functions
Simple squamous epithelium	Air sacs of the lungs and the lining of the heart, blood vessels and lymphatic vessels	1. Allowing materials to pass through by diffusion and filtration 2. Secretion of lubricating substances

Type of epithelial tissue	Location	Functions
Simple cuboidal epithelium	In ducts and secretory portions of small glands and in kidney tubules	1. Secretion 2. Absorption
Simple columnar epithelium	Ciliated tissues including the bronchi, uterine tubes and uterus; smooth (non-ciliated tissues), and are in the digestive tract bladder	1. Absorption 2. Secretion of mucous and enzymes
Pseudostratified columnar epithelium	Ciliated tissues line the trachea and much of the upper respiratory tract	Secretion of mucous—ciliated tissues move mucous
Stratified squamous epithelium	Lines the esophagus, mouth and vagina	Protects against abrasion
Stratified cuboidal epithelium	Sweat glands, salivary glands and mammary glands	Protection
Stratified columnar epithelium	The male urethra and the ducts of some glands	1. Secretion 2. Protection
Transitional epithelium	Lines the bladder, urethra and ureters	Allowing the urinary organs to expand and stretch

Simple Epithelial Tissue

It consists of a single layer of cells. It is typically present where the organ requires carrying out absorption, secretion and filtration.

Simple epithelial tissues are generally classified by the shape of their cells. The four major classes of simple epithelium are: 1) simple squamous 2) simple cuboidal 3) simple columnar and 4) pseudostratified.

Simple squamous

Simple squamous epithelium cells are flat in shape and arranged in a single layer. This single layer is thin enough to form a membrane that compounds can move through via passive diffusion. This epithelial type is found in the walls of capillaries, linings of the pericardium and the linings of the alveoli of the lungs.

Simple cuboidal

Simple cuboidal epithelium consists of a single layer of cells that are as tall as they are wide. The important functions of the simple cuboidal epithelium are secretion and absorption. This epithelial type is found in the small collecting ducts of the kidneys, pancreas and salivary glands.

Simple columnar

Simple columnar epithelium is a single row of tall, closely packed cells, aligned in a row. These cells are found in areas with high secretory function (such as the wall of the stomach), or absorptive areas (as in the small intestine). They possess cellular extensions (e.g., microvilli in the small intestine, or the cilia found almost exclusively in the female reproductive tract).

Pseudostratified

These are simple columnar epithelial cells whose nuclei appear at different heights, giving the misleading (hence pseudo) impression that the epithelium is stratified when the cells are viewed in cross section.

Pseudostratified epithelium can also possess fine hair-like extensions of their apical (luminal) membrane called cilia. In this case, the epithelium is described as ciliated pseudostratified epithelium. Ciliated epithelium is found in the airways (nose, bronchi), but is also found in the uterus and fallopian tubes of females, where the cilia propel the ovum to the uterus.

Stratified epithelium

Stratified epithelium differs from simple epithelium by being multilayered. It is therefore found where body linings have to withstand mechanical or chemical insults.

Stratified epithelia are more durable and protection is one of their major functions. Since stratified epithelium consists of two or more layers, the basal cells divide and push towards the apex, and in the process, flatten the apical cells.

Stratified epithelia can be columnar, cuboidal or squamous.

CONNECTIVE TISSUE

Connective tissues link and support other tissues or organs of the body. Connective tissues include cartilage, bone, adipose and blood. All connective tissues except blood secrete structural proteins called collagen or elastin.

Types of Connective Tissue

Connective tissues are classified into three types—loose connective tissue, dense connective tissue and specialized connective tissue.

Loose connective tissue

These tissues have cells and fibres that are loosely arranged in a semi-fluid ground substance.

- **Areolar tissue:** Present beneath the skin; serves as a framework support for epithelium
- **Adipose tissue:** Specialized to store fats

Dense Connective Tissue

Fibres and fibroblasts are packed compactly in dense connective tissue. Tendons are dense regular tissue that attach skeletal muscle to bones and ligaments attach bone to bone. Collagen is the dense irregular tissue present in the skin.

Specialized Connective Tissue

Cartilage, bones and blood are types of specialized connective tissue.

- **Cartilage:** Cartilage is present on the tip of the nose, outer ear joints and between bones of the vertebral column.
- **Bones:** They are hard and non-pliable, rich in calcium salts and collagen fibres. They provide a structural frame to the body. The bone cells are osteocytes. The bone marrow in some bones is the site of production of blood cells.
- **Blood:** It is a fluid connective tissue. It contains plasma, red blood corpuscles, white blood corpuscles and platelets.

MUSCLE TISSUE

Muscle tissues are made of long cylindrical fibres, arranged in parallel arrays. These fibres are composed of fine fibrils known as myofibrils. Muscles contract and relax to move the body to adjust to the changes in environment or to respond to stimuli. Muscles are of three types: skeletal, smooth and cardiac.

- **Skeletal muscle:** Skeletal muscles are also known as striated muscles. They are attached to bones.
- **Smooth muscle:** Smooth muscle fibres are not striated. Walls of internal organs of our body contain smooth muscles.

- **Cardiac muscle:** Cardiac muscle tissue is a tissue present only in the heart.

NEURAL TISSUE

There are two main branches of the nervous system in our body—the central nervous system (CNS) comprising the brain and spinal cord, and the peripheral nervous system (PNS) which has the branching peripheral nerves. Neural tissue or nervous tissue or nerve tissue is the main tissue component of these two nervous systems. It is composed of neurons or nerve cells, which receive and transmit impulses, and neuroglia, also known as glial cells, or more commonly, as just glia, which assist the propagation of the nerve impulse and provide nutrients to the neuron.

Nervous tissue is made up of different types of nerve cells, all of which have an axon, the long stem-like part of the cell that sends action potential signals to the next cell. Bundles of axons make up the nerves.

The nervous system performs various functions, the most important ones being of sensory input, integration, control of muscles and glands, homeostasis and mental activity.

There are four components of neural tissue. These are: neurons, neurosecretory cells, neuroglia and ependymal cells.

NUTRITION

INTRODUCTION

All organisms need energy to perform various processes in their lives. Regardless of whether an organism is working or at rest, energy is necessary for metabolic activities, and hence the survival of the organism. Plants require energy. Animals require energy. We require energy even during sleep because a number of biological activities occur continuously in our body. For example, respiration and beating of the heart keeps on happening always without any break. All these processes of living beings need a continuous flow of energy. Energy comes from food. Food, after a complex biological process, breaks down into the form of energy that the body can use. Therefore food is the source of this energy. In this chapter we will learn about food and nutrition.

NUTRITION

Nutrition is the process by which food intake takes place and also the process of taking in and utilizing the various nutrients by an organism. Nutrients are substances that provide energy to the organism. They also help in the biosynthesis of various constituents of the body. These are obtained by organisms from their surroundings. Food is an important source of various nutrients required for growth, maintenance and repair of the body. It is also required to build resistance in the body against various diseases and foreign pathogens. Thus, nutrition is a process by which organisms obtain substances that are utilized for their growth and reproduction, and other metabolic activities, and to fight various diseases. Substances which provide nutrition are called nutrients.

MODES OF NUTRITION

Organisms have different modes of nutrition. They are classified into two major groups on the basis of their food intake—autotrophic nutrition and heterotrophic nutrition.

1. **Autotrophic nutrition:** In this mode of nutrition, organisms synthesize their own food in their own bodies from simpler inorganic substances. Such organisms are known as autotrophs.

    Autotrophic nutrition is further classified into photoautotrophic nutrition and chemoautotrophic nutrition, depending on the source of energy used.

    (i) *Photoautotrophic nutrition*: In this case, organisms can directly use solar energy in the presence of chlorophyll to make their organic food from simpler inorganic substances—water and carbon dioxide. The green pigment present in these organisms is for trapping solar energy.

    (ii) *Chemoautotrophic nutrition or chemosynthesis*: In this case, solar energy is not used. Certain bacteria can make organic food from simpler organic substances without using solar energy. Instead, they use energy produced by the breakdown of these inorganic substances.

2. **Heterotrophic nutrition**: In this mode of nutrition, organisms depend on others for food. These organisms cannot make their own food. Such organisms are known as heterotrophs. Thus, in heterotrophic nutrition, food from other sources is taken in, and after digestion this food is converted into the simplest form which can provide energy for metabolic and physiological activities of the organism.

Different types of heterotrophic nutrition are as listed below:

   (i) Saprophytic nutrition
   (ii) Parasitic nutrition
   (iii) Holozoic nutrition

   (i) *Saprophytic nutrition:* In this mode of nutrition, organisms obtain nutrition from dead and decaying organic matter. Examples of organisms that are saprophytic are fungi and bacteria.

   (ii) *Parasitic nutrition:* In this mode of nutrition, organisms take food from others. The organism that takes food is known as the parasite and the organism from which food is taken is known as the host. Not only does the parasite take food, but it also lives in the body of the host. However, the host does not get any benefit from the parasite in return. The host may be an animal or a plant. Parasite nutrition is found in bacteria, fungi, roundworm and plasmodium.

(iii) *Holozoic nutrition*: This mode of nutrition is found in most of the animals. They take solid or liquid food in this type of nutrition. In holozoic nutrition, complex food is taken in, which is then digested and absorbed by the body. Depending upon the source of food, holozoic nutrition is further categorized into the following types.

(a) Herbivorous
(b) Carnivorous
(c) Omnivorous

PHOTOSYNTHESIS

Photosynthesis is the process by which plants, some bacteria and algae produce sugar and chemical energy, using the energy from sunlight and by the actions of the green pigment chlorophyll. The photosynthetic process uses water and carbon dioxide, and releases oxygen. The overall reaction of this process can be written as:

$$6H_2O + 6CO_2 \text{ (in the presence of chlorophyll)} \xrightarrow{sunlight} C_6H_{12}O_6 + 6O_2$$

The raw materials of photosynthesis are water and carbon dioxide, which enter the cells of the leaf. After the photosynthesis process is over, the products of photosynthesis, i.e. sugar and oxygen, leave the leaf.

Water is absorbed by the root and is transported up to the leaves by the xylem. Carbon dioxide can enter the leaf through an opening, called the stomata, flanked by two guard cells. Carbon dioxide cannot pass through the protective waxy layer covering the leaf (cuticle). Land plants have evolved stomata, a specialized structure to allow gas to enter and leave the leaf. Similar to carbon dioxide, oxygen produced during photosynthesis can pass out of the leaf through the opened stomata.

The chlorophyll pigment can absorb light. Actually it absorbs all wavelengths of visible light except green, which it reflects, to be detected by our eyes. Thus it appears as a green pigment. The thylakoid is the structural unit of photosynthesis. Both photosynthetic prokaryotes and eukaryotes have these flattened sacs/vesicles containing photosynthetic chemicals. Only eukaryotes have chloroplasts with a surrounding membrane. Thylakoids are stacked like pancakes in stacks known collectively as grana. The areas between grana are referred to as stroma. While the mitochondrion has two membrane systems, the chloroplast has three, forming three compartments.

THE PROCESS OF PHOTOSYNTHESIS

Photosynthesis is a two-stage process. The first stage depends on light and is called light reactions. It requires the sunlight to make energy carrier molecules that are used in the second process. The dark reactions, reactions that occur independent of light, occur when the products of the light reaction are used to form C-C bonds of carbohydrates. In the light reactions, light strikes chlorophyll in such a way as to excite electrons to a higher energy state. In a series of reactions the energy is converted into adenosine tri phosphate (ATP) and nicotinamide adenine di nucleotide phosphate hydrogen (NADPH). Water is split in the process, releasing oxygen as a by-product of the reaction. The ATP and NADPH are used to make C-C bonds in the dark reactions. In the dark reaction, carbon dioxide from the atmosphere (or water for aquatic/marine organisms) is captured and modified by the addition of hydrogen to form carbohydrates. The incorporation of carbon dioxide into organic compounds is known as carbon fixation. The energy for this comes from the first phase of the photosynthetic process. Living systems cannot directly utilize light energy, but can, through a complicated series of reactions, convert it into C-C bond energy that can be released by glycolysis and other metabolic processes. In the dark phase six molecules of carbon dioxide enter into the reaction, producing one molecule of glucose. Figure 5.1 depicts the process of photosynthesis in green plants.

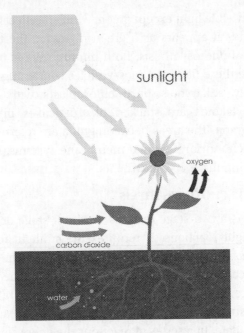

Fig. 5.1: Photosynthesis (Wikimedia commons)

DIGESTION IN HUMANS

Our digestive system comprises the following compartments: (1) the buccal cavity (2) the food pipe or oesophagus (3) the stomach (4) the small intestine (5) the large intestine ending in the rectum (6) the anus. These parts together form the alimentary canal (digestive tract). The food that we take in passes through a continuous canal which begins at the buccal cavity and ends at the anus. Digestion is a gradual process and the food components get digested as food travels through the various compartments. The inner walls of the stomach and the small intestine, and the various glands such as salivary glands, the liver and the pancreas, which secrete digestive juices, also form part of the digestive system. In other words, the digestive tract and the associated glands together constitute the digestive system.

THE PROCESS OF DIGESTION

Food is taken into the body through the mouth, and this process of taking food into the body is called ingestion. We chew the food with our teeth and break it down mechanically into small pieces. There are various types of teeth to perform different functions. Primarily the following types of teeth are found: cutting and biting teeth; piercing and tearing teeth; chewing and grinding teeth. The tongue plays an important role in swallowing the chewed food. The functions of the tongue include talking as well. Besides that, it mixes saliva with the food during chewing and helps in swallowing the food. We also taste food by our tongue. It has taste buds that detect different tastes in food.

The swallowed food passes into the food pipe or oesophagus. The food pipe runs along the neck and the chest, and it finally opens into the stomach. The chewed and swallowed food keeps moving through the alimentary canal by the process of peristalsis.

The stomach is a thick-walled, flattened U-shaped, bag-like organ. It receives food from the food pipe at one end and opens into the small intestine at the other. The inner lining of the stomach secretes mucous, hydrochloric acid and digestive juices. The mucous protects the lining of the stomach. The acid kills many bacteria that enter along with the food and makes the medium in the stomach acidic. The digestive juices secreted from the stomach break down food into simpler substances. Saliva also contains a digestive enzyme that works on carbohydrates and breaks it into simpler substance.

The small intestine is the next organ in the alimentary canal after stomach. It is highly coiled and is about 7.5 m long. It receives digestive juices from the liver and the pancreas. Besides, its wall also secretes juices. These juices continue to break food into simpler substances so that they can be absorbed by the cells. The liver is a reddish-brown gland situated in the upper part of the abdomen on the right side. It is the largest gland in the body. It secretes bile juice that is stored in a sac called the gall bladder. Bile plays an important role in the digestion of fats. The pancreas is a large cream-coloured gland located just below the stomach. The pancreatic juice acts on carbohydrates and proteins and changes them into simpler forms. The simpler forms of food in which they are absorbed by our body are: carbohydrates (glucose), fats (fatty acids and glycerol) and proteins (amino acids).

This next stage in the process of digestion is called absorption, in which the digested food passes into the blood vessels in the wall of the intestine. The inner walls of the small intestine have finger-like projections, called villi. The villi increase the surface area for absorption of the digested food. The absorbed substances are transported by blood vessels to different organs of the body. The food that remains undigested and unabsorbed then enters into the large intestine.

The large intestine is wider yet shorter in length than the small intestine. It is about 1.5 m in length. Its function is to absorb water and some salts from the undigested food material. The remaining waste passes into the rectum and remains there as semi-solid faeces. The faecal matter is removed through the anus from time to time. This is called egestion, which is the last process in digestion. Figure 5.2 shows the digestive system in humans.

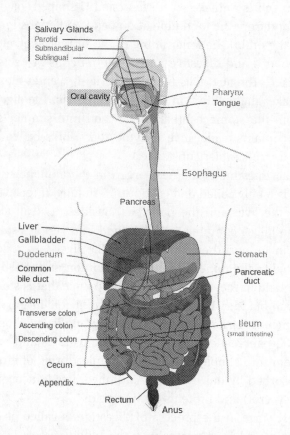

Fig. 5.2: Digestive system in humans (Wikimedia commons)

6

RESPIRATION

INTRODUCTION

All organisms need energy to perform various processes of their lives. The food that we eat is burnt to produce energy which takes care of our need of energy to carry out physical activities. For burning of food, oxygen is required (aerobic respiration), and we get this oxygen from the air by respiration. Respiration is a life process. Respiration is the biochemical process through which all cells of living organisms get the energy to perform essential life processes. In biochemical language, what happens in the process of respiration is the following: glucose from the food undergoes reaction with oxygen to form carbon dioxide and water, and in this process energy is released. Of course it happens through a series of complex cellular processes, and that is why it is called cellular respiration.

TYPES OF RESPIRATION

Different organisms can obtain energy in different ways. Certain organisms, humans, for example, need air to live. Since oxygen is essential for these organisms, this type of respiration is called aerobic respiration. However, there are some lower organisms, like certain species of bacteria and algae, or some prokaryotes, that do not need oxygen to generate energy, and hence, to live. So, these organisms get energy through what is called anaerobic respiration.

ANAEROBIC RESPIRATION

Here, the first step is the conversion of glucose, a 6-carbon molecule, into a simpler sugar called pyruvate, a 3-carbon molecule, in the cytoplasm. Then, in the absence of oxygen, pyruvate gets converted to other substances, and energy is released in this process. The pyruvate is the intermediate product of anaerobic respiration. This is the process of fermentation. In yeast, pyruvate gets broken down into ethanol and carbon dioxide, and energy is released.

Glucose → Pyruvate + Energy → Ethanol + Carbon dioxide + Energy

Sometimes anaerobic respiration occurs in the human body also. This, however, happens only in certain emergency situations of excess energy requirement. For example, when we exercise too heavily, the oxygen supply in our muscle cells falls short of requirement. So, our body temporarily generates energy in the absence of oxygen by means of anaerobic cellular respiration. You may have noticed or experienced muscle cramps during heavy exercise. It is due to the lactic acid released during the process of anaerobic cellular respiration. Only when we take sufficient rest and allow the muscles to relax well does cellular aerobic respiration resume and lactic acid is removed from the body.

Glucose → Pyruvate + Energy → Lactic acid + Energy

AEROBIC RESPIRATION

In aerobic respiration, energy is released by the breakdown of glucose into carbon dioxide and water. This process occurs in the mitochondria. However, it is not a simple one-step reaction. It occurs by a series of enzyme-controlled biochemical reactions, and in steps to release the energy stored up in food that is absorbed by cells in their simplest forms.

The overall reaction in aerobic respiration may be represented by the following general equation:

$$C_6H_{12}O_6 + 6O_2 \rightarrow 6CO_2 + 6H_2O + Energy$$

Glycolysis, the Krebs cycle and the oxidative phosphorylation comprise aerobic cellular respiration.

Glycolysis

In this process each glucose molecule (six-carbon molecule) splits into two pyruvates (three-carbon molecules) during a sequence of enzyme-controlled reactions. Interestingly this occurs in both aerobic and anaerobic respiration.

The Krebs Cycle

It is a complicated cyclic process, and is also known as the tricarboxylic acid cycle or TCA cycle. All aerobic organisms release stored energy through the oxidation of acetyl-CoA derived from carbohydrates, fats and proteins into carbon dioxide and chemical energy in the form of adenosine triphosphate (ATP). Pyruvate from glycolysis enters the Krebs cycle by first getting converted into acetyl-CoA by the pyruvate dehydrogenase complex which is an oxidative process wherein NADH and CO_2 are formed. In addition, the cycle provides precursors of certain amino acids, as well as the reducing agent NADH, which are used in numerous other biochemical reactions.

During aerobic respiration, oxidation of one molecule of glucose produces 38 ATP molecules (net).

Interestingly, the first step of aerobic and anaerobic respiration remains the same, i.e. the conversion of glucose into pyruvate. But the amount of energy released during aerobic respiration is a lot greater than that during anaerobic respiration.

RESPIRATORY SYSTEM

Air is taken in through our nostrils that are lined with fine hair and mucous in order to prevent foreign substances from entering our body. This air enters an air passage through the throat and reaches the lungs eventually. Rings of cartilage present in the air passage prevent it from collapsing.

The air passage, on reaching the lungs, divides into two tubes called bronchi, which further divide into smaller tubes called bronchioles. These bronchioles end in alveoli or structures that are shaped like balloons. These expand when we breathe in and contract when we breathe out, thus allowing the exchange of gases to take place. Human lungs have an estimated 3,00,000,000 alveoli.

The surfaces of the alveoli have an extensive number of blood cells, which absorb oxygen from inhaled air and give away carbon dioxide when we breathe out. The oxygen is taken up by blood because of the presence of haemoglobin, a carrier which has a high affinity for oxygen. Carbon dioxide that is soluble in water is transported in the dissolved form in our blood. This is brought to the alveoli by blood from all over the body. During the breathing cycle, the lungs always contain a residual volume of air so that there is sufficient time for oxygen to be absorbed and for carbon dioxide to be released.

Expansion of the chest lowers the pressure between the lungs and the chest wall, as well as the pressure within the lungs. This causes atmospheric air to flow into the lungs. The chief muscles of inspiration are the diaphragm and the external intercostal muscles. The diaphragm is a dome-like sheet of muscle separating the abdominal and chest cavities that moves downward as it contracts. The downward motion enlarges the chest cavity and depresses the organs below. As the external intercostal muscles contract, the ribs rotate upward and laterally, increasing the chest circumference. During severe exercise other muscles may also be used. Inspiration ends with the closing of the glottis.

In expiration, the glottis opens, and the inspiratory muscles relax; the stored energy of the chest wall and lungs generates the power for expiration. During exercise or when respiration is laboured, the internal intercostal muscles and the abdominal muscles are activated. The internal intercostal muscles produce a depression of the rib cage and a decrease in chest circumference. Figure 6.1 shows a typical human respiratory system.

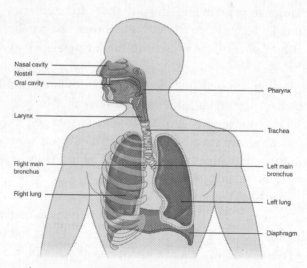

Fig. 6.1: Human respiratory system (Wikimedia commons)

BIOLOGY

7

CIRCULATION

INTRODUCTION

How do different cells of the human body receive oxygen for cellular respiration and how does carbon dioxide come out from cells through breathing out mechanism? How do our cells receive nutrients? It's all with the help of the circulatory system. The circulatory system is a network of organs and vessels that causes the flow of blood, nutrients, hormones, oxygen and other gases to and from cells. The circulatory system helps the body fight disease and maintain proper temperature and pH level.

COMPONENTS OF HUMAN CARDIOVASCULAR SYSTEM

The essential components of the human cardiovascular system are the heart, blood and blood vessels. The human cardiovascular system comprises the network for pulmonary circulation and systemic circulation. While the former circuit loops through the lungs where blood is oxygenated, the latter is a loop through the rest of the body to provide oxygenated blood. The amount of blood in an average human adult is approximately 4.7 to 5.7 litres. Blood consists of plasma, red blood cells, white blood cells and platelets.

The cardiovascular systems of humans are closed, meaning that the blood never leaves the network of blood vessels. In contrast, oxygen and nutrients diffuse across the blood vessel layers and enter interstitial fluid, which carries oxygen and nutrients to the target cells, and carbon dioxide and wastes in the opposite direction. The other component of the circulatory system, the lymphatic system, is open.

The heart pumps blood to all parts of the body and collects blood from all parts of the body through vessels. The arteries, which receive oxygenated blood at high pressure and velocity, carry it throughout the body. Arteries have thick walls that are composed of elastic fibrous tissue and muscle cells. The arteries branch into arterioles, from which blood enters capillaries. These capillaries actually exchange cellular nutrients and waste products. From the capillaries, the deoxygenated blood which carries waste products enters small vessels called venules that converge to form veins. These veins carry the blood back to the heart.

THE HUMAN HEART

The dimension of an adult human heart is normally about $13 \times 9 \times 6$ cm and weighing approximately 300 grams. It is located in the thoracic cavity behind the sternum, in front of the trachea, the esophagus, and the descending aorta, between the lungs, and above the diaphragm (the muscular partition between the chest and abdominal cavities). About two-thirds of the heart lies to the left of the midline. The heart is suspended in its own membranous sac, the pericardium.

Chambers of The Heart

Looking at the outside of the heart, you can see that the heart is made of muscle. The strong muscular walls contract to pump blood to the rest of the body. On the surface of the heart, there are coronary arteries, which supply oxygen-rich blood to the heart muscle itself. The major blood vessels that enter the heart are the superior vena cava, the inferior vena cava and the pulmonary veins. The pulmonary artery and the aorta exit the heart and carry oxygen-rich blood to the rest of the body.

On the inside, the heart is a four-chambered, hollow organ. It is divided into the left and the right side by a muscular wall called the septum. The right and left sides of the heart are further divided into two top chambers called the atria, which receive blood from the veins, and two bottom chambers called ventricles, which pump blood into the arteries.

The atria and ventricles work together, contracting and relaxing to pump blood out of the heart. As blood leaves each chamber of the heart, it passes through a valve. There are four valves within the heart: mitral valve, tricuspid valve, aortic valve and pulmonic valve. The tricuspid and mitral valves lie between the atria and ventricles. The aortic and pulmonic valves lie between the ventricles and the major blood vessels leaving the heart. The heart valves work as one-way valves and prevent blood from flowing in the wrong direction.

There are three main types of blood vessels:

Arteries: They begin with the aorta, the large artery leaving the heart. Arteries carry oxygen-rich blood away from the heart to all of the body's tissues. They branch several times, becoming smaller and smaller as they carry blood further from the heart and into organs.

Capillaries: These are small, thin blood vessels that connect the arteries and the veins. Their thin walls allow oxygen, nutrients, carbon dioxide and other waste products to pass to and from our organ's cells.

Veins: These are blood vessels that take blood back to the heart; this blood has lower oxygen content and is rich in waste products that are to be excreted or removed from the body. Veins become larger and larger as they get closer to the heart. The superior vena cava is the large vein that brings blood from the head and arms to the heart, and the inferior vena cava brings blood from the abdomen and legs into the heart.

The Mechanism of Blood Flow Through Heart

The right and left sides of the heart work together. The sequence described below is repeated again and again, causing blood to flow continuously to the heart, lungs and the rest of the body.

Right Side of the Heart

> Blood enters the heart through two large veins, the inferior and superior vena cava, emptying oxygen-deficient blood from the body into the right atrium of the heart.

> As the atrium contracts, blood flows from the right atrium into the right ventricle through the open tricuspid valve.

> When the ventricle is full, the tricuspid valve closes to prevent blood from flowing backward into the atria while the ventricle contracts.

> As the ventricle contracts, blood leaves the heart through the pulmonic valve, into the pulmonary artery and to the lungs, where it is oxygenated and then returns to the left atrium through the pulmonary veins.

Left Side of the Heart

> The pulmonary veins empty oxygen-rich blood from the lungs into the left atrium of the heart.

> As the atrium contracts, blood flows from the left atrium into the left ventricle through the open mitral valve.

> When the ventricle is full, the mitral valve shuts to prevent blood from flowing backward into the atrium while the ventricle contracts.

> As the ventricle contracts, blood leaves the heart through the aortic valve, into the aorta and to the body.

BLOOD

Blood is one of the most vital tissues of the human body and a constituent of the circulatory system. The main function of blood is transportation. It transports oxygen and nutrients to the cells and carries away carbon dioxide and other waste products. It also transports hormones.

Blood is made up of red blood cells, white blood cells, platelets and plasma. The characteristic red colour of blood of humans and other animals is due to the presence of haemoglobin. The main constituent of haemoglobin is an iron-containing protein. The plasma, which is the fluid portion of blood, is a clear, slightly sticky, yellowish liquid. It is a complex solution containing more than 90 per cent water. Other than water, it also contains protein and lipids. Several inorganic materials are essential constituents of plasma, and each has special functional roles. The predominant ion of the plasma is sodium, which has a vital role in the body. Potassium, the principal intracellular cation, occurs in plasma at a much lower concentration than sodium. Calcium, magnesium, iron, copper and zinc ions are also present in plasma. Among the many other constituents of plasma are numerous enzymes.

Blood Cells

There are four major types of blood cells: red blood cells (erythrocytes), platelets (thrombocytes), lymphocytes and phagocytic cells. Collectively, the lymphocytes and phagocytic cells constitute the white blood cells (leukocytes). Each type of blood cell has a specialized function: red cells take up oxygen from the lungs and deliver it to the tissues; platelets participate in forming blood clots; lymphocytes are involved with immunity and phagocytic cells occur in two varieties—granulocytes and monocytes—and ingest and break down microorganisms and foreign particles.

The red blood cells are highly specific for their primary function of transporting oxygen from the lungs to all of the body tissues. The red blood cell is enclosed in a thin membrane that is composed of chemically complex lipids, proteins and carbohydrates in a highly organized structure. A large percentage of the weight of a red blood cell is due to haemoglobin. The metal ion associated with haemoglobin is iron. Haemoglobin is the substance responsible for transport of oxygen to cells from lungs. It is the iron atom that reversibly binds oxygen as the blood travels between the lungs and the tissues. However, haemoglobin has a higher affinity for carbon monoxide than for oxygen. Carbon monoxide, having higher affinity, once it binds itself with haemoglobin, leaves with no more binding sites available for oxygen, thereby preventing oxygen transport.

White blood cells (leukocytes) have nucleus. These cells are involved in the body's defence mechanism. The white blood corpuscles comprise three classes of cells: granulocytes (which are further classified into three types—neutrophils, eosinophils and basophils), monocytes and lymphocytes. Granulocytes are larger than red cells.

The neutrophils are very short-lived. To guard against rapid depletion of the neutrophils (for example, during infection), the bone marrow holds a large number of them in reserve to be mobilized in response to inflammation or infection. Within the body, the neutrophils migrate to areas of infection or tissue injury. Neutrophils are actively phagocytic; they engulf bacteria and other microorganisms and microscopic particles.

Eosinophils, like other granulocytes, are produced in the bone marrow until they are released into circulation. Like neutrophils, eosinophils respond to chemotactic signals released at the site of cell destruction. They are actively motile and phagocytic. Eosinophils are involved in defense against parasites, and they participate in hypersensitivity and inflammatory reactions, primarily by dampening their destructive effects.

Basophils incite immediate hypersensitivity reactions in association with platelets, macrophages and neutrophils.

Monocytes are the largest cells of blood. Monocytes are actively motile and phagocytic. They are capable of ingesting infectious agents as well as red blood cells and other large particles, but they cannot replace the function of the neutrophils in the removal and destruction of bacteria.

Lymphocytes constitute about 28-42 per cent of the white cells of the blood, and they are part of the immune response to foreign substances in the body. Most lymphocytes are small, only slightly larger than erythrocytes, with a nucleus that occupies most of the cell. The lymphocytes are responsible for reactions to invading organisms. All lymphocytes begin their development in the bone marrow.

The blood platelets are the smallest cells of the blood. However, they occupy a much smaller fraction of the volume of the blood. They adhere to each other but not to red cells and white cells. The function of the platelets is to prevent and control bleeding. Platelets are formed in the bone marrow. There are no reserve stores of platelets except in the spleen.

BLOOD GROUPS

THE ABO SYSTEM

There are four main blood groups: A, B, AB and O. A person's blood group is determined by the genes that person inherits from his or her parents. A person's blood group is identified by antibodies and antigens in the blood. Antibodies are proteins found in plasma. Antigens are protein molecules found on the surface of red blood cells.

Table 7.1: Blood group (ABO) system

Blood group	Antigens on the RBC	Antibody in the plasma
A	A	Anti-B
B	B	Anti-A
AB	Both A and B	No antibodies
O	No antigens	Both Anti-A and Anti-B

Blood group O is called the universal donor and AB the universal acceptor.

Group A blood must never be given to someone who has group B blood, and vice versa.

THE RH SYSTEM

Red blood cells sometimes have another antigen, a protein known as the RhD antigen. If this is present, the blood group is RhD positive. If it's absent, the blood group is RhD negative.

Therefore, by including the RhD factor, the following eight blood groups can finally occur:

A+
A-
B+
B-
O+
O-
AB+
AB-

where the + and – signs indicate the presence and absence of the RhD factor, respectively.

Thus it can be concluded that in most cases, O- can safely be given to anyone. It's often used in medical emergencies when the blood type isn't immediately known for an exact match.

8

EXCRETORY SYSTEM

INTRODUCTION

Humans must get rid of two types of waste. Waste from the digestive system (faeces) and waste from metabolic activities (sweat and urine). Removing digestive waste (pooping) is called egestion. Removing metabolic waste is called excretion. In this chapter we will learn about the human excretory system.

HUMAN EXCRETORY ORGANS

There are four excretory organs in humans: the skin, the lungs, the liver and the kidney (urinary system).

THE SKIN

The skin excretes the sweat outside the body through numerous pores in its surface. Sweat is a mixture of three metabolic wastes: water, salts and urea. So, as we sweat, our body maintains two things: 1) cooling of the body 2) excretion of metabolic wastes.

The skin is formed of two layers: the thin epidermis at the top and the thicker dermis below. The inner layer of skin (dermis) contains the oil glands, hair follicles, fatty layers, nerves and sweat glands. The sweat gland leads to the sweat duct (tube) which opens on the skin surface through a pore.

Sweat Formation

Sweat glands are tubular structures tangled with blood capillaries. This close association of tubes allows wastes (namely water, salts and urea) to diffuse from the blood into the sweat gland. When body temperature rises, the fluid (sweat) is released from the gland, travels through the duct, and reaches the skin surface through openings called pores.

THE LUNGS

Cellular respiration occurs in every living cell in our body. It is the reaction that provides energy (in the form of ATP molecules) for cellular activities. As respiration produces carbon dioxide as a waste product, it has to be thrown out of the body. Carbon dioxide accumulates in body cells, it diffuses out of the cells and into the bloodstream, which eventually circulates in the lungs. In the alveoli of the lungs, carbon dioxide diffuses from the blood into the lung tissue, and then leaves the body every time we exhale. Some water vapour also exits the body during exhalation.

THE LIVER

The liver is an interesting and important organ in our body. Its takes part in the circulatory, digestive and excretory activities. Liver as an excretory organ acts to break down some proteins and other nitrogenous compounds by a process called deamination. As a result of these reactions, a nitrogenous waste called urea is formed. The liver also helps in excreting other toxic substances, drugs and their derivatives, bile pigments and cholesterol.

THE URINARY SYSTEM IN HUMANS

The major functions of the excretory system can be summarized as follows:

1. Maintenance of proper concentration of individual ions (Na^+, K^+, Cl, H^+, etc.).
2. Maintenance of proper body volume by regulating water content.
3. Maintenance of osmotic concentrations, which result from the ability of the excretory system to control water and electrolyte content in the body.
4. Removal of metabolic end products (e.g., urea, uric acid, etc.).
5. Removal of foreign substances and/or their metabolic products.

The Kidney: External Structure

Two kidneys: They are dark red, bean-shaped, and lie in the upper part of the abdominal cavity against the dorsal body wall. A layer of fat and connective tissue in which the kidneys are embedded provides them with the necessary protection. The right kidney is slightly on a lower level than the left. Each kidney is about 4½ inches long, 2½ inches broad, and over one inch thick. The weight of each kidney in an adult human is about 150 g, so they represent about 0.5 per cent of the total weight of the body.

Two ureters: They are two slender muscular tubes which take their origin at the hilum of each kidney (from the renal pelvis) and run down to join the urinary bladder.

The urinary bladder: The bladder has an elastic wall and is placed in the lower part of the abdominal cavity. It is supplied with sphincter muscles at its connection with both the ureters and the urethra.

The urethra: It is a muscular tube that carries the urine from the bladder to the outside.

Renal vein and artery: Each kidney receives a renal artery from the aorta, which brings the blood into the kidney. From each kidney, a renal vein is extended to the inferior vena cava, which carries the blood back to the heart. Figure 8.1 shows the external structure of the human excretory system.

Components of the Urinary System

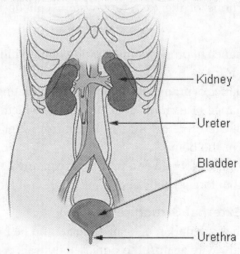

Fig. 8.1: The human excretory system (Wikimedia commons)

The Kidney: Internal Structure

Examination of vertical section of the kidney shows that the kidney is made up of the following components.

An outer cortex: It is made of a dark red tissue, due to the presence of all glomeruli which contain tufts of blood capillaries. The cortex contains all the proximal tubules and distal tubules, and cortical collecting ducts.

An inner medulla: It is made of lighter tissue, due to its relative low blood supply. The medulla has a radial appearance due to the presence of loops of Henle, the vasa recta, and medullary collecting tubules. It is subdivided into: (i) an outer medulla, which lies next to the cortex and (ii) an inner medulla which extends out into the renal sinus, forming renal papillae. The medulla is differentiated to form a number of cone-like structures known as renal pyramids with their apical ends projecting as renal papillae into the calyces of the pelvis.

The pelvis: It is a funnel-shaped structure which has, at its free end, number of cup-like cavities called calyces (singular calyx). The pelvis leads to the ureter.

Functions of Kidneys

Excretion of waste products: Kidneys excrete the waste products which contain nitrogen and sulphur, as well as ketone bodies. They aid in excretion of drugs, toxic substances, and their derivatives, e.g., penicillin.

Maintenance of constant volume of fluids and composition inside the body: The kidneys maintain constant volume of body fluids, osmotic pressure and blood pressure, hence they protect the body from diseases, by excreting excess water and electrolytes. For instance, (i) excess intake of sodium salts (NaCl) leads to hypernatermia accompanied with increased water retention which lead to increase in blood pressure and osmotic pressure, as well as development of oedema. As kidneys capable of removing the excess NaCl, they prevent the mentioned syndromes; (ii) excess intake of potassium (K+) produces hyperkalemia which leads to weakness of muscles and this causes trouble in the heart and abdominal muscles. Kidneys remove the excess K+ and keep normal muscle function, e.g., heartbeat.

Regulation of arterial blood pressure: In case of hypoxia due to hypotension, the kidneys secrete the enzyme renin, via the juxtaglomerular tissue, which converts plasma angiotensigogen to angiotensin I that are converted by convertase into angiotensin II. Angiotensin II acts as (i) a vasoconstrictor leading to raising the blood pressure and (ii) a stimulator for the secretion of both aldosterone from the adrenal cortex and antidiuretic hormone from the posterior pituitary, which cause Na+ and water retention, increasing blood volume and then restoring the blood pressure.

Synthesis of a number of prostaglandins (PGs): These are vasoactive substances that act to increase the ABP. PGE2 acts as a vasodilator that can modulate the vasoconstriction induced by sympathetic stimulation.

Regulation of blood pH through preserving acid-base balance: In case of acidosis, they secrete H+ and make it react with ammonia (NH3), forming ammonium (NH4), excreted as NH4 salts in the urine. While in the case of alkalosis, the kidneys decrease the secretion of H+, synthesis of NH4, and reabsorption of bicarbonate (HCO3-); and they increases reabsorption of Cl.

Enzyme formation: The kidneys synthesize enzymes such as histaminase to destroy the histamine, phosphatase to remove inorganic phosphate from organic compounds, and cholinesterase to destroy acetylcholine.

Endocrine function: They regulate the conversion of vitamin D to 1,25 dihydroxycholecalciferol (and also 24,25 dihydroxcholecalciferol) which facilitate the intestinal absorption of calcium and phosphate. It also acts on the bone by mobilizing the calcium ion. Parathyroid hormone (PTH) is required for renal synthesis of 1,25 dihydroxcholecalciferol.

Detoxification: In the kidney, toxic substances are converted to a non-toxic compound. For example, the kidneys convert benzoic acid to hippuric acid by combining with glycine and excrete it through urine. This process occurs mainly in the liver.

The Nephron

The kidney is made up of a number of structural and functional units called nephrons. Each human kidney contains one million nephrons or more. The nephrons are concerned with the separation of urine from the blood.

It should be noted that there are two basic types of nephrons: cortical nephrons and juxtamedullary nephrons.

Structure of the nephron: I - Malpighian corpuscle, II - Coiled uriniferous tubule (proximal tubule, loops of Henle and distal tubule). Malpighian corpuscles are placed in the cortex and each one is composed of Bowman's capsule.

Bowman's capsule: Bowman's capsule is composed of a double-walled sac, enclosing inside its cavity a network of blood capillaries, the glomerulus. The capsule is formed of two layers.

(1) An internal or visceral layer which is formed from epithelial cells that rest on a dense basement membrane. The latter membrane is the only intact barrier between blood inside the capillaries and the filtrate in Bowman's capsule.

Epithelial cells do not provide a continuous covering for the basement membrane and capillaries, being attached to them only by means of processes (pedicles or feet, Figure 8), so they are called podocytes. The visceral layer is highly involved in filtrate formation.

(2) An external or parietal layer of Bowman's capsule which is formed of simple squamous epithelium surrounded by reticular fibres. It plays no role in filtrate formation. Between these two layers, there is a space known as capsular space which receives the fluid filtered from the capillaries.

Glomerulus: The Bowman's capsule receives a small arteriole, afferent arteriole, which branches into a tuft of capillary loops about 50 in number, the glomerulus, within the capsule. The capillaries then reunite and form another small arteriole, the efferent arteriole, which leaves the capsule. The afferent arteriole is wider than the efferent one, and as a result, a pressure builds up within the capillaries which causes filtration of the water and dissolved substances out of the capillaries and into the capsule. The average diameter of the glomerulus is about 200μm and the total surface of glomerular capillaries in the two human kidneys is estimated to be about 1.5 m^2.

9

SKELETAL SYSTEM

INTRODUCTION

The structure and shape of the human body is provided by the skeletal system. The bones and associated cartilages of the skeleton create a supportive framework for the muscles and organs of the body. The bones are rigid while the cartilage components of the skeleton are flexible. The joints form the junctions between individual bones. The muscles pull against the bone levers to cause movement. In this chapter we will learn about the human skeletal system.

THE SKELETAL SYSTEM

The skeletal system consists of the axial skeleton and the appendicular skeleton. The average human adult has 206 bones that are divided into two different parts, the axial and the appendicular skeleton. While the axial skeleton consists of the skull, vertebral column and ribcage, the appendicular skeleton consists of the arms, legs and supporting structures in the shoulders and pelvis. The axial skeleton has 80 bones and it forms a vertical axis that includes the head, neck, back and chest. It consists of the skull, vertebral column and thoracic cage. The adult vertebral column consists of 24 vertebrae plus the sacrum and coccyx. The thoracic cage is formed by 12 pairs of ribs and the sternum. The appendicular skeleton consists of 126 bones in the adult and includes all of the bones of the upper and lower limbs plus the bones that anchor each limb to the axial skeleton.

The functions of the skeletal system are to act as a lever system, as surface area for attachment of muscle, tendons and ligaments, and to give shape and support to the body. Also, red/white blood cells are manufactured within the bone marrow, and bones store fats and minerals.

TYPES OF BONES AND PRINCIPAL FUNCTIONS

> Long bones, for example, the femur, act as a lever.
> Short bones, for example, carpals, have strength and lightness.
> Flat bones, for example, the pelvis, have a large surface area for muscle and tendon attachments, and the cranium protects the brain.
> Irregular bones, for example, the vertebrae, protect the spinal cord, and the patella (a sesamoid bone) increases the mechanical advantage of the quadriceps tendon.

STRUCTURE AND FUNCTION OF BONE TISSUE

> The periosteum is an outer protective covering of the bone that provides attachment for muscle tendons and ligaments.
> The deeper layers of the periosteum are responsible for growth in bone width.
> The epiphyseal disc or growth plate is the segment of a bone in which an increase in bone length takes place.
> A compact bone consists of solid bone tissue, located down the shaft of a long bone and the outer layers of short, flat and irregular bones. Its dense structure gives strength and support.
> A cancellous bone has a lattice-like/spongy appearance. It is lightweight and is located at the ends of a long bone, in addition to providing the internal bone tissue in short, flat and irregular bones.

Bone is made of collagen fibres filled with minerals, mainly calcium salts. There are five types of bone in the skeleton that are classified according to their shape. One of these types is the long bone, which is longer than it is wide and consists of a shaft, called the diaphysis and two ends, each called the epiphysis. The epiphysis is covered by articular cartilage that acts as a cushion to absorb shock and also prevents friction during joint movement. It is one of the three types of cartilage that we have in our bodies. Children and young adults have a region between the diaphysis and each epiphysis called the growth plate, which is responsible for promoting longitudinal bone growth until physical maturity. Bones also contain cavities that are filled with bone marrow, which generates new blood cells. Long bones have a large cavity in the diaphysis and a network of small cavities in each epiphysis.

ARTICULATIONS OR JOINTS

Articulations, or joints, are the junctions between two bones. Some are designed for movement; while others are merely connections between the bones. The suture lines of the skull are an example of immoveable joints. This type of joint is found in places in which bones need to be connected to form a larger unit (e.g., the skull) and where movement could prove harmful to other tissues in the area (i.e. the brain). The joints between the vertebrae are examples of partially moveable joints. The movement here is restricted because a large piece of cartilage (i.e., the intervertebral disc) is obstructing the movement of the bones. The pubic symphysis is another example of this type of joint.

Most of the other joints in the body are freely moveable joints in which there is a wide range of motion. The types of motion that can occur in these joints is determined by the shape of the bone surfaces and the placement of the ligaments (fibrous bands that connect bones together) within the joint. Some examples of the freely moveable joints would include:

- Ball and socket: shoulder and hip (round head moves within a cup) – this type of joint has the greatest freedom of motion (i.e., up/down, side to side, front to back and circular)
- Hinge: humerus to ulna articulation (trough and cylinder) – this is much like the movement of a door, back and forth
- Pivot: humerus to radius articulation (flat head of radius spins on the humerus) – this allows the turning over of the hand
- Gliding: carpal bones (flat surfaces slide across one another) – the sliding of these bones is restricted by the connective tissue band surrounding the bones

Joints are mostly of three types: fibrous, cartilaginous and synovial. Fibrous joints offer no movement, cartilaginous joints offer little movement, while synovial joints offer free movement. Figure 9.1 shows the human skeletal system.

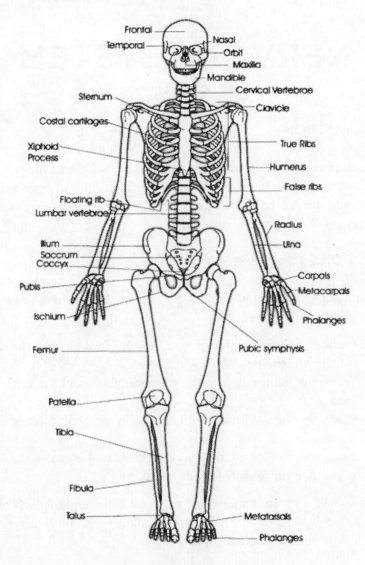

Fig. 9.1: Human skeletal system

10

NERVOUS SYSTEM

INTRODUCTION

The human nervous system is one of the most developed nervous systems in the living world. It has evolved over many thousands of years and the current structure of the human nervous system has gone through several changes and evolutions.

FUNCTIONS OF THE NERVOUS SYSTEM

The functions of the nervous system can be categorized under the following heads:

- Gathers information from both inside and outside the body (sensory function)
- Transmits information to the processing areas of the brain and spine
- Processes the information in the brain and spine (integration function)
- Sends information to the muscles, glands and organs so they can respond appropriately (motor function)

In a nutshell, it controls and coordinates all essential functions of the body including that of all the body systems allowing the body to maintain homeostasis or its delicate balance.

DIVISIONS OF THE NERVOUS SYSTEM

The nervous system is divided into two main divisions: the Central Nervous System (CNS) and the Peripheral Nervous System (PNS).

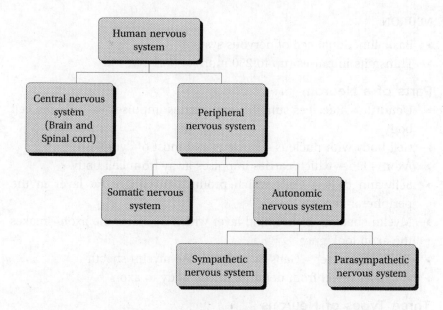

Fig. 10.1: The human nervous system

The central nervous system develops from the neural tube, while the peripheral nervous system develops from the neural crest cells.

FUNCTIONAL DIVISIONS OF THE NERVOUS SYSTEM

1. The Voluntary Nervous System or somatic division: Wilful control of effectors (skeletal muscles), and conscious perception; mediates voluntary reflexes
2. The Autonomic Nervous System: Control of autonomic effectors (smooth muscles, cardiac muscles, glands), responsible for 'visceral' reflexes

BASIC CELLS OF THE NERVOUS SYSTEM

1. Neurons – The functional cells of the nervous system
2. Neuroglia – Described as supporting cells of the nervous system; there is also a functional interdependence of neuroglial cells and neurons

NEURON

> Basic functional cell of nervous system
> Transmits impulses (up to 250 mph)

Parts of a Neuron

> Dendrite – Receives stimulus and carries impulses towards the cell body
> Cell body with nucleus – Nucleus and most of cytoplasm
> Axon – Fiber which carries impulses away from cell body
> Schwann cells – Cells which produce myelin or fat layer in the peripheral nervous system
> Myelin sheath – Dense lipid layer which insulates the axon—makes the axon look gray
> Node of Ranvier – Gaps or nodes in the myelin sheath
> Impulses travel from dendrite to cell body to axon

Three Types of Neurons

> Sensory neurons – Bring messages to CNS
> Motor neurons – Carry messages from CNS
> Interneurons – Between sensory and motor neurons in the CNS

Figure 10.1 shows the structure of a neuron.

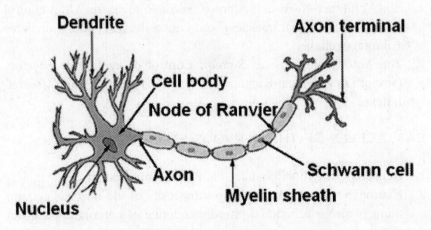

Fig. 10.2: Structure of a neuron (Wikimedia commons)

In order to connect to other cells, receptors and effectors, neurons have cytoplasmic extensions which attach to an enlarged area known as the cell body or cyton. Within the cell body is the nucleus and the neuron's biosynthetic machinery, the rough endoplasmic reticulum and the Golgi bodies. These organelles are so highly concentrated, they can be visualized with a light microscope when stained with a specific technique. Called Nissl substance after the scientist who invented the staining technique, they manufacture the neurotransmitters which the neuron must secrete in large quantities. The neurotransmitter molecules are transported to the axon terminus by microfilaments and microtubules.

There are two basic types of cytoplasmic extensions: the dendrites and the axon. Dendrites are short branching processes which receive stimuli from receptors or other neurons. They can perform this function because they, like the exposed membrane of the cell body, possess chemically-gated ion channels which respond to stimulation by neurotransmitters. So the dendrites increase the area on which a neuron can be stimulated, and together with the rest of the membrane of the cell body, constitute the neuron's receptive region.

A neuron will usually have only one axon, although it may branch extensively. The axon has voltage regulated ion gates (voltage-gated ion channels) and therefore is responsible for carrying an impulse to another neuron or effector. The axon represents the neuron's conducting region. At the end of the axon, the axon terminus is the secretory region where the neurotransmitters are released into the synapse.

A multipolar neuron has many dendrites and one axon. Multipolar neurons are found as motor neurons and interneurons.

THE SPINAL CORD

The spinal cord is the connection centre for the reflexes as well as the afferent (sensory) and efferent (motor) pathways for most of the body below the head and neck. The spinal cord begins at the brainstem and ends at about the second lumbar vertebra. The sensory, motor and interneurons are found in specific parts of the spinal cord and nearby structures. Sensory neurons have their cell bodies in the spinal (dorsal root) ganglion. Their axons travel through the dorsal root into the gray matter of the cord. Within the gray matter are interneurons with which the sensory neurons may connect. Also located in the gray matter are the motor neurons whose axons travel out of the cord through the ventral root. The white matter surrounds the gray matter. It contains the spinal tracts which ascend and descend the spinal cord. Surrounding both the spinal cord and the brain are the meninges, a three-layered covering of connective tissue. The dura mater is the tough outer layer. Beneath the dura is the arachnoid which is like a spider web in consistency. The arachnoid has abundant space within and beneath its thickened outer portion (the subarachnoid space) which contains cerebrospinal fluid, as does the space beneath the dura mater (subdural space). This cerebrospinal fluid supplies buoyancy for the spinal cord and brain to help provide shock absorption. The pia mater is a very thin layer which adheres tightly to the surface of the brain and spinal cord. It follows all contours and fissures (sulci) of the brain and cord.

CENTRAL NERVOUS SYSTEM

> Brain
>   • Brain stem – Medulla, pons, midbrain
>   • Diencephalon – Thalamus and hypothalamus
>   • Cerebellum
>   • Cerebrum
> Spine
>   • Spinal cord
>   ▪ Meninges – The three coverings around the brain and spine which help cushion, protect and nourish the brain and spinal cord.
>   § Dura mater is the outermost layer; very tough
>   § Arachnoid mater is the middle layer and adheres to the dura mater and has web-like attachments to the innermost layer, the pia mater
>   § Pia mater is very thin, transparent, but tough, and covers the entire brain, following it into all its crevices (sulci) and spinal cord
> Cerebrospinal fluid, which buffers, nourishes, and detoxifies the brain

and spinal cord, flows through the subarachnoid space, between the arachnoid mater and the pia mater

REGIONS OF THE BRAIN

Cerebellum – Coordination of movement and aspects of motor learning

Cerebrum – Conscious activity including perception, emotion, thought and planning

Thalamus – Brain's switchboard which filters and then relays information to various brain regions

Medulla – Vital reflexes like heartbeat and respiration

Brainstem – Consists of the medulla, pons and midbrain (involuntary responses) and relays information from spine to upper brain

Hypothalamus – Involved in regulating activities of internal organs, monitoring information from the autonomic nervous system, controlling the pituitary gland and its hormones, and regulating sleep and appetite

Cerebrum

➤ The largest portion of the brain; encompasses about two-thirds of the brain mass
➤ Consists of two hemispheres divided by a fissure—corpus callosum
➤ Includes the cerebral cortex, the medullary body and basal ganglia
   • Cerebral cortex is the layer of the brain often referred to as gray matter because it has cell bodies and synapses but no myelin
➤ The cortex (thin layer of tissue) is gray because nerves in this area lack the insulation or white fatty myelin sheath that makes most other parts of the brain appear to be white
➤ The cortex covers the outer portion (1.5 mm to 5 mm) of the cerebrum and cerebellum
➤ The cortex consists of folded bulges called gyri that create deep furrows or fissures called sulci
➤ The folds in the brain add to its surface area which increases the amount of gray matter and the quantity of information that can be processed
   • Medullary body is the white matter of the cerebrum and consists of myelinated axons
➤ Commisural fibers conduct impulses between the hemispheres and form the corpus callosum

> Projection fibers conduct impulses in and out of the cerebral hemispheres
> Association fibers conduct impulses within the hemispheres
>   • Basal ganglia are masses of gray matter in each hemisphere which are involved in the control of voluntary muscle movements

Lobes of the Cerebrum

> Frontal – Motor area involved in movement and in planning and coordinating behaviour
> Parietal – Sensory processing, attention and language
> Temporal – Auditory perception, speech and complex visual perceptions
> Occipital – Visual centre; plays a role in processing visual information

PERIPHERAL NERVOUS SYSTEM

CRANIAL NERVES

> 12 pairs
> Attached to undersurface of brain

SPINAL NERVES

> 31 pairs
> Attached to spinal cord

SOMATIC NERVOUS SYSTEM (VOLUNTARY)

> Relays information from skin, sense organs and skeletal muscles to CNS
> Brings responses back to skeletal muscles for voluntary responses

AUTONOMIC NERVOUS SYSTEM (INVOLUNTARY)

> Regulates body's involuntary responses
> Relays information to internal organs

There are two divisions:

- o Sympathetic nervous system – In times of stress
  - § Emergency response
  - § Fight or flight
- o Parasympathetic nervous system – When the body is at rest or performs normal functions
  - § Normal everyday conditions

SENSE ORGANS

Sense organs are responsible for sensation and perception.

- Vision – Eye
- Hearing – Ear
- Taste – Taste receptors (new)
- Smell – Olfactory system
- Skin – Hot, cold, pressure, pain

EYE

This is the organ used to sense light.

It has three layers:

1. Outer layer consists of sclera and cornea
2. Middle layer consists of choroid, ciliary body and iris
3. Inner layer consists of retina

Functions of the Major Parts of the Eye

Sclera or scleroid layer (white of the eye) – A tough protective layer of connective tissue that helps maintain the shape of the eye and provides an attachment for the muscles that move the eye

Cornea – The clear, dome-shaped part of the sclera covering the front of the eye through which light enters the eye

Anterior chamber – A small chamber between the cornea and the pupil

Aqueous humour – The clear fluid that fills that anterior chamber of the eye and helps to maintain the shape of the cornea, providing most of the nutrients for the lens and the cornea and involved in waste management in the front of the eye

Choroid layer – Middle layer of the eye containing may blood vessels

Ciliary body – The ciliary body is a circular band of muscle that is connected and sits immediately behind the iris—produces aqueous humour and changes the shape of lens for focusing

Iris – The pigmented front portion of the choroid layer contains the blood vessels—it determines the eye colour and it controls the amount of light that enters the eye by changing the size of the pupil (an albino only has the blood vessels, not pigment, so it appears red or pink because of the blood vessels)

Lens – A crystalline structure located just behind the iris; it focuses light onto the retina

Pupil – The opening in the centre of the iris; it changes size as the amount of light changes (the more the light, the smaller the hole)

Vitreous – A thick, transparent liquid that fills the centre of the eye; it is mostly water and gives the eye its form and shape (also called the vitreous humour)

Retina – Sensory tissue that lines the back of the eye. It contains millions of photoreceptors (rods for black and white and cones for colour) that convert light rays into electrical impulses that are relayed to the brain via the optic nerve

Optic nerve – The nerve that transmits electrical impulses from the retina to the brain

Common eye defects include myopia or nearsightedness where the eyeball is too long or the cornea is too steep; hyperopia or farsightedness where the eyeball is short or the lens cannot become round enough; cataracts where the lens becomes fogged; presbyopia where the muscles controlling the bulging of the lens become weak as we age; nyctalopia or night blindness where vision is impaired in dim light and in the dark due to the pigment rhodospin in the rods not functioning properly.

EAR

Outer ear and ear canal – Brings sound into the eardrums

Eardrum – Vibrates to amplify sound and separates inner and middle ear

Middle ear – Has three small bones or ossicles—anvil, stirrup and stapes—which amplify (small bones) and vibrate sound

Eustachian tube – Connects middle ear to throat and equalizes pressure on eardrum

Inner ear or cochlea – Has receptors for sound and sends signals to the brain via the auditory nerve

Process of Hearing

➤ Sound waves enter your outer ear and travel through your ear canal to the middle ear.

➤ The ear canal channels the waves to your eardrum, a thin, sensitive membrane stretched tightly over the entrance to your middle ear.

➤ The waves cause your eardrum to vibrate.

➤ The vibrations are passed on to the hammer, one of the three tiny bones in your ear. The hammer vibrating causes the anvil, the small bone touching the hammer, to vibrate. The anvil passes these vibrations to the stirrup, another small bone which touches the anvil. From the stirrup, the vibrations pass into the inner ear.

➤ The stirrup touches a liquid-filled sack and the vibrations travel into the cochlea, which is shaped like a shell.

➤ Inside the cochlea, a vestibular system is formed by three semicircular canals that are approximately at right angles to each other and are responsible for the sense of balance and spatial orientation.

The ear has chambers filled with a viscous fluid and small particles (otoliths) containing calcium carbonate. The movement of these particles over small hair cells in the inner ear sends signals to the brain that are interpreted as motion and acceleration. The brain processes the information from the ear and lets us distinguish between different types of sounds.

11

ENDOCRINE SYSTEM

INTRODUCTION

The endocrine system is a system of internal ductless glands of the body that secrete hormones within specific organs. Hormones are carried by the blood to different cells in the body. Hormones play a crucial and vital role in our body. Without hormones, we cannot grow, maintain a constant body temperature, produce offspring or perform the basic actions and functions that are essential for life.

The endocrine system provides an electrochemical connection from the hypothalamus of the brain to all the organs that control the body's metabolism, growth and development, and reproduction.

TYPES OF GLANDS

There are two types of glands—exocrine glands and endocrine glands.

Exocrine glands are those glands that release their cellular secretions through a duct which empties to the outside or into the lumen (empty internal space) of an organ. These include certain sweat glands, salivary and pancreatic glands and mammary glands. They are not considered a part of the endocrine system.

Endocrine glands are those glands that have no duct and release their secretions directly into the intercellular fluid or into the blood. All the endocrine glands put together constitute the endocrine system.

ENDOCRINE GLANDS

The main endocrine glands are the pituitary (anterior and posterior lobes), thyroid, parathyroid, adrenal (cortex and medulla), pancreas and gonads.

- The pituitary gland is attached to the hypothalamus of the lower forebrain.
- The thyroid gland consists of two lateral masses, connected by a cross bridge, that are attached to the trachea. They are slightly inferior to the larynx.
- The parathyroid glands are four masses of tissue, two embedded to the posterior of each lateral mass of the thyroid gland.
- One adrenal gland is located on top of each kidney. The cortex is the outer layer of the adrenal gland. The medulla is the inner core.
- The pancreas is along the lower curvature of the stomach, close to where it meets the first region of the small intestine, the duodenum.
- The gonads are found in the pelvic cavity.

Hormones released by different endocrine glands and their functions are given in Table 11.1.

Table 11.1: Endocrine glands and their hormones

Endocrine gland	Hormone released	Major function of hormone
Hypothalamus	Hypothalamic releasing and inhibiting hormones	Regulate anterior pituitary hormone
Posterior pituitary	Antidiuretic (ADH)	Stimulates water reabsorption by kidneys
	Oxytocin	Stimulates uterine muscle contractions and release of milk by mammary glands
Anterior pituitary	Thyroid stimulating (TSH)	Stimulates thyroid
	Adrenocorticotropic (ACTH)	Stimulates adrenal cortex
	Gonadotropic (FSH, LH)	Egg and sperm production, sex hormone production
	Prolactin (PRL)	Milk production
	Growth (GH)	Cell division, protein synthesis and bone growth
Thyroid	Thyroxine (T4) and Triiodothyronie (T3)	Increases metabolic rate, regulates growth and development
	Calcitonin	Lowers blood calcium level

Endocrine gland	Hormone released	Major function of hormone
Parathyroids	Parathyroid (PTH)	Raises blood calcium level
Adrenal cortex	Glucocorticoids (cortisol)	Raises blood glucose level, stimulates breakdown of protein
	Mineralocorticoids (aldosterone)	Reabsorbs sodium and excretes potassium
	Sex Hormones	Stimulates reproductive organs and brings on sex characteristics
Adrenal medulla	Epinephrine and norepinephrine	Released in emergency situations, raises blood glucose level, 'fight or flight' response
Pancreas	Insulin	Lowers blood glucose levels, promotes formation of glycogen
	Glucagon	Raises blood glucose levels
Testes	Androgens (testosterone)	Stimulates male sex characteristics
Ovaries	Estrogen and progesterone	Stimulates female sex characteristics
Thymus	Thymosins	Stimulates production and maturation of T lymphocytes
Pineal gland	Melatonin	Controls circadian and circannual rhythms, possibly involved in maturation of sexual organs

Figure 11.1 shows the human endocrine system.

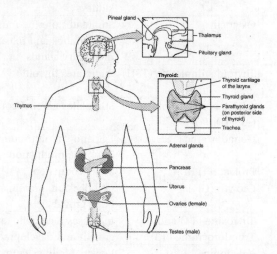

Fig. 11.1: Human endocrine system (Wikimedia commons)

Endocrine Disorders

Even the slightest problem with the functioning of one or more of the endocrine glands can cause a major disorder in the body and throw off the delicate balance of hormones in our body. This results in disorders in our systems and endocrine disease.

Causes of Endocrine Disorders

Endocrine disorders are typically grouped into two categories:

Endocrine disease that results when a gland produces too much or too little of an endocrine hormone, called a hormone imbalance.

Endocrine disease that is due to the development of lesions (such as nodules or tumours) in the endocrine system, which may or may not affect hormone levels.

Increased or decreased levels of endocrine hormone may be caused by one or more than one of the following factors:

- A problem with the endocrine feedback system
- Disease
- Failure of a gland to stimulate another gland to release hormones (for example, a problem with the hypothalamus can disrupt hormone production in the pituitary gland)
- A genetic disorder, such as multiple endocrine neoplasia (MEN) or congenital hypothyroidism
- Infection
- Injury to an endocrine gland
- Tumour of an endocrine gland
- Most endocrine tumours and nodules (lumps) are non-cancerous. They usually do not spread to other parts of the body. However, a tumour or nodule on the gland may interfere with the gland's hormone production.

Types of Endocrine Disorders

There are many different types of endocrine disorders. Diabetes is the most common endocrine disorder. Other endocrine disorders include the following.

Adrenal insufficiency: The adrenal gland releases too little of the hormone cortisol and sometimes, aldosterone. Symptoms include fatigue, stomach upset, dehydration and skin changes. Addison's disease is a type of adrenal insufficiency.

Cushing's disease: Overproduction of a pituitary gland hormone leads to an overactive adrenal gland. A similar condition called Cushing's syndrome may occur in people, particularly children, who take high doses of corticosteroid medication.

Gigantism (acromegaly) and other growth hormone problems: If the pituitary gland produces too much growth hormone, a child's bones and body parts may grow abnormally fast. If growth hormone levels are too low, a child can stop growing in height.

Hyperthyroidism: The thyroid gland produces too much thyroid hormone, leading to weight loss, fast heart rate, sweating and nervousness. The most common cause for an overactive thyroid is an autoimmune disorder called Grave's disease.

Hypothyroidism: The thyroid gland does not produce enough thyroid hormone, leading to fatigue, constipation, dry skin and depression. The underactive gland can cause slowed development in children. Some types of hypothyroidism are present at birth.

Hypopituitarism: The pituitary gland releases little or no hormones. It may be caused by a number of different diseases. Women with this condition may stop getting their periods.

Multiple Endocrine Neoplasia I and II (MEN I and MEN II): These rare, genetic conditions are passed down in families. They cause tumours of the parathyroid, adrenal and thyroid glands, leading to overproduction of hormones.

Polycystic Ovary Syndrome (PCOS): Overproduction of androgens interferes with the development of eggs and their release from the female ovaries. PCOS is a leading cause of infertility.

Precocious puberty: Abnormally early puberty occurs when glands tell the body to release sex hormones too early in life.

12

REPRODUCTIVE SYSTEM

INTRODUCTION

Reproduction is one of the fundamental processes of life where an organism gives birth to its offspring. The process of reproduction in humans is complex. It involves specialized and different anatomies in the two sexes, a hormone regulation system and specialized behaviours regulated by the brain and endocrine system. Humans are sexually reproducing and viviparous. The reproductive events in humans include the following steps:

- Gametogenesis, by which formation of gametes i.e., sperms in males and ovum in females, takes place
- Insemination by which transfer of sperms into the female genital tract takes place
- Fertilization which causes fusion of male and female gametes, leading to formation of zygote
- Implantation is the process of formation and development of a blastocyst and its attachment to the uterine wall
- Gestation, i.e., embryonic development
- Parturition, i.e., delivery of the baby

Although it is a vast as well as complex subject, we will confine ourselves to learning about the human reproductive system.

THE MALE REPRODUCTIVE SYSTEM

The male reproductive system is located in the pelvis region. A pair of testes, along with accessory ducts, glands and the external genitalia, together constitute the male reproductive system. The testes are situated outside the abdominal cavity within a pouch called the scrotum. In adults, the testis is oval in shape. The male germ cells undergo meiotic divisions, finally leading to sperm formation, while Sertoli cells provide nutrition to the germ cells. The regions outside the seminiferous tubules called interstitial spaces contain small blood vessels and interstitial cells or Leydig cells. Leydig cells synthesize and secrete testicular hormones called androgens. Other immunologically competent cells are also present.

The male sex accessory ducts include rete testis, vasa efferentia, epididymis and vas deferens. The seminiferous tubules of the testes open into the vasa efferentia through the rete testis. The vasa efferentia leave the testis and open into the epididymis located along the posterior surface of each testis. The epididymis leads to vas deferens that ascends to the abdomen and loops over the urinary bladder. It receives a duct from the seminal vesicle and opens into the urethra as the ejaculatory duct. These ducts store and transport the sperms from the testis to the outside through the urethra. The urethra originates from the urinary bladder and extends through the penis to its external opening called the urethral meatus.

The penis is the male external genitalia. It is made up of special spongy tissue that helps in the erection of the penis to facilitate insemination. The enlarged end of the penis called the glans penis is covered by a loose fold of skin called the foreskin. The male accessory glands include paired seminal vesicles, a prostate and paired bulbourethral glands. Secretions of these glands constitute the seminal plasma which is rich in fructose, calcium and certain enzymes. The secretions of bulbourethral glands also help in the lubrication of the penis. Figure 12.1 shows the male reproductive system in human beings.

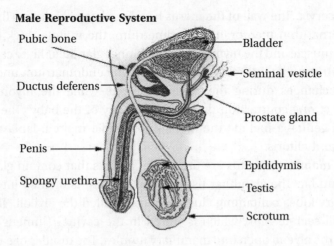

Male Reproductive System

Pubic bone

Bladder

Seminal vesicle

Ductus deferens

Prostate gland

Penis

Epididymis

Spongy urethra

Testis

Scrotum

Fig. 12.1: Male reproductive system (Wikimedia commons)

THE FEMALE REPRODUCTIVE SYSTEM

The female reproductive system consists of a pair of ovaries along with a pair of oviducts, uterus, cervix, vagina and the external genitalia located in the pelvic region. Ovaries are the primary female sex organs that produce the female gamete (ovum) and several ovarian hormones. The ovaries are located one on each side of the lower abdomen. Each ovary is about 2–4 cm in length and is connected to the pelvic wall and uterus by ligaments. Each ovary is covered by a thin epithelium that encloses the ovarian stroma. The stroma is divided into two zones—a peripheral cortex and an inner medulla. The oviducts (fallopian tubes), uterus and vagina constitute the female accessory ducts. Each fallopian tube is about 10–12 cm long and extends from the periphery of each ovary to the uterus. The part closer to the ovary is the funnel-shaped infundibulum. The edges of the infundibulum possess finger-like projections called fimbriae, which help in the collection of the ovum after ovulation. The infundibulum leads to a wider part of the oviduct called the ampulla. The last part of the oviduct, the isthmus, has a narrow lumen and it joins the uterus. The uterus is single and it is also called the womb. The shape of the uterus is like an inverted pear. It is supported by ligaments attached to the pelvic wall. The uterus opens into the vagina through a narrow cervix. The wall of the uterus has three layers of tissue. These are the external thin membranous perimetrium, the middle thick layer of smooth muscle and the myometrium and inner glandular layer called the endometrium that lines the uterine cavity. The endometrium undergoes cyclical changes during the menstrual cycle while the myometrium exhibits strong contraction during the delivery of the baby. The female external genitalia include the mons pubis, labia majora, labia minora, hymen and clitoris.

The mammary glands are the pair of breasts that contain glandular tissue and fat. The glandular tissue of each breast is divided into 15-20 mammary lobes containing clusters of cells called the alveoli. The cells of alveoli secrete milk, which is stored in the cavities (lumens) of the alveoli. The alveoli open into mammary tubules. The tubules of each lobe join to form a mammary duct. Several mammary ducts join to form a wider mammary ampulla which is connected to lactiferous duct through which milk is sucked out. Figure 12.2 shows the structure of the female reproductive system.

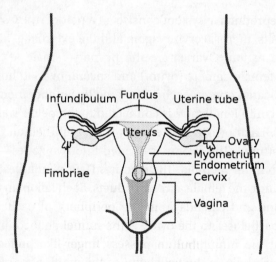

Fig. 12.2: Female reproductive system (Wikimedia commons)

THE MENSTRUAL CYCLE

The reproductive cycle in females is also called the menstrual cycle. The cycle is present in apes as well. The first menstruation at puberty is called the menarche. Thereafter, menstruation is repeated at an average interval of about 28/29 days. The cycle of events starting from one menstruation till the next one is called the menstrual cycle. One ovum is released (ovulation) during the middle of each menstrual cycle. The major events of the menstrual cycle and the changes that happen are shown in Figure 12.3. The cycle starts with the menstrual phase, when menstrual flow occurs, and it lasts for 3–5 days. The menstrual flow results due to the breakdown of the endometrial lining of the uterus and its blood vessels which forms a liquid that comes out through the vagina. Menstruation only occurs if the released ovum is not fertilized. Absense of menstruation may be indicative of pregnancy. However, it may also be caused because of a variety of other reasons like stress, poor health, etc. The menstrual phase is followed by the follicular phase.

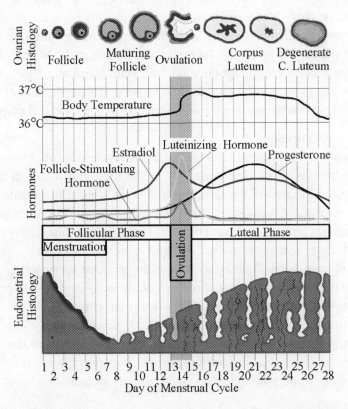

Fig. 12.3: Menstrual cycle in human females (Wikimedia commons)

STRUCTURE OF THE HUMAN SPERM

The sperm or the male gamete has a microscopic structure which has a head, a neck, a middle piece and a tail. A plasma membrane covers the whole body of sperm. The sperm head has an elongated nucleus which is haploid. The anterior portion of the nucleus is covered by a cap-like structure, the acrosome. The acrosome of the sperm is filled with enzymes. These enzymes help in fertilization of the ovum. The middle piece of sperm possesses numerous mitochondria, which produce energy for the movement of tail that facilitate sperm motility essential for fertilization.

GAMETOGENESIS (SPERMATOGENESIS AND OOGENESIS)

Gametogenesis, the production of sperm and eggs, involves the process of meiosis. During meiosis, two nuclear divisions separate the paired chromosomes in the nucleus and then separate the chromatids that were made during an earlier stage of the cell's life cycle. Meiosis and its associated cell divisions produce haploid cells with half of each pair of chromosomes normally found in diploid cells. The production of sperm is called spermatogenesis and the production of eggs is called oogenesis.

Spermatogenesis

Spermatogenesis occurs in the wall of the seminiferous tubules, with the most primitive cells at the periphery of the tube and the most mature sperm at the lumen of the tube. Immediately under the capsule of the tubule are diploid, undifferentiated cells. These stem cells, each called a spermatogonium (pluralspermatogonia), go through mitosis to produce one cell that remains as a stem cell and a second cell called a primary spermatocyte that will undergo meiosis to produce sperms.

The diploid primary spermatocyte goes through meiosis I to produce two haploid cells called secondary spermatocytes. Each secondary spermatocyte divides after meiosis II to produce two cells called spermatids. The spermatids eventually reach the lumen of the tubule and grow a flagellum, becoming sperm cells. Four sperms result from each primary spermatocyte that goes through meiosis.

Oogenesis

Oogenesis occurs in the outermost layers of the ovaries. As with sperm production, oogenesis starts with a germ cell. In oogenesis, this germ cell is called an oogonium and forms during the embryological development of the individual. The oogonium undergoes mitosis to produce about one to two million oocytes by the time of birth.

The primary oocytes begin meiosis before birth. However, the meiotic division is arrested in its progress in the first prophase stage. At the time of birth, all future eggs are in prophase I. This situation is in contrast with the male reproductive system in which sperms are produced continuously throughout the life of the individual. Starting at adolescence, anterior pituitary hormones cause the development of a few follicles in an ovary each month. This results in a primary oocyte finishing the first meiotic division. The cell divides unequally, with most of the cytoplasm and organelles going to one cell, called a secondary oocyte, and only one set of chromosomes and a small amount of cytoplasm going to the other cell. This second cell is called a polar body and usually dies. Cell division is again arrested, this time at metaphase II. At ovulation, this secondary oocyte is released and travels toward the uterus through the oviduct. If the secondary oocyte is fertilized, the cell continues through meiosis II, producing a second polar body and haploid egg, which fuses with the haploid sperm to form a fertilized egg (zygote) containing all 46 chromosomes.

FERTILIZATION

The fusion of a haploid male gamete, or a sperm, and the haploid female gamete, or an ovum, is called fertilization. The motile sperms swim and pass the cervix to enter into the uterus and finally reach the ovum released by the ovary in the ampulla-isthmic junction. Fertilization takes place in the ampulla-isthmic junction. The sperm, after reaching the ovary in the ampulla-isthmic junction, comes in contact with the zona-pellucida layer of the ovum and blocks the entry of the additional sperms. Thus, only one sperm fertilizes the ovum. The secretions of acrosome help the sperm to enter into the ovum through zonapellucida and the plasma membrane and thus the secondary oocyte completes meiosis II and results in the formation of a second polar body and haploid ovum. The haploid nucleus of the sperm and the ovum fuse together to form a zygote which develops into a new individual.

PREGNANCY AND EMBRYONIC DEVELOPMENT

After implantation, finger-like projections appear on the trophoblast called chorionic villi. Uterine tissue and maternal blood surround the chorionic villi. The chorionic villi and uterine tissue together form a structural and functional organic structure between the developing embryo and tissues of the mother called the placenta. The placenta facilitates the supply of oxygen and nutrients to the embryo. It helps in the removal of carbon dioxide and excretory/waste materials produced by the embryo. The placenta is connected to the embryo through an umbilical cord which helps in the transport of substances to and from the embryo. The placenta also acts as an endocrine tissue and produces several hormones like human chorionic gonadotropin (hCG), human placental lactogen (hPL), estrogens, progestogen, etc. A hormone called relaxin is secreted by the ovary in the later phase of pregnancy. hCG, hPL and relaxin are produced in women only during pregnancy. Levels of other hormones like estrogens, progestogens, cortisol, prolactin, thyroxine, etc., are increased several folds in the maternal blood. Increased production of all the hormones is essential for supporting the foetal growth, metabolic changes in the mother and maintenance of pregnancy.

After implantation, the inner cell mass is differentiated into an outer layer called the ectoderm and an inner layer called the endoderm with a middle layer. The three layers give rise to all organs in adults. The cells which have the potency to give rise to any type of cells in the body are called stem cells. Human pregnancy lasts for nine months, the heart develops after one month of pregnancy, limbs develop by the end of the second month and major organ systems are formed by the end of the third month. First movement and appearance of hair happen during the fifth month of pregnancy. By the end of 24 weeks, the body is covered with fine hair, eyelids are separated and eyelashes formed. At the end of nine months, the foetus fully develops.

PARTURITION AND LACTATION

The average duration of human pregnancy is about nine months and is known as the gestation period. Vigorous contraction of the uterus at the end of pregnancy causes expulsion/delivery of the foetus, called parturition. The signals for parturition originate from the fully developed foetus, and the placenta which induces mild uterine contraction is called foetal ejection reflex. Foetal ejection reflex releases oxytocin hormone from the pituitary gland of the mother which acts on the uterine muscle and causes contraction of the uterus which, in turn, stimulates further oxytocin secretion. Production of milk at the end of pregnancy by the mammary glands is called lactation. The milk produced during the first few days of lactation is called colostrum. Colostrum contains antibodies necessary to develop resistance against diseases of the newborn baby.

13

GENETICS

INTRODUCTION

Since time immemorial, we have known, a lioness always gave birth to a lion cub and never to some other animal. Similarly, a date plant grows from a date seed only. Our curiosity further takes us to the question whether the offspring are identical to their parents. Or is there any difference in some of their characteristics? These and several related questions are dealt with scientifically in a branch of biology known as genetics. Therefore, genetics is the scientific study of heredity.

The modern approach to genetics can be traced to the mid-nineteenth century, with Gregor Johann Mendel's experiments and analyses of inheritance in peas. Mendel's experiments were simple and direct and they brought forth the most significant principles that determine how traits are passed from one generation to the next. He is known as the father of genetics.

MENDEL'S LAWS OF INHERITANCE

Mendel conducted hybridization experiments on garden peas and proposed the laws of inheritance in living organisms. Mendel investigated characters in the garden pea plant that were manifested as two opposing traits, e.g., tall or dwarf plants and yellow or green seed coats. Mendel selected 14 true-breeding pea plant varieties as pairs which were similar except for one character with contrasting traits. Some of the contrasting traits are given in Table 13.1.

Table 13.1: Contrasting traits studied by Mendel in pea

S. No.	Characters	Contrasting traits
1.	Stem height	Tall/dwarf
2.	Flower colour	Violet/white
3.	Flower position	Axial/terminal
4.	Pod shape	Inflated/constricted
5.	Pod colour	Green/yellow
6.	Seed shape	Round/wrinkled
7.	Seed colour	Yellow/green

Let us explain the results of Mendel's hybridization between tall and dwarf pea plants to study the inheritance of one gene. The seeds produced as a result of hybridization between tall and dwarf plants were grown to generate plants of the first hybrid generation. This generation is called the Filial 1 progeny or the F1. Mendel observed that all the F1 progeny plants were tall, like one of their parents; none were dwarf. He concluded that the F1 always resembled either one of the parents, and that the trait of the other parent was not seen in them.

The tall F1 plants were self-pollinated after that and to his surprise Mendel found that in the Filial 2 generation some of the offspring were 'dwarf'; the character that was not seen in the F1 generation now reappeared. The self-pollinated F1 plants (or cross-pollinated with other F1 plants) produce an F2 generation with three out of four of the plants tall and one out of four short. Therefore the ratio of tall to dwarf plants in the F2 generation was ¾ to ¼.

Let us now turn our attention to understand the phenotype and genotype of the F1 and F2 generations. Let us use uppercase T for the tall trait and lowercase t for the dwarf; T and t are alleles of each other. Hence, in plants, the pair of alleles for height would be TT, Tt or tt. Mendel proposed that in a true breeding, tall or dwarf pea variety the allelic pair of genes for height are identical or homozygous, TT and tt, respectively. TT and tt are called the genotype of the plant while the descriptive terms tall and dwarf are the phenotype. According to Mendel, in a pair of dissimilar factors, one dominates the other (as in the F1) and hence is called the dominant factor while the other factor is recessive. T (for tallness) is dominant over t (for dwarfness), that is recessive.

Therefore, in F1 generation all the plants are tall.

The phenotype of the experiment in F1 and F2 generation can be represented as in Fig 13.1 below.

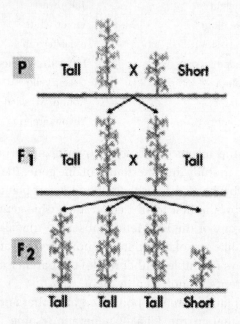

Fig. 13.1: Mendel's experiment and the phenotype in F1 and F2 generation

The probability of all possible genotypes of offspring in a genetic cross was developed by a British geneticist, Reginald C. Punnett. For Mendel's experiment, the production of gametes by the parents, the formation of the zygotes, the F2 plants can be understood from the Punnett Square as shown in Figure 13.2.

	T	t
T	**TT**	**Tt**
t	**Tt**	**tt**

Fig. 13.2: Punnett square showing distribution of genotype in F2 generation

MENDEL'S FIRST LAW: LAW OF DOMINANCE

According to this law, when two alternative forms of a trait are present in an organism, only one factor expresses itself in the F1 progeny. This trait is called dominant. The other trait which remains hidden is called recessive.

MENDEL'S SECOND LAW: LAW OF SEGREGATION

Law of segregation states that the pair of alleles segregates from each other during meiosis (gamete formation) so that only one allele will be present in each gamete. In a monohybrid cross, both the alleles are expressed in the F2 generation without any blending. Thus, the law of segregation is based on the fact that each gamete contains only one allele.

MENDEL'S THIRD LAW: LAW OF INDEPENDENT ASSORTMENT

The law of independent assortment states that during a dihybrid cross (crossing of two pairs of traits), an assortment of each pair of traits is independent of the other. In other words, during gamete formation, one pair of trait segregates from another pair of traits independently. This gives each pair of characters a chance of expression.

The dihybrid crosses between the parental genotype RRYY (round yellow seeds) and rryy (green wrinkled seeds) explain the law. Here the chances of formation of gametes with the gene R and the gene r are 50:50. Also, the chances of formation of gametes with the gene Y and the gene y are 50:50. Thus, each gamete should have either R or r and Y or y. The law of independent assortment states that the segregation of R and r is independent of the segregation of Y and y. This results in four types of gametes: RY, Ry, rY and ry. These combinations of alleles are different from their parental combinations (RR, YY, rr and yy).

The results of the dihybrid cross experiment are shown in Figure 13.3.

THE MOLECULAR BASIS OF GENETIC INHERITANCE

The genome is the blueprint for all cellular structures and activities and is stored in the nucleus of every cell. It is made up of tightly wound strands of deoxyribonucleic acid (DNA) organized, in humans, into 23 pairs of chromosomes: 22 autosome pairs (numbered 1–22) and one sex chromosome pair (XX in females and XY in males). The basic form of a DNA molecule is that of a twisted ladder or double helix, proposed by Watson and Creek. Each strand of the helix is a linear arrangement of repeating units called nucleotides that consist of one sugar, one phosphate and a nitrogen-containing molecule called a base. There are four possible bases—adenine (A), guanine (G), cytosine (C) and thymine (T)—and it is the order of these bases along the sugar-phosphate backbone that makes the DNA sequence. This sequence specifies the genetic instructions required to create a protein and, ultimately, to create an entire organism. In the DNA double helix, the bases are always paired (T with A, and G with C) and are often referred to as base pairs.

Genes are composed of exons (coding regions) linked by introns (non-coding regions). Specific triplets of nucleotides encode different amino acids, which are the building blocks of the gene products (proteins). During transcription of the DNA, the introns are removed and the coding exons are spliced together to form a messenger RNA (mRNA) that is an exact mirror image of the successive triplet codons in the exons. The mRNA is exported out of the nucleus into the cytoplasm, where triplet codons are translated into the amino acids of the protein on the ribosomes. Variations in the nucleotide sequence of DNA are common, and when they occur in introns or intervening sequence, they usually are silent. When they affect the coding or regulatory regions of genes, however, they can lead to a change in the gene's function. Copies of specific genes with such a difference in nucleotide sequence are called alleles. In general, each individual carries only two copies of an autosomal gene, and therefore only two alleles, but many different alleles can exist in the population. By definition, non-deleterious alterations, or sequence variants, in alleles occurring in more than 1 per cent of the population are called polymorphisms. When the altered nucleotide responsible for the allelic difference is part of a triplet codon in a coding exon, it can cause a mutation or deleterious change to the amino acid sequence of the resulting protein. In contrast to the normal or wild-type copy, the allele carrying such a change is called the mutant allele. For instance, the mutant allele of the β-globin gene has an A-to-T transition at codon 6, which causes the amino acid glutamine to be replaced by valine at position 6 of the protein (Glu6Val); this one change leads to sickle cell haemoglobin (HbS). Such small-scale changes of only one or a few nucleotides, referred to as point mutations, are a typical cause of Mendelian disorders. When the nucleotide change results in a codon for a different amino acid, as with the sickle cell disease mutation in β-globin, it is called a missense mutation. A nonsense mutation is a nucleotide change resulting in a stop codon (TGA or TAA) that signals the ribosome to stop translating the mRNA and thus truncates the protein. A deletion or insertion of one or two base pairs (or another number that cannot be divided by three) shifts the reading frame of the mRNA and changes an entire series of amino acids until a stop codon is reached in the novel reading frame (frameshift mutation). In general, once a de novo mutation has occurred, it is stably inherited with each mitotic and meiotic cell division.

EXCEPTIONS TO MENDEL'S LAWS

In many ways Mendel was successful in stating his genetic laws. However, things are not always so clear-cut and simple in the world of genetics. Therefore, we find a number of exceptions to Mendel's laws.

INCOMPLETE DOMINANCE

With incomplete dominance, a cross between organisms with two different phenotypes produces offspring with a third phenotype that is a blending of the parental traits. For example, in the snapdragon, *Antirrhinum majus*, a cross between a homozygous white-flowered plant and a homozygous red-flowered plant will produce offspring with pink flowers. This type of relationship between alleles, with a heterozygote phenotype intermediate between the two homozygote phenotypes, is called incomplete dominance. It's like mixing of paints; red × white will make pink. Red doesn't totally block (dominate) the white; instead there is incomplete dominance, and we end up with something in-between.

CODOMINANCE

The meaning of the prefix 'co' is 'together'. S codominance would mean where both the alleles dominate.

A hybrid organism shows a third phenotype, not the usual 'dominant' one and not the 'recessive' one, but a third, different phenotype. With incomplete dominance we saw blending of the dominant and recessive traits so that the third phenotype is something in the middle (red × white = pink). However, in codominance, the 'recessive' and 'dominant' traits appear together in the phenotype of hybrid organisms.

It is very much like red × white → red and white spotted.

With codominance, a cross between organisms with two different phenotypes produces offspring with a third phenotype in which both of the parental traits appear together. Blood group AB is the resulting phenotype for A and B alleles of blood group.

MULTIPLE ALLELES

If more than two alternate forms of a gene are present on the same locus, those alleles are called multiple alleles. There is absence of crossing over in multiple alleles and the mode of inheritance is called multiple allelism. A well-known example is the human ABO blood group system.

The ABO system in humans is controlled by three alleles, usually referred to as I^A, I^B and I^O (the 'I' stands for isohaemagglutinin). I^A and I^B are codominant and produce type A and type B antigens, respectively, which migrate to the surface of red blood cells, while I^O is the recessive allele and produces no antigen. The blood groups (phenotype) arising from the different possible genotypes are summarized in Table 13.2.

Table 13.2: ABO blood groups from multiple alleles

Genotype	Blood group
$I^A I^A$	A
$I^A I^O$	A
$I^B I^B$	B
$I^B I^O$	B
$I^A I^B$	AB
$I^O I^O$	O

The ABO group system is an excellent example where complete dominance, codominance and multiple alleles, all the three exist as shown in Table 13.3.

Table 13.3: Multiple alleles, complete dominance and co-dominance in ABO blood grouping system

Multiple alleles	I^A, I^B and I^O
Complete dominance	Between I^A and I^O
Complete dominance	Between I^B and I^O
Codominance	Between I^A and I^B

MUTATION

Mutation is an alteration in the genetic material (the genome) of a cell of a living organism. The alteration becomes more or less permanent and it gets transmitted to the descendants. This transmission to descendant cells happens by DNA replication and hence results in a sector or patch of cells having abnormal function. Mutations in egg or sperm cells (germinal mutations) may result in an individual offspring, all of whose cells carry the mutation, which often confers some serious malfunction, as in the case of a human genetic disease. Mutations result either from accidents during the normal chemical transactions of DNA, often during replication, or from exposure to high-energy electromagnetic radiation (e.g., ultraviolet light or X-rays) or particle radiation or to highly reactive chemicals in the environment. Because mutations are random changes, they are expected to be mostly deleterious, but some may be beneficial in certain environments. In general, mutation is the main source of genetic variation, which is the raw material for evolution by natural selection.

14

HEREDITY AND EVOLUTION

INTRODUCTION

Gregor J. Mendel is the father of heredity. At the heart of Mendel's results which determined various traits and how they were carried from one generation to another was the genetic material which was not known at the time of Mendel's experiment. The material which is responsible for this is now known as the DNA which is the abbreviation of deoxyribonucleic acid. This molecule encodes the genetic information and passes on the same information from one generation to another. The term heredity refers to the transmission of traits or characters from parents to offspring. Evolution is the process of gradual change from simple life forms to complex organisms. In this chapter we will learn about heredity and evolution.

DEOXYRIBONUCLEIC ACID (DNA)

DNA consists of two polynucleotide chains or strands, wound around each other such that they resemble a twisted ladder. This structure is referred to as the double helix. The backbone of each of these strands is a repeating pattern of a 5-carbon sugar, deoxyribose, and a phosphate group. Each sugar is attached to one of the four nitrogen-containing bases: adenine (A), thymine (T), guanine (G) and cytosine (C). The sugar present in the nucleotide is a deoxyribose, hence the name deoxyribonucleic acid (DNA). In the double helix DNA structure, all four bases are confined to the inside of the double helix, held in place by hydrogen bonds linking complimentary bases on the two strands. Adenine and thymine are paired by two hydrogen bonds, whereas cytosine and guanine are paired by three hydrogen bonds. The bases are stacked up the ladder and the hydrophobic bonding between the bases gives the DNA molecule stability. The ordering of the bases is the most crucial aspect in heredity as this determines the DNA's instructions, or genetic code. Similar to the way the order of letters in the alphabet can be used to form a word, the order of nitrogen bases in a DNA sequence forms genes, which, in the language of the cell, tells cells how to make proteins. Another type of nucleic acid, ribonucleic acid, or RNA, translates genetic information from DNA into proteins.

The two DNA strands in the double helix run in opposite directions (antiparallel to each other) to help the bases in each base pair fit into the double helix. This means the nucleotides in each strand of DNA are exactly complementary to that in the other strand. In the double helix structure as a ladder, the phosphate and sugar molecules would be the sides, while the bases would be the rungs. The bases on one strand pair with the bases on another strand: adenine pairs with thymine, and guanine pairs with cytosine. Figure 14.1 shows the double helix structure of DNA.

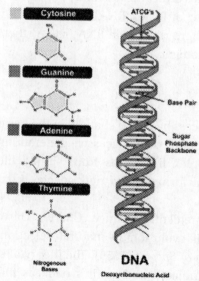

Fig. 14.1: Double helix structure of DNA

To fit inside cells, DNA is coiled tightly to form chromosomes. Each chromosome contains a single DNA molecule. Humans have 23 pairs of chromosomes, which are found inside the cell's nucleus.

RIBONUCLEIC ACID (RNA)

Ribonucleic acid (RNA) is a polymeric molecule that is pivotal in hereditary roles carrying out coding, decoding, regulation and expression of genes. RNA, very much like DNA, is a nucleic acid. However, unlike DNA, RNA is found in nature as a single strand folded onto itself, rather than a paired double-strand (structure of DNA). The four bases that constitute an RNA molecule are adenine (A), uracil (U), guanine (G) and cytosine (C). Cellular organisms use messenger RNA (mRNA) to convey genetic information using the nitrogenous bases. The genetic information directs synthesis of specific proteins. Some RNA molecules play an active role within cells by catalyzing biological reactions, controlling gene expression, or sensing and communicating responses to cellular signals. One of these active processes is protein synthesis, a universal function where RNA molecules direct the assembly of proteins on ribosomes. This process uses transfer of RNA (tRNA) molecules to deliver amino acids to the ribosome, where ribosomal RNA (rRNA) then links amino acids together to form proteins.

EVOLUTION

Evolution is the process by which changes in the heritable characteristics of biological populations over successive generations takes place, giving rise to more complex life forms from simple life forms. Evolution comprises repeated formation of new species, change within species and loss of species.

In the mid-nineteenth century, Charles Darwin formulated the scientific theory of evolution by natural selection, published in his book *On the Origin of Species* (1859). The theory of evolution by natural selection, first formulated in Darwin's book, is the process by which organisms change over time as a result of changes in heritable physical or behavioural traits. Changes that allow an organism to better adapt to its environment will help it survive and have more offspring. Evolution by natural selection is one of the best substantiated theories in the history of science. The theory has been supported by evidence from a wide variety of scientific studies in various disciplines.

THEORIES OF EVOLUTION

Based on the evidences of evolution, various theories have been put forward by scientists about the evolution of life. The most important theories were postulated by Lamarck and Darwin.

Lamarck's Theories

Changes in the structure or function of any organ acquired during the lifetime of an individual in response to changes in the environment are inherited by the offspring and keep on adding over a period of time. These changes lead to the origin of new species.

Lamarck's postulates are:

1. New needs: There are changes occurring in the environment that creates new needs; these allow them to adapt better to the changed environment. These efforts lead to a change in habits or behaviour.

2. Acquisition of new characters or organs: new characters can be acquired in two ways.

    By use and disuse of organs: Continuous use or disuse of an organ can keep them functional and efficient or lead to a gradual reduction in size and disappearance. Vestigial organs are examples of such structures.

    Effect of environment: Changes in temperature, light, medium, food, etc. influence the functioning and behaviour of the organisms. These changes in functioning and behaviour changes lead to development of new characters.

3. Inheritance of acquired characters: The characters acquired by the organism are inherited to the next generation. Thus, in every generation, new characters are added and the species gets modified to a new one.

4. Speciation: In every generation, new characters are acquired and transmitted to the next generation, so that new characters accumulate generation after generation. After a number of generations, a new species is formed.

There are certain evidences in favour of Lamarck's postulates.

1. Evolution of long neck in giraffe: According to Lamarck, giraffes evolved from deer-like ancestors. These organisms had short necks and forelimbs and grazed on grass. As the climatic conditions changed, the rich vegetation changed to a few trees. The leaves of these trees were the only source of food for these giraffes. The ancestors of the giraffe had to stretch their neck to obtain the leaves on the trees. This gradual stretching of the neck led to increase in the sizes of the neck and forelimbs. This was then transmitted to the next generation and thus giraffes have long neck and forelimbs.

2. Evolution of feet of modern horse. They developed the power of running fast to protect themselves from enemies. Thus gradually there was lengthening of limbs and the middle digit with the reduction of other digits.

3. Evolution of snakes. According to Lamarck, the ancestors of snakes were limbed and lizard-like. They lived in thick jungles. Out of fear of mammals, these snakes started creeping on the jungle floor and living in narrow crevices or burrows. For creeping among the vegetation or burrowing in the narrow crevices, they stretched their bodies, which gradually became elongated. The limbs were of no use and were a hindrance in creeping and burrowing; thus they gradually disappeared.

4. Webbed feet in aquatic birds. Aquatic birds like ducks, swans and geese, etc., have arisen from terrestrial ancestors by developing a web between the toes for wading in water (adaptation to aquatic mode of life through continuous use). The web developed because the ancestral forms had to spread their toes and stretch the skin between them to rest on water; reduction in the size of wings was due to their continuous disuse.

Theory of Darwin

Darwin's postulates are the following:

1. **Overproduction:** All living beings have an inherent tendency to produce offspring of their own kind in large numbers for the perpetuation of their race. The number of their offspring is much

more than can be supported by a particular environment and can possibly survive.

2. **Limited food and space:** The space in the universe remains constant. The ultimate source of food for plants and animals also remains constant. Thus, the carrying capacity of the environment does not allow the population to grow indefinitely. In spite of enormous reproductive potential of living beings under natural conditions the number of individuals of each species remains nearly constant over a long period of time.

3. **Struggle for existence:** According to Darwin, individuals multiply in geometric ratio whereas space and food availability remains constant, so there is an intense competition and three-fold struggle for existence. The struggle is within the same species, within two different species, and with the environment.

4. **Variations:** The struggle for existence results in competition among the organisms. Thus the organisms adapt and differ from each other in shape, size, behaviour, etc.

5. **Natural selection and survival of the fittest:** According to Darwin, nature selects only those individuals who are with more favourable variations and are best adapted to the environment. The less fit and unfit organisms are left out by selection. This sorting out of individuals with useful variations was called natural selection by Darwin and survival of the fittest by Wallace.

6. **Inheritance of useful variations:** The individuals who survive the struggle for existence transmit their useful variations to the offspring, which will also prove to be fit. Thus offsprings of selected individual are born fit to the environment.

7. **Formation or origin of new species:** Darwin suggested the appearance of new variations in every generation. These variations keep on accumulating, and after a number of generations, the offsprings become markedly different, forming a new species. The origin of new species by gradual modification of older ones is called speciation.

Neo-Darwinism

The Dutch botanist Hugo de Vries proposed the mutation theory, according to which new species arose due to appearance of sudden inheritable changes. According to him, new species are not formed by continuous variations but by sudden appearance of variations, which he named mutations. Hugo de Vries stated that mutations are heritable and persist in successive generations. On the basis of Darwin's theory and de Vries' theory the modern concept of evolution or Neo-Darwinism was formed.

The salient features of de Vries' theory are the following:

On the basis of the above observations, Hugo de Vries (1901) put forward a theory of evolution, called mutation theory. The theory states that evolution is a jerky process where new varieties and species are formed by mutations (discontinuous variations) that function as the raw material for evolution. The salient features of mutation theory are:

1. Mutations or discontinuous variations are the raw material of evolution. Mutations appear all of a sudden. They become operational immediately.
2. Mutations do not revolve around the mean or normal character of the species. The same type of mutations can appear in a number of individuals of a species.
3. All mutations are inheritable. Useful mutations are selected by nature. Lethal mutations are eliminated. However, useless and less harmful ones can persist in the progeny.
4. Evolution is a jerky and discontinuous process.

SECTION IV

COMPUTER SCIENCE

1

BASICS OF COMPUTER

INTRODUCTION TO COMPUTERS

All of us know that our daily life without computers is unthinkable today. They are everywhere and so much so that we use computers even for the smallest activity today. Someone might argue that it is an overstatement. Whether this statement is an overstatement or not, or how much of this is correct and how much is not may be the subject of an academic discussion, but from our daily life experience it may be safely concluded that computers have reshaped our lives at work, school, home and outside.

In this chapter we will learn some basics of computer, how computers evolved, and what the latest in computing is.

WHAT IS A COMPUTER?

In layman's terms, a computer is a machine that processes data. In slightly more scientific terms, it is an electronic device that is capable of converting data into information that can be used. It processes a set of data instructed and controlled by instructions, called programs. Therefore, for a complete understanding of the working of a computer, we may say that it is an electronic device that is designed to receive data as input from users, process the data as per instruction based on built-in commands or programs, and produce a result as the desired output. The output may be obtained as required on an output device, whether it is a monitor or a printer or any other external output device attached to the computer. We should also remember that a computer is a device that can be programmed, thereby making it perform arithmetic and logical operations, which is also a data processor, as it can store, process and retrieve data as per the instructions of the user.

The generalized term 'computer' indicates digital computers. These are mostly all around us. Scientifically, they process every bit of information in terms of numbers. Another type of computer is the analog computer. These are not only lesser known or less popular today, but they also work differently from digital computers.

HISTORY OF COMPUTER EVOLUTION

Computers have been around for a lot longer than what we commonly believe. However, the computer was not created in a day. Neither was it the result of one single invention. Rather, computers that we find today are complex machines, which are the result of a large number of inventions and developments that started as early as the sixteenth century. The abacus, which is the first recognized calculating device used for addition and subtraction, is considered to be the forefather of modern-day computers. Since then, a lot of inventions contributed to the development of modern-day computers. Since the entire history of development of machines and devices that contributed to modern-day computers is out of the scope of this book, we confine ourselves to the most significant inventions of the sixteenth century and onwards that contributed to the modern day computer.

Table 1.1: Inventors and their inventions

Name	Invention	Year
Babylonians	Abacus	
John Napier	Napier bones	1617
	Side ruler	1632
Blaise Pascal	Adding machine (Pascaline)	1642
Gottfried Wilhems	Improved Pascal machine and it was called (Step reckoner)	1674
Joseph Jacquard	Mechanical loom	1801
Charles Babbage	Difference engine	1822
Charles Babbage	Analytical engine	.1833

Charles Babbage, the father of the computer, and Ada Augusta Lovelace, the first computer programmer, designed programs for the Analytical Engine.		
Herman Hollerith	Tabulating machine	1890
Herman Hollerith was the one who established the IBM (International Business Machines)		
Howard Aiken	Sequence Controlled Calculator (Mark I)	1944
John Vincent Atanasoff and Cliff Berry	Atanasoff-Berry Computer (ABC)	Between 1937–1942
John Von Neumann	A concent—to get different tasks performed by using its stored programs without effecting any physical changes to the computer	1942
Moor school of electrical engineering of the University of Pennsylvania	The world's first electronic digital computer, ENIVAC (Electronical Numerical Integrator and Computer) could carry out about 5,000 calculations per second and used about 18,000 vacuum tubes	

GENERATIONS OF COMPUTER

Various developments in calculating devices, technologies, hardwares, etc. directly or indirectly have made significant contributions in the evolution of computers. In order to group together a number of technological developments, computers are categorized in generations. In other words, one generation of computers differs significantly from another generation of computers. The next generation is said to start only when the technology of the new generation is upgraded and significantly different from the previous generation. Based on technology upgradation, we have first generation computers, second generation computers, etc., and the current generation is the fifth generation of computers. The following table gives a brief history of the generations of computers.

Table 1.2: Computers by generation

Generation	1	2	3	4	5
Duration	1945–1956	1956–1963	1964–1971	1971–present	Present and futuristic
Memory device	Vacuum tubes or valves	Silicon transistor	IC (Integrated circuits)	Silicon chip VLSI or microprocessor	Biochips
Features	• Used vaccum tubes as electronic circuit • Magnetic drum for primary storage • Mercury delay lined for memory • Punch card used as secondary storage • Machine level programming used • Operating speed was used in terms of millisecond	• Magnet core memory used as internal storage • Magnetic tapes used as secondary storage • Little faster I/O devices • High level language used as programming • Processing speed measured in microsecond	• Semiconductor memory used as primary storage • Magnetic discs were used as secondary storage • Massive use of high level language • Processing speed increased to nanosecond and even faster	• Massive use of magnetic and optical storage devices with capacity more than 100 GB • Advancement in software and high level language • Use of 4th generation language (4GL) • Operation speed increased beyond picoseconds and MIPS (Millions of Instructions Per Second)	• AI will make computer intelligent and knowledge based • Very high speed, PROLOG (programming language)
Example	Mark-I, UNIVAC, ENIAC	IMB 1401, ICL 2950/10	IBM 360 series, UNIVAC 9000	IMB PC, Pentium PC, Apple/ Macintosh	

COMPONENTS OF A COMPUTER SYSTEM

A computer system comprises mainly of two kinds of components: hardware and software.

HARDWARE

The physical components of a computer system are known as its hardware. The following are the different types of hardware components (which carry out specific functions).

Monitor: It displays (visual) the result.

CPU: It is the acronym for Central Processing Unit. The term suggests that it controls the computer's central functions and transmits data for further actions.

Motherboard: It is mainly accountable for establishing communication between components and transmission of information.

RAM: It is the acronym for Random Access Memory. RAM is responsible for temporarily storing data and information of currently-running programs.

Hard disk drive: It is a permanent memory storage device.

Floppy disk drive: It is a data storage device, but is obsolete today.

Optical disks: This is also a device that stores data.

Input and output devices

The following table categorically lists down the commonly used input and output devices.

Table 1.3: Input and output devices

Input device	Output device
Mouse	Monitor
Keyboard	Printer
Scanner	Projector
Touchpad	Plotter
Microphone	Speaker
Camera	Earphone
Joystick	

SOFTWARE

Software consists of programs that perform commands or instructions provided by a user. These commands work based on certain built-in instructions in the computer system. A computer system cannot function without software. Software controls the sequence of operations of a computer.

Types of Software

Depending on the basic features and functionality, software can be broadly categorized into Operating Systems (OS) and Application Software (AS).

Operating System

This software helps to load the basic program automatically as soon as the computer is started. The following are the major types of operating system:

Table 1.4: Operating systems

Operating system software	Example
Microsoft Windows	XP, Vista, Windows 98, Windows 10, etc.
Mac OS X	Panther, cheetah, snow leopard, etc.
Linux	Debian, ubuntu, fedora, knoppix, etc.
UNIX	

Application Software

An application software consists of a program written for a certain specific purpose and for carrying out some specialized function. Such a program can be used on an installed operating system. Following are the examples of some of the common and widely used application software.

Table 1.5: Application softwares

Application software	Examples
Office program	Microsoft Office, OpenOffice, LibreOffice, etc.
Web browser	Internet Explorer, Mozilla Firefox, Google Chrome, Opera, Safari, etc.
Antivirus program	Norton, McAfee, Quick Heal, Avira, Kaspersky, etc.

In addition to these, there are many other application softwares. Some of these are educational software, some engineering software, some medical software, and some gaming software.

CLASSIFICATION OF COMPUTERS

Computers are so widely used and in almost every field—from personal data processing to scientific computational work to business to complex medical and engineering issues—such that it is not possible to classify computers in just one way.

Based on the purpose that computers serve, they are classified either as general purpose or specific purpose computers.

Based on the technique of data handling and functionality, computers are classified as analog, digital and hybrid, which is a mixture of analog and digital.

Analog Computer: An analog computer is a form of computer that uses electrical signals in its architecture.

Digital Computer: For a digital computer, everything is in binary. It performs calculations and logical operations by executing each instruction represented as digits, usually in the binary number system.

Hybrid Computer: A hybrid computer is a combination of computers that are capable of handling analog as well as digital signals.

On the basis of size, computers can be classified into the following types:

Super Computer: These computers exhibit the fastest speed in data processing and have large memory so they are the most powerful type of computer. Super computers are employed for complex and specialized applications that require huge volume of computational work and mathematical calculations.

Mainframe Computer: Mainframe computers are capable of supporting a large number of users simultaneously. In the order of performance these computers come just below supercomputers. While supercomputers are specialized to carry out particularly highly complex and computation-intensive jobs at a very fast rate, mainframe computers can host a large number of programs and users simultaneously.

Mini Computer: As the name suggests, these are mid-sized computers. These computers are capable of executing multiple processes simultaneously and can support a large number of users at the same time for computational work.

Micro Computer or Personal Computer: These can be further classified as:

- Desktop Computer: A personal or micro-mini computer sufficient to fit on a desk.

- Laptop Computer: A portable computer that has a screen as an output device, a keyboard and a mouse as input devices. The mouse features may be built-in and come as a factory-fitted touchpad. It is generally smaller in size than a desktop computer and larger than a notebook computer.
- Palmtop Computer/Digital Diary/Notebook /PDAs: A hand-sized computer. Palmtops have no separately attached keyboard but the screen serves both as an input and an output device.

USES OF COMPUTERS

As we have already learnt, and it is common knowledge today, computers have become an essential part of modern human life. Ever since its invention, the computer has been at the centre stage of attempts by scientists to use it in various fields. Ever-increasing computing power and decrease in its size have worked to its advantage when computers have been put to use in various fields. In short, life in today's world would be unimaginable without computers. Uses of computer in different fields of work are just gigantic in proportion. It would not only be futile to make an attempt to list all the uses of computers in various fields, but also out of the scope of this book. Therefore, we will try to touch upon some of the more common uses. Computers are used for scientific and mathematical research and computation, designing, for word processing and emailing in offices, accounting, e-commerce, etc.

Computers in Education: A major use of computers is in the field of teaching and learning. Computers can significantly contribute to what is called Computer Aided Learning (CAL), e-learning, distance learning, assessment, etc.

Computers in Telecommunication: In the era of digital telecommunication, handling a large number of calls simultaneously through a network is possible with the use of computer technology. Today's communication technology largely collaborates with communication satellites, etc. Without computers in these space research activities, it would not have been possible to go to that advanced level. Teleconferencing and video conferencing are some of the other areas of telecommunication where computer systems are in big use.

Computers in Health and Medicine: In today's world of Internet and digitization with high-resolution images and videos, doctors and healthcare professionals can get in touch with each other and exchange information about complicated medical conditions of patients and help each other with expert opinion. Medical equipments now come fitted with computers to analyse data and give insights about patients' condition. Scientists of late are trying to use Artificial Intelligence (AI) in a big way in healthcare not only to cure patients, but also to predict a healthy person's likely health problems in the time to come based on his or her health parameters at the present time. Medical transcription is another field where use of computers is widely seen. Digitization of health records of patients in various hospitals helps them to keep records of a huge volume of patients easily, enabling them to sift through past health issues, medical history, past treatments, etc. easily and quickly.

Computers in Financial Institutions: Banks and other financial institutions use computers for various purposes. They store customer information in a database which is available at any time. With operations automated and the database being available at all times, it is possible to carry out transactions not only during banking office hours, for which one may not necessarily have to visit the bank's office, but also at a time beyond normal banking hours and without visiting the bank.

Computers in Entertainment Industry: We often come across terms like film editing, SFX, mixing, etc. These all pertain to the entertainment and film industry. With the advent of sophisticated computers equipped with high quality graphics and software for video editing, audio editing, audio integration, sound effects, etc., professionals create unbelievable visual effects, special effects, etc. in films of today. High quality computer and trained professionals to use them have only made it possible. Furthermore, we all listen to music and sometimes watch movies on our computer, which has become possible by digitization and computer technology.

Computers in Gaming: Computer games are a major hit among people. These are a favourite pastime for many people and are quite engrossing. Some of them are quite complicated and need huge mathematical calculations through complex algorithms at the programming level.

Computers in Transport: We all book tickets for journey by train, bus, flight, etc. using our computer. We get timely updates from the transport provider about the status. High speed computer and specific software programs have made it possible.

Computers in Personal Use: Computers are used for many personal purposes also. Apart from storing our favourite music or movie, we also store our bank records, house records, personal photos, books, etc.

Computers in Business and Workplace: At a time when time is the most precious commodity, nobody wants to lose it. One way to be with time in doing work is its proper organization, and no one can do it better than a computer. Business communication in both private offices and government offices is done through e-mail. Other than that, in every field of business there are specific software applications available, which make the working systematic, planned and properly organized.

Computers in Defence: Highly potential defence systems, weapons, surveillance and spying, and the entire defence establishments of a country are fully dependent on computers. Without sophisticated computer programs and complex algorithms, weapons cannot be launched to attack a target at a long distance with accuracy and precision. Coupled with the modern communication system which again depends on high quality computer systems, the defence network of a country rests on very powerful computer networks which are managed and used by highly trained professionals of that field.

Computers in E-Commerce: We are all familiar with the term e-commerce today. We do shopping online by ordering what we need using our computer. But that is just one aspect of it. From collecting orders to processing them to collecting payment to warehousing to delivery, everything is connected, and advanced computer technology has made it all possible.

There are many other complicated aspects in the use of computers in each and every field mentioned above. We have tried to give readers some idea about various aspects of our life in which the computer has become inseparable from us and we are fully dependent on it.

2

COMPUTER HARDWARE

INTRODUCTION

At the beginning of this chapter we will give the readers some basic concept about computer architecture. As we have learnt in the previous chapter, a fully functional computer is made of its hardware and software. The architecture of a computer describes how its hardware and software interact so that the computer system works flawlessly. In other words, computer architecture refers to the design of a computer system. It also tells about the technologies that it is compatible with.

Computer systems can be classified into two separate categories based on their application. In the first and most obvious category comes a computer itself. For example, a desktop computer or a laptop. In the second category come embedded computer systems. Embedded computer systems are not so-called computers themselves, but are integrated with another system so that control and/or monitoring of that system can be carried out. Embedded computers may appear to be less in number as we do not see them in their well-known form of the computer, but they are far more numerous than desktops. Ask any person—if he does not have a computer in his home, he will respond by saying he does not have one, but the fact is, he may have many more computers than he thinks; hidden inside his TVs, VCRs, DVD players, remote controls, washing machines, cell phones, air conditioners, game consoles, ovens, toys and a host of other devices.

COMPUTER ARCHITECTURE

A computer system is made up of five basic units. These units or components help the computer to carry out operations.

- Input Unit
- Output Unit
- Storage Unit
- Arithmetic and Logic Unit
- Control Unit

We will discuss in detail the function of each unit in the following section.

INPUT UNIT

An input unit is the means to provide input in the form of data and instructions to the computer system. An input unit is therefore an external device that connects with the internal components of the computer. Some of the commonly used input devices are keyboard, mouse, etc.

An input unit performs the following tasks:

- Accepts data from outside
- Accepts instructions from outside
- Supplies the data to the computer system

Some common input units are as follows:

Keyboard

There are a number of types of keyboards available, but the most common type is called the QWERTY keyboard. The name stems from the fact that in this type of keyboard the first row of alphabets from the top row contains keys that have these letters; one on each key, in the order of letters given.

Mouse

Another commonly used input device is the mouse. There are several types of mouse, out of which the ball-and-roller mechanical mouse, optical mouse, cordless mouse and trackball mouse are the most important ones.

Scanner

A scanner is another type of input device very common today. Scanners scan through pictures and pages containing text as input, and convert them into a file in digital format. This file can be stored in the computer or can be displayed on the screen as an output also. The technique it uses is called optical character recognition (OCR), to convert images into digital files. Some of the common types of scanners are the flatbed scanner, handheld scanner, drum scanner, photo scanner, etc.

Joystick

People who are familiar with computer games may know about joysticks. A joystick is a pointing input device like a mouse, but it is structurally different from the latter. It has a stick with a spherical base, which is fitted in a socket. In this arrangement, the stick can move freely. Hence, by moving the stick, the movement of the cursor or pointer on the screen can be controlled.

Microphone

Another common input device for computers is a microphone. It provides sound as input to the computer. The vibrations due to sound are converted into digital signals or digital data and stored in the computer for further processing. Microphones are also used for teleconferencing or web conferencing through the computer.

Magnetic Ink Character Recognition (MICR)

It is a more advanced input device and is used for a specific purpose. For example, we all are familiar with the MICR code written at the bottom of a leaf of a bank cheque. It contains all the relevant information of the account and about the account holder. The input device is designed to read the text printed with magnetic ink. The device reads the details stored in the magnetic characters and sends them to a computer for processing.

Optical Character Reader (OCR)

It is another specialized technique used for a specific purpose. The OCR computer input device is designed to convert the scanned images of handwritten, typed or printed text into digital text. It is widely used in digitization of office records, books and old documents into electronic documents. Historical records and old legal records are all stored in digitized form using this technique.

OUTPUT UNIT

An output unit is a device that produces the output of a computer operation in the form that can be read, understood and interpreted by humans. It acts as a connect between the internal system of a computer and the external environment. Some output devices are printers, monitors, etc.

Monitor

The most common output device of a computer is the monitor. There are four types of monitors.

- CRT monitor
- LCD monitor
- LED monitor
- Plasma monitor

CRT monitors are the earliest ones. These use the cathode ray technology. However, these monitors are almost obsolete today and we use much more technologically-upgraded ones today.

LCD monitors have a flat screen, are compact and lightweight. LCD stands for liquid crystal display. As the name suggests, these monitors are based on liquid crystal display technology. An improved version in the LCDs contains thin film transistors (TFTs) with capacitors.

An LED monitor is an improved version of an LCD monitor. It is similar to an LCD in many aspects. However, the differentiating factor is the source of backlight. The backlight illuminates the display. While an LCD monitor uses cold cathode fluorescent light, an LED monitor has many LED panels at the back end, and each panel has several LEDs to backlight the display.

The latest technology used in monitors is the plasma display technology, hence the name plasma monitors. Plasma displays are brighter than liquid crystal displays (LCD) and also offer a wider viewing angle than an LCD.

Printer

Printers are among the oldest output devices used with computers. Printers have undergone huge changes and today we get a variety of printers doing from very simple to complex printing work as output device to computers.

Some of the commonly used printers today are:

- Dot matrix printers
- Laser printers
- Inkjet printers

A dot matrix printer, as the name suggests, prints characters and images as patterns of dots. The print head runs over a ribbon which is soaked in ink and produces dots on a page, in such a way that the position of dots together makes it look like characters consisting of alphabets, numerical digits, etc., and images. The more the pins in the print head, the better the print quality. However, these printers are slow in their output and often lack clarity in the output produced. These printers are almost obsolete these days.

A laser printer uses laser beam technology to print characters. These printers are equipped with a drum, which rolls in toner and prints characters and images on paper. For the purpose of printing, laser printers use powdered toner instead of liquid ink. The quality of print produced is much better than that produced by dot matrix printers. These are much faster also in producing outputs.

An inkjet printer, as the name suggests, produces print output by spraying fine droplets of ink that come out as a jet. The print head itself is equipped with tiny nozzles to produce this jet. When the printer head moves back and forth and sprays droplets of ink on the paper, printing of alphanumeric characters and images takes place. The advantage of inkjet technology is that it can produce colour prints of high quality.

Projector

This is another very commonly used output device in computers, called a projector. It is used to project the output from a computer onto a big screen. Sometimes even a smooth white surface of a wall can be used for display purpose. In this way magnified texts, images, etc. can be produced so that many people can have a look at the output sitting in a big room and without having to bother looking at the computer monitor. Newer and newer technology advancements have enabled producing these outputs through HDMI ports so that users can experience High Definition (HD) outputs on big screens.

STORAGE UNIT

A storage unit, as the name suggests, is responsible for storing the data and instructions. It also stores the intermediate results of computation before these are sent to the output devices. Another function of a storage unit is to store data for later use.

The storage unit of a computer system can be divided into two categories:

Primary Storage

Primary storage memory, also called temporary storage memory, is used to store data which is being used in the current process. The data stored here is of current operation and will not be stored permanently. On the other hand, the data will be erased when the computer is switched off. Random Access Memory (RAM) is used as primary storage memory.

Secondary Storage

Secondary storage memory is used to permanently store data, until and unless it is erased by the user. It may be an internal component of the computer system, such as a hard disk, or an external component, such as a CD. Examples of other secondary storage devices are floppy disks, magnetic tape, optical disk, etc.

Hard disk

It is a rigid magnetic disc that is used to store data. It permanently stores data and is located inside a computer. Some hard disks are also available which can be plugged in with the computer from outside.

Other storage devices are optical disks, pen drive, etc.

Central Processing Unit (CPU)

It is the Central Processing Unit of the computer. It has two components— the control unit and the ALU. It can be easily understood that the CPU is the central and most important component of a computer system, so much so that it can be called the brain of the computer. Its functions are to control operations, and do arithmetic and logical operations.

The process flow occurring among the various components of a computer system can be shown by the schematic diagram below.

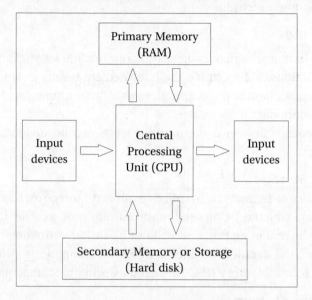

Fig. 2.1: Processes in a computer system

ARITHMETIC LOGIC UNIT (ALU)

Actual computational work is done here. All the calculations are performed in the ALU of the computer system. As the name suggests, an ALU can perform both arithmetic as well as logical operations.

CONTROL UNIT

It has to its authority the command and control of all other units of the computer. It controls the transmission of data and instructions to and from the storage unit to the ALU.

COMPUTER MEMORY

Memory is that component of a computer that can hold data and instructions. Both data and instructions are needed to carry out operations and produce output. Depending on the requirement, memory can sometimes be permanent and sometimes temporary. Therefore, computer memory is of two types: volatile (RAM) or temporary and non-volatile (ROM) or permanent. The hard disk of a computer is a storage device and does not act as the memory.

One of the commonest terms in computers is cache memory. It stores data and instruction in such a way that when required it can be accessed quickly by a computer. This way data and instructions that are needed to be accessed frequently by the CPU are made available, thus making the operation fast and efficient. Hence, it speeds up the system performance. Data and instructions can be erased from the cache memory.

Another common term in computer architecture is Random Access Memory (RAM). It is also known as volatile memory. It does not store data or instructions permanently. The CPU utilizes data and instruction stored here to perform the operations but as soon as the computer system is shut down, the RAM loses all the data.

Read Only Memory or ROM is non-volatile in nature. It means that data and instruction stored here are not erasable. Systems come with data and instructions pre-loaded and this uses ROM. One of the most important parts written in the ROM is the set of instructions to boot the system or load the operating system.

MEMORY UNITS

In our common parlance we use terms like 6GB RAM, 8GB RAM, 1TB hard disk, etc. What are these GB, TB, etc.? These are called memory units. In order to understand memory units, one must remember that computers work in the binary system (0 and 1). From the words **B**inary and dig**ITS** computer scientists derived the word BITS. Therefore each storage unit in a computer is defined in terms of BITS. Some of the commonly used memory units are:

- Bit: The computer memory unit starts from bit. A bit is the smallest memory unit to store data. The smallest memory location of a bit can store only one binary value: either 0 or 1.
- Byte: 1 byte = 8 bits. Thus, a byte can represent 2^8 or 256 values.
- Kilobyte: A kilobyte has 1024 bytes.
- Megabyte: A megabyte has 1024 kilobytes.
- Gigabyte: A gigabyte has 1024 megabytes.
- Terabyte: A terabyte has 1024 gigabytes.
- Petabyte: A petabyte has 1024 terabytes.

3

COMPUTER SOFTWARE

INTRODUCTION

As we have mentioned in an earlier section, a functional computer system is made of its hardware and the instructions given to the hardware, as to how to process data, etc. These sets of instructions are known as computer software. Plainly speaking, computer software is actually a set of programs that enables the hardware to perform a specific task.

TYPES OF COMPUTER SOFTWARE

As can be understood from the introductory line, certain instructions that are required by the computer are mandatory. In other words, without these instructions, the computer cannot function. There are other softwares that perform other specific tasks as required by a user. Therefore, there are two types of software: system software and application software.

SYSTEM SOFTWARE

System software is the main software that runs the computer. Often these are a collection of programs that work in tandem. When a computer system is turned on, a system software activates the hardware and establishes controls and coordination within various units. System software programs are written in low-level languages, which interact with the hardware at a very fundamental level. These are also called firmware. An operating system is an example of system software. Other examples are compilers, assemblers, etc.

We will try here to give the reader a basic understanding of how instructions flow due to system software. When a computer is started (switched on), the Basic Input/Output System (BIOS) gets activated. Transmission of data between the operating system and the attached devices such as the hard disk, monitor, keyboard, mouse, printer, etc. is controlled and managed by the BIOS. Following this, the boot program loads the operating system into the computer's RAM.

Operating System (OS)

The operating system is the system software that makes the system ready to interface with users to enable communication with the computer. Commonly used operating systems are Microsoft Windows, Linux, UNIX, Ubuntu and Apple Mac OS. If an operating system is tampered with, or uninstalled completely or partially, or if it does not function properly, the computer will not work.

APPLICATION SOFTWARE

An application software is a set of programs written with a specific purpose to perform a specific task. It may not control or coordinate the working of a computer but it does interface with the operating system of the computer. A computer may or may not have an application software, depending on the requirement. These softwares can be installed or uninstalled whenever required.

Some common examples of application softwares are: accounting software, payroll software, income tax software, railways reservation software, Microsoft Office suite programs, e-mail applications, Internet applications (browsers), etc.

Some of the softwares are available for free. These are called freeware.

Some of the softwares are licensed versions but the license is for use, and the user cannot have the source code with him. These are called shareware.

An application software is generally written in a high-level programming language. A high-level language is one that is readable by people. However, since computers do not understand high-level language, these high-level instructions and programs are converted into machine language instructions, which the computer can read and understand. Obviously, this is in binary code for the computer to be able to process these instructions.

Examples of programming languages:

- C
- C++
- C#
- FORTRAN
- BASIC
- JAVA
- Visual Basic
- Phyton
- HTML
- PHP

Some Common Application Software

The world of application software is so vast that no single book can give the readers knowledge about all the softwares that are used for various purposes. Naturally, that is also outside the scope of this book. However, in this section, we will attempt to familiarize the reader with some of the most commonly used application software.

Table 3.1: Application software types

Application software type	Examples
Word processing software	MS Word, WordPad and Notepad
Database software	Oracle, MS Access, etc.
Spreadsheet software	Microsoft Excel
Multimedia software	Real player, VLC media player
Presentation software	Microsoft Power Point
Information Worker software	Documentation tools, resource management tools
Educational software	Dictionaries: Encarta, Britannica Mathematical: MATLAB Others: Google Earth, NASA World Wind
Simulation software	Flight and scientific simulators
Content Access software	Accessing content through media players, web browsers
Application suites	OpenOffice, Microsoft Office

4

NUMBER SYSTEM

INTRODUCTION

We have already understood about high-level language and low-level language in the context of computer operations. When we key in some characters, letters, words, sentences, numbers, etc., the computer translates them into numbers as computers can understand only numbers. In this chapter we will learn about number systems that are used by computers.

TYPES OF NUMBER SYSTEM

There are three components required to understand the value of each digit in a number. These are the following:

- The digit
- The position of the digit in the number
- The base of the number system (where the base is defined as the total number of digits available in the number system)

In this section we will discuss in detail the third bullet point.

DECIMAL NUMBER SYSTEM

This is the number system we use in our daily life and it is the easiest to understand and work on. The decimal number system has base 10 as there are 10 digits in use, from 0 to 9. In the decimal number system, the successive positions to the left of the decimal point represent units, tens, hundreds, thousands, ten thousands, and so on.

Each position represents a specific power of the base (10). For example, the decimal number 6789 consists of the digit 9 in the units position, 8 in the tens position, 7 in the hundreds position, and 6 in the thousands position. Its value can be written as:

$(6 \times 1000) + (7 \times 100) + (8 \times 10) + (9 \times 1)$
i.e., $(6 \times 10^3) + (7 \times 10^2) + (8 \times 10^1) + (9 \times 1)$
i.e., $6000 + 700 + 80 + 9$
i.e., 6789

In the context of computer architecture and operations, you should understand the following number systems.

Table 4.1: Number systems

S. no.	Number system	Description
1	Binary number system	Base 2. Digits used: 0 and 1
2	Octal number system	Base 8. Digits used: 0 to 7
3	Hexadecimal number system	Base 16. Digits used: 0 to 9, Letters used: A–F

BINARY NUMBER SYSTEM

It uses two digits, 0 and 1. It is also known as the base 2 number system.

Example of a binary number: 110100

Note: As we have already stated earlier, a bit is a single binary digit. The number in the example given above has 6 bits.

Each position in a binary number represents a power of the base (2). So, instead of powers of ten (10^n), for example: 1, 10, 100, 1000 (n = 0, 1, 2, 3, respectively) etc., binary numbers use powers of two (2^n). This effectively doubles the value of each successive bit as it goes, for example: 1, 2, 4, 8, 16, 32, etc., for 2^0, 2^1, 2^2, 2^3, 2^4, 2^5 respectively.

Let us take an example.

Binary number: 10101_2

As we do not write base 10 for decimal system, we will omit the base 2 also for binary system.

We will show here what the decimal equivalent of the above binary number is.

Table 4.2: Binary to decimal

Step	Binary number	Decimal number
Step 1	10101	$((1 \times 2^4) + (0 \times 2^3) + (1 \times 2^2) + (0 \times 2^1) + (1 \times 2^0))$
Step 2	10101	$(16 + 0 + 4 + 0 + 1)$
Step 3	10101	21

OCTAL NUMBER SYSTEM

It uses eight digits, 0, 1, 2, 3, 4, 5, 6 and 7. It is also called the base 8 number system. Each position in an octal number represents a 0 power of the base (8).

Each position in an octal number represents a power of the base (8). So, instead of powers of ten (10^n), for example: 1, 10, 100, 1000 (n = 0, 1, 2, 3, respectively) etc., octal numbers use powers of eight (8^n).

We will explain how the octal number system works with the help of an example.

Octal number: 12570_8

Note: Here also we will ignore writing the base 8.

Table 4.3: Octal to decimal

Step	Octal number	Decimal number
Step 1	12570	$((1 \times 8^4) + (2 \times 8^3) + (5 \times 8^2) + (7 \times 8^1) + (0 \times 8^0))$
Step 2	12570	$(4096 + 1024 + 320 + 56 + 0)$
Step 3	12570	5496

HEXADECIMAL NUMBER SYSTEM

It uses 10 digits and 6 letters: 0, 1, 2, 3, 4, 5, 6, 7, 8, 9, A, B, C, D, E and F, where the letters represent the numbers starting from 10, that is, A = 10, B = 11, C = 12, D = 13, E = 14, F = 15. It is also called the base 16 number system.

We will explain the equivalent decimal number of a hexadecimal number.

Hexadecimal number: $19FDE_{16}$

Table 4.4: Binary to decimal

Step	Binary number	Decimal number
Step 1	19FDE	$((1 \times 16^4) + (9 \times 16^3) + (F \times 16^2) + (D \times 16^1) + (E \times 16^0))$
Step 2	19FDE	$((1 \times 16^4) + (9 \times 16^3) + (15 \times 16^2) + (13 \times 16^1) + (14 \times 16^0))$
Step 3	19FDE	$(65536 + 36864 + 3840 + 208 + 14)$
Step 4	19FDE	106462

COMPUTER CODES

Before we understand various types of codes used in a computer, we need to understand what the different types of data used in computers are.

- Computers use alphabets: A, a, B, b, C, c, etc., both in uppercase and lowercase
- Computers use numeric characters 0, 1, 2, 3, etc.
- Computers use special characters such as *, &, (,), ^, %, $, #, @ ! ~, etc.

Computer codes are used for internal representation of data in computers. ASCII, BCD, EBCDIC and Unicode are different types of computer codes.

ASCII

ASCII is the American Standard Code for Information Interchange. The characters encoded are numbers 0–9, a–z, A–Z, basic punctuation symbols and control codes.

BCD

BCD stands for Binary Coded Decimal. It is represented by a 4-bit number and so we can represent sixteen numbers (0000 to 1111).

EBCDIC

EBCDIC stands for Extended Binary-Coded Decimal Interchange Code. It has an 8-bit code. It was used by IBM.

UNICODE

Unicode is a standard for representing the characters of all the languages of the world. Unicode uses 16-bits per character to represent 65,536 (216) unique characters.

5

COMPUTER NETWORK AND DATA COMMUNICATION

INTRODUCTION

Today we are living in an era where there is hardly any time we work in isolation on our computer. A computer can be connected to another computer or a number of computers which enable all the computers so connected to share their resources.

A computer which is not connected to any other computer is called a closed system. On the other hand, if a computer is connected to another or a number of other computers, and is open for communication, it is called an open system.

In this chapter we will learn about computer network and data communication.

A network is the interconnection of multiple computers, generally termed hosts or nodes, connected by multiple modes. Such interconnected computers are capable of sending/receiving digital files.

Each device, aka a host, in the network, is associated with a unique device name known as 'hostname'. If you type 'hostname' in the command prompt and press 'Enter', this will display the hostname of your machine.

It may be noted here that not only computer systems; any other device may also be a part of the network. For example, printers are commonly seen to be connected in network.

COMPONENTS OF DATA COMMUNICATION

A data communications system has five components.

Message: The message is the information (data) that will be communicated by one computer and received by another. Generally information includes text and numbers, pictures, audio and video.

Sender: The sender is the device that sends the information. It can be a computer, workstation, telephone handset, video camera, and so on.

Receiver: The receiver is the device that receives the information. It can be a computer, workstation, telephone handset, television, and so on.

Transmission medium: The transmission medium is the physical medium or path by which information travels from sender to receiver. Some examples of transmission media include twisted-pair wire, coaxial cable, fiber-optic cable and radio waves.

Protocol: A protocol means what to follow to do a certain thing. It is, therefore, a set of rules that govern data communications. It establishes an agreement between the communicating devices. In the absence of a protocol, two devices may be connected but not communicating because they would not know what to follow in the communication between them.

DATA FLOW

Simplex: In simplex mode, the communication is unidirectional. Only one of the two devices on a link can transmit; the other can only receive. For example, keyboards and monitors. The keyboard can only give input; the monitor can only produce output.

Half-duplex: In the half-duplex mode of data flow, each device can both transmit and receive. However, this cannot happen at the same time. When one device is sending information, the other can only receive, and vice versa.

Full-duplex: In the full-duplex mode of data communication, the shortcoming of the half-duplex mode is rectified. In this case, both devices can transmit and receive information simultaneously.

TYPES OF COMPUTER NETWORK

Depending on the geographical area of the network, networks can be of the following types.

- Personal Area Network (PAN)
- Area Network (LAN)
- Metropolitan Area Network (MAN)
- Wide Area Network (WAN)
- Internetworks

PERSONAL AREA NETWORK (PAN)

This network is very 'personal'. Mostly a single user connects two or three of his devices in a small area, by means of, say, a bluetooth. It may be connected through a wire also.

LOCAL AREA NETWORK (LAN)

As the name suggests, the local area network is 'local'; that is, confined to a small geographical area like within an office, school, college, etc.

METROPOLITAN AREA NETWORK (MAN)

Metropolitan area network extends over a metropolitan area like a city or a town. It is set up by connecting the local area networks of the city or town. It is ideal for the people of a particular region to share data or information.

WIDE AREA NETWORK (WAN)

Wide area network covers a large geographical area. It is not confined within an office, a school or a town. It is mainly set up by telecommunication lines. Big organizations like banks and multinational companies communicate with their branches and customers through WAN. The Internet that we use is also a WAN.

INTERNETWORKS

It is a network of networks. The short form of Internetworks is the Internet. Obviously it is the largest network. The Internet connects all WANs in a big way.

UNIQUE IDENTIFIERS OF NETWORK

HOST NAME

As has already been mentioned, each device in the network can be identified by a unique device name called hostname.

IP ADDRESS (INTERNET PROTOCOL ADDRESS)

It is the network address of the system across the network. It is also known as the logical address.

To identify each device in the World Wide Web (WWW), the Internet Assigned Numbers Authority (IANA) assigns IPV4 (Version 4) address as a unique identifier for each device on the Internet. The length of the IP address is 32-bits. (Hence we have 2^{32} IP addresses available.) If you type 'ipconfig' in the command prompt and press 'Enter', you can see the IP address of the device.

Example of an IP address is 204.160.240.95. These are four bytes, with a period separating each byte.

MAC ADDRESS (MEDIA ACCESS CONTROL ADDRESS)

It is the unique identifier of each host and is associated with the NIC (Network Interface Card). A MAC address is assigned to the NIC at the time of manufacturing.

PORT

A port is a logical channel through which data can be sent to and received by an application. We have seen that a device is capable of running multiple applications simultaneously. Each of these applications is identified using the port number on which they are running. The port number is a 16-bit integer; hence we have 2^{16} ports available.

SOCKET

The combination of the IP address and the port number makes it unique. This combined IP address and port number is termed a socket and it can have connection to LANs.

DOMAIN NAME SYSTEM (DNS)

Textual addresses can be simply remembered by human beings. Hence these are provided to human beings for Internet addresses, in lieu of complicated numbers which are difficult to remember. DNS servers, however, act as the bridge between the two. They are responsible for translating textual Internet addresses into numeric Internet addresses.

In the system of networking, there are certain protocols that are followed by computers which are connected. While the details of protocols will be outside the scope of this book, according to the protocols involved, networks interconnection is achieved using one or several of the following devices:

Bridge: A computer or device that links two similar LANs based on the same protocol.

Router: A communication computer that connects different types of networks using different protocols.

Bridge router or brouter: A single device that combines both the functions of the bridge and the router.

Gateway: A network device that connects two different systems, using direct and systematic translation between protocols.

NETWORK TOPOLOGY

A network topology is the arrangement with which computer systems or network devices are connected to each other. Various types of commonly used topologies are as follows:

POINT-TO-POINT TOPOLOGY

Point-to-point networks contain exactly two hosts. Figure 5.1 shows point-to-point topology.

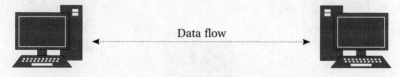

Fig. 5.1: Point-to-point topology

BUS TOPOLOGY

In the case of bus topology, all devices are connected to a single communication line or cable. Figure 5.2 shows bus topology.

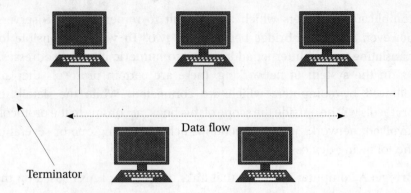

Fig. 5.2: Bus topology

STAR TOPOLOGY

All hosts in star topology are connected to a central device, known as the hub, using a point-to-point connection. In other words, there is a point-to-point connection between hosts and the hub. Figure 5.3 shows the structure of the network in star topology.

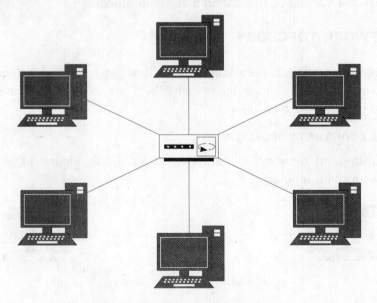

Fig. 5.3: Star topology

RING TOPOLOGY

In ring topology, each host connects exactly to two other machines, creating a circular network structure. Hence it is also called circular topology. Figure 5.4 shows ring topology.

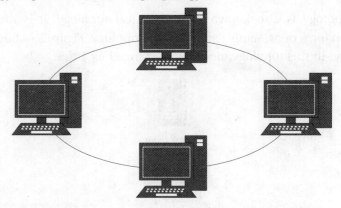

Fig. 5.4: Ring topology

MESH TOPOLOGY

In mesh topology, a host is connected to one or multiple hosts. This topology has hosts in point-to-point connection with every other host or may also have hosts which are in point-to-point connection with a few hosts only. Figure 5.5 shows mesh topology.

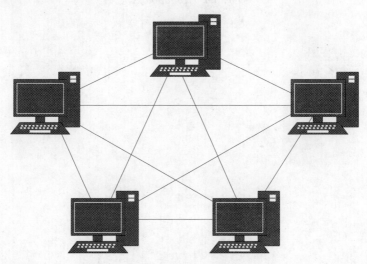

Fig. 5.5: Mesh topology

When every host is connected to every other host, it is called full mesh topology. If all hosts do not have point-to-point connection with every other host, it is called partial mesh topology.

TREE TOPOLOGY

This topology is also known as hierarchical topology. It is the most common form of presently used network topology. Figure 5.6 shows tree topology. In this topology, nodes are arranged as a tree.

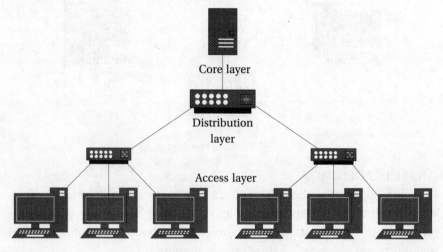

Fig. 5.6: Tree topology

6

INTERNET

INTRODUCTION

Probably no other invention of the modern day has impacted our daily lives as much as the Internet has—rich and poor, students and teachers, males and females alike. All of us use the Internet for getting information or for many other purposes. It has affected the way we carry out our profession, our work as well as the way we spend our leisure time.

The Internet is a communication system which is a network of networks, which has brought a wealth of information to our fingertips and organized it for our use.

A BRIEF HISTORY OF THE INTERNET

The first time Internet came into existence was in the year 1969. To understand the developments that led to the Internet, we have to go back a little. In the mid-1960s, when mainframe computers in research organizations were being used as standalone devices, scientists were trying to find ways to connect computers so that one can benefit from the research of another. The Advanced Research Projects Agency (ARPA) in the Department of Defense (DoD) was doing this. In 1967, at an Association for Computing Machinery (ACM) meeting, the ARPA presented its ideas for ARPANET, a small network of connected computers. That was the first successful attempt ever to connect remote computer systems. By 1969, ARPANET was a reality. Four nodes, at the University of California at Los Angeles (UCLA), the University of California at Santa Barbara (UCSB), Stanford Research Institute (SRI) and the University of Utah were connected to form a network.

In 1972, Vint Cerf and Bob Kahn, both of whom were part of the core

ARPANET group, successfully collaborated on what is now known to be their Internetting Project. In the next year, 1973, Cerf and Kahn published their landmark research paper outlining the protocols to achieve end-to-end delivery of packets. This paper on Transmission Control Protocol (TCP) is considered even today as one of the most pioneering and path-breaking research papers in Internet communication. Further developments quickly followed. It was the split of TCP into two protocols—Transmission Control Protocol (TCP) and Internetworking Protocol (IP).

However, the Internet today has crossed many more milestones and is a complex network of many wide- and local-area networks joined by connecting devices and switching stations. In 1993 the University of Illinois made Mosaic widely available. Mosaic was a new type of computer program, known as a browser that ran on most types of computers, and it simplified access, retrieval and display of files through the Internet. That started a whole new chapter in Internet communication technology. Tim Berners-Lee added to the already rich list of innovations, a new Internet application, the WWW. In 1994, Netscape Communications Corporation started working on further developing the Mosaic browser and server software for commercial use. Shortly thereafter, Microsoft Corporation came up with its Internet Explorer web browser (based initially on Mosaic).

By the late 1990s it became clear that the Internet is the future of communication technology and there were approximately 10,000 Internet service providers (ISPs) around the world, more than half of them located in the United States.

DIFFERENT TYPES OF INTERNET CONNECTIONS

We are familiar with many ways to connect to the Internet. With time, faster and faster connecting devices are coming up.

DIAL-UP

Dial-up used to be one of the earliest methods to access the Internet. In this method, a modem (internal or external) connects to the Internet after the computer dials a phone number. It is not only slow, but also has the drawback of a dial-up connection, which is that the phone line cannot be used for dual purposes once connected to the Internet or vice versa.

BROADBAND

Improvement to the dial-up connection to the Internet came as broadband. As the name rightly suggests, broadband offers faster Internet speed and significantly improves user experience of uploading and downloading data over the Internet.

DSL

DSL is the acronym for Digital Subscriber Line. It rectifies the dual inaccessibility issue of a dial-up connection. It always remains 'on'. This uses a splitter to bifurcate the phone line, so that it connects to the Internet as well as allows a subscriber to use his telephone line for voice communication. Also, there is no need to dial a phone number to connect. DSL uses a router to transport data. It is faster compared to a dial-up connection.

CABLE

Many of us use cable Internet at home and at the workplace. It uses a cable modem and operates over cable TV lines. Cable Internet lines offer faster Internet speed than DSL lines.

FIBRE OPTICAL NETWORK

Normal cables have been replaced by fibre optical cables to enable faster speed and transmission of a large volume of data.

WIRELESS

One of the most widely used and familiar terms today is the Wi-Fi. It stands for wireless connection. As the name suggests, it does not use telephone lines or cables to connect to the Internet. Instead, it uses radio frequency waves. Wireless is also an always-on connection and it can be accessed from just about anywhere.

CELLULAR

Cellular technology has enabled wireless Internet access through cell phones. The speed depends on multiple factors, but the most common now are 3G and 4G. G here stands for generation. 3G means third generation and 4G stands for fourth generation cellular technology. Now, of course, 5G technology is also around, although not being extensively used.

ADVANTAGES OF THE INTERNET

Although in this section we make an attempt to list the advantages of the Internet, it is not only impossible to list out all of them here, but it also depends on the way one looks at it or uses it. While some people use the Internet for information retrieval and academic purpose, some others use it for leisure. To both the types of people, the Internet is useful and offers advantages, but the context varies. Therefore, we will try to confine ourselves to a more generic discussion.

The Internet can let a person communicate with people in virtually any part of the world through e-mail, chat, etc. Through e-mail one can communicate with anyone in any part of the world from his own place and at lightning speed. E-mail is today the official medium of communication in all offices. Furthermore, chat and video conferencing are some of the latest additions in this technology and these have allowed people to communicate in real time. Another communication method is called messenger service that also works over the Internet.

Getting information on almost everything is one of the biggest advantages that the Internet offers. The Internet enables access to an unbelievably huge amount of information. Any kind of information, on any topic, at any time, at any place is available on the Internet. Who has not heard about Google? Or Yahoo? Or MSN? We depend so much on search engines today that searching for something over the Internet is loosely called googling.

Students can benefit enormously from the Internet, not only because of their access to information, but also by getting access to various advanced and scientifically proven methodology of education including e-learning, audio, video, animation, etc. Books are also available, which they can study over the Internet or download, depending on the availability and subject to the conditions for download and their use. Distance learning programs offered by many higher educational institutes have been possible and are a reality today because of the Internet. Students who cannot physically go and take admission in various institutes of great repute for multiple reasons can today get themselves enrolled in different programs that the Internet has made possible.

Forums or groups allow peoples to discuss issues and share their thoughts and information with others located at different geographies and in different time zones.

The Internet is a giant source of entertainment. Be it games or music or movies, the Internet has made it all possible and brought all of that inside your living room. One may not decide to step out to catch up with his favourite movie show, but can still watch it on his TV or even on his mobile phone.

Who, among us, has not done online shopping yet? I believe you will not find even one among those who have smartphones and use the Internet. Well, the Internet has been the big business enabler for the e-commerce industry. Amazon, Flipkart, etc. are household names today.

DISADVANTAGES OF THE INTERNET

Like everything that comes with certain positives, the Internet also has negatives. For all its advantages and positive aspects, the Internet has its dark and ugly sides too. Again we will confine ourselves to a very generic discussion. But we should try to use the Internet for its positive aspects, the negatives notwithstanding.

The Internet has made communication fast and unrestricted. Taking advantage of this, rumour-mongers misuse the Internet to spread hatred, fake information, misinformation and falsehood on any topic they want, thereby misleading people. At times it turns out that it is too late before any control by the authorities is put in place to curb such negative campaigns.

The Internet offers a sea of information. Anyone can post information over the Internet. There are no checks and balances to verify the correctness of information. Therefore, sometimes people fall prey to wrong information and unverified facts.

The Internet at times turns out to be addictive. Students in particular should use the Internet for specific purposes related to their studies and not indulge in playing games or watching movies, etc. Being on the Internet for long hours has, at times, barred students from taking part in outdoor games and sports, which is very essential for students.

Another disadvantage of the Internet is the huge volume of

information itself. Sometimes we do not know where to stop, and we spend hours and hours on the same topic over the Internet and do not know where to draw the line.

Another disadvantage of the Internet is the unrestricted access to all kinds of content, especially to students and young children. One of the greatest threats that the Internet poses for children is easy access to all kinds of material that should otherwise be far from the reach of children. Content that requires viewers' discretion can be accessed by children. This not only spoils their own life and career, but is also a threat to society, as this gives rise to crimes.

Social networking sites like Facebook, WhatsApp, Instagram, etc., sometimes prove to be harmful for those who let their vision get blurred and cannot discriminate between good and bad people.

Cybercrimes are on the rise in society. We do not blame the Internet for any crime, but people must not forget that everything that comes with a good side has a bad side as well. Not everybody indulges in cybercrime, true, but authorities must put proper checks and balances to curb this menace.

WEB BROWSERS

Web browsers are software programs that are specifically written to allow access to the web using the Internet. These are either downloadable and can be installed easily, or come with the operating system.

There are a few leading web browsers—Chrome (by Google), Internet Explorer (by Microsoft), Firefox, Netscape and Safari, but there are a few others also available, which may be not as popular as these. The browser that one uses in his computer must be compatible with the operating system in use.

The popularity of a browser is based on multiple factors. Some of these are as follows:

- Fast browsing
- Private browsing
- Phishing/malware filter
- Add-ons
- Chat extensions

- RSS headlines
- Ad blocker
- Download manager

Most of the browsers offer these features; some might be offering more than another. In the following section, we will learn about some of the commonly used browsers.

CHROME

It is one of the most popular browsers by Google. It focuses on the enhanced performance of web applications. It comes equipped with a few extensions and many other extensions can be added for free from Chrome Store and can be used for personal work.

MOZILLA FIREFOX

This web browser is an open source browser. It is designed for fast browsing experience, browser security, extensibility and versatility. It is compatible with Microsoft Windows, Linux as well as Android. There are lots of plugins and extensions with some powerful developer tools. Users get constant updates and high performance is delivered. Its customizable interface is an advantage for advanced users.

OPERA

It is constantly evolving and improving and is one of the web browsers gaining popularity by the day. It is also a free and fast browser with good support for updates.

SAFARI

Safari is a web browser developed by Apple Inc. It is the most popular browser with MAC users. Safari is a very fast browser. It comes with the features like tabbed browsing, pop-up blocking and built-in search functionality. It also has one of the best RSS-reading features available online.

INTERNET EXPLORER

This browser is by Microsoft and is the default browser for Windows OS. It is still very popular with many Internet users.

7

COMPUTER VIRUS

INTRODUCTION

A computer virus is a program designed to act like a virus by spreading from one computer to another, and it has the ability to replicate itself. The word 'virus' is used for such maliciously designed codes due to the similarity between how a real virus works and how such a computer program works. It is very much similar to an actual virus that requires a host body to thrive and make its activities felt. A computer virus also cannot reproduce and spread without a file or a document. In other words, a computer virus changes the way a computer should operate. And with time it spreads from one computer to another, thereby damaging all these computers.

A computer virus makes its way either secretly when one accesses certain programs and infected software, or by way of a residual virus already in that system but which was dormant due to lack of proper circumstances for it to thrive. The damaging effects that a virus may cause on a computer may be like harming the system software by corrupting or destroying data. Stealing passwords or data, corrupting files, spamming e-mail contacts, and even taking over the machine are just some of the devastating and dangerous things a virus can do. Sometimes they erase data or cause irreversible damage to a hard disk or boot sector.

HOW DOES A COMPUTER VIRUS ATTACK?

Once a virus has successfully attached itself to a program, file or document, it will lie dormant and its effect will be invisible until circumstances cause the computer to execute that file with which the virus was attached, thereby activating its code. In order for a virus to infect the computer, the infected program has to be run, which, in turn, causes the virus code to be executed and hence activated to carry out its malicious function. Sometimes a virus can lie dormant for a long period of time, without letting the user of the computer know that such a code has been there, secretly waiting for a long time to strike at an appropriate time.

HOW DO COMPUTER VIRUSES SPREAD?

In a constantly connected world, one computer can contract a computer virus in many ways, some more obvious than others. Viruses look for opportune and favourable circumstances to spread themselves from one computer to another. For this they need a medium, that is, a file with which they can get attached, and when that file is passed on to another computer, viruses reach that hitherto unaffected computer and start their activity there. They can be spread through e-mail and text message attachments, Internet file downloads and social media scam links. Mobile devices and smartphones can become infected with mobile viruses through shady app downloads. Viruses can hide disguised as attachments of socially shareable content such as funny images, greeting cards or audio and video files, etc. They can come to users in the guise of passing on monetary benefits to them, such that they are required to open the attachment and fill in the form therein and submit it to get the payment for having won an obscure lottery, etc.

WHAT ARE THE SIGNS THAT A COMPUTER HAS A VIRUS?

A computer virus attack can have a variety of symptoms. Here are some of them. The list below cannot be exhaustive and it consists of only the most common symptoms,

- Frequent pop-up windows, unless you have knowingly opted for one from a reliable and known source
- Changes to your homepage
- Mass e-mails sent from your e-mail account
- Frequent crashes
- Unusually slow computer performance
- Unknown programs that start up when you turn on your computer
- Unusual activities like password changes

WHAT TO DO TO KEEP A COMPUTER SAFE FROM VIRUSES?

To avoid contact with a virus, it's important to exercise caution when surfing the web, downloading files and opening links or attachments. Do not open or accept files from unknown, unreliable, inauthentic, untrustworthy and unsecure sources. To help stay safe, never download text or e-mail attachments that you're not expecting, or files from websites you don't trust. Like any machine, computers also come with standard operating procedures, or what we commonly call SOPs. Therefore there are certain do's and don'ts which we advise users to follow.

- Instal an antivirus program in your computer
- Keep the antivirus program updated with the latest virus definitions
- Take regular backup of your work and save them in multiple places
- Avoid clicking on any pop-up advertisements
- Always scan your e-mail attachments before opening them.
- Always scan the files that you download using file-sharing programs

ABBREVIATIONS USED IN COMPUTER SCIENCE

We use many abbreviations while describing computer architecture, language, operations, etc. Some of these are given below.

ADSL – Asymmetric Digital Subscriber Line (form of DSL)

AGP – Advanced Graphics Port

ANSI – American National Standards Institute

AOL – America Online

ASCII – American Standard Code for Information Interchange

ASP – Association of Shareware Professionals

ASPI – Advanced SCSI Programming Interface [Adaptec]

ATA – Advanced Technology Attachment (original hard drive interface)

BDSL – Broadband DSL

BIOS – Basic Input/Output System (system chips)

BPS – Bits Per Second/Bytes Per Second

CAD – Computer Aided Design

CADD – Computer Aided Design and Drafting

CC – Carbon Copy (e-mail usage)

CD-R – Compact Disk – Recordable

CD-ROM – Compact Disk – Read Only Memory

CDMA – Code-Division Multiple Access (wireless/cell phone protocol)

CERN – The European Particle Physics Laboratory (initials originally from Conseil European pour la Recherche Nucleaire)

CERT – Computer Emergency Response Team

CGI-BIN – Common Gateway Interface – Binary (programming for Web forms)

CMOS – Complementary Metal-Oxide Semiconductor (type of non-volatile memory chip) + PC configuration stored on CMOS

CMYK – Cyan-Magenta-Yellow-Black (colour model)

COAX – Coaxial Cable (for ethernet and similar networks)

COM1 – First serial port (asynchronous port)

COM2 – Second serial port

CRT – Cathode Ray Tube: standard type computer monitor display

CPU – Central Processing Unit

CSV – Comma-Separated Value/Variable (file type)

CTRL – Control (computer keyboard key)

CYMK – Cyan-Yellow-Magenta-Black (colour model)

DAC – Data Acquisition and Control + Digital to Analog Converter

dB – Decibel

DBMS – Data Base Management System

DDR – Double Data Rate (double speed of RAM)

DDR-SDRAM – Double Data Rate – SDRAM

DLL – Dynamic Link Library

DMA – Direct Memory Access/Addressing

DNS – Domain Naming System (Internet address names)

DOS – Disk Operating System

DPI – Dots Per Inch

DRAM – Dynamic Random Access Memory

DSL – Digital Subscriber Line

DVD – Digital Video Disk; Digital Versatile Disk; 4.7 GB CD format

EBCDIC – Extended Binary Coded Decimal Interchange Code [IBM] (is to ASCII as Sanskrit is to English)

EEPROM – Electrically Erasable Programmable Read-Only Memory

EISA – Extended Industry Standard Architecture (PC bus design)

EPROM – Electrically Programmable Read Only Memory + Erasable Programmable Read Only Memory

ESDI – Enhanced Small Device Interface

FAQ – Frequently Asked Question

FAT – File Allocation Table

FDC – Floppy Disk Controller

FDISK – Fixed Disk (DOS utility)

FIFO – First-In, First-Out

FLOPS – Floating Point Operations/Second

GIS – Geographic Information System

GNU – Gnu's Not Unix (operating system that really is Unix)

GPS – Global Positioning Satellite/System

GUI – Graphical User Interface

HDSL – High-Data-Rate Digital Subscriber Line (DSL) + High-Speed Digital Subscriber Loop

HDTV – High Definition Television

HEX – Hexadecimal

HTML – HyperText Markup Language

HTTP – HyperText Transport Protocol

HTTP-NG – HTTP Next Generation

HTTPS – HyperText Transfer Protocol Secure

IMAP – Internet Message Access Protocol [Internet; a step up from POP]

I/O – Input/Output (serial and parallel ports)

IP – Internet Protocol (as in TCP/IP)

IrDA – Infrared Data Association (Ir port standard)

ISDN – Integrated Services Digital Network (digital phone line)

ISP – Internet Service Provider

IT – Information Technology

I-WAY – Information Highway

JPEG – Joint Photographic Experts Group

KB – Keyboard + Kilobyte (1,024 bytes; also kB)

kHz – Kilohertz

LAN – Local Area Network

LCD – Liquid Crystal Display

LED – Light Emitting Diode

LINUX (Free-source version of UNIX operating system named after Linus Torvalds)

LPT – Line Printer

LPT1 – First Parallel Printer Port

LPT2 – Second Parallel Printer Port

LQ – Letter Quality

LSI – Large Scale Integration

MB – Megabyte (also mB; 1,024 kilobytes)

MBASIC – Microsoft BASIC [Microsoft]

MBps – Megabytes Per Second

Mbps – Megabits Per Second

MEG – Megabyte

MFS – Macintosh File System [Macintosh]

MHz – Megahertz (million cycles per second)

MIDI – Musical Instrument Digital Interface

MIME – Multipurpose Internet Mail Extension [e-mail attachment protocol]

MIPS – Million Instructions Per Second

MMX – Multimedia Extensions (additional CPU instructions)

MODEM – Modulator Demodulator

MPC – Multimedia Personal Computer (Microsoft)

MPEG – Moving Picture Experts Group

MSCDEX – Microsoft Compact Disc Extension

MS-DOS – Microsoft – Disk Operating System

MSG – Message

MSIE – Microsoft Internet Explorer [Microsoft]

NCSA – National Center for Supercomputing Applications

NNTP – Network News Transfer Protocol [Internet]

NSFNET – National Science Foundation Network

PC-DOS – Personal Computer – Disk Operating System [IBM]

PCI – Peripheral Component Interconnect/Interface (PC Bus)

PD – Public Domain

PDA – Personal Digital Assistant

PGP – Pretty Good Privacy (name of encryption program)

PIM – Personal Information Manager

PING – Packet Internet Groper

PIXEL – Picture Element

POP – Post Office Protocol (protocol for distributing e-mail)

Popmail – e-mail via POP

PPM – Pages Per Minute

PRN – Printer

PRTSC – Print Screen

RAM – Random Access Memory

RDRAM – Rambus Dynamic Random Access Memory

RGB – Red-Green-Blue (colour model)

RISC – Reduced Instruction Set Computer

RJ-11 – Standard US phone connector

RJ-45 – Standard Ethernet connector

RAID – Redundant Arrays of Independent Disks + Redundant Arrays of Independent Drives + Redundant Arrays of Inexpensive Disks

ROM – Read Only Memory (chip)

SCSI – Small Computer System Interface (for hard drives, scanners, etc.)

SDRAM – Synchronous Dynamic Random Access Memory

SGML – Standard Generalized Markup Language

SGRAM – Synchronous Graphics RAM

SIMM – Single In-line Memory Module

SIPP – Single In-line Pin Package

SLIP – Serial Line Interface Protocol

SMTP – Simple Mail Transfer Protocol (basic e-mail protocol)

SNOBOL – String Oriented Symbolic Language (Programming Language)

SRAM – Static Random Access Memory

SSL – Secure Sockets Layer

SVGA – Super Video Graphics Array

SYSOP – System Operator

TCP/IP – Transmission Control Protocol/Internet Protocol

TEMP – Temporary

TIFF – Tagged Image File Format

TMP – Temporary

UNIX – (AT&T Bell Laboratories Operating System)

UPS – Uninterruptible Power Supply

USB – Universal Serial Bus serial port standard

USENET – User's Network [Internet]

VGA – Video Graphics Array: IBM/Windows 640 × 480 colour graphics display standard

VRAM – Video Random Access Memory

WPM – Words Per Minute

WYSIWYG – What You See Is What You Get

XGA – Extended Graphics Array [IBM]: generically, 1024 × 768 colour standard

ZIF – Zero-Insertion Force (socket)

FILE EXTENSIONS

There are many different file formats depending on the program that we use. And every program comes with its own extension. Given below is a list of the most common file extensions. They are grouped together for the type of programs these files use.

Audio files

.aif – AIF audio file

.cda – CD audio track file

.mid or .midi – MIDI audio file

.mp3 – MP3 audio file

.mpa – MPEG-2 audio file

.ogg – Ogg Vorbis audio file

.wav – WAV file

.wma – WMA audio file

.wpl – Windows Media Player playlist

Compressed files

.deb – Debian software package file

.pkg – Package file

.rar – RAR file

.rpm – Red Hat Package Manager

.tar.gz – Tarball compressed file

.z – Z compressed file

.zip – Zip compressed file

Disc and media file extensions

.bin – Binary disc image

.dmg – macOS X disk image

.iso – ISO disc image

.vcd – Virtual CD

Data and database file extensions

.csv – Comma separated value file
.dat – Data file
.db or .dbf – Database file
.log – Log file
.mdb – Microsoft Access database file
.sav – Save file (e.g., game save file)
.sql – SQL database file
.tar – Linux / Unix tarball file archive
.xml – XML file

Executable file extensions

.apk – Android package file
.bat – Batch file
.bin – Binary file
.cgi or .pl – Perl script file
.com – MS-DOS command file
.exe – Executable file
.jar – Java Archive file
.py – Python file
.wsf – Windows Script file

Font file extensions

.fnt – Windows font file
.fon – Generic font file
.otf – Open type font file
.ttf – TrueType font file

Image file formats by file extension

.ai – Adobe Illustrator file
.bmp – Bitmap image
.gif – GIF image
.ico – Icon file
.jpeg or .jpg – JPEG image
.png – PNG image

.ps – PostScript file
.psd – PSD image
.svg – Scalable Vector Graphics file
.tif or .tiff – TIFF image

Internet-related file extensions

.asp and .aspx – Active Server Page file
.cer – Internet security certificate
.cfm – ColdFusion Markup file
.cgi or .pl – Perl script file
.css – Cascading Style Sheet file
.htm and .html – HTML file
.js – JavaScript file
.jsp – Java Server Page file
.part – Partially downloaded file
.php – PHP file
.py – Python file
.rss – RSS file
.xhtml – XHTML file

Presentation file

.key – Keynote presentation
.odp – OpenOffice Impress presentation file
.pps – PowerPoint slide show
.ppt – PowerPoint presentation
.pptx – PowerPoint Open XML presentation

Programming files by file extensions

.c – C and C++ source code file
.class – Java class file
.cpp – C++ source code file
.cs – Visual C# source code file
.h – C, C++, and Objective-C header file
.java – Java Source code file
.sh – Bash shell script
.swift – Swift source code file
.vb – Visual Basic file

Spreadsheet file formats by file extension

.ods – OpenOffice Calc spreadsheet file

.xlr – Microsoft Works spreadsheet file

.xls – Microsoft Excel file

.xlsx – Microsoft Excel Open XML spreadsheet file

System-related file formats and file extensions

.bak – Backup file

.cab – Windows Cabinet file

.cfg – Configuration file

.cpl – Windows Control panel file

.cur – Windows cursor file

.dll – DLL file

.dmp – Dump file

.drv – Device driver file

.icns – macOS X icon resource file

.ico – Icon file

.ini – Initialization file

.lnk – Windows shortcut file

.msi – Windows installer package

.sys – Windows system file

.tmp – Temporary file

Video file formats by file extension

.3g2 – 3GPP2 multimedia file

.3gp – 3GPP multimedia file

.avi – AVI file

.flv – Adobe Flash file

.h264 – H.264 video file

.m4v – Apple MP4 video file

.mkv – Matroska Multimedia Container

.mov – Apple QuickTime movie file

.mp4 – MPEG4 video file

.mpg or .mpeg – MPEG video file

.rm – RealMedia file

.swf – Shockwave flash file

.vob – DVD Video Object

.wmv – Windows Media Video file

Word processor and text file formats by file extension

.doc and .docx – Microsoft Word file

.odt – OpenOffice Writer document file

.pdf – PDF file

.rtf – Rich Text Format

.tex – A LaTeX document file

.txt – Plain text file

.wks and .wps – Microsoft Works file

.wpd – WordPerfect document